COUNTRY LIVING
MAGAZINE

Guide to Rural England

EAST
ANGLIA

Norfolk, Suffolk, Essex and Cambridgeshire

By Peter Long

© Travel Pu...

Published by:

Travel Publishing Ltd

7a Apollo House, Calleva Park

Aldermaston, Berkshire RG7 8TN

ISBN 1-904-43447-9

© Travel Publishing Ltd

Country Living is a registered trademark of The National
Magazine Company Limited.

First Published: 2001
Second Edition: 2004
Third Edition: 2006

COUNTRY LIVING GUIDES:

East Anglia	Scotland
Heart of England	The South of England
Ireland	The South East of England
The North East of England	The West Country
The North West of England	Wales

PLEASE NOTE:

All advertisements in this publication have been accepted in good faith by Travel Publishing and
they have not necessarily been endorsed by *Country Living* Magazine.

All information is included by the publishers in good faith and is believed to be correct at the time
of going to press. No responsibility can be accepted for errors.

Editor:	Peter Long
Printing by:	Scotprint, Haddington
Location Maps:	© Maps in Minutes ™ (2006) © Crown Copyright, Ordnance Survey 2006
Walks:	Walks have been reproduced with kind permission of the internet walking site www.walkingworld.com
Walk Maps:	Reproduced from Ordnance Survey mapping on behalf of the Controller of Her Majesty's Stationery Office, © Crown Copyright. Licence Number MC 100035812
Cover Design:	Lines & Words, Aldermaston
Cover Photo:	Church and Poppy Field, Lyng, Norfolk © www.britainonview.com
Text Photos:	Text photos have been kindly supplied by the Pictures of Britain photo library © www.picturesofbritain.co.uk

Foreword

From a bracing walk across the hills and tarns of The Lake District to a relaxing weekend spent discovering the unspoilt hamlets of East Anglia, nothing quite matches getting off the beaten track and exploring Britain's areas of outstanding beauty.

Each month, *Country Living Magazine* celebrates the richness and diversity of our countryside with features on rural Britain and the traditions that have their roots there. So it is with great pleasure that I introduce you to the *Country Living Magazine Guide to Rural England* series. Packed with information about unusual and unique aspects of our countryside, the guides will point both fair-weather and intrepid travellers in the right direction.

Each chapter provides a fascinating tour of the East Anglia area, with insights into local heritage and history and easy-to-read facts on a wealth of places to visit, stay, eat, drink and shop.

I hope that this guide will help make your visit a rewarding and stimulating experience and that you will return inspired, refreshed and ready to head off on your next countryside adventure.

Susy Smith

Susy Smith
Editor, Country Living magazine

PS To subscribe to *Country Living Magazine* each month, call 01858 438844

Introduction

This is the 3rd edition of the *Country Living Guide to Rural England – East Anglia* and we are sure that it will be as popular as its predecessors. Regular readers will note that the page layouts have been attractively redesigned and that we have provided more information on the places, people, and activities covered. Also, in the introduction to each village or town we have summarized and categorized the main attractions to be found there which makes it easier for readers to plan their visit. Peter Long, the editor, is an experienced travel writer who spent many years as an inspector and writer with Egon Ronay's Hotels & Restaurants Guides before joining the Travel Publishing editorial team. Peter has, of course, completely updated the contents of the guide and ensured that it is packed with vivid descriptions, historical stories, amusing anecdotes and interesting facts on hundreds of places in Norfolk, Suffolk, Cambridgeshire and Essex.

Norfolk is famous for the Norfolk Broads but has a rich and interesting past, gentle hills as well as expansive horizons, delightful pastoral scenes, a beautiful coastline rich in wildlife and many interesting hidden places to visit. Suffolk was made famous by the brush of John Constable and is blessed with incomparable rural beauty which encompasses wide open spaces broken by gentle hills and tidal rivers meandering from a coastline teeming with birdlife. Cambridgeshire is famous for its ancient university and being the birthplace of Oliver Cromwell and Samuel Pepys but offers a wealth of peaceful and attractive countryside with many towns and villages steeped in history. Essex, containing England's oldest recorded town (Colchester), has a strong maritime tradition, pretty villages, a coastline with attractive estuaries and a rich history going back to Roman times.

The advertising panels within each chapter provide further information on places to see, stay, eat, drink, shop. We have also selected a number of walks from walkingworld.com (full details of this website may be found to the rear of the guide) which we highly recommend if you wish to appreciate fully the beauty and charm of the varied rural landscapes and coastlines of East Anglia.

The guide however is not simply an "armchair tour". Its prime aim is to encourage the reader to visit the places described and discover much more about the wonderful towns, villages and countryside of East Anglia in person. In this respect we would like to thank all the Tourist Information Centres who helped us to provide you with up to date information. Whether you decide to explore this region by wheeled transport or on foot we are sure you will find it a very uplifting experience!

We are always interested in receiving comments on places covered (or not covered) in our guides so please do not hesitate to use the reader reaction forms provided at the rear of this guide to give us your considered comments. This will help us refine and improve the content of the next edition. We also welcome any general comments which will help improve the overall presentation of the guides themselves.

For more information on the full range of travel guides published by Travel Publishing please refer to the order form at the rear of this guide or log on to our website (see below).

Travel Publishing

Did you know that you can also search our website for details of thousands of places to see, stay, eat or drink throughout Britain and Ireland? Our site has become increasingly popular and now receives over 160,000 hits per day. Try it!

website: **www.travelpublishing.co.uk**

Contents

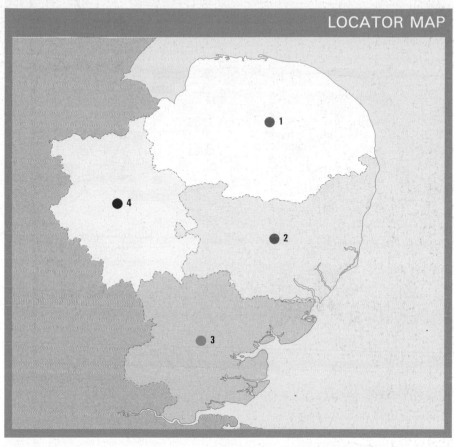

LOCATOR MAP

LOCATOR MAP

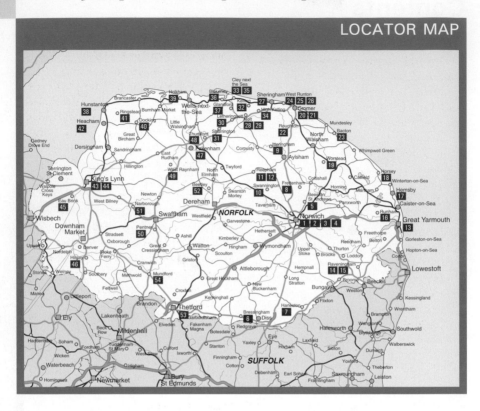

ADVERTISERS AND PLACES OF INTEREST

🏛 historic building   🏛 museum   🏛 historic site   🜲 scenic attraction   🌿 flora and fauna

1| Norfolk

With two sides bordered by the sea and a third by the Fens, Norfolk has a wealth of attractions for the visitor: miles of sandy beaches, great walking and boating, nature reserves, wonderful villages of thatch and flint, great houses, Norman castles and over 600 medieval churches.

The area that lies between the county capital of Norwich and the border with Suffolk is effectively a plateau, where the major centres of population include Diss, an old market town with a mix of Tudor, Georgian and Victorian houses, and Wymondham, with its timber-framed houses, picturesque market place and an abbey church that stands up well to comparison even with the majestic Norwich Cathedral. Norwich, once an important centre of the worsted trade, retains many medieval buildings, a number of which now serve as museums relating the fascinating history of the region.

The area to the east of this fine city contains the unique Norfolk Broads, beautiful stretches of shallow water that form Britain's finest wetland area. On the coast due east of Norwich is the old port and modern holiday resort of Great Yarmouth, where the visitor will find miles of sandy beaches, a breezy promenade, two grand old traditional piers and all the fun of the fair, as well as a rich maritime heritage that lives on to this day.

Miles of sandy beaches, spectacular sea views and fresh sea air are the rewards awaiting visitors to the Norfolk coast, which stretches from Great Yarmouth in the east up to Cromer on the edge of the county and west to Sheringham, Hunstanton and beyond.

Substantial stretches of the coast are in the

📖 stories and anecdotes   🦢 famous people   🎨 art and craft   ✒ entertainment and sport   🚶 walks care of the National Trust, including the highest point in the county at West Runton, and the North Norfolk coast is renowned for its birdlife. Felbrigg Hall is a superb 17th century house with Grand Tour paintings and marvellous grounds. The house is near Cromer, a charming resort with a 100-year-old pier and a proud fishing tradition: Cromer crabs are known far and wide.

The northwest coast is an exhilarating coast, with huge skies, ozone-tangy breezes sweeping in from the North Sea, and an abundance of wildlife. An admirable way to experience the area to the full is to walk all or part of the Coastal Footpath which follows the coastline for some

Norfolk Broads

36 miles from Cromer in the east to Holme-next-the-Sea, for most of its route well away from any roads.

King's Lynn, on the Great Ouse three miles inland from The Wash, was one of England's most important ports in medieval times, sitting at the southern end of an underwater maze of sandbanks. To the northeast of King's Lynn is the prosperous market town of Fakenham, around which lie a remarkable variety of places of interest – religious, industrial and scenic. Breckland, which extends for more than 360 square miles in southwest Norfolk and northwest Suffolk, is underlain by chalk with only a light covering of soil. The name 'Breckland' comes from the become exhausted. This quiet corner of the county is bounded by the rivers Little Ouse and Waveney, which separate Norfolk from Suffolk.

Norwich

- 🏛 Norwich Castle 🏛 Norwich Cathedral
- 📷 Bridewell Museum 🏛 Venta Icenorum
- 📷 City of Norwich Aviation Museum
- 📷 Castle Museum & Art Gallery 🎨 The Forum
- 📷 Royal Norfolk Regimental Museum
- 📷 John Jarrold Printing Museum
- 🎭 The Mustard Shop 🎨 Sainsbury Centre
- 🚶 Whitlingham Country Park

"Norwich has the most Dickensian atmosphere of any city I know," declared J B Priestley in his *English Journey* of 1933. "What a grand, higgledy-piggledy, sensible old place Norwich is!" More than half a century later, in a European Commission study of 'most habitable' cities, Norwich topped the list of British contenders, well ahead of more favoured candidates such as Bath and York. The political, social and cultural capital of Norfolk, Norwich has an individual charm that is difficult to define, a beguiling atmosphere created in part by its prodigal wealth of sublime buildings, and partly by its intriguing dual personality as both an old-fashioned cathedral town and a vibrant, modern city. Back in prehistoric times, there were several settlements around the confluence of the Rivers Wensum and Yare. By the late fourth century, one of them was important enough to have its own mint. This was *Northwic*. By the time of the *Domesday Book* 700 years later, Northwic/Norwich, had become the third-most populous city in

THE JADE TREE

39 Elm Hill, Norwich, Norfolk NR3 1HG
Tel: 01603 664615
e-mail: info@thejadetree.co.uk
website: www.thejadetree.co.uk

A showcase of exquisite, innovative and unique fine art and craft, much of it made in the studios on the premises. Choose an unusual gift in the relaxed atmosphere of the beautiful shop, a 17th century merchants house, nestled between the river and the Cathedral. Elm Hill is Norwich at its most beautiful and individual. Step into the picture postcard; browse the art galleries and antique shops or relax in the cafes and bistros.

You will recognise The Jade Tree by the mascot bronze piglet welcoming you on the step. Meet the artists in their studios. Commission a painting or something from the collection of fashion accessories for men and women to suit your personal taste. There is a bespoke wedding stationery service. You could choose to have a consultation/treatment in the Kiju skincare salon. Browse the fabulous range of contemporary jewellery, skincare, textiles and fashion accessories. Be spoilt for choice by the paintings, sculpture, cards and ceramics.

The Jade Tree partners are Jacqui Fenn Designs (figurative, abstract and landscape paintings in oil), Jean Cummings (figurative and abstract paintings in acrylic), Tamara Rampley (embroidered textiles and botanical illustrations), Textile Treasures (designer accessories) and Kiju (ethical skincare). All the products are handmade locally and therefore each is unique. You can also see the current selection on the website.

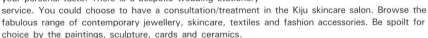

🎭 stories and anecdotes 🐦 famous people 🎨 art and craft 🎭 entertainment and sport 🚶 walks

PINOCCHIO'S RESTAURANT

11 St Benedicts Street, Norwich,
Norfolk NR2 4PE
Tel/Fax: 01603 613318
e-mail: jayner@talktalk.net

Jayne and Nigel Raffles have been running restaurants in Norwich since 1990. They started with one, and the summer of 2006 saw the opening of their fourth outlet. Each is different in look and style, with its own character and appeal, but all share the common assets of high-quality food, a comfortable, relaxing ambience and friendly, efficient staff. Behind a listed shop front, **Pinocchio's** is a stylish Italian brasserie with picture windows, a hand-made mahogany bar, pitch-pine flooring and a huge Picasso-style mural. The menu covers a fine range of pasta (starter or main course), pizzas and an interesting à la carte choice typified by chargrilled squid and chorizo salad, grilled lamb chops primavera and hazelnut semifreddo with a hazelnut sauce. This place really buzzes, particularly on the live jazz evenings (every Monday and every other Thursday).

Next door to Pinocchio's is **St Benedicts Restaurant** (9 St Benedicts Street, Tel: 01603 765377, easy to spot with its smart navy blue paintwork and large, distinctive awning. Inside, it has the look and feel of a French bistro, with warm yellow and blue décor and an enticing menu of beautifully prepared and presented dishes that reflect the owners' passion for quality and fine, fresh flavours. Typical choices might include calves' liver with sweet and sour pink grapefruit, wing of skate grenobloise and a delectable trio of lemon puddings (with equally delectable pudding wines to accompany).

Pulse Café Bar (The Old Fire Station Stables, Labour in Vain Yard, Guildhall Hill, Tel: 01603 765562) has been busy ever since it opened in 2004. A café by day and a bar/restaurant in the evening, it serves a wide selection of funky vegetarian food of worldwide inspiration, with fresh, vibrant flavours, accompanied by organic wines, beers and soft

drinks. A mecca for students, shoppers, office workers and tourists, it was originally home to the horses that pulled the city's first fire engines. When the sun shines, diners can enjoy a meal in the sun in the courtyard.

The Library (2a Guildhall Hill, Tel: 01603 616606) is Jayne and Nigel's most recent and biggest project to date, a large bar/brasserie/restaurant where much of the food is cooked on a specially imported wooden grill. Behind its 1830s frontage, with Doric columns at the entrance, The Library has a modern 'clubby' feel, with the old book shelves still in place. Besides the main eating area, it has a private dining space, a bar and outside seating in a courtyard that overlooks the busy market place.

---

 historic building   museum   historic site   scenic attraction   flora and fauna

England, only outnumbered by London and York. To the Norman conquerors, such a major centre of population (about 5,500 residents) needed a **castle** to ensure that its Saxon inhabitants could be kept in order.

The first castle structure, in wood, was replaced in the late 1100s by a mighty fortress in stone which, unlike most blank-walled castles of the period, is decorated with a rich façade of blind arcades and ornamental pilasters. This great fort never saw any military action, and as early as the 13th century was being used as the county gaol, a role it continued to fill until 1889. From its walls, in December 1549, the leader of the rebellion against land enclosures, Robert Kett, was hung in chains and left to starve to death.

The Castle is now home to the **Castle Museum and Art Gallery**, home to some of the most outstanding regional collections of fine art, archaeological exhibits and natural history displays. The former dungeons contain a forbidding display of instruments of torture, along with the death masks of some of the prisoners who were executed here. Among the countless other fascinating exhibits are those devoted to Queen Boudicca, which features the life of the Iceni tribe with an interactive chariot ride, the Egyptian gallery with its mummy Ankh Hor, and new and interactive displays in the Castle keep and keep basement, recently made accessible to the public, and a collection of teapots and porcelain.

The Art Gallery has an incomparable collection of paintings by the celebrated Norwich artist, John Sell Cotman (1782-1842), and others in the group known as the Norwich School. Their subjects were mostly landscape scenes, such as John Crome's *The Poringland Oak*. Quite apart from the artistic quality of their works, they have left a fascinating pictorial record of early 19th century Norfolk.

Next door to the Castle Museum is the **Royal Norfolk Regimental Museum** on Market Avenue, telling the story of the regiment from its founding in 1685. Exhibits include an extensive collection of medals and other memorabilia and an important photographic collection. The great open space of the Market Square, where every weekday a colourful jumble of traders' stalls can be found, offers just about every conceivable item for sale. Dominating the western side of the Market Square is City Hall, modelled on Stockholm City Hall and opened by King George VI in 1938. Opinions differ about its architectural merits, but there are no such

---

ELM HILL CRAFT SHOP

12 Elm Hill, Norwich, Norfolk NR3 1HN
Tel: 01603 621076 Fax: 01603 762417

Established originally just for crafts in 1936, **Elm Hill Craft Shop** is now an exclusive gift shop selling a wide and imaginative selection of gifts and toys. Christina Morris, the owner since 1981, puts her seal of approval on everything on display in the well-lit interior, and each visit is a browser's delight, with something new to discover every time. The stock includes Maisy, Miffy, Elmer and Babar ranges, Russian dolls, dolls' houses and miniature furniture, Irish spongeware pottery by Nicolas Mosse, activity books, stationery, greetings cards, gift wrap, jewellery and toiletries. The shop occupies a corner site in a cobbled street close to the Norman Cathedral and backed by the River Wensum.

📖 stories and anecdotes 🐦 famous people 🎨 art and craft ✒ entertainment and sport 🚶 walks

doubts about the nearby Guildhall, a fine example of 15th century flintwork that now houses a tea room.

Around the corner from London Street, in Bridewell Alley, is the **Bridewell Museum**, a late 14th century merchant's house now dedicated to Norfolk's crafts and industries. Another museum/shop, this one located in the Royal Arcade, a tiled riot of Art Nouveau fantasy, celebrates the county's great contribution to world cuisine - mustard. Back in the early 1800s, Jeremiah Colman perfected his blend of mustard flours and spice to produce a condiment that was smooth in texture and tart in flavour. Together with his nephew James he founded J & J Colman in 1823; 150 years later **The Mustard Shop** was

established to commemorate the company's history. The shop has an appropriately late-Victorian atmosphere and a fascinating display of vintage containers and advertisements, some of them from 'Mustard Club' featuring such characters as Lord Bacon of Cookham and Miss Di Gester, created by no less distinguished a writer than Dorothy L Sayers. All in all, a most piquant exhibition.

Millennium Plain just off Theatre Street is where visitors will find **The Forum**, an architecturally stunning modern building designed by Sir Michael Hopkins. Combining a unique horseshoe shape with an all-glass façade, this spectacular structure has, at its heart, the Atrium and Bridge, meeting places where you can enjoy a meal or drink anytime

through to midnight, seven days a week. At the Origins Visitor Centre, an attractive multi-media display on three floors, affords the opportunity to experience the life and times of Norwich and the wider Norfolk region during the past 2,000 years. Here can also be found the Tourist Information Centre. The Norfolk & Norwich Millennium Library houses 120,000 books and offers the best in information and communication technology.

Also on the site is the Second Air Division Memorial library, a memorial to the Americans based in East Anglia during the Second World War. The Assembly House in Theatre Street is one of the city's finest historical houses and also a leading venue for the arts. With two concert halls, three galleries featuring changing exhibitions and a restaurant and tea rooms, this magnificent Georgian home must be included in any visit to the city. John Jarrold was a pioneering figure in British printing, and the **John Jarrold Printing Museum** charts the history of the printing industry over the last 160 years.

While the Castle has been used for many purposes over the years, the **Cathedral** remains what it has always been: the focus of ecclesiastical life in the county. It's even older than the castle, its service of consecration taking place over 900 years ago, in 1101. This peerless building, its flint walls clad in creamy white stone from Caen is, after Durham, the most completely Norman cathedral in England, its appeal enhanced by later Gothic features such as the flying buttresses. The Norman cloisters are the largest in the country and notable for the 400 coloured and gilded bosses depicting scenes from medieval life. Another 1,200 of these wondrous carvings decorate the glorious vaulted roof of the nave.

It's impossible to list all the Cathedral's treasures here, but do seek out the Saxon Bishop's Throne in the Presbytery, the lovely 14th century altar painting in St Luke's Chapel, and the richly carved canopies in the Choir.

Outside, beneath the slender 315-foot spire soaring heavenwards, the **Cathedral Close** is timeless in its sense of peace. There are some 80 houses inside the Close, some medieval, many Georgian, their residents enjoying an idyllic refuge free from cars. At peace here lie the remains of Nurse Edith Cavell. A daughter of the rector of Swardeston, a few miles south of Norwich, Nurse Cavell worked at a Red Cross hospital in occupied Brussels during the First World War. She helped some 200 Allied soldiers to escape to neutral Holland before being detected and court-martialled by the Germans. As she faced execution by firing squad on 12 October 1915, she spoke her own resonant epitaph: 'Standing as I do, in the view of God and eternity, I realise that patriotism is not enough. I must have no hatred or bitterness towards anyone.'

A stroll around the Close will take you to Pull's Ferry with its picturesque flint gateway fronting the River Wensum. In medieval times a canal ran inland from here so that provisions, goods and, in the earliest days, building materials, could be moved direct to the Cathedral. A short stroll along the riverside walk will bring you to Cow Tower, built around 1378 and the most massive of the old city towers.

At the western end of the Cathedral Close is the magnificent Erpingham Gate, presented to the city in 1420 by a hero of the Battle of Agincourt, Sir Thomas Erpingham. Beyond this gate, in Tombland (originally Toom or wasteland), is Samson and Hercules House, its entrance flanked by two 1674 carvings of these giants. Diagonally opposite stands the 15th century Maid's Head Hotel. A 14th century door within a 15th century opening on King Street leads to the only medieval merchants' trading halls known to survive in Western Europe. Dragon Hall was built for the merchant Robert Toppes in the mid 15th century.

Norwich is home to some 32 medieval churches in all, every one of them worth attention, although many are now used for purposes other than worship. Outstanding among them are St Peter Mancroft, a masterpiece of Gothic architecture built between 1430 and 1455 (and the largest church in Norwich), and St Peter Hungate, a handsome 15th century church standing at the top of Elm Hill, a narrow, unbelievably

picturesque lane where in medieval times the city's wool merchants built their homes, close to their warehouses beside the River Wensum.

St Gregory's Church in Pottergate is another Norwich church to have been deconsecrated, and its fate might well have been a sad one. Happily, it is now the home to an arts centre where local artists, actors, musicians, dancers and other arts groups stage a variety of performances and exhibitions throughout the year.

When the basic structure of the present St Gregory's was built in the late 14th century, the general rule seems to have been that any parish of around 1,000 people would have its own place of worship. St Gregory's was founded on the site of a Saxon church in 1210 and rebuilt in its present form in 1394. The church takes it name from Gregory the Great, the 6th century Pope best known for his campaign to convert the heathen Anglo-Saxons of 'Angle-land' to Christianity, despatching a party of 40 monks to Angle-land in AD596, led by Augustine, whom the Pope consecrated as the first Archbishop of Canterbury. St Julian's Church is adjoined by a rebuilt cell that is the shrine to Mother Julian, whose 14th century *Revelations of Love Divine* is thought to be the first English book written by a woman.

The Inspire Discovery

Elm Hill, Norwich

🏠 historic building   🏛 museum   🏛 historic site   🍃 scenic attraction   🌱 flora and fauna

Centre, housed in the medieval church of St Michael in Coslany Street, just across the Wensum northeast of the city centre, is full of exciting hands-on displays and activities that make scientific enquiry come to life.

There are also a large number of beautiful and well-maintained parks in the city, some of which offer chess, lawn tennis and hard tennis courts, bowls, pitch and putt, rowing and more, together with a programme of entertainments ranging from theatre to concerts. One worth particular mention is The Plantation Garden in Earlham Road, three acres of Victorian plantings restored after having fallen into disrepair, and thought to be the only one in the nation with a Grade II listing.

On the western edge of the city stands the University of East Anglia. It's well worth making your way here to visit the **Sainsbury Centre for Visual Arts**. Housed in a huge hall of aluminium and glass designed by Norman Foster, the Centre contains the eclectic collection of a 'passionate acquirer' of art, Sir Robert Sainsbury. For more than 50 years, Sir Robert purchased whatever works of art took his fancy, ignoring fashionable trends. Thus the visitor finds sculptures and pictures by Henry Moore, Bacon and Giacometti, along with African and pre-Columbian artefacts, Egyptian, Etruscan and Roman bronzes, works by Native Americans and the Inuit, and sculptures from the Cyclades, the South Seas, the Orient and medieval Europe. This

HFG FARM SHOP

North Walsham Road, Beeston St Andrews,
nr Norwich, Norfolk NR12 7BY
Tel/Fax: 01603 424608
e-mail: farmshop@h-f-g.co.uk
website: www.h-f-g.co.uk

HFG – Horstead Farming Group – is a cooperative of seven local farmers who came together in 2002 and took over a farm shop that had been established many years before. The long, low building is well signposted on the B1150 about two miles north of Norwich, and the displays inside are bright, fresh and modern. Accurately described as 'a farmers' market under one roof', it specialises in the group's own seasonal fruit and vegetables, beef, pork and free-range poultry. Most of the fruit comes from the owners farms, the rest being locally grown, and everything is fresh, excellent and well priced, grown by mainly traditional methods and on sale the day it's harvested.

Beef comes from the farm at Frettenham, pork from the Pig Farmer of the Year at Blythburgh. There's Mrs Temple's Norfolk cheese, Norfolk Garden preserves, 12 types of olives, bread baked daily at the Whalebone bakery, 15 types of locally produced flour from Letheringsett Watermill, cakes, biscuits, apple juices, sweets, chocolates....and plenty more besides. Visits can be arranged to the vegetable fields and fruit farm. March 2006 saw the opening of a new HFG farm shop at the Leisure village, Old Yarmouth Road, Blofield. Countryside Alliance Rural Retailer of the Year - highly commended and EDP Food Awards Farm Shop of the Year - 2006 winner.

extraordinary collection was donated to the University by Sir Robert and Lady Lisa Sainsbury in 1973; their son David complemented his parents' generosity by paying for the building in which it is housed.

To the south of Norwich in the village of Caistor St Edmund are the remains of **Venta Icenorum**, the Roman town established here after Boudicca's rebellion in AD61. Unusually, this extensive site has not been disturbed by later developments, so archaeologists have been able to identify the full scale of the original settlement. Sadly very little remains above ground, although in dry summers the grid pattern of the streets show up as brown lines in the grass. Most of the finds discovered during excavations in the 1920s and 1930s are now in Norwich Castle Museum, but the riverside site still merits a visit.

Just to the north of the city, on the Cromer road, lies the **City of Norwich Aviation Museum**. A massive Vulcan bomber dominates the collection, which also includes a variety of aircraft both military and civil and displays showing the development of aviation in Norfolk. On the southern outskirts, **Whitlingham Country Park** is a great place for walking, cycling and boating, with woodland, meadows, trails and two broads.

Around Norwich

PORINGLAND
6 miles SE of Norwich on the B1332

The name of this sizable village will be familiar to those who love the paintings of the Norwich artist John Crome (1794-1842), whose Arcadian painting of *The Poringland Oak* hangs in the Norwich Castle Art Gallery.

To the southwest of Poringland is The Playbarn, an indoor and outdoor adventure centre specially designed for the under-sevens. All the play equipment is based on a farmyard theme, with a miniature farm, bouncy tractors, soft-play sheep pens, and donkey rides among the attractions. Refreshments and light lunches are available, or you can bring along your own picnic.

WYMONDHAM
9 miles SW of Norwich off the A11

| 🏛 Becket's Chapel | 🏛 Railway Station |
| 🏛 Wymondham Heritage Museum | 🏛 The Bridewell |

The exterior of **Wymondham Abbey** presents one of the oddest ecclesiastical buildings in the county; the interior reveals one of the most glorious. The original building on the site was a Saxon church, replaced when William d'Albini, Chief Butler to Henry I, built a priory for the Benedictine monastery of St Albans. The Benedictines - or Black Monks, as they were known because of the colour of their habits – were the richest and most aristocratic of the monastic orders, who apparently experienced some difficulty in respecting their solemn vows of poverty and humility; especially the latter. Constantly in dispute with the people of Wymondham, the dissension between them grew so bitter that in 1249 Pope Innocent IV himself attempted to reconcile their differences. When his efforts failed, a wall was built across the interior of the building, dividing it into an area for the monks and another for the parishioners. Even this drastic measure failed to bring peace, however. Both parties wanted to ring their own bells, so each built a tower. The villagers erected a stately rectangular tower at the west end; the monks an octagonal one over the crossing, thus creating the curious exterior appearance.

Step inside and you find a magnificent Norman nave, 112 feet long. (It was originally twice as long, but the eastern end, along with most of what had become the Abbey buildings, was demolished after the Dissolution of the Monasteries.) The

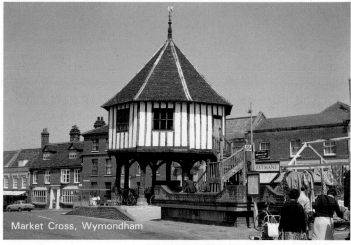

Market Cross, Wymondham

superb hammerbeam roof is supported by 76 beautifully carved angels. There's also an interesting 16th century tomb, of the last Abbot, in delicate terracotta work, and a striking modern memorial: a gilded and coloured reredos and tester commemorating the local men who lost their lives in the First World War.

The rectangular western tower of the Abbey was the setting for one of the last acts in the ill-fated Kett's Rebellion of 1549. From its walls, William Kett was hung in chains and left to die: his brother Robert, the leading figure in the uprising, suffered the same fate at Norwich Castle.

Although many of Wymondham's oldest houses were lost in the fire of 1615, when some 300 dwellings were destroyed, there are still some attractive Elizabethan buildings in the heart of the town. The Market Place (Friday is market day, and on the first Friday of every month there's an antiques and collectors' fair held in Central Hall) is given dignity by the picturesque octagonal Market Cross, rebuilt two years after the fire.

Crowned by a pyramid roof, this appealing timber-framed building is open on all sides on the ground floor, and its upper floor is reached by an outside stairway. Also of interest is **Becket's Chapel**, founded in 1174 and restored in 1559. In its long history it has served as a pilgrim's chapel, grammar school, and coal store. Currently, it houses the town library. **The Bridewell**, or House of Correction, in Bridewell Street was built as a model prison in 1785 along lines recommended by the prison reformer, John Howard, who had condemned the earlier gaol on the site as 'one of the vilest in the country'. Wymondham's Bridewell is said to have served as a model for the penitentiaries established in the United States. Now owned by the town's Heritage Society, Bridewell is home to several community projects, including the **Wymondham Heritage Museum**.

Railway buffs will also want to visit the historic **Railway Station**, built in 1845 on the Great Eastern's Norwich-Ely line. At its peak, the station and its section employed over 100

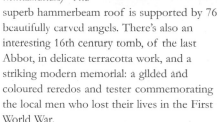

people. Still providing a rail link to Norwich, Cambridge, London and the Midlands, the station has been restored, and its buildings house a railway museum, restaurant and tea room, and a piano showroom. The Mid-Norfolk Heritage Railway runs from Wymondham to Dereham (see under Dereham).

DISS
20 miles S of Norwich on the A1066

🏛 St Mary's Church

The much-loved Poet Laureate John Betjeman declared Diss his favourite Norfolk town, and it's easy to understand his enthusiasm. The River Waveney running alongside forms the boundary between Norfolk and Suffolk, but this attractive old market town – winner of Best Kept Market Town in Norfolk, whose town centre is now a designated conservation area – keeps itself firmly on the northern bank of the river. The town is a pleasing mixture of Tudor, Georgian and Victorian houses grouped around The Mere, which gives the town its name, derived from the Anglo-Saxon word for 'standing water'.

The old town grew up on the hill above the Mere, perhaps because, as an 18th century resident observed, "all the filth of the town centring in the Mere, beside the many conveniences that are placed over it, make the water very bad and altogether useless ... it stinks exceedingly, and sometimes the fish rise in great numbers, so thick that they are easily taken; they are chiefly roach and eels." A proper sewerage system was finally installed in 1851 at this six-acre lake, which is said to be the second deepest in the country, counting the depth of water and mud.

There's a public park beside The Mere, and from it a narrow street leads to the small Market Place. This former poultry market is dominated by the somewhat over-restored **St Mary's Church**. The oldest parts date back some 700 years, and the St Nicholas Chapel is particularly enjoyable with its wonderful corbels, angels in the roof, and gargoyles. In the early 1500s, the Rector here was John Skelton, Court poet and tutor to Prince Henry, later Henry VIII. A bitter, quarrelsome man, Skelton was appointed Poet Laureate through the patronage of Cardinal Wolsey, despite the fact that most of Skelton's output has been described as 'breathless doggerel'. Appointed Rector of Diss in 1502, he appears to have been suspended nine years later for having a concubine. Not far from his church is the delightful Victorian Shambles with a cast-iron veranda and a small museum inside.

BRESSINGHAM
5 miles W of Diss off the A1066

🏛 Bressingham Gardens & Steam Museum

🏛 Fire Museum

Bressingham Gardens and Steam Museum (see panel opposite) boasts one of the world's finest collections of British and Continental locomotives, amongst them the famous 'Royal Scot'. All are housed under cover in the museum's extensive locomotive sheds, which also contain many steam-driven industrial engines, traction engines, a Victorian steam roundabout and **The Fire Museum**, whose collection of fire engines and fire-fighting equipment could form a complete museum in its own right. Visitors can view the interior of the Royal Coach and ride along five miles of track through the woods and gardens. Three narrow-gauge railways run through the gardens, woods, meadows and lakes. Alan Bloom's world-famous six-acre Dell Garden has 47 island beds of perennials, and Foggy

Bressingham Steam & Gardens

Thetford Road, Bressingham, Norfolk IP22 2AB
Tel: 01379 686900 Fax: 01379 686907
website: www.bressingham.co.uk

A day to remember is guaranteed at **Bressingham**, where gardeners will be in paradise and children past and present can experience the thrill of the golden age of steam. Alan Bloom, one of the most respected plantsmen of his age, created the Dell Garden and its famous Island Beds between 1955 and 1962, and his garden is now world-renowned for its collection of nearly 5,000 species and varieties of hardy perennials. The Garden Centre has a comprehensive collection of hardy perennials including the Blooms Heritage Collection, plus plants for the house and conservatory and all sorts of gardening gifts and accessories, as well as a café and bookshop.

 Alan's son-in-law Jaime Blake carries on the family tradition as Curator of Dell Garden, while son Adrian has created a garden for all seasons at nearby Foggy Bottom, where trees, conifers and shrubs provide a backdrop which is enhanced by plantings of perennials and ornamental grasses. The two gardens are open from April to October, the Garden Centre and Steam Experience all year round. There's a full programme of special events, lectures, talks and demonstrations. This really is a place to linger, and Alan Bloom offers B&B accommodation at his Georgian home, Bressingham Hall.

Bottom is a seasonal combination of trees, conifers, shrubs, perennials and ornamental grasses. A two-acre plant centre adjoins the gardens and here there are thousands of plant specimens, many of them rare, available for purchase. Another major attraction here is the national Dads Army collection – a tribute to Captain Mainwaring and his men at Walmington-on-Sea.

SCOLE
2 miles E of Diss on the A140

Scole's history goes back to Roman times, since it grew up alongside the Imperial highway from Ipswich to Norwich at the point where it bridged the River Waveney. Traffic on this road (the A140) became unbearable in the 1980s, but a bypass has now mercifully restored some peace to the village. There are two hostelries of note: a coaching inn of 1655, built in an extravagant style of Dutch gables, giant pilasters and towering chimney stacks, and the Crossways Inn, which must have a good claim to being the prettiest pub in the county.

LANGMERE
6 miles NE of Diss on minor road off the A140 (through Dickleburgh)

100th Bomb Group Memorial Museum

Veterans of the Second World War and their families and friends will be interested in the **100th Bomb Group Memorial Museum**, a small museum on the edge of Dickleburgh

stories and anecdotes   famous people   art and craft   entertainment and sport   walks

Airfield (now disused). The Museum is a tribute to the US 8th Air Force which was stationed here during the war, and includes displays of USAAF decorations and uniforms, equipment, combat records and other memorabilia. Facilities include refreshments, a museum shop, visitor centre and a picnic area.

HARLESTON
7 miles NE of Diss off the A143

This pretty market town with some notable half-timbered and Georgian houses, and a splendid 12th century coaching inn, was a favourite of the renowned architectural authority, Nikolaus Pevsner, who particularly admired the early Georgian Candlers House at the northern end of the town. Another writer has described the area around the marketplace as 'the finest street scene in East Anglia'. The town lies in the heart of the Waveney Valley, a lovely area which inspired many paintings by the locally-born artist, Sir Alfred Munnings.

COLTISHALL
8 miles N of Norwich on the B1150/B1354

🏠 Ancient Lime Kiln

This charming village beside the River Bure captivates visitors with its riverside setting, leafy lanes, elegant Dutch-gabled houses, village green and thatched church. Coltishall has a good claim to its title of 'Gateway to Broadland', since for most cruisers this is the beginning of the navigable portion of the

POLLY PRINGLE SILVER

5a Market Place, Harleston, Norfolk IP20 9AD
Tel: 01379 851955
e-mail: polly@pollypringle.fsnet.co.uk
website: www.pollypringlesilver.co.uk

The summer of 2005 saw the opening of **Polly Pringle Silver** in a Tudor-style building on Harleston's market place, just off the A143 Diss-Bungay road. The owner, who has for many years also run a stall in London's Camden Lock, stocks a wide range of silver jewellery including costume and vintage pieces, displayed to elegant effect on solid oak blocks against a simple white background. Prices are very reasonable, and Polly or her assistants are on hand with help and advice. Polly Pringle Silver is open every day except Sunday (the Camden Lock stall operates on Saturday and Sunday).

GLEBE FARM HOLIDAY COTTAGES

Church Lane, Frettenham, Norfolk NR12 7NW
Tel/Fax: 01603 897641   e-mail: rona.norton@btinteret.com
website: www.glebefarm-cottages.co.uk

Glebe Farm Holiday Cottages are the ideal choice for unwinding in the idyllic Norfolk countryside and discovering the magic of the area. Glebe House has two double rooms, a twin and a triple, sleeping up to nine guests plus a cot, and the adjoining Glebe Farm Cottage sleeps four plus a cot. This handsome period property stands in a large south-facing garden with patio furniture and a barbecue area. On a neighbouring site is the two-bedroom Rectory Cottage, also standing in a large private garden and with a barbecue facility and garden furniture. All three properties are fully equipped for a comfortable, stress-free self-catering holiday.

🏠 historic building   📷 museum   🏛 historic site   🦢 scenic attraction   🌿 flora and fauna

Bure. Anyone interested in Norfolk's industrial heritage will want to seek out the **Ancient Lime Kiln**, next door to the Railway Tavern in Station Road. Lime, formerly an important part of Norfolk's rural economy, is obtained by heating chalk to a very high temperature in a kiln. Most of the county sits on a bed of chalk, but in the area around Coltishall and Horstead it is of a particularly high quality. The kiln at Coltishall, one of the few surviving in the country, is a listed building of finely finished brickwork, built in a style unique to Norfolk.

The top of the tapered kiln pot is level with the ground, and down below a vaulted walkway allowed access to the grills through which the lime was raked out. This was uncomfortable and even dangerous work since fresh lime, when it comes into contact with a moist surface, such as a human body, becomes burning hot. The lime had to be slaked with water before it could be used as a fertiliser, for mortar or as whitewash. Access to the kiln is by way of the Railway Tavern, but during the months from October to March you may find that the building has been taken over by a colony of hibernating bats which, by law, may not be disturbed.

AYLSHAM
14 miles N of Norwich on the A140

- Blickling Hall
- Mannington
- Bure Valley Railway
- Wolterton Park
- Little Barningham

The attractive little town of Aylsham is set beside the River Bure, the northern terminus of the **Bure Valley Railway**. It has an unspoilt Market Place, surrounded by late 17th and early 18th century houses, reflecting the prosperity the town enjoyed in those years from the cloth trade, and a 14th/15th century church, St Michael's, said to have been built by John O'Gaunt. In the churchyard is the tomb of one of the greatest of the 18th century landscape gardeners, Humphrey Repton, the creator of some 200 parks and gardens around the country.

One of Repton's many commissions was to landscape the grounds of **Blickling Hall**, a 'dream of architectural beauty' which stands a mile or so outside Aylsham. Many visitors have marvelled at their first sight of the great Hall built for Sir Henry Hobart in the 1620s. "No-one is prepared on coming downhill past the church into the village, to find the main front of this finest of Jacobean mansions,

ITTERINGHAM MILL

The Mill, The Common, Itteringham, Norfolk NR11 7AR
Tel: 01263 587688
e-mail: downspeter@talk21.com
website: www.itteringham.com/business/mill.html

Country-lovers, birdwatchers, walkers and tourists all enjoy the hospitality in generous supply at **Itteringham Mill**, which enjoys a quiet, scenic setting in a tiny rural hamlet. The 18th century mill has been stylishly converted into a distinguished country mansion where owners Peter and Lis Downs have three very spacious and comfortable bedrooms for Bed & Breakfast guests. All rooms have river views and ensuite facilities. A splendid multi-choice breakfast is served in the lovely lounge that also makes the most of the location. Two holiday cottages in a converted barn are also available. Non-smoking. Cash and cheques only.

stories and anecdotes   famous people   art and craft   entertainment and sport   walks

actually looking upon the road, unobstructedly, from behind its velvet lawns," enthused Charles Harper in 1904. "No theatrical manager cunning in all the artful accessories of the stage could devise anything more dramatic."

Inside, the most spectacular feature is the Long Gallery, which extends for 135 feet and originally provided space for indoor exercise in bad weather. Its glory is the plaster ceiling, an intricately patterned expanse of heraldic panels bearing the Hobart arms, along with others displaying bizarre and inscrutable emblems such as a naked lady riding a two-legged dragon.

Blickling Hall

Other treasures at Blickling include a dramatic double-flight carved oak staircase, the Chinese Bedroom lined with 18th century hand-painted wallpaper, and the dazzling Peter the Great Room. A descendant of Sir Henry Hobart, the 2nd Earl of Buckinghamshire, was appointed Ambassador to Russia in 1746, and he returned from that posting with a magnificent tapestry, the gift of Empress Catherine the Great. This room was redesigned so as to display the Earl's sumptuous souvenir to its full effect, and portraits of himself and his Countess by Gainsborough were added later.

The Earl was a martyr to gout, and his death in 1793 at the age of 50 occurred when, finding the pain unbearable, he thrust his bloated foot into a bucket of icy water, and suffered a heart attack. He was buried beneath the idiosyncratic Egyptian Pyramid in the grounds, a 45-foot structure designed by Ignatius Bonomi that combines Egyptian and classical elements to create a mausoleum which, if nothing else, is certainly distinctive.

Within a few miles of Blickling Hall are two other stately homes, both the properties of Lord and Lady Walpole. **Mannington Gardens and Countryside** are set around a medieval moated manor house and feature a wide variety of plants, trees and shrubs, including thousands of roses, and particularly classic varieties. The Heritage Rose Garden and Twentieth-Century Rose Garden are set in small gardens reflecting their period of origin. There are also Garden Shops, with plants, souvenirs and crafts, and tea rooms. The Hall itself is open by appointment, while the grounds are open Sundays between May-September and also Wednesdays-Fridays from June-August.

Two miles from Mannington, **Wolterton Park**, the stately 18th century Hall built for Horatio Walpole, brother of Sir Robert,

England's first Prime Minister, stands in grounds landscaped by Humphry Repton. Here can be found walks and trails, orienteering, an adventure playground and various special events are held throughout the year. The Hall is open for tours every Friday from April to the end of October.

Over 20 miles of waymarked public footpaths and permissive paths run around Mannington and Wolterton linking into the Weavers Way long-distance footpath and Holt circular walk.

Just north of Mannington Hall stands the village of **Little Barningham**, where St Mary's Church is a magnet for collectors of ecclesiastical curiosities. Inside, perched on the corner of an ancient box pew, stands a remarkable wood-carved skeletal figure of the Grim Reaper. Its fleshless skull stares hollow-eyed at visitors with a defiant, mirthless grin: a scythe gripped in one clutch of bones, and an hour-glass in the other, symbolise the inescapable fate that awaits us all. This gruesomely powerful *memento mori* was donated to the church in 1640 by one Stephen Crosbie who, for good measure, added the inscription: 'As you are now, even so was I, Remember death for ye must dye.' Those words were a conventional enough adjuration at that time, but what is one supposed to make of Stephen's postscript inscribed on the back of the pew: 'For couples joined in wedlock this seat I did intend'?

GREAT WITCHINGHAM
11 miles NW of Norwich off the A1067

🐦 Norfolk Wildlife Centre 🐿 Weston Longville

Norfolk Wildlife Centre & Country Park is home to an interesting collection of rare and ancient breeds of farm livestock such as white-faced woodland and Shetland sheep, pygmy

goats and Exmoor ponies. Set in 40 acres of peaceful parkland, the Centre also has reindeer, otters and badgers, pools teeming with wildfowl and a huge colony of wild herons nesting in the trees. There are also 'Commando' and Adventure Play Areas, one of the finest collections of trees and flowering shrubs in the county, a café and gift shop. The Centre is also home to the most spectacular birds of-prey flying display in Norfolk.

A little further southeast, the Dinosaur Adventure Park near Lenwade doesn't have any living creatures, but as you wander through the woods here you will come across some startlingly convincing life-size models of dinosaurs. One of them, the 'Climb-a-Saurus', is a children's activity centre. A woodland maze, picnic area with gas-fired barbecues, a play area for toddlers, a restaurant and a 'Dinostore' offering a wide variety of dinosaur models, books and gifts are among the park's other attractions.

Anyone who has ever read Parson Woodforde's enchanting *Diary of a Country Parson* will want to make a short diversion to the tiny village of **Weston Longville**, a mile or so south of the Dinosaur Park. The Revd James Woodforde was vicar of this remote parish from 1774 until his death in 1803, and throughout that time he conscientiously maintained a daily diary detailing a wonderful mixture of the momentous and the trivial. "Very great Rebellion in France" he notes when, 10 days after the Fall of the Bastille, the dramatic news eventually arrived at Weston Longville. More often he records his copious meals ("We had for dinner a Calf's head, boiled Fowl and Tongue, a saddle of Mutton roasted on the side table, and a fine Swan roasted with Currant Jelly Sauce for the first Course. The Second Course a couple of Wild

Alderford Common

Distance: *3.1 miles (4.83 kilometres)*

Typical time: *90 mins*

Height gain: *20 metres*

Map: *Explorer 238*

Walk: *www.walkingworld.com ID:1504*

Contributor: *Joy & Charles Boldero*

ACCESS INFORMATION:

There is no bus route to the car parking area, however there is a bus route to Swannington and the walk could be started at Point 7. The car park is on Alderford Common which is situated on the Reepham to Hellesdon road 3 miles southeast of Reepham.

DESCRIPTION:

This is a nice easy short rural walk not far from Norwich. The route is through woodland, along tracks, across meadows and through the rural village of Swannington.

ADDITIONAL INFORMATION:

Alderford Common is a haven for wildlife. Parts of it have been listed as a site of Special Scientific Interest since 1957. On the south side there is an overgrown Bronze Age barrow. In 1988, the National Nightingale survey stated that this area had more pairs of nightingales than any other in east Norfolk.

Swannington Hall was probably built in the late 1500's for a family named, Richers. Some years ago it became a popular 'pub' but now it is again a private house; part of the old

moat can still be seen. St Margaret's Church has stood here since the 13th century and inside the font is of that age too.

FEATURES:

Church, Wildlife, Birds, Flowers, Great Views, Butterflies

WALK DIRECTIONS:

1 | From the car park turn right along the road.

2 | Just before cancellation sign turn left at the finger post sign into a woodland path. It goes through the bracken then across open spaces, at the second of which the path keeps to the top of the bank. The path then goes up and down finally going up steps.

3 | Turn left at the road then after about 10 paces turn right at the fingerpost along track.

4 | Turn right along a country lane. Opposite the yellow hydrant marker in Upgate turn left across grass to a yellow marker on finger post sign in the far hedgeline. Go over a plank bridge, up the bank and continue along the field edge.

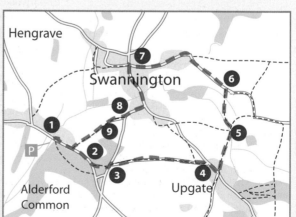

5 | Turn right at the yellow marker signs, over a bridge and through a gate. Turn left along a meadow, go through a gate and diagonally right under wires to the next gate. Cross the next meadow to a gate ahead.

6 | Turn left along a tarmac lane.

7 | Turn left along a country lane, by a church walking through Swannington. Keep along The Street then bear right along Broad Lane (Near here is the bus stop).

8 | At the bend turn right at the fingerpost along a track.

9 | At a footpath marker on the ground turn left through a hedge gap. Take the path round against the hedge on the left in the two fields. Cross the road to the car park.

Fowl, Larks, Blamange, Tarts etc. etc.'"), the weather (during the winter of 1785, for example, the frost was so severe that it froze the chamberpots under the beds), and his frequent dealings with the smuggler Andrews, who kept the good parson well-supplied with contraband tea, gin and cognac.

Inside the simple village church there's a portrait of Parson Woodforde, painted by his nephew, and across the road the inn has been named after this beguiling character.

SWANNINGTON

11 miles NW of Norwich off the A1067/B1149

Swannington Manor

The gardens of **Swannington Manor** are famous for the 300-year-old yew and box topiary hedge. Other features of this small

---

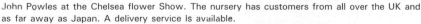

stories and anecdotes   famous people   art and craft   entertainment and sport   walks

town are the 13th century St Margaret's church, Swannington Hall – where can be seen the remains of the former moat – and the charming thatched village water pump.

Swannington's Ketts Lane was named after Robert Kett, leader of the peasants' revolt, who reputedly was captured in a barn nearby.

REEPHAM
12 miles NW of Norwich on the B1145

🏃 Marriott's Way

Reepham is an attractive town set in the rich countryside between the Wensum and Bure Valleys. Lovely 18th century houses border the Market Place, and there is delightful walking along the **Marriott's Way** cycle path. Market day is Wednesdays, and regular antiques fairs are held at the Old Reepham Brewery.

SALLE
13 miles NW of Norwich off the B1145

🏛 Church of St Peter and St Paul

In the village of Salle stands one of Norfolk's finest churches. Norfolk's 'rural cathedral', the Barnack-stone **Church of St Peter and St Paul**, stands in splendid isolation in the Norfolk countryside. Among its many treasures are the seven-sacrament font, the chancel roof with its 160 angels, the carved bosses and a three-decker pulpit.

VERY NICE THINGS

Market Place, Reepham, nr Norwich, Norfolk NR10 4JJ
Tel/Fax: 01603 873390

Beautiful, interesting locally-made gifts fill the display space at **Very Nice Things**, a large and charming shop situated on the old market place alongside the parish church. Originally a private residence, it retains a relaxed and welcoming atmosphere, making it a real pleasure to browse and buy among the extensive range of decorative hand-painted pottery, kitchenware, teapots, silk scarves, silver jewellery, blankets, candles, soaps, a vast selection of lovely cards, and much, much more. Customers are sure to find something special for any occasion at Very Nice Things.

REEPHAM FISHERY

Beck Farm, Norwich Road, Reepham, Norfolk NR10 4NR
Tel: 01603 870829
e-mail: enquiries@reephamfishery.co.uk
website: www.reephamfishery.co.uk

A day's great fishing or a fishing holiday to remember – **Reepham Fishery** is the ideal place for both, geared firmly towards the pleasure angler. In a beautiful, tranquil setting in the heart of the Norfolk countryside, this is one of Norfolk's premier fishing sites, established for many years on spring-fed lakes. Day tickets are available for a full day's fishing, while for those taking a break in this delightful place there's a choice between two luxury caravan homes bookable between March and October and four luxury bungalows open 11 months a year.

🏛 historic building   🏛 museum   🏛 historic site   🌀 scenic attraction   🌿 flora and fauna

CAWSTON
12 miles NW of Norwich on the B1145

🏠 St Agnes' Church

"Lovers of the Norfolk churches can never agree which is the best," wrote Sir John Betjeman. "I have heard it said that you are either a Salle man or a Cawston man." In this county so rich in exceptionally beautiful churches, Salle and Cawston are indeed in a class of their own. **St Agnes' Church** in Cawston, among many other treasures, boasts a magnificent double hammerbeam roof, where angels with protective wings eight feet across float serenely from the roof, and a gorgeous 15th century rood screen embellished with lovely painted panels of saints and Fathers of the Church. The two churches are just a couple of miles apart, so you can easily decide for yourself whether you are 'a Salle man or a Cawston man'. Surprisingly for such a genial character, Sir John seems to have overlooked the possibility that other visitors to these two remarkable churches might define themselves as either 'a Salle woman or a Cawston woman'. By the B1149 close to its junction with the B1145 stands a huge stone known as the Duelling Stone. It marks the occasion of a duel that took place in 1698 between two local dignitaries, Sir Henry Hobart (see under Aylsham) and Oliver Le Neve.

Great Yarmouth

🏛 Norfolk Nelson Museum 🏛 The Tolhouse
🏛 Time and Tide Museum 🕯 Nelson's Monument
🏚 The Quay 🏚 The Rows 🐟 Sealife centre
🕯 Anna Sewell House

The topography of Great Yarmouth is rather curious. Back in Saxon times, it was actually an island, a large sandbank dotted with fishermen's cottages. Later, the narrow estuary of the River Bure at the northern end was blocked off, causing it to flow down the western side of the town. It runs parallel to the sea for two miles before joining the larger River Yare, and then their united waters curve around the southern edge of the town for another three miles before finally entering the sea.

So Yarmouth is now a promontory, its eastern and western sides displaying markedly different characters. The seaward side is a five-mile stretch of sandy beaches, tourist attractions and countless amusements, with a breezy promenade from which one can watch the constant traffic of ships in Yarmouth Roads. There are two fine old traditional piers, the Britannia (810 feet long) and the Wellington (600 feet long), as well as The Jetty, first built in the 16th century for landing goods and passengers. A host of activities are on offer for families: **The Sealife Centre** with many kinds of marine life including octopus and seahorses, and an underwater viewing channel passing through shark-infested 'oceans'; Amazonia, an indoor tropical paradise featuring the largest collection of reptiles in Britain; Merrivale Model Village, which offers an acre of attractive landscaped gardens with over 200 realistic models of town and country in miniature, which are illuminated at dusk, and the Pleasure Beach, featuring over 70 rides and attractions combining all the thrills of modern high-tech amusement park rides with the fun of traditional fairground attractions.

For heritage enthusiasts, Great Yarmouth has a rich and proud maritime history. The **Norfolk Nelson Museum** on South Quay features displays, paintings and contemporary memorabilia relating to the life and times of

🗟 stories and anecdotes 🕯 famous people 🖉 art and craft 🖉 entertainment and sport 🚶 walks

Horatio Lord Nelson. Also on South Quay is the **Elizabethan House Museum**, built by a wealthy merchant and now a museum of domestic life, with 16th century panelled rooms and a Victorian kitchen. In Row 117, South Quay, the Old Merchant's House is an excellent example of a 17th century dwelling and a showplace for local wood and metalwork. Nearby is **The Tolhouse**, originally built in 1262 as a gaol and later used as a courthouse. It is now a museum with original dungeons.

At South Denes the 144-foot **Nelson's Monument** crowned by a statue, not of Norfolk's most famous son, but of Britannia.

Most of Yarmouth's older buildings are concentrated in the western, or riverside, part of the town. Here you will find **The Quay**, which moved Daniel Defoe, in 1724, to describe it as "the finest quay in England, if not Europe". It is more than a mile long and in places 150 yards wide. The Town Hall is well known for its grand staircase, Court Room and Assembly Room; the building itself is in use by the Local Authority. **The Rows**, a medieval network of tiny courtyards and narrow alleys, are a mere two feet wide in places. Badly damaged during a bombing raid in 1942, enough remains to show their unique character. There were originally 145 of these rows, about seven miles in total, all of them built at right angles to the sea and therefore freely ventilated by onshore breezes which, given the urban sanitary conditions of those times, must have been extremely welcome.

The bombing raid of 1942 also completely destroyed the interior of St Nicholas' church, but left its walls standing. Between 1957 and 1960 this huge building - the largest parish church in England - was completely restored and furnished in traditional style largely by using pieces garnered from redundant churches and other sources. The partly Norman font, for example, came from

Great Yarmouth Row Houses

Great Yarmouth, Norfolk NR30 2RQ
Tel: 01493 857900
website: www.english-heritage.org.uk

Experience the sights and sounds of yesterday's Great Yarmouth.

Visit these unique and vividly-presented houses, one set in c.1870 and the other in 1942, just before incendiary bombing. Find out how Yarmouth's 'Herring Girls' lived, hear an original BBC wartime broadcast and 'Mr Rope's sea shanties', See the amazing collection of artefacts rescued

from Row houses after World War II bombing, and contrast tenement conditions with 'respectable' merchant's interiors.

Open daily April to September

🏛 historic building   🏛 museum   🏛 historic site   🍃 scenic attraction   🐑 flora and fauna

Highway church in Wiltshire, the organ from St Mary-the-Boltons in Kensington.

Just south of the church, off the Market Place, is the half-timbered **Anna Sewell House**, built in 1641, in which the author of *Black Beauty* lived. Sewell was born in the town in 1820, but it was only when she was in her late fifties that she transmuted her concern for the more humane treatment of horses into a classic and seemingly timeless novel. Anna was paid just £20 for the rights to a book which, in the five months that elapsed between its publication and her death in 1878, had already sold an incredible 100,000 copies.

Birthplace of Anna Sewell

Another famous author associated with the town is Charles Dickens, who stayed at the Royal Hotel on Marine Parade in 1847-48 while writing *David Copperfield*. Dickens had visited the town as a child and had actually seen an upturned boat on the beach being used as a dwelling, complete with a chimney emerging from its keel. In his novel, this becomes Peggotty's house to which young Copperfield is brought following the death of his mother. "One thing I particularly noticed in this delightful house," he writes, "was the smell of fish; which was so searching, that when I took out my pocket-handkerchief to wipe my nose, I found it smelt exactly as if it had wrapped up a lobster."

In fact, the whole town at that time was pervaded with the aroma of smoked herring, the silvery fish that were the basis of Yarmouth's prosperity. Around the time of

Dickens' stay here, the author of the town's directory tried to pre-empt any discouraging effect this might have on visitors by claiming that "The wholesome exhalations arising from the fish during the operation of curing are said to have a tendency to dissipate contagious disorders, and to be generally beneficial to the human constitution which is here sometimes preserved to extreme longevity."

Across the town, some 60 curing houses were busy gutting, salting and spicing herrings to produce Yarmouth's great contribution to the English breakfast, the kipper. The process had been invented by a Yarmouth man, John Woodger: a rival of his, a Mr Bishop, developed a different method which left the fish wonderfully moist and flavoursome, and so created the famous Yarmouth bloater.

For centuries, incredible quantities of herring were landed, nearly a billion in 1913 alone. In earlier years the trade had involved so many fishermen that there were more boats (1,123) registered at Yarmouth than at London. But the scale of the over-fishing produced the inevitable result: within the space of two decades Yarmouth's herring industry foundered, and by the late 1960s found itself dead in the water. Luckily, the end of that historic trade coincided with the beginning of North Sea oil and gas exploitation, a business which has kept the town in reasonably good economic health up to the present day. The **Time and Tide Museum of Great Yarmouth Life** explains the town's fishing and maritime heritage. Here, too, is the Great Yarmouth Potteries & Herring Smokehouse Museum.

Around Great Yarmouth

CAISTER-ON-SEA
3 miles N of Great Yarmouth off the A149

🏠 Caister Castle   🌿 Thrigby Hall

In Boudicca's time, this modern holiday resort with its stretch of fine sands was an important fishing port for her people, the Iceni. After the Romans had vanquished her unruly tribe, they settled here sometime in the 2nd century and built a *castra*, or castle, or Caister, of which only a few foundations and remains have yet been found. **Caister Castle**, which stands in a picturesque setting about a mile to the west of the town, is a much later construction, built in 1432-5 by the legendary Sir John Fastolf with his spoils from the French wars in which he had served, very profitably, as Governor of Normandy and also distinguished himself leading the English bowmen at the Battle of

Agincourt. Academics have enjoyed themselves for centuries disputing whether this Sir John was the model for Shakespeare's immortal rogue, Falstaff. Certainly the real Sir John was a larger-than-life character, but there's no evidence that he shared Falstaff's other characteristics of cowardliness, boastfulness or general over-indulgence.

Caister Castle was the first in England to be built of brick, and is in fact one of the earliest brick buildings in the county. The 90-foot tower remains, together with much of the moated wall and gatehouse, now lapped by still waters and with ivy relentlessly encroaching. The castle is open daily from May to September and, as an additional attraction, there is a Car Collection in the grounds which features an impressive collection of cars from an 1893 Panhard et Levassor to Edwardian and vintage cars, an antique fire engine, the original car used in the film of Ian Fleming's *Chitty Chitty Bang Bang*, Jim Clark's Lotus and the very first Ford Fiesta.

About three miles west of Caister Castle, the pleasantly landscaped grounds surrounding an 1876 Victorian mansion have been transformed into the **Thrigby Hall Wildlife Gardens**, home for a renowned collection of Asian mammals, birds and reptiles. There are snow leopards and rare tigers; gibbons and crocodiles; deer and otters; and other attractions include a tropical house, aviaries, waterfowl lake, willow pattern garden, gift shop and café. The Gardens are open every day, all year round.

FRITTON
6 miles SW of Great Yarmouth off the A143

🌊 Fritton Lake   🌿 Redwings Horse Sanctuary

At **Fritton Lake Countryworld**, visitors will find a large undercover falconry centre with

🏠 historic building   📷 museum   🏛 historic site   🌊 scenic attraction   🌿 flora and fauna

MATTHEW HIGHAM ANTIQUES

Unit 10, The Raveningham Centre, Beccles Road,
Raveningham, Norfolk NR14 6NU
Tel/Fax: 01986 896655
e-mail: info@matthewhighamantiques.co.uk
website: www.matthewhighamantiques.co.uk

Owner Matthew Higham, Manager Julia Headland and a fine team of experts run **Matthew Higham Antiques**, which has over 20 years' experience of sourcing and importing rare and interesting European pine and hardwood furniture, mainly from France, Hungary, Romania, Russia and the Czech Republic. Each month around 250 pieces, including armoires, food cupboards, dressers, bookcases, benches, tables, boxes and chests of drawers arrive at their UK warehouse, where a team of specialised cabinet-makers and painters will paint or customise items to individual customer requirements. The company is renowned for the skill and taste it employs in reviving the grace and integrity of each piece through specially developed restoration processes; since each item will enjoy a special place in any home, the experts will modify furniture and develop paint colours to suit a wide range of interiors, from classic homes to modern urban spaces.

A new range of Chinese antique furniture represents styles and forms from almost every province in China. Restoration carried out in Beijing is very sympathetic to the original surface patina of each piece, so re-lacquering is largely rejected in favour of reconditioning the crackled and worn finishes. Prices at Matthew Higham Antiques cover a wide range, and customers include interior designers, quality antique and interiors outlets, dealers and the trade in the UK and around the world, as well as private individuals.

EAST INDIA TRADING DEPOT

Castell Farm, The Raveningham Centre,
Beccles Road, Raveningham, Norfolk NR14 6NU
Tel: 01508 548406
e-mail: mal@norfolkrugs.co.uk
website: www.norfolkrugs.co.uk

For the past 20 years Mal and Liz Cannell have run the **East India Trading Depot**, making it a mecca for people looking to find a beautiful object for the home away from the usual high street hassle. In the stables of a large farmhouse in the heart of rural Norfolk, the showrooms are packed with the region's best display of rugs and carpets from Afghanistan and Persia. Customers will also find a range of exquisite textiles and antiques from around the world.

The friendly, helpful owners believe that being surrounded by rich colours and beautiful objects enriches and stimulates a life and should be available to all – a philosophy that leads to reasonable prices as well as assured taste and quality. Browsers can take a break in the little tea room with a cup of tea or coffee and a chat with the owners. East India Trading Depot is open from 10am to 6pm Friday to Monday, and otherwise 'by luck or appointment'

stories and anecdotes   famous people   art and craft   entertainment and sport   walks

birds-of-prey flying displays twice daily. There are also heavy horse stables and a children's farm, a nine-hole pitch and putt course, lakeside gardens, boating and a large adventure playground. Open end-March to end-September every day, and weekends and half-term in October. Opposite Countryworld is the Caldecott Visitor Centre of the **Redwings Horse Sanctuary**, where 70 acres of paddocks are home to some very special rescued horses, ponies, donkeys and mules, some of which are available for adoption.

The Broads

The Broads area covers more than 33 square kilometres that include 200 kilometres of waterways. The broads themselves are shallow lakes formed in medieval times when peat was dug out to provide fuel and over the years the diggings became flooded as the water level rose. These waterways have always been important transport routes, and each village had its own staithe, or quay, many of which are still in use.

The traditional Broads boat, originally used for commercial purposes, was the wherry, a large, single-sail vessel of shallow draught which plied the broads with cargoes of corn, coal and reed. As rail and road transport gradually took over and the holiday trade began to boom, the wherry's original role was lost and many were converted for leisure use or purpose-built for that purpose, with all mod cons. A few - perhaps no more than half a dozen - still survive, available for regular tours or for private charter, and there really is no finer way to savour the delights of the Broads than from the deck of a wherry.

The Broads, with their wonderful mixture of open water, woodland, fen and marsh, have virtually the status of a National Park; they are protected by the Broads Authority, which is responsible for conservation, recreation and navigation in this unique part of the world. Besides providing peaceful waterborne holidays the area offers great opportunities for walking and cycling, and there are many points from which fishing is permitted. Some of the individual broads are nature reserves, and the waterways are home to an amazing variety of bird, fish and plant life.

REEDHAM
8 miles SW of Great Yarmouth off the B1140

Here in Reedham is the single remaining car and passenger ferry in the Broads. There's also an interesting craft showroom at the Old Brewery, and a great pub in The Reedham Ferry Inn.

BURGH CASTLE
4 miles W of Great Yarmouth off the A12 or A143

When the Romans established their fortress of Garionnonum, now known as Burgh Castle, the surrounding marshes were still under water. The fort then stood on one bank of a vast estuary, commanding a strategic position at the head of an important waterway running into the heart of East Anglia. The ruins are impressive, with walls of alternating flint and brick layers rising 15 feet high in places, and spreading more than 11 feet wide at their base. The Romans abandoned Garionnonum around AD 408 and some two centuries later the Irish missionary St Fursey (or Fursa) founded a monastery within its walls. Later generations cannibalised both his building, and much of the crumbling Roman castle, as materials for their own churches and houses.

LOW ROAD FARM HOLIDAYS

Low Road Farm, Runham, nr Great Yarmouth,
Norfolk NR29 3EQ
Tel: 01493 368104

Low Road Farm Holidays are an ideal choice for a family holiday amidst the wonderful mix of water, woodland, fen and marsh that makes up the Norfolk Broads. Originally a dairy farm and part of the Herringby Estate, the family-run Low Road Farm has two cottages – Peach Tree Cottage in the old dairy with two en suite bedrooms and Owl Barn with one bedroom. Both are provided with everything needed for a stress-free, come-as-you-please stay in lovely quiet surroundings.

A patio with furniture for summer days and evenings looks out over the large, well-kept garden, which contains an ornamental pond and some splendid fruit trees. This is an excellent area for walking and wildlife watching and the coast and countryside hereabouts offer a wide variety of ways to fill the day. Great Yarmouth has plenty of family attractions, Caister has its Castle, and other places of interest include the impressive remains of Burgh Castle and Thrigby Hall Wildlife Gardens, home to a renowned collection of mammals, reptiles and birds.

ACLE

10 miles W of Great Yarmouth off the A47

🏛 Church of St Edmund

A thousand years ago, this small market town, now 10 miles inland, was a small fishing port on the coast. Gradually, land has been reclaimed from the estuaries of the Rivers Bure, Waveney and Yare, so that today large expanses of flat land stretch away from Acle towards the sea. The town's importance as a boating centre began in the 19th century with boat-building yards springing up beside the bridge. When Acle's first Regatta was held in 1890, some 150 yachts took part. The town became known as the 'Gateway to the Broads' and also as the gateway to 'Windmill Land', a picturesque stretch of the River Bure dotted with windmills. The medieval bridge that formerly crossed the Bure at Acle has less agreeable associations, since it was used for numerous executions with the unfortunate victims left to dangle over the river.

Acle was granted permission for a market in 1272, and it's still held every Thursday, attracting visitors from miles around. Others come to see the unusual **Church of St Edmund** with its Saxon round tower, built some time around AD 900, crowned with a 15th century belfry from which eight carved figures look down on the beautifully thatched roof of the nave. The treasures inside include a superbly carved font, six feet high, and inscribed with the date 1410, and a fine 15th century screen.

🎬 stories and anecdotes   🦢 famous people   ✍ art and craft   🎭 entertainment and sport   🚶 walks

WROXHAM
8 miles NE of Norwich on the A1151

🐾 Wroxham Broad   🐾 Bure Valley Railway

🌿 Hoveton Hall Gardens   ✍ Wroxham Barns

This riverside village, linked to its twin, Hoveton, by a hump-backed bridge over the River Bure, is the self-styled 'capital' of the Norfolk Broads and as such gets extremely busy during the season. The banks of the river are chock-a-block with boatyards full of cruisers of all shapes and sizes, there's a constant traffic of boats making their way to the open spaces of **Wroxham Broad**, and in July the scene becomes even more hectic when the annual Regatta is under way.

Wroxham is also the southern terminus of the **Bure Valley Railway**, a nine-mile long, narrow-gauge (15-inch) steam train service that closely follows the course of the River Bure through lovely countryside to the market town of Aylsham. It runs along the trackbed of the old East Norfolk Railway, has two half-scale locomotives, and specially constructed passenger coaches with large windows to provide the best possible views.

A couple of miles north of Wroxham is **Wroxham Barns**, a delightful collection of beautifully restored 18th century barns set in 10 acres of countryside, and housing a community of craftspeople. There are numerous workshops, producing between them a wide range of crafts, from stained glass

to woodturning, stitchcraft to handmade children's clothes, pottery to floral artistry, and much more. The complex also includes a cider-pressing centre, a junior farm with lots of hands-on activities, a traditional Family Fair (with individually priced rides), a gift and craft shop, and a tearoom.

A mile or so east of Wroxham Barns, **Hoveton Hall Gardens** offer visitors a splendid combination of plants, shrubs and trees, with rare rhododendrons, azaleas, water plants and dazzling herbaceous borders within a walled garden. There are woodland and lakeside walks, plant sales, gardening books and a tearoom.

Anyone interested in dried flower arrangements should make their way to the tiny hamlet of Cangate, another couple of miles to the east, where Willow Farm Flowers provides an opportunity of seeing the whole process, from the flowers in the field to the

Wroxham

final colourful displays. The farm shop has an abundance of dried, silk, parchment and wooden flowers, beautifully arranged, and more than 50 varieties of dried flowers are available in bunches or made into arrangements of all shapes and sizes, or to special order. Willow Farm also has a picnic and play area, a guided farm walk, lays on flower arranging demonstrations and also runs one day classes for those interested in learning more about mastering this delicate-fingered skill.

SOUTH WALSHAM
9 miles E of Norwich on the B1140

🏛 St Benet's Abbey   🌿 Fairhaven

🌿 South Walsham Inner Broad

This small village is notable for having two parish churches built within yards of each other. Just to the north of the village is the **Fairhaven Woodland and Water Garden**, an expanse of delightful water gardens lying beside the private **South Walsham Inner Broad**. Its centrepiece is the 900-year-old King Oak, lording it over the surrounding displays of rare shrubs and plants, native wild flowers, rhododendrons and giant lilies. There are tree-lined walks, a bird sanctuary, plants for sale, and a restaurant. A vintage-style riverboat runs trips every half hour around the Broad.

The best way to see the remains of **St Benet's Abbey** is from a boat along the River Bure (indeed, it's quite difficult to reach it any other way). Rebuilt in 1020 by King Canute, after the Vikings had destroyed an earlier Saxon building, St Benet's became one of the richest abbeys in East Anglia. When Henry VIII closed it down in 1536 he made an unusual deal with its last Abbot. In return for creating the Abbot Bishop of Norwich, the Cathedral estates were to be handed over to the King, but St Benet's properties could remain in the Abbot/Bishop's possession. Even today, the Bishop of Norwich retains the additional title of Abbot of St Benet's, and on the first Sunday in August each year travels the last part of the journey by boat to hold an open-air service near the stately ruins of the Abbey gatehouse.

RANWORTH
9 miles E of Norwich off the B1140

🏛 St Helen's Church

🌿 Broadland Conservation Centre

This beautiful Broadland village is famous for its church and its position on Ranworth Broad. From the tower of **St Helen's Church** it is possible to see five Norfolk Broads, Horsey Mill, the sea at Great Yarmouth and, on a clear day, the spire of Norwich Cathedral. Inside, the church houses one of Norfolk's greatest ecclesiastical treasures, a breathtaking early 15th century Gothic choir screen, the most beautiful and the best preserved in the county. In glowing reds, greens and golds, gifted medieval artists painted a gallery of more than 30 saints and martyrs, inserting tiny cameos of such everyday scenes as falcons seizing hares, dogs chasing ducks and, oddly for Norfolk, lions. Cromwell's men, offended by such idolatrous images, smothered them with brown paint - an ideal preservative for these wonderful paintings, as became apparent when they were once again revealed during the course of a 19th century restoration of the church.

Just to the north of the village is the **Broadland Conservation Centre** (Norfolk Naturalists Trust), a thatched building floating on pontoons at the edge of Ranworth Broad. It houses an informative exhibition on the

---

🎭 stories and anecdotes   👤 famous people   🎨 art and craft   🎵 entertainment and sport   🚶 walks

Ludham Marshes

Reserve on the edge of the River Thurne. In the summer months the air is buzzing with insects and butterflies and many varieties of birds are to be seen all year round. Deer can also sometimes be spotted in the nearby wood, while on the river, you will see sailing craft and water birds. The undergrowth can get quite high along the riverbank in the summer, so leg covering is recommended. Short enough for a gentle afternoon stroll, this walk offers something for everyone.

Distance: *3.5 miles (5.5 kilometres)*

Typical time: *90 mins*

Height gain: *0 metres*

Map: *Outdoor Leisure 40 The Broads*

Walk: *www.walkingworld.com ID:800*

Contributor: *Stephanie Kedik*

ACCESS INFORMATION:

Ludham can be reached by car from Norwich (A1151/A1062) or by bus (tel: Norfolk Bus Information 0845 300 6116)

DESCRIPTION:

Ludham is a beautiful, peaceful village at the heart of the Norfolk Broads. A teashop, small restaurant and pub provide a choice of refreshments. The pub with beer garden and children's outside play area, caters for families with young children. The walk takes you from the village centre, down a lane and past a small marina where day boats can be hired. Further down you enter Ludham Marshes Nature

FEATURES:

River, Pub, Toilets, Play Area, Church, Wildlife, Birds, Flowers, Butterflies, Gift Shop Food Shop, Good for Kids, Nature Trail, Tea Shop

WALK DIRECTIONS:

1 | After arriving in the centre of Ludham, take the Yarmouth Road, past the Ludham village sign at Bakers Arms Green. Further down, on your right is a little path leading off and alongside the road. Follow this until you get to a right turn where Horse Fen Road meets the main Yarmouth Road.

2 | Turn right, into Horse Fen Road. Continue along the lane, past Womack Staithe boat hire and camping site.

3 | Follow the public bridleway down onto Ludham Marshes National Nature Reserve. As you take the path round the corner and into the reserve, first a garden and then a wood will be on your left beyond the drainage ditch. Deer can sometimes be seen in these woods. On your right, the marshes stretch out across to the River Thurne.

4 | Follow the footpath through the reserve. Where you meet the gravel track, take a turn to the right through

the gate (that says 'Danger unstable road!').
Continue along this track and through another
gate. At Horse Fen pumping station, turn right
to follow the green footpath sign.

5 | Across the bridge, follow the footpath
along the river, keeping the river on your left.
This stretch can be a bit overgrown in
summer, although it is compensated for by the
views of the river. This footpath will take you
back from the river, up the creek and out of
the reserve at the side of Hunters Yard.

6 | Walk back up Horse Fen Road, past
Womack Staithe and the boatyard.

7 | At the top of Horse Fen Road, turn left and
onto the road leading back into Ludham.

history of the Broads, and there's also an
interesting Nature Trail which shows how
these wetlands gradually developed over the
centuries.

HORNING

12 miles NE of Norwich off the A1062

📷 RAF Air Defence Radar Museum

The travel writer Arthur Mee described
Horning as "Venice in Broadland", where
"waterways wandering from the river into the
gardens are crossed by tiny bridges." With its
pretty reed-thatched cottages lining the bank
of the River Bure and its position in the
heart of the Broads, there are few more
attractive places from which to explore this
magical area.

At RAF Neatishead, near Horning, the **Air
Defence Radar Museum** tells the story of
radar and air defence from 1935 to the present
day. It is housed in the original 1942 Radar
Operations building.

POTTER HEIGHAM

14 miles NE of Norwich off the A149

Modern Potter Heigham has sprung up
around the medieval bridge over the River
Thurne, a low-arched structure with a
clearance of only seven feet at its highest, a
notorious test for novice sailors. The Thurne
is a major artery through the Broads, linking
them in a continuous waterway from Horsey
Mere in the east to Wroxham Broad in the
west. A pleasant excursion from Potter
Heigham is a visit to **Horsey Mere**, about six
miles to the east, and **Horsey Windpump**
(both National Trust). From this early 20th
century drainage mill, now restored and fully

THE OLD VICARAGE HOTEL

The Street, Hemsby, nr Great Yarmouth, Norfolk NR29 4EU
Tel: 01493 731557   e-mail: info@theoldvicaragehotel.net
website: www.theoldvicaragehotel.net

The **Old Vicarage Hotel** is a handsome and substantial redbrick
house standing in extensive grounds with lawns and mature trees.
Built in 1850 for the local vicar, it is now a very comfortable and
civilised hotel owned and run by Jason and Justine Ingram. The bedrooms all have en suite
facilities, TV, beverage tray and bottled water, and the whole place has an inviting feel. The
hotel offers a three-course table d'hote evening meal with four choices for each course, and the
chef makes excellent use of the fine Norfolk produce available in the local markets. The hotel is
well situated for exploring all the scenic splendour of Norfolk's coast and countryside.

📖 stories and anecdotes   🕊 famous people   🎨 art and craft   🎭 entertainment and sport   🚶 walks

THE OLD CHAPEL GUEST HOUSE

Horsey Corner, Horsey, Norfolk NR29 4EH
Tel: 01493 393498
e-mail: enquiries@norfolkbedbreakfast.com
website: www.norfolkbedbreakfast.com

Set in a designated Area of Outstanding Natural Beauty, the **Old Chapel Guest House** is a perfect spot to relax and unwind, to enjoy the bracing Norfolk air, to discover the abundant bird life and to explore the many local delights of coast and countryside. Trish and Colin Wearmouth welcome guests with a cup of tea and a slice of homemade cake, and the three en suite guest rooms, all on the ground floor, provide dune views, home-from-home comfort and up-to-the-minute amenities. A varied breakfast starts the day, and excellent evening meals are available by arrangement.

working, there are lovely views across the Mere. A circular walk follows the north side of Horsey Mere, passes another windmill, and returns through the village. There's a small shop at the Windpump, and light refreshments are available.

WORSTEAD
12 miles NE of Norwich off the A149/B1150

🏛 Norfolk's Golden Fleece Heritage Museum

Hard to imagine now, but Worstead was a busy little industrial centre in the Middle Ages. The

THE OLLANDS GUEST HOUSE

Swanns Yard, Worstead, nr North Walsham,
Norfolk NR28 9RP
Tel: 01692 535150
e-mail: theollands@btinternet.com
website: www.ollandsfarm.com

Worstead was a busy little industrial centre in the Middle Ages, giving its name to the hard-wearing cloth produced in the region. The lovely 14th century Church of St Mary provides ample evidence of Worstead's former prosperity, and **The Ollands Guest House** is a very comfortable, civilised base for a break in this picturesque part of the world. The accommodation at Susan Smith's home comprises three double rooms, two of them en suite, the other with its own private bathroom. All three rooms have TV, clock radio, beverage tray, hairdryer and shoe cleaning kit, and guests have the use of a pleasant lounge with a open fire.

A selection of books, magazines and games is provided for guests' use, and the garden is a pleasant spot for a quiet stroll. An excellent breakfast includes home-produced eggs and home-baked bread, packed lunches can be provided on request and a two-course evening meal is available by arrangement. There are some lovely walks in the vicinity of the house, and the Broads, the coast and the city of Norwich are all within an easy drive.

village lent its name to the hard-wearing cloth produced in the region, and many of the original weavers' cottages can still be seen in the narrow side-streets. Worsted cloth, woven from tightly-twisted yarn, was introduced by Flemish immigrants and became popular throughout England from the 13th century onwards. The Flemish weavers settled happily into the East Anglian way of life and seem to have influenced its architecture almost as strongly as its weaving industry.

The lovely 14th century church of St Mary provides ample evidence of Worstead's former prosperity. Its many treasures include a fine hammerbeam roof, a chancel screen with a remarkable painted dado, and a magnificent traceried font complete with cover. **Norfolk's Golden Fleece Heritage Museum** has a collection relating to the place of the Chapel in local life and a collection reflecting the importance of spinning, weaving and dyeing in Norfolk. In the 'Weaver's loft' members of the Worstead Guild of Weavers, Spinners and Dyers can be seen at work.

The village stages an annual weekend of events in July to raise money for the restoration of the church.

SUTTON
15 miles NE of Norwich off the A149

🏠 Sutton Windmill and Broads Museum

Sutton Windmill, the tallest in Britain and a famous Norfolk landmark, was built in 1789 and was in commercial use until 1940. On the same site, the **Broads Museum** has numerous displays, including woodworking, the leather trade, razors and shaving, coopers', tinsmiths' and blacksmiths' tools, plumbing, animal traps, taxidermy, medical, veterinary, banknotes and the story of tobacco.

STALHAM
15 miles NE of Norwich off the A149

🏠 Museum of the Broads

🏠 Stalham Fire House Museum

In a range of traditional buildings long associated with the wherry trade, the **Museum of the Broads** tells the story of the history, culture and environment of the Broads. Displays include the old racing yacht *Maria* and the steam launch *Falcon*. The **Fire House Museum** relates the history of the Stalham fire service in an 1830s building that housed the town's first fire engine.

Sutton Windmill

🏚 stories and anecdotes   🐦 famous people   ✏ art and craft   ✐ entertainment and sport   🚶 walks

Cromer

🐦 Henry Blogg Museum 🔍 Cromer Museum

As you enter a seaside town, what more reassuring sight could there be than to see the pier still standing? **Cromer Pier** is the genuine article, complete with Lifeboat Station and the Pavilion Theatre, which still stages traditional end-of-the-pier shows. The Pier's survival is all the more impressive since it was badly damaged in 1953 and 1989, and in 1993 sliced in two by a drilling rig which had broken adrift in a storm.

Cromer has been a significant resort since the late 1700s and in its early days even received an unsolicited testimonial from Jane Austen. In her novel *Emma* (1816), a character declares that "Perry was a week at Cromer once, and he holds it to be the best of all the sea-bathing places." A succession of celebrities, ranging from Lord Tennyson and Oscar Wilde to Winston Churchill and the German Kaiser, all came to see for themselves.

The inviting sandy beach remains much as they saw it (horse-drawn bathing machines aside), as does the Church of St Peter & St

RICHARD & JULIE DAVIES

7 Garden Street, Cromer, Norfolk NR27 9HN
Tel: 01263 512727 Fax: 01263 514789

Quality and freshness are paramount at the outstanding fish shop that carries the name of owners **Richard & Julie Davies**. Chef Rick Stein included this excellent establishment in his quest to find the best seafood in Britain, and its renown is well-deserved, as here are sold the very best fish and shellfish, including Cromer crabs, lobster and whelks. Much of the fish is caught by the owners' son John, who represents the eighth generation of the family in the fishing business.

Cromer Museum

East Cottages, Tucker Street, Cromer,
Norfolk NR27 9HB
Tel: 01263 513543
e-mail: cromer.museum@norfolk.gov.uk
website: www.museums.norfolk.gov.uk

A row of restored fishermen's cottages houses **Cromer Museum**, where the look and feel of a fisherman's home life 100 years ago is enhanced by the gentle glow of real gas lights. The rooms in the cottages tell the story of Cromer and the area from the bones of prehistoric animals that once roamed this part of the world to the development of the town, the coming of the railway and the building of the grand Victorian hotels. Thousands of pictures of old Cromer are stored in the museum's computer, and visitors can find out about the geology and natural history of the local beaches in the Beachcombers' Shed. The museum has a small, well-stocked shop.

🏨 historic building   📷 museum   🏛 historic site   🏞 scenic attraction   🌱 flora and fauna

Cromer Pier

Paul, which boasts the tallest tower in Norfolk, 160 feet high. And then as now, Cromer Crabs were reckoned to be the most succulent in England. During the season, between April and September, crab-boats are launched from the shore (there's no harbour here), sail out to the crab banks about three miles offshore, and there the two-man teams on each boat deal with some 200 pots.

Next to the old boathouse is the new **RNLI Henry Blogg Museum**. It tells the dramatic story of the courageous men who manned the town's rescue service. Pre-eminent among them was Harry Blogg, who was coxswain of the lifeboat for 37 years, from 1910 to 1947.

During those years his boat, the *II F Bailey*, was called out 128 times and saved 518 lives. The most decorated lifeboatman, he won three Gold and four Silver RNLI Gallantry medals, the George Cross and the British Empire Medal. The *II F Bailey* is displayed alongside lifeboat models, historic photographs, paintings and other memorabilia.

Also well worth visiting is the **Cromer Museum** (see panel opposite), housed in a row of restored fishermen's cottages near the church, where you can follow the story of Cromer from the days of the dinosaurs, some of whose bones were found nearby, up to the present, and access the computer for thousands of pictures and facts about this attractive town.

Around Cromer

HAPPISBURGH
14 miles SE of Cromer on the B1159

🏛 St Mary's Church

The coastal waters off Happisburgh (or 'Hazeborough', to give the village its correct

GROVELAND FARM SHOPS
Thorpe Market Road, Roughton, nr Cromer, Norfolk NR11 8TB
Tel: 01263 833777

Groveland Farm Shops comprise several outlets under one roof in a flint-walled 17th century barn just off the A140 south of Cromer. The Farm Shop itself sells a wide variety of home-grown fruit and vegetables, own-label jams, chutneys and apple juice, an excellent deli range, organic and health foods, kitchenware and outdoor clothing. Best sellers in the Butchers Shop include home-produced beef and turkey, local lamb and pork and home-cooked ham. The restaurant highlights this produce in its excellent home cooking, and also on site are the Wine Cellar, with own-label, local and imported wines; a garden centre specialising in bonsai and unusual plants; English Rose Hair and Beauty Salon; and Seasons Ladies Fashions selling classic womens' clothes. Groveland's owners also have a farm shop in Feathers Yard in Holt.

Bacton Woods

Distance: *3.1 miles (4.83 kilometres)*

Typical time: *90 mins*

Height gain: *20 metres*

Map: *Explorer 25*

Walk: *www.walkingworld.com ID:1208*

Contributor: *Joy & Charles Boldero*

ACCESS INFORMATION:

Parking in National Trust car park by the Quay. Go along the B1150 east from North Walsham and then follow the signs, 'Bacton Wood' and 'picnic centre' to the car park.

ADDITIONAL INFORMATION:

There has been a woodland here since Saxon times. It is thought that because the soil is so poor the area was not converted to agriculture. The Forestry Commission bought the wood in the 1950s. In the larch woodlands goldcrests and warblers can be spotted. There are two sessile oaks standing, they have been there for over 200 years. The sessile and the English oak are true native species. The sessile oak was planted like a crop in centuries past because the wood is so good for making charcoal. Oak bark of course was used for the tanning of leather before manmade chemicals were used. Mountain cycling is permitted, also horse riding by permit.

There is a permanent orienteering course, maps for this and permits are obtained from the Countryside Project Officer at North Norfolk District council 01263 513811

DESCRIPTION:

This walk is mostly around the ancient Bacton woodland although the route has a short section along a country lane.

FEATURES:

Wildlife, Birds, Flowers, Great Views, Butterflies, Woodland

WALK DIRECTIONS:

1 | Go to the notice board. Turn left along the path with a red and yellow band on a small post.

2 | At the left hand bend turn right through two small posts and along a narrow path. Turn left along a wider path ignoring all paths off it.

3 | At the T junction turn right along a track.

4 | At a country lane turn left.

5 | At Wood Mill Farm track turn left along the bridleway. This leads into the wood. Ignore all the paths off it. Keep along it until you reach the road, then the path curves left still in woodland beside the road.

6 | Turn left, the path takes you back into the wood again.

7 | Take the right fork.

8 | At the T junction turn left, following red marker posts. Turn right. Turn left downhill. Cross the track and go up the bank opposite and back to the car park.

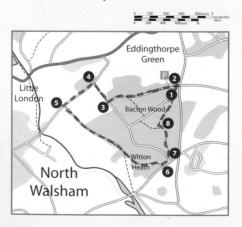

pronunciation), have seen many a shipwreck over the centuries, and the victims lie buried in the graveyard of **St Mary's Church**. The large grassy mound on the north side of the church contains the bodies of the ill-fated crew of HMS *Invincible*, wrecked on the treacherous sandbanks here in 1801. The ship was on its way to join up with Nelson's fleet at Copenhagen when the tragedy occurred, resulting in the deaths of 119 sailors. Happisburgh's distinctive lighthouse, built in 1791 and striped like a barber's pole, certainly proved ineffectual on that occasion; as did the soaring 110-foot tower of the church itself, which could normally be relied on as a 'back-up' warning to mariners.

Inside the Church is a splendid 15th century octagonal font carved with the figures of lions, satyrs and 'wild men'; embedded in the pillars along the aisle are the marks left by shrapnel from German bombs dropped on the village in 1940.

LESSINGHAM
14 miles SE of Cromer off the B1159

From this small village a lane winds down through spectacular dunes to the sands at Eccles Beach and, a little further north, to Cart Gap with its gently sloping beach and colourful lines of beach huts.

NORTH WALSHAM
9 miles SE of Cromer on the A149

🐾 Paston School

This busy country town with its attractive Market Cross of 1600 has some interesting historical associations. Back in 1381, despite its remoteness from London, North Walsham became the focus of an uprising in support of Wat Tyler's Peasants' Revolt. These North Norfolk rebels were led by John Litester, a local

dyer, and their object was the abolition of serfdom. Their actions were mainly symbolic: invading manor houses, monasteries and town halls and burning the documents that recorded their subservient status. In a mass demonstration they gathered on Mousehold Heath outside Norwich, presented a petition to the King, and then retreated to North Walsham to await his answer. It came in the form of the sanguinary Bishop of Norwich, Henry Despenser, who, as his admiring biographer recorded, led an assault on the rebels, "grinding his teeth like a wild boar, and sparing neither himself nor his enemies ... stabbing some, unhorsing others, hacking and hewing". John Litester was captured, summarily executed and, on the orders of the Bishop, "divided into four parts, and sent throughout the country to Norwich, Yarmouth, Lynn and to the site of his own house".

A more glorious fate awaited the town's most famous resident, Horatio Nelson, who came to the Paston School here in 1768 as a boy of 10. Horatio was already dreaming of a naval career and, three years later when he read in the county newspaper that his Uncle Maurice had been appointed commander of a warship, he prevailed on his father to let him join the *Raisonnable*.

The **Paston School** had been founded in 1606 by Sir William Paston. His ancestors were the writers of the extraordinary collection of more than 1,000 letters, written between 1422 and 1509, which present an astonishingly vivid picture of East Anglian life at the end of the turbulent Middle Ages. Sir William himself is buried in the parish church where he personally supervised (and paid for) the construction of the impressive marble and alabaster monument he desired to be erected in his memory.

About four miles east of North Walsham, near the village of Erpingham on the A140, **Alby Crafts & Gardens** has a Crafts Gallery promoting the excellence of mainly East Anglian and British craftsmanship - lacework, woodturning, jewellery, canework and much more. The Plantsman's Garden displays a fine collection of unusual shrubs, plants and bulbs in a four-acre site; there are also workshops where you can watch craftsmen at work, a Bottle Museum (small charge for admission) and a tearoom.

PASTON
9 miles SE of Cromer on the B1159

It was in this small village that the Paston family entered historical record. The vivid collection of letters they wrote to each other during the years that England was being wracked by the Wars of the Roses has already

been mentioned, and the village boasts another magnificent legacy from this remarkable family. In 1581, Sir William Paston built a cavernous tithe-barn here with flint walls and a thatched roof. It still stands, its roof still thatched: 160 feet long, almost 60 feet high - the longest, most imposing barn in Norfolk. In the nearby church, the most striking of the family memorials is the one dedicated to Katherine Paston. Sculpted in alabaster by Nicholas Stone in 1628, Katherine lies dressed to kill in her Jacobean finery of starched ruff, embroidered bodice, puffed sleeves and pearl necklaces. The monument cost £340, a staggering sum of money at that time. In the nearby village of **Bacton** are the remains of Bromholm Priory, founded in the 12th century and once one of the grandest and most famous of European ecclesiastical buildings.

BACTON FARM SHOP
Beach Road, Bacton, Norfolk Nr12 0EP
Tel: 01692 650271

Bacton Farm Shop is a modern brick and glass building behind the pumps of the associated service station. The shop specialises in local produce, including pork and pork products from owner Nick Alexander's farm.

Lamb and beef, fresh fruit and vegetables are all locally produced or sourced, as are many of the preserves and pickles. There's a good selection of nuts, pulses, flour and coffee, and the deli counter includes a fine variety of cheeses – local or from elsewhere in the British Isles, including Binham Blue, Wighton, Walsingham, Warham and a new Montgomery.

A new and increasingly popular part of the business is the wide range of ready meals that cater for customers who don't always have the time to prepare a meal but who don't want to stint on quality. Chicken in a creamy mushroom sauce and minced beef and carrot pie are just two examples of the dishes prepared by Nick's assistant Sara and friends in their homes.

Cakes are also made specially for the shop, and sandwiches are made to order to provide tasty quick lunches or daytime snacks.

🏠 historic building   🏛 museum   🏚 historic site   ♨ scenic attraction   🌱 flora and fauna

MUNDESLEY
7 miles SE of Cromer on the B1159

🏛 Maritime Museum

"The finest air in the kingdom has been wasted for centuries," said a speaker celebrating the arrival of the railway at Mundesley in 1898, "because nobody had the courage to bring the people to the district." The railway has been and gone, but the fresh breezes off the North Sea remain as invigorating as ever.

After the hazards of the coastline, immediately to the north where cliffs, fields and houses have all been eroded by the relentless sea, it's a pleasure to arrive at this unassuming holiday resort with its superb sandy beach, considered by many the very best in Norfolk. Mundesley village is quite small (appropriately, its **Maritime Museum**, housed in a former coastguard lookout, is believed to be the smallest museum in the country), but it provides all the facilities conducive to a relaxing family holiday. Best of all, there is safe swimming in the sea, and when the tide is out children can spend many a happy hour exploring the many 'lowes', or shallow lagoons, left behind.

WEST RUNTON
3 miles W of Cromer on the A149

🔍 Beacon Hill   🐎 Norfolk Shire Horse Centre

The parish of West Runton can boast that within its boundaries lies the highest point in

The Norfolk Shire Horse Centre

West Runton, Cromer, Norfolk NR27 9QH
Tel: 01263 837339 Fax: 01263 837132
e-mail: bakewell@norfolkshirehorse.fsnet.co.uk
website: www.norfolk-shirehorse-centre.co.uk

Shires, Suffolk Punches and Clydesdales are among the stars of the show at the **Norfolk Shire Horse Centre**, and visitors can meet these wonderful, gentle giants at close quarters in the front yard stables. Two large museum sheds contain a video room and an indoor demonstration area, and also on show are carts, coaches, gypsy caravans and farm machinery of yesteryear. Next to the museum is a children's play area.

A short walk through a meadow brings visitors to the area where the small animals are kept in their sheds and pens and aviaries. This really is a paradise for animal lovers: native pony mares with their foals, donkeys, Dexter cows, pigs, goats, lambs, guinea pigs, rabbits, chipmunks, chinchillas, cage birds. The ducks and geese have a great time in their own little pond. Twice a day the centre's proprietor, David Blakewell, accompanies demonstrations with a friendly, informative talk about the heavy horses; themes include harnessing and working the horses with the old machinery. Children can have a ride in a cart and join in the feeding of small animals. Numerous specials events are held throughout the summer, including foal days, blacksmiths days, sheepdog days, plough days and harvesting with the heavy horses. Dogs are welcome on leads; the site has a two-acre car park, a café and a gift shop.

MIRABELLE RESTAURANT & BISTRO

Station Road, West Runton, nr Cromer, Norfolk NR27 9QD
Tel/Fax: 01263 837396

Lovers of good food from all over Norfolk and beyond come to **Mirabelle Restaurant & Bistro** to enjoy the really excellent menus and the extensive wine list. Manfred Hollwoger, who established the restaurant 35 years ago, has retired and sold the business to Jackie Tuck and Jake Wright. The place has been totally refurbished in classic style, and re-opened on April 6th, 2006. Only the finest, freshest ingredients – including locally caught fish and shellfish – go into the kitchen to create a range of dishes that are expertly prepared, cooked to order and presented with flair.

Typical dishes – the choice changes according to what's best in the markets – might include Morston mussels, roast Norfolk duck, Dover sole meunière, steaks, rack of lamb and seasonal game. In the bistro, a similar high quality of cooking is served in delightfully relaxed, informal surroundings. Mirabelle is open for lunch and dinner Tuesday to Sunday (closed Sunday evenings November to May). In September 2006 three well-equipped en suite guest bedrooms will open above the restaurant.

Jackie and Jake also own the restaurant Jacque in Garden Street, Cromer – a modern restaurant where dinners before the show at the Pavilion Theatre are popular. Tel: 01263 512149

THE PEPPERPOT RESTAURANT

Water Lane, West Runton, nr Cromer,
Norfolk NR27 9QP
Tel: 01263 837578   Fax: 01263 838317
e-mail: fchr5@aol.com
website: www.the-pepperpot.com

Normandy-born Antoine Foucher and his wife Debbie are the talented team who have put the **Pepperpot Restaurant** on the gastronomic map of Norfolk. Antoine trained in some of the top kitchens in France and England, and Debbie is a hostess par excellence, and after many years working for others they decided that this part of Norfolk provided the perfect environment for running a business and bringing up a family. They fell in love with the Pepperpot as soon as they saw it, and their daughter Sophie is very much part of the team.

Antoine seeks out the finest seasonal produce for his menus and cooks everything freshly to order. His specialities include baked Cromer crab, dishes using Gloucester Old Spot pork, the French classic confit of duck and, for a memorable finale, chocolate and orange terrine.

The relaxing family atmosphere, the friendly, efficient service, and above all the superb cooking make the Pepperpot a lovely place to visit – for a romantic dinner for two, for entertaining friends, to celebrate a special occasion, or just because you love the food.

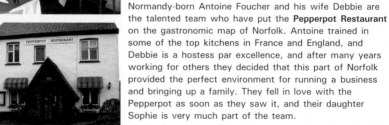

🏠 historic building   🏛 museum   🏛 historic site   🌲 scenic attraction   🌿 flora and fauna

Norfolk - **Beacon Hill**. This eminence is all of 330 feet high, so you won't be needing any oxygen equipment to reach the summit, but there are some excellent views. Nearby is the Roman Camp (National Trust), a misleading name since there's no evidence that the Romans ever occupied these 70 acres of heathland. Excavations have shown, however, that in Saxon and medieval times this was an iron-working settlement.

West Runton's major tourist attraction is undoubtedly the **Norfolk Shire Horse Centre** (see panel on page 41), where twice a day, during the season, these noble beasts are harnessed up and give a half-hour demonstration of the important role they played in agricultural life right up until the 1930s. They are the largest (19 hands/6 feet 4 inches high) and heaviest horses in the world, weighing more than a ton, and for generations were highly valued both as war-horses and draught animals. Several other heavy breeds, such as the Suffolk Punch, Clydesdale and Percheron, also have their home here, along with no fewer than nine different breeds of pony. The Centre also has a video room showing a 30-minute film, a small animals' enclosure and an adventure playground for children, a cafe and gift shop. A horse-drawn cart will transport you around the village and at the West Runton Riding School (on site) you can hire riding horses by the hour or obtain instruction in riding.

AYLMERTON

3 miles W of Cromer on minor road off the A148

🏠 Felbrigg Hall

Aylmerton is home to one of Norfolk's grandest houses, **Felbrigg Hall**. Thomas Windham began rebuilding the old manor house at Felbrigg in the 1620s, erecting in its place a grand Jacobean mansion with huge mullioned windows, pillared porch, and at roof-level a dedication in openwork stone: *Gloria Deo in Excelsis*, 'Glory to God in the Highest'. Later that century, Thomas' grandson William Windham I married a wealthy heiress and added the beautifully proportioned Carolean West Wing, where visitors can see portraits of the happily married couple painted by Sir Peter Lely. Their son, William Windham II, returning from his four-year-long Grand Tour, filled the house with treasures he had collected - so many of them that he had to extend the Hall yet again.

The Windham family's ownership of Felbrigg Hall came to a tragi-comic end in the 1860s when William Frederick Windham inherited the estate. William was one of the great English eccentrics. He loved uniforms. Accoutred in the Felbrigg blue and red livery, he would insist on serving at table; in guard's uniform he caused chaos on the local railway with his arbitrary whistle-blasts; dressed as a policeman, he sternly rounded up the ladies of easy virtue patrolling London's Haymarket. Inevitably, 'Mad' Windham fell prey to a pretty fortune-hunter and Felbrigg was only saved from complete bankruptcy by his death at the age of 26.

The Hall was acquired by the National Trust in 1969, complete with its 18th century furnishings, collection of paintings by artists such as Kneller and van der Velde, and a wonderful Gothic library. There are extensive grounds which include a Walled Garden containing an elegant octagonal dove-house, an Orangery of 1707 sheltering an outstanding collection of camellias, many woodland and lakeside walks, and a restaurant, tea room and shop.

SHERINGHAM
5 miles W of Cromer on the A149

🗘 The Poppy Line (North Norfolk Railway)

🗘 Pretty Corner   🗘 Sheringham Park

Sheringham has made the transition from fishing village to popular seaside resort with grace and style. There are plenty of activities on offer, yet Sheringham has managed to avoid the brasher excesses of many English seaside towns. The beach here is among the cleanest in England, and markedly different from the shingle beaches elsewhere on this part of the coast. Consisting mainly of gently sloping sand, it is excellent for bathing and the team of lifeguards makes it ideal for families with children. Rainfall at Sheringham is one of the lowest in the county, and the bracing air has also recommended the town to sufferers from rheumatism and respiratory problems.

A small fleet of fishing boats still operates from here, mostly concentrating on crabs and lobsters, but also bringing in catches of cod, skate, plaice, mackerel and herring. Several original fishermen's cottages remain, some with lofts where the nets were mended. Sheringham has never had a harbour, so boats are launched from the shore where stacks of creels stand as they have for generations. A 'golden lobster' in the town's coat of arms celebrates this traditional industry.

Like so many other former fishing villages in England, Sheringham owes its transformation into a resort to the arrival of the railway. During the Edwardian peak years of rail travel, some 64 trains a day steamed into the station but the line became yet another victim of the Beeching closures of the 1960s. Devotees of steam trains joined together and, by dint of great effort and enthusiasm, managed to re-open the line in 1975 as the **North Norfolk Railway**, better known as **The Poppy Line**.

The name refers to 'Poppyland", a term given to the area by the Victorian journalist Clement Scott who visited in pre-herbicide days when the summer fields were ablaze with poppies. In 1883, Scott travelled to Cromer on the newly-opened Great Eastern Railway's

Sheringham Station - The Poppy Line

🏢 historic building   🏛 museum   🏚 historic site   🗘 scenic attraction   🌱 flora and fauna

extension from Norwich. Walking out of the town, he was entranced by the tranquillity of the countryside. In his dispatch to the *Daily Telegraph* he wrote: "It is difficult to convey an idea of the silence of the fields through which I passed, or the beauty of the prospect that surrounded me - a blue sky without a cloud across it, a sea sparkling under a haze of heat, wild flowers in profusion around me, poppies predominating everywhere ..." Spurred by Scott's enthusiasm, a succession of notable Victorians made their way here - painters, writers, actors, even a youthful Winston Churchill. Later, during the Second World War, Churchill returned to the area, staying at Pear Tree Cottage in Mundesley.

Although greatly diminished in number, plenty of brilliant poppies can still be seen when travelling the scenic five-mile journey from Sheringham to Holt. The railway operates up to eight trains daily in each direction during the season, March to October, and there are special Saturday evening and Sunday lunchtime services when you can dine in style in one of the Pullman coaches from the old 'Brighton Belle'. On West Slipway, the Henry Ramey Upcher Lifeboat Museum houses this private lifeboat built in 1894 and in service until 1935. It is housed in its original boatshed.

Just to the west of the town, at Upper Sheringham, footpaths lead to the lovely grounds of **Sheringham Park** (National Trust). The Park was landscaped by Humphry Repton, who declared it to be his "favourite and darling child in Norfolk".

stories and anecdotes 　 famous people 　 art and craft 　 entertainment and sport 　 walks

There are grand views along the coast, dense growths of oak, beech and fir trees and banks of rhododendrons which are at their most dazzling in late May and June.

There's yet more grand scenery at the aptly-named **Pretty Corner**, just to the east of the A1082 at its junction with the A148. This is a particularly beautiful area of woodland and also offers superb views over the surrounding countryside.

WEYBOURNE
9 miles W of Cromer on the A149

The Muckleburgh Collection

Here, the shingle beach known as Weybourne Hope (or Hoop) slopes so steeply that an invading fleet could bring its ships right up to the shore. Which is exactly what the Danes did many times during the 9th and 10th centuries. A local adage states that "He who would Old England win, Must at Weybourne Hoop begin," and over the centuries care has been taken to protect this stretch of the coast. A map dated 1st, May 1588 clearly shows 'Waborne Fort', and Holt's Parish Register for that year of the Armada notes that "in this yeare was the town of Waborne fortified with a continuall garrison of men bothe of horse and foote with sconces (earthworks) ordinaunce and all manner of appoyntment to defend the Spannyards landing theare".

As it turned out, the 'Spannyards' never got close, but during both World Wars the same concern was shown for defending this vulnerable beach. The garrison then became the Anti-Aircraft Permanent Range and Radar Training Wing, providing instruction for National Servicemen until the camp finally closed in 1959. It was reckoned that by then some 1,500,000 shells had been fired out to sea. The site has since been returned to agricultural use, but the original NAAFI building remains and now houses **The Muckleburgh Collection**, a fascinating museum of military vehicles, weapons and equipment, most of which have seen action in battlefields all over the world. All of the tanks, armoured cars and amphibious vehicles on display can be inspected at close quarters, and there are regular tank demonstrations and rides on various vehicles. Meals and snacks are

All Saints Church, Weybourne

🏛 historic building   🏛 museum   🏛 historic site   🔱 scenic attraction   🌿 flora and fauna

available - served in a NAAFI-style canteen. Incidentally, despite its exposed position, Weybourne has in fact only been attacked once, by the Luftwaffe on 11th July, 1940. A stick of bombs landed in the main street and badly damaged two cottages.

HOLT
10 miles W of Cromer on the A148

A perennial finalist in the Anglia in Bloom competition, Holt's town centre always looks a picture, with hanging baskets and flowers everywhere. Back in 1892, a guide-book to the county described Holt as "A clean and very prettily situated market town, being planted in a well undulating and very woody neighbourhood". More than a century later, one can't quarrel with that characterisation.

The worst day in the town's history was May 1st, 1708, when a raging fire consumed most of the town's ancient houses. The consequent rebuilding replaced them with some elegant Georgian houses, gracious buildings which played a large part in earning the town its designation as a Conservation Area.

The town's most famous building, Gresham's School, somehow escaped the disastrous conflagration of 1708. Founded in 1555 by Sir John Gresham, the school began as an altruistic educational establishment, its pupils accepted solely on the basis of their academic promise. Since then, the school has abandoned both its town centre location and

---

THE NORTH NORFOLK FISH COMPANY
8 Old Stable Yard, Holt, Norfolk NR25 6BN
Tel: 01263 711913
e-mail: john@northnorfolkfish.co.uk

Seafood doesn't come much fresher than the fish and shellfish on sale at the **North Norfolk Fish Company** in the attractive market town of Holt. John and Fiona Griffin have built up a loyal book of regular customers in their 10 years here, supplying a large number of private and public establishments and offering an outside catering service, in addition to the over-the-counter sales. The fish and shellfish, including sole, sea bass, sea trout, crab, lobster and oysters, are sourced locally and from around the British Isles, and among the top-quality home-made products are fish cakes, pâtés, lasagne, curries and sauces.

MOO MOOS
15 High Street, Holt, Norfolk NR25 6BN
Tel: 01263 713178

Nerissa Brittain owns and runs two delightful shops (the other is in Aldeburgh) with a wonderful eye for all that's beautiful and elegant for the home, family and friends as well as those well-deserved personal treats. **Moo Moos** stocks a wonderful range of goods for all aspects of modern lifestyle. Lovely things for the home include quilts, linen, clothes, handbags, luggage, jewellery accessories, china, and small items of furniture – a quirky, eclectic and totally delightful mix assembled from all over the world. The Holt Moo Moos, opened in an old town house in 2003, has proved such a success that in 2005 Nerissa opened a second shop, run by her eldest daughter, in Aldeburgh's High Street.

BACK TO THE GARDEN

Breck Farm, Letheringsett, Holt, Norfolk NR25 7JJ
Tel: 01328 822125 Fax: 01328 822146
e-mail: astleyestate@farming.co.uk

A lovely name for a splendid establishment on the main A148 a couple of miles west of Holt. Fresh organic food brings customers from a wide local area to **Back to the Garden**, which occupies a superb Norfolk barn with original brickwork and beams. Fresh fruit and vegetables, locally and often home-grown, taste as good as they look, and the organic beef, lamb, pork and chicken are also of the highest quality. A wide range of other local and regional food, including preserves and pickles, fruit juices, eggs and bread, is on sale in this beautiful and very accessible place.

THE GARDEN COTTAGE

Chequers, Sharrington, Norfolk NR24 2PG
Tel: 01263 860308
e-mail: rosemary@kimminsl.wanadoo.co.uk

Garden Cottage offers comfortable, self-contained self-catering accommodation in a quiet village close to Holt and the North Norfolk coast. The recently converted 18th century brick and flint building contains one double and one twin bedroom, a bathroom with shower over the bath, a second WC, fully-fitted kitchen-diner with electric stove, microwave, fridge and dishwasher, sitting room with TV and video, and a patio looking out over the beautiful, secluded garden. Décor and furnishings are of the highest order throughout, and oil-fired central heating keeps the cottage warm at any time of the year.

The region offers something for everyone, with lovely walks in the country, uncrowded sandy beaches, medieval churches and magnificent country houses. The delightful Georgian town of Holt is only four miles away, and Blakeney and the coast are within a 10-minute drive. There's also some of the best bird-watching in the country. Dinghy hire and tuition are available at various points on the coast, and cycles can be hired in Holt. Garden Cottage is a non-smoking establishment; no children under 16 or dogs.

its founder's commitment to educating, free, those bright children who could not otherwise afford it. Among the school's many distinguished alumni are the dour creator of the BBC, Lord Reith, the poets W H Auden and Stephen Spender, and the composer Benjamin Britten.

Look out for one of Holt's most unusual buildings, Home Place. Designed and built between 1903 and 1905 by E S Prior, an architect follower of the Arts & Crafts movement, the exterior of the house is completely covered with an ingeniously contrived cladding of local pebbles.

🏠 historic building   🏛 museum   🏛 historic site   ❧ scenic attraction   🌱 flora and fauna

The Stable Gallery. *'A Unique Collection'*
The Kelling Estate, Kelling, Norfolk NR25 7EW
01263 710610 www.norfolkeye.co.uk
Set within the grounds of the historic Kelling Estate, the gallery houses a varied collection of photography, original paintings, prints and greetings cards. In-house framing workshop, and fine art publishing. Also soft furnishings, fabrics and textiles, cast iron garden statuary and a gift shop stocked with a large range of affordable jewellery and design-led giftware.

pinkfoot Gallery
High Street, Cley next the Sea, NR25 7RB
01263 740947 www.pinkfootgallery.co.uk
We are a small, friendly gallery based in beautiful Cley. We specialise in natural history, koi carp, sea- and landscapes and sculptures.
Our bronze bird and animal sculptures by Robert Aberdein and Robin Bouttell are highly collectable and certainly worth a look.
Also books, cards and prints. Open everyday.

HIGH KELLING NURSERY

Selbrigg Road, High Kelling, nr Holt, Norfolk NR25 6RJ
Tel: 01263 712629   Fax: 01263 711314
e-mail: enquiries@highkellingnursery.co.uk

'Buy it, plant it, enjoy it' that's the motto of **High Kelling Nursery**, a traditional working nursery set in three acres of tranquil woodland in High Kelling, a short drive from Holt. The vast majority of the plants on sale are pot-grown on the premises, and the peat-free compost used can be bought at the nursery. Owners John and Paula Pierrepont put their many years' expertise and experience at the disposal of customers with advice and help on any questions about gardening. Only closed Mondays.

CLEY-NEXT-THE-SEA
12 miles W of Cromer on the A149

🏠 St Mary's Church 🪶 Blakeney Point

Cley's name is no longer appropriate. Cley-a-mile-away-from-the-Sea would be more truthful. But in early medieval times, Cley (pronounced Cly, and meaning clay) was a more important port than King's Lynn, with a busy trade exporting wool to the Netherlands. In return, Cley imported a predilection for houses with curved gables, Flemish bricks and pantiles. The windmill overlooking the harbour adds to the sense that a little piece of Holland has strayed across the North Sea. This is the famous Cley Mill, the subject of thousands of paintings. Built in 1713 and in use until 1921, the Mill is open to visitors during the season (afternoons only), and also offers bed and breakfast.

The village's prosperity in the past is reflected in the enormous scale of its 14th/

Blakeney

Distance: *3.1 miles (4.83 kilometres)*

Typical time: *90 mins*

Height gain: *15 metres*

Map: *Explorer 24*

Walk: *www.walkingworld.com ID:2103*

Contributor: *Joy & Charles Boldero*

DESCRIPTION:

This is a very pleasurable walk with good paths and no stiles. There are fine views of the coastline. Blakeney is a very popular and pretty village on the North Norfolk coast. The River Glaven is tidal and fills the quayside channel at high tide. It is a place for sailing, safe for small children to bathe and fish and where the boats wait to take passengers out to Blakeney Point to see the seals. The outer route is along field edges and returns along the Norfolk Coastal Path which runs beside the marshes.

FEATURES:

River, Pub, Toilets, Church, National Trust/ NTS, Wildlife, Birds, F lowers, Great Views, Butterflies, Food Shop

WALK DIRECTIONS:

1 | Turn left up the narrow street with its attractive flinted cottages. Just past the Methodist church and opposite Coronation Cottage turn right along Little Lane. At the T junction turn left along New Road, then right along a residential road.

2 | Turn right at a finger-post sign along a gravel track with pretty flinted cottages. It then becomes a rough path alongside a field.

3 | Turn left along the road and very soon turn right at a finger-post sign along a driveway. There are fine views here of the marshes. As the driveway goes right keep ahead to a house, and then go left at a yellow marker sign beside the field edge with a hedge on the right. The path winds and the hedge is then on the left with a thatched house on the hill ahead. Just before the gate the path goes left.

4 | Turn right along the road, then left at a finger-post sign ahead along a grass path leading downhill.

5 | At a T junction of paths turn right along the Norfolk Coastal Path which takes you into Blakeney. This path goes beside the marshes where sea lavender and wading birds can be seen.

6 | Turn left along the pavement and beside the Quay.

7 | Turn right up the narrow street with the White House Hotel ahead and back to the car park.

CLEY SMOKEHOUSE

High Street, Cley-next-the-Sea, nr Holt, Norfolk NR25 7RF
Tel: 01263 740282
e-mail: enquiries@cleysmokehouse.com
website: www.cleysmokehouse.com

An excellent range of freshly smoked fish, shellfish and cured meats, delicious home-made pâtés all hand crafted to highest of standards, are some of the things that await customers at **Cley Smokehouse**. Situated on the High Street at Cley-next-the-Sea (now actually a mile from the sea), the building dates back to the late-1600s and was once part of the customs bonded warehouse.

Owner Glen Weston is from a well-known local fishing family and has his own fishing boat. He knows the best and freshest fish when he sees it, and chooses only the best for smoking.

Glen and his team do all the prepatation and smoking on the premises in the new and completely refurbished preparation areas at the rear of the shop. Kippers and eels are two specialities, but delicious bloaters, mackerel, haddock, salmon, herring, trout and cod roe are also sold here. Other tempting fare includes taramasalata, potted shrimp, smoked cheese, pickled herring, home-made soup and much, much more. Staff are always friendly and helpful, and the shop also offers an excellent mail order service.

15th century parish church, **St Mary's**, whose south porch is particularly notable for its fine stonework and 16 armorial crests. The gorgeous fan-vaulted roof is decorated with bosses carved with angels, flowers, and a lively scene of an old woman throwing her distaff at a fox running away with her chickens.

From Cley it's possible to walk along the shoreline to **Blakeney Point**, the most northerly extremity of East Anglia. This spit of land that stretches three miles out into the sea is a bird-watcher's paradise. Some 256 species of birds have been spotted here, and the variety of flora is scarcely less impressive: almost 200 flowering species have been recorded.

BLAKENEY

14 miles W of Cromer on the A149

One of the most enchanting of the North Norfolk coastal villages, Blakeney was a commercial port until the beginning of the 20th century, when silting up of the estuary prevented all but pleasure craft from gaining access. The silting has left a fascinating landscape of serpentine creeks and channels twisting their way through mud banks and sand hills. In a side street off the quay is the 14th century Guildhall (English Heritage), which was probably a private house and contains an interesting undercroft, or cellar, which is notable as an early example of a brick-built vaulted ceiling.

The beautifully restored Church of St Nicholas, set on a hill overlooking village and marshland, offers the visitor a lovely Early English chancel, built in 1220, and the magnificent west tower, 100 feet high, a landmark for miles around. In a small turret on the northeast corner of the chancel a light

BLAKENEY COTTAGE COMPANY

69a High Street, Blakeney, Norfolk NR25 7NA
Tel: 01263 741773 Fax: 01263 741777
e-mail: kitty@blakeneycottagecompany.co.uk
website: www.blakeneycottagecompany.co.uk

Kitty and Justin Player used to let out their holiday home through the **Blakeney Cottage Company**, and they knew exactly how they wanted the business to develop when they took it over in 2005. The company specialises in providing select local properties to holidaymakers and weekenders looking for a really special base in this lovely part of Norfolk. The owners take the greatest care in matching their customers to exactly the right property for their requirements, and two-way personal communication is key to their success.

The properties are always presented in absolutely immaculate condition, and no detail is overlooked. Top-quality bed linen and towels are provided, and the welcome package includes flowers, chocolates and wine; personal requests, perhaps to mark a special celebration, can also be arranged. The properties range from snug retreats for two to bigger places that provide space and comfort for families or groups of friends. Kitty has a very special flair for interior design, and her beautiful soft furnishings, bed linen and small household items can be bought in the company's High Street premises.

would once burn as a beacon to guide ships safely into Blakeney Harbour.

GLANDFORD

12 miles W of Cromer off the B1156

🏠 Glandford Shell Museum

🌿 Natural Surroundings Wild Flower Centre

Near this delightful village, the **Natural Surroundings Wild Flower Centre** is dedicated to gardening with a strong ecological emphasis. There are wild flower meadows and gardens, organic vegetable and herb gardens, nurseries, a nature trail alongside the unspoilt River Glaven, and the Centre also organises a wide range of events with a conservation theme. A short walk down the valley from the Centre is the **Glandford Shell Museum**, a lovely Dutch-style building

which houses the private collection of Sir Alfred Jodrell, a unique accumulation of sea shells gathered from beaches all around the world, together with a fascinating variety of artefacts, fossils, scraps of ingeniously carved scrimshaw, tiny figures made out of shells and 19th century cameo brooches.

A couple of miles south of Glandford you'll find a building of 1802 which, year after year, has been awarded the title of 'Top Tourist Attraction in North Norfolk'. Letheringsett Watermill stands on the site of an earlier mill recorded in the *Domesday Book*, and was rescued from near-dereliction in the 1980s. This fully functional, water-powered mill produces 100% wholewheat flour from locally grown wheat; there are regular demonstrations of the milling process, with a

THE BIRDSCAPES GALLERY

*Manor Farm Barns, Glandford, nr Holt,
Norfolk NR25 7JP
Tel: 01263 741742
website: www.birdscapesgallery.co.uk*

'*Spoonbills' by Robert Gillmor*

Liz and Steve Harris have been interested in bird art ever since they bought a painting of geese over Norfolk mud-flats in 1974. They have lived overlooking the marshes at Salthouse for over 25 years. Liz was a teacher and Steve worked in wildlife and landscape conservation. They opened the **BIRDscapes Gallery** in October 2005. Wild birds and wild places are the main themes, although pure landscapes and other wildlife are included. BIRDscapes displays works by many of the leading bird artists working in Britain today, as well as landscapes with a local flavour. Original paintings and prints are the mainstay, but sculptures, reproductions, wildlife art books and cards are also available.

The pine-clad exhibition area is spacious, well lit and welcoming, with chairs to encourage an unhurried visit in a warm, relaxed atmosphere. Monthly exhibitions are held, with featured artists, and mixed shows that display the talents of the Gallery's many regular contributors. The gallery has 'green' aspirations, and in conjunction with the UK's largest binocular and telescope shop, Cley Spy in Glandford, manages an adjacent six acres as a 'Farmland Bird Reserve'. The yard marks the start of a three-mile bird walk that explores the lovely Bayfield Estate and its varied birdlife.

running commentary from the miller; and the end product can be purchased in the gift shop.

LANGHAM
14 miles W of Cromer off the A149/A148

📍 Langham Glass

The minor road south from Morston leads to **Langham Glass**, where, in a wonderful collection of restored 18th century barn workshops, visitors can watch a variety of craftspeople exercising their traditional skills. In addition to the now famous Langham Glass works where a master glass-maker will give a running commentary, there's a pyrographer, wood-turner, stained glass maker, and glass engraver. The Factory Gift Shop is well stocked with their creations, the Antiques & Collectables Shop offers a wide variety of

items from Victorian china to Lalique, and there's also a rose and clematis walled garden, a seven-acre maize maze with three miles of walkways through corn maize interspersed with sunflowers, an adventure playground, tea rooms and café.

MORSTON
13 miles W of Cromer on the A149

Great stretches of salt marshes and mud flats lie between this pleasant village and the sea, which is reached by way of a tidal creek that almost disappears at low tide. Morston is a particularly pleasing village with quiet lanes and clusters of cottages built from local flint cobbles. If the church tower looks rather patched-up, that's because it was struck by lightning in 1743. It's said that local people took this as a sign that the Second Coming of Christ was imminent, and that repairing their church was therefore pointless. It was many years before restoration work was finally undertaken, by which time the fabric of the tower had deteriorated even further.

STIFFKEY

16 miles W of Cromer on the A149

🏛 Binham Priory   🌱 Stiffkey Salt Marshes

Regarded as one of the prettiest villages in the county, Stiffkey lies beside the little river of the same name. Pronounced 'Stewkey', the name means 'island of tree stumps' and is most likely derived from the marshy river valley of reed beds and fallen trees, which indeed gives the village the appearance of an island. At the east end of the village is the church of St John the Baptist; from the churchyard there are fine views of the river and of Stiffkey Hall to the south. All that now remains of this once-impressive building, built by the Bacon family in 1578, are the towers, one wing of the house, and the 17th century gatehouse. The stately ruins of the great hall have been transformed into a rose terrace and sunken garden and are open to the public.

The former Rectory is a grand Georgian building, famous as the residence of the Revd Harold Davidson, Rector of Stiffkey during the 1920s and 1930s. Rather like the central character in Michael Palin's film *The Missionary*, Harold launched a personal crusade to save the fallen women of London, and caused much gossip and scandal by doing so. Despite the fact that his notoriety regularly filled the church to capacity, he constantly fell foul of the ecclesiastical authorities and eventually lost his living. There is a rather bizarre ending to his story. After handing over the keys of Stiffkey Rectory, Harold joined a travelling show and was later killed by a lion whose cage he was sharing.

To the north of the village are the **Stiffkey Salt Marshes**, a National Trust nature reserve which turns a delicate shade of purple in July when the sea lavender is in bloom. Here on

Stiffkey Marshes

🏛 historic building   🏛 museum   🏛 historic site   ❀ scenic attraction   🌱 flora and fauna

the sandflats can be found the famous 'Stewkey blues' - cockles which are highly regarded as a delicacy by connoisseurs of succulent bivalve molluscs.

A couple of miles south of Stiffkey stand the picturesque ruins of **Binham Priory** (English Heritage), its magnificent nave still serving as the parish church. This represents only about one-sixth of the original Priory, founded in 1091 by a nephew of William the Conqueror. The church is well worth a visit to see its unusually lofty interior with a Monk's Walk at roof level, its Seven Sacraments font, and noble west front.

Hunstanton

🐦 Sea Life Sanctuary

The busy seaside resort of Hunstanton can boast two unique features: one, it has the only cliffs in England made up of colourful levels of red, white and brown strata, and two, it is the only east coast resort that faces west, looking across The Wash to the Lincolnshire coast and the unmistakable tower of the 272-foot Boston Stump (more properly described as the Church of St Botolph).

Hunstanton town is a comparative newcomer, developed in the 1860s by Mr Hamon L'Estrange of nearby Hunstanton Hall to take advantage of the arrival of the railway here, and to exploit the natural appeal of its broad, sandy beaches. The centre is well-planned with mock-Tudor houses grouped around a green that falls away to the shore.

Hunstanton's social standing was assured after the Prince of Wales, later Edward VII, came here to recover from typhoid fever. He stayed at the Sandringham Hotel which, sadly, has since been demolished, along with the grand Victorian pier and the railway. But Hunston, as locals call the town, still has a distinct 19th century charm about it and plenty to entertain visitors.

The huge stretches of sandy beach, framed by those multi coloured cliffs, are just heaven for children who will also be fascinated by the **Sea Life Sanctuary**, on Southern Promenade, where an underwater glass tunnel provides a wonderful opportunity to watch the varied and often weird forms of marine life that inhabit Britain's waters. A popular excursion from Hunstanton is the boat trip to Seal Island, a sandbank in The Wash where seals can indeed often be seen sunbathing at low tide.

🎭 stories and anecdotes   🐟 famous people   🎨 art and craft   🎵 entertainment and sport   🚶 walks

Around Hunstanton

WELLS-NEXT-THE-SEA
17 miles E of Hunstanton on the A149

There's no doubt about the appeal of Wells' picturesque quayside, narrow streets and ancient houses. Wells has been a working port since at least the 13th century, but over the years the town's full name of Wells-next-the-Sea has become increasingly inapt - its harbour now stands more than a mile from the sea. In 1859, to prevent the harbour silting up altogether, Lord Leicester of Holkham Hall built an Embankment cutting off some 600 acres of marshland. This now provides a pleasant walk down to the sea.

The Embankment gave no protection, however, against the great floods of 1953 and 1978. On the 11th January, 1978 the sea rose 16 feet 1 inch above high tide, a few inches less than the 16 feet 10 inches recorded on the 31st January, 1953 when the flood-waters lifted a ship on to the quay. A silo on the harbour is marked with these abnormal levels.

Running alongside the Embankment is the Harbour Railway, which trundles from the small museum on the quay to the lifeboat station by the beach. This narrow-gauge railway is operated by the same company as the Wells-Walsingham Light Railway, which carries passengers on a particularly lovely ride along the route of the former Great Eastern Railway to Little Walsingham. The four-mile journey takes about 20 minutes with stops at Warham St Mary and Wighton. Both the WWR and the Harbour Railway services are seasonal. In a curious change of function, the former GER station at Wells is now home to the well-known Burnham Pottery, the former signal box is now the station, while the old station at Walsingham is now a church!

In addition to being the largest of North Norfolk's ports, Wells is also a popular resort

Holkham Hall & Bygones Museum

Wells-next-the-Sea, Norfolk NR23 1AB
Tel: 01328 710227 Fax: 01328 711707
website: www.holkham.co.uk

In a lakeside deer park on the beautiful North Norfolk coast stands **Holkham Hall**, one of Britain's most majestic stately homes, seat of seven generations of the Earls of Leicester. This classic 18th century mansion in Palladian style is a veritable treasure house of artistic and architectural history, and each part has its separate character and appeal, from the stunning grandeur of the Marble Hall and the magnificence of the State Rooms to the old kitchen with its original pots and pans and the elegant formal gardens. In addition to the superb house and gardens there are other attractions at Holkham, including a Bygones Museum crammed with over 4,000 domestic and agricultural artefacts, nursery gardens, a pottery shop, restaurant and tearooms.

🏛 historic building   🏛 museum   🏛 historic site   🐾 scenic attraction   🌱 flora and fauna

Wells-Next-The-Sea

Palladio. Working with his friend Lord Burlington - another fervent admirer of Palladio - and the architect William Kent, Coke's monumental project slowly took shape. Building began in 1734 but was not completed until 1762, three years after Coke's death.

with one of the best beaches in England, bordered by the curiously named Holkham Meals, a plantation of pines established here in the 1860s to stabilise the dunes.

HOLKHAM

16 miles E of Hunstanton on the A149

Holkham Hall

If the concept of the Grand Tour ever needed any justification, **Holkham Hall** (see panel opposite) amply provides it. For six years, from 1712 to 1718, young Thomas Coke (pronounced Cook) travelled extensively in Italy, France and Germany, studying and absorbing at first hand the glories of European civilisation. And, wherever possible, buying them. When he returned to England, Coke realised that his family's modest Elizabethan manor could not possibly house the collection of treasures he had amassed. The manor would have to be demolished and a more worthy building erected in its place.

During his travels in Italy, Coke had been deeply impressed by the cool, classical lines favoured by the Renaissance architect Andrea

The completed building, its classical balance and restraint emphasised by the pale honey local brick used throughout, has been described as 'the ultimate achievement of the English Palladian movement'. As you step into the stunning entrance hall, the tone is set for the rest of the house. Modelled on a Roman Temple of Justice, the lofty coved ceiling is supported by 18 huge fluted columns of pink Derbyshire alabaster, transported to nearby Wells by river and sea.

Historically the most important room at Holkham is the Statue Gallery, which contains one of the finest collections of classical sculpture still in private ownership. In this sparsely furnished room there is nothing to distract one's attention from the sublime statuary that has survived for millennia, among it a bust of Thucydides (one of the earliest portrayals of man) and a statue of Diana, both of which have been dated to 4BC.

Each room reveals new treasures: Rubens and Van Dyck in the Saloon, the Landscape Room with its incomparable collection of

stories and anecdotes ❧ famous people ✍ art and craft ✐ entertainment and sport ✦ walks paintings by Lorrain, Poussin and other masters, the Brussels tapestries in the State Sitting Room and, on a more domestic note, the vast, high-ceilinged kitchen which remained in use until 1939 and still displays the original pots and pans.

Astonishingly, the interior of the house remains almost exactly as Thomas Coke planned it, his descendants having respected the integrity of his vision. They concentrated their reforming zeal on improving the enormous estate. It was Coke's great-nephew, Thomas William Coke (1754-1842), who was mainly responsible for the elegant layout of the 3,000-acre park visitors see today. Universally known as 'Coke of Norfolk', Thomas was a pioneer of the Agricultural Revolution, best known for introducing the idea of a four-crop rotation. He was also a generous patron of agricultural innovations, and the 'Sheep Shearings' he inaugurated - gatherings to which several hundred people came to exchange ideas on all aspects of agriculture, were the direct forerunners of the modern agricultural show.

The Thomas Coke who had built the house had been created Earl of Leicester in 1744, but as his only son died before him, the title lapsed. However, when his grand-nephew, 'Coke of Norfolk' was elevated to the peerage by Queen Victoria in 1837, he adopted the same title. The present Earl, the 7th, lives at Holkham in the private apartments known as the Family Wing, but still uses the State Rooms when entertaining guests. The Earl continues in the tradition of 'Coke of Norfolk' by overseeing the vast estate with its 30 tenant farmers and more than 300 houses: the Countess has established a new tradition by setting up the Holkham Pottery in the former brickworks.

BURNHAM THORPE
11 miles E of Hunstanton off the B1355

🏛 Creake Abbey

From the tower of All Saints' Church, the White Ensign flaps in the breeze; the only pub in the village is the *Lord Nelson*; and the shop next door to it is called the Trafalgar Stores. No prizes for deducing that Burnham Thorpe was the birthplace of Horatio Nelson. His father, the Revd Edmund Nelson, was the Rector here for 46 years; Horatio was the sixth of his 11 children.

Parsonage House, where Horatio was born seven weeks' premature in 1758, was demolished during his lifetime, but the pub (one of more than 200 hostelries across the country bearing the hero's name) has become a kind of shrine to Nelson's memory, its walls covered with portraits, battle scenes and other marine paintings.

There's more Nelson memorabilia in the church, among it a crucifix and lectern made with wood from *HMS Victory*, a great chest from the pulpit used by the Revd Nelson, and two flags from *HMS Nelson*. Every year on Trafalgar Day, October 21st, members of the Nelson Society gather at this riverside church for a service in commemoration of the man who had specified in his will that he wanted to be buried in its country graveyard "unless the King decrees otherwise". George III did indeed decree otherwise, and the great hero was interred in St Paul's Cathedral.

A little over a mile to the south of Burnham Thorpe stand the picturesque ruins of **Creake Abbey** (English Heritage), an Augustinian monastery founded in 1206. The Abbey's working life came to an abrupt end in 1504 when, within a single week, every one of the monks died of the plague.

BURNHAM MARKET

9 miles E of Hunstanton on the B1155

There are seven Burnhams in all, strung along the valley of the little River Burn. Burnham Market is the largest of them, its past importance reflected in the wealth of Georgian buildings surrounding the green and the two churches that lie at each end of its broad main street, just 600 yards apart. In the opinion of many, Burnham Market has the best collection of small Georgian houses in Norfolk, and it's a delight to wander through the yards and alleys that link the town's three east-west streets.

Burnham Market also boasts two excellent bookshops. Auctions are held on the village green every other Monday in summer.

BRANCASTER STAITHE

9 miles NE of Hunstanton on the A149

In Roman times a castle was built near Brancaster to try and control the Iceni, Boudicca's turbulent tribe. Nothing of it remains, although a Romano-British cemetery was discovered nearby in 1960. In the 18th century, this delightful village was a port of some standing, hence the 'Staithe', or quay, in its name. The waterborne traffic in the harbour is now almost exclusively pleasure craft, although whelks are still dredged from the sea bed, 15 miles out, and mussels are farmed in the harbour itself.

From the harbour a short boat trip will take you to Scolt Head Island (National Trust), a three-and-a-half mile sand and shingle bar separated from the mainland by a narrow tidal creek. It was originally much smaller, but over the centuries deposits of silt and sand have steadily increased its size, and continue to do so. Scolt Head is home to England's largest colony of Sandwich terns, which flock here to breed during May, June and July. A Nature Trail leads past the ternery (closed during the breeding season) and on to a fascinating area where a rich variety of plantlife and wildlife abounds. During the summer the sea asters, sea

Brancaster Staithe

🎬 stories and anecdotes   🦜 famous people   🎨 art and craft   🎭 entertainment and sport   🥾 walks

THE GREAT ESCAPE HOLIDAY COMPANY

The Granary, Docking, nr King's Lynn, Norfolk PE31 8LY
Tel: 01485 518717 Fax: 01485 518937
e-mail: bookings@thegreatescapeholiday.co.uk
website: www.thegreatescapeholiday.co.uk

The Great Escape Holiday Company was set up to rent out second homes in Norfolk The company cares for them as if they were their own and indulges every whim of the guests who stay in them. The owners of the properties are aware that sharing a second home with others can be of great benefit both to themselves and to visitors. The houses are often unoccupied for up to 48 weeks a year, so it makes excellent sense to make them available for paying guests, providing income to pay for the costs of owning and running a second home.

The Great Escape Holiday Company prides itself on the standard of service it offers its clients: each year they audit and review the services they offer both to the house owners and to the guests who occupy them when the owners are absent. Most of the properties on the company's books have a unique charm and character that makes guests feel instantly at home. The properties cover a very broad range: a tiny flint cottage for two close to the beach; a roomy converted barn for two close to a gourmet restaurant; a newly built home with everything provided for the perfect family summer holiday; a mansion that's ideal for family or group reunions; a converted stable block that's perfect for board meetings. From a tiny cottage to a grand stately home, all the properties are loved by owners who are happy to share their homes in their absence and confident in the care taken by the company. Beds are made up with crisp white cotton sheets, there are fluffy towels and locally made toiletries in the bathrooms, the fire is laid or lit, and on the kitchen table a basket contains the makings of the first supper and breakfast. In addition to the services that ensure that everything is in perfect order for incoming guests, the company has added other options.

The Concierge Service includes greeting all house guests, making them welcome at their chosen holiday home and conducting a guided tour of the property. A choice of ready meals can be made at the time of booking, and partner companies specialise in wines, in tour packages, in the hire of vintage and thoroughbred cars, in arranging tuition in riding and clay-pigeon shooting, and in chartering flights or trips out to sea. Guests at Great Escape properties know that northing is overlooked in ensuring that their holiday will be a memorable one, and the owners are equally confident that their second homes could not be in better hands.

lavender and sea pinks put on a colourful display, attracting many different types of moths and butterflies.

TITCHWELL
7 miles E of Hunstanton on the A149

🐾 Titchwell Marsh

Perhaps in keeping with the village's name, the church of St Mary at Titchwell is quite tiny - and very pretty indeed. Its circular, probably Norman tower is topped by a little 'whisker' of a spire, and inside is some fine late 19th century glass.

Just to the west of the village is a path leading to **Titchwell Marsh**, a nationally important RSPB reserve comprising some 420 acres of shingle beach, reed beds, freshwater and salt-marsh. These different habitats encourage a wide variety of birds to visit the area throughout the year, and many of them breed on or around the reserve. Brent geese, ringed plovers, marsh harriers, terns, waders and shore larks may all be seen, and two of the three hides available are accessible to wheelchairs.

DOCKING
9 miles SE of Hunstanton on the B1454/B1153

One of the larger inland villages, Docking was at one time called Dry Docking because, perched on a hilltop 300 feet above sea level, it had no water supply of its own. The nearest permanent stream was at Fring, almost three miles away, so in 1760 the villagers began boring for a well. They had to dig some 230 feet down before they finally struck water, which was then sold at a farthing (0.1p) per bucket. A pump was installed in 1928, but a mains supply didn't reach Docking until the 1930s.

HOLME-NEXT-THE-SEA
3 miles NE of Hunstanton off the A149

🚶 Peddar's Way and Norfolk Coastal Footpath

This village is notable chiefly as the northern end of the **Peddar's Way**, the 50-mile pedestrian trail that starts close to the Suffolk border at Knettisham Heath near Thetford and, almost arrow-straight for much of its length, slices across northwest Norfolk to Holme, with only an occasional deviation to negotiate a necessary ford or bridge. This determinedly straight route was already long-trodden for centuries before the Romans arrived, but they incorporated long stretches of it into their own network of roads. It was from the Latin word *pedester* that the route takes its name. With few gradients of any consequence to negotiate, the Peddar's Way is ideal for the casual walker. At Holme, the Peddar's Way meets with the **Norfolk Coastal Footpath**, a much more recent creation. Starting at Hunstanton, it closely follows the coastline all the way to Cromer. Numerous sections of the Peddars Way are open to cyclists, and a special route is available for horse riders. Several lengths of both routes are accessible to wheelchair users.

Holme-next-the-Sea is famous in part as the site of 'Sea Henge', a 4,500-year-old Bronze Age tree circle discovered on Holme Beach.

RINGSTEAD
3 miles E of Hunstanton off the A149

🐾 Ringstead Downs

Another appealing village, with pink and white-washed cottages built in wonderfully decorative Norfolk carrstone. A rare Norman round tower, all that survives of St

WARDS NURSERIES

Foundry Lane, Ringstead, nr Hunstanton,
Norfolk PE36 5LE
Tel: 01485 525242 Fax: 01485 525395

On a two-acre site at Ringstead, three miles inland from Hunstanton, **Wards Nurseries** is a family-run business that has been trading successfully for more than 50 years. The nursery grows and sells a wide range of flowers, shrubs and trees, along with seeds, made-to-order hanging baskets and National Garden gift vouchers. Ringstead, on the Peddars Way, with delightful countryside all around and the sea close by, is a lovely part of the world to visit, and anyone with an interest in plants and gardens should definitely make a point of looking in at Wards. They also sell their plants at markets in King's Lynn (Tuesday), Downham Market (Friday) and Swaffham (Saturday). Open: Mon - Fri 9am-5pm, Sat - Sun 9am-4pm (closed Sunday afternoons July/August).

Peter's church, stands in the grounds of the former Rectory and adds to the visual charm.

In a region well-provided with excellent nature reserves, the one on **Ringstead Downs** is particularly attractive, and popular with picnickers. The chalky soil of the valley provides a perfect habitat for the plants that thrive here and for the exquisitely marked butterflies they attract.

OLD HUNSTANTON
1 mile N of Hunstanton off the A149

With its mellow old houses and narrow winding lanes, Old Hunstanton is utterly charming. The sand dunes and creeks provide a perfect habitat for interesting varieties of colourful flora - sea poppies, samphire, marram and sea lavender and more. The glorious sands continue here, and the Norfolk Coastal Footpath leads eastwards all the way to Cromer, some 36 miles distant.

GREAT BIRCHAM
7 miles SE of Hunstanton off the B1153

A couple of miles south of Docking stands the five-storey Great Bircham Windmill, one of the few in Norfolk to have found a hill to perch on,

and it's still working. If you arrive on a day when there's a stiff breeze blowing, the windmill's great arms will be groaning around; on calm days, content yourself with tea and home-made cakes in the tearoom, and take home some bread baked at the Mill's own bakery.

HEACHAM
3 miles S of Hunstanton off the A149

🐾 Norfolk Lavender

Heacham Park Fishery on Pocahontas Lake is set within the original boundary of Heacham Hall. This three-and-a-half acre freshwater lake was re-established in 1996. Spring 1997 saw the introduction to the lake of specimen carp, to be followed in 1998 by rudd, bream, perch and roach. The lake takes its name from the renowned Native American princess, who married into the Rolfe family, owners of Heacham Hall, and lived here in the 1600s.

Just outside this charming village is the famous **Norfolk Lavender** (see panel opposite), the largest lavender-growing and distilling operation in the country. Established in 1932, it is also the oldest. The information point at the western entrance is sited in an attractive listed building built of local carrstone in the 19th century that was originally a water mill. On entering the site, visitors instinctively breathe in, savouring the unmistakable aroma that fills the air. Guided tours of the grounds run throughout the day from the Spring Bank Holiday until the end of September, and during the lavender harvest, visitors can tour the distillery and see how the wonderful fragrance is made.

As well as being a working farm, this is also the home of the National Collection of Lavenders, a living botanical dictionary which displays the many different colours, sizes and smells of this lovely plant. Among other attractions at Norfolk Lavender are a Fragrant Meadow Garden, a Fragrant Plant Centre in the conservatory, a Herb Garden with 55 individual beds of herbs, a gift shop selling a wide variety of products, and a tearoom

serving cream teas and even lavender-and-lemon scones!

SNETTISHAM
5 miles S of Hunstanton off the A149

🐦 RSPB Bird Sanctuary

Snettisham is best known nowadays for its spacious, sandy beaches and the **RSPB Bird Sanctuary**, both about two miles west of the village itself. But for centuries Snettisham was much more famous as a prime quarry for carrstone, an attractive soft-red building-block that provided the 'light relief' for the walls of thousands of Georgian houses around the country, and for nearby Sandringham House. The carrstone quarry is still working, its product now destined mainly for goldfish ponds and the entrance-banks of the more pretentious types of bungalow. Unfortunately,

Norfolk Lavender

Caley Mill, Heacham, Norfolk PE31 7JE (on A149 at junction with B1454. Plenty of on site parking available) Tel: 01485 570384 Fax: 01485 571176 e.mail: info@norfolk-lavender.co.uk website: www.norfolk-lavender.co.uk

Norfolk Lavender is England's premier lavender farm and home of the National Collection of Lavender.

There is a tearoom offering main meals, cream teas and snacks, as well as gift shops, a conservatory plant sales area, a herb garden & a fragrant meadow.

Tours of the grounds (including distillery & drying barn) are availble from May to September, and minibus tours to the lavender fields and surrounding villages can be taken from July to the end of harvest (pre - booking advisable) . Please phone for more details.

Free Admission and Free Parking.

Open daily (except25/26 Dec & 1 Jan) April to October 9am to 5pm; November to March 9am to 4pm.

🏠 stories and anecdotes 🦜 famous people 🎨 art and craft 🎭 entertainment and sport 🚶 walks

one has to go to the British Museum in London to see Snettisham's greatest gift to the national heritage: an opulent collection of gold and silver ornaments from the 1st century AD, the largest hoard of treasure trove ever found in Britain, discovered here in 1991. The attractions at Snettisham Park include a renowned red deer herd, a discovery trail, horse and pony rides, friendly farm animals, a huge adventure playground, a leather workshop, gift and farm shop, visitor centre and tea room.

DERSINGHAM
7 miles S of Hunstanton off the A149

This large village just north of Sandringham was actually the source of the latter's name: in the *Domesday Book*, the manor was inscribed as 'Sant-Dersingham'. Norfolk tongues found 'Sandringham' much easier to get around. Dersingham village has expanded greatly in recent years and modern housing has claimed much of Dersingham Common, although there are still many pleasant walks here through Dersingham Wood and the adjoining Sandringham Country Park.

SANDRINGHAM
8 miles S of Hunstanton off the A149/B1140

🏠 Sandringham House

🍂 Sandringham Country Park

A couple of miles north of Castle Rising is the entrance to **Sandringham Country Park** and **Sandringham House**, the royal family's country retreat. Unlike the State Rooms at Windsor Castle and Buckingham Palace, where visitors marvel at the awesome trappings of majesty, at Sandringham they can savour the atmosphere of a family home. The rooms the visitor sees at Sandringham are those used by the royal family when in residence, complete with family portraits and

photographs, and comfy armchairs. Successive royal owners have furnished the house with an intriguing medley of the grand, the domestic and the unusual. Entering the principal reception room, The Saloon, for example, you pass a weighing-machine with a leather-covered seat, apparently a common amenity in great houses of the 19th century. In the same room, with its attractively carved Minstrels' Gallery, hangs a fine family portrait by one of Queen Victoria's favourite artists, Heinrich von Angeli. It shows the Prince of Wales (later Edward VII), his wife Alexandra and two of their children, with Sandringham in the background. The numerous porcelain, jade and crystal oriental figures were collected by Queen Alexandra and Queen Mary, and the collection of oriental arms and armour was brought back from the Far East by the Prince in 1876.

The Prince first saw Sandringham on 4th February 1862. At Victoria's instigation, the 20-year-old heir to the throne had been searching for some time for a country property, a refuge of the kind his parents already enjoyed at Balmoral and Osborne. A courtier accompanying the Prince reported back that although the outside of the house was ugly, it was pleasant and convenient within, and set in 'pretty grounds'. The surrounding countryside was plain, he went on, but the property was in excellent order and the opportunity of securing it should not be missed. Within days, the purchase was completed.

Most of the 'ugly' house disappeared a few years later when the Prince and Princess rebuilt the main residence in 1870; the 'pretty grounds' have matured into one of the most beautiful landscaped areas in the country. And the 'plain' countryside around - open heath and grassland overrun by rabbits - has been transformed into a wooded country park, part of the coastal Area of Outstanding Natural Beauty.

One of the additions the Prince made to the house in 1883 was a Ballroom, much to the relief of Princess Alexandra. "It is beautiful I think & a great success." she wrote, "& avoids pulling the hall to pieces each time there is a ball or anything." This attractive room is now used for cinema shows and the estate

Sandringham House

workers' Christmas party. Displayed on the walls is a remarkable collection of Indian weapons, presented to the Prince during his state visit in 1875-6; hidden away in a recess are the two flags planted at the South Pole by the Shackleton expedition.

Just across from the house, the old coach-houses and stables have been converted into a fascinating museum. There are some truly splendid royal vehicles here, including the first car bought by a member of the royal family - a 1900 Daimler Phaeton. There's also a splendid 1939 Merryweather fire engine used by the Estate's own fire brigade, several childen's cars and the old estate game cart. There are Arts and Crafts ceramic tiles and plaques, commemorative china, an exhibition of the Sandringham Company of the 5th Norfolk Regiment and an evocative series of old

photographs depicting the life of the royal family at Sandringham from 1862 until Christmas 1951. Other attractions at Sandringham include a visitor centre, adventure playground, nature walks, souvenir shop, restaurant and tearoom. The beautiful medieval church where the Royal Family worships is open during the visitor season

King's Lynn

🏛 Custom House 🏛 St George's Guildhall

🏛 Hanseatic Warehouse 🏛 Museum of Lynn Life

🎭 Church of St Margaret ✍ King's Lynn Arts Centre

In the opinion of James Lee-Milne, the National Trust's architectural authority, "The finest old streets anywhere in England" are to be found at King's Lynn. Tudor, Jacobean and

THE TUDOR ROSE HOTEL

*St Nicholas Street, off Tuesday Market Place,
King's Lynn, Norfolk PE30 1LR
Tel: 01553 762824 Fax: 01553 764894*

The historic market town of King's Lynn has an abundance of places of interest for the visitor, and the **Tudor Rose Hotel** provides the ideal base for tourists. It combines a central location close to the railway station and the largest market town square in the UK with a welcoming ambience, exceptional comfort and service, good food and a wealth of history. Frances Bloom and Gordon Hale took over this Grade II listed building in August 2001 and the top-to-toe refurbishment they put in place means that everything is in pristine condition.

The hotel stands on the site of a former winter palace built by the Bishops of Norwich in the 12th century and stands in the oldest part of town opposite the magnificent St Nicholas Chapel. The main part of what is now the hotel was the work of a local merchant in about 1500, and behind its timber-farmed frontage there was originally a shop below and living quarters above. A brick extension added in the 1640s is now the oldest part of the hotel; remains of the Dutch gable can be seen from the courtyard. The guest accommodation comprises 14 bedrooms, each with its own style and character, and all with en suite facilities, telephone, television, hairdryer and hot drinks tray.

The restaurant, which is open both to residents and non-residents, is an elegant setting fro enjoying an excellent meal chosen from interesting menus that include dishes inspired by the cuisines of Britain, France and Italy. Bar snacks, with daily specials supplementing the regular printed menu, are available as lighter options. A well-chosen selection of wines complements the fine food, and the lounge bar is a favourite spot for relaxing with friends over a drink. The hotel is renowned for the quality of its real ales, and the choice of four always includes Timothy Taylor and Batemans XB. They are kept in perfect condition by Roger, who treats his ales like a French sommelier treats his wine.

This friendly hotel, where even the resident ghosts have smiles on their faces, is handily placed for seeing the sights of King's Lynn and is also a perfect start point for exploring further afield into North and West Norfolk. The glorious north coast is only a short drive away, and two nearby attractions are the royal residence of Sandringham and the superb Holkham Hall with its fabulous sculptures, Old Master paintings and wonderful gardens.

🏛 historic building   🏛 museum   🏛 historic site   � scenic attraction   🦚 flora and fauna

Flemish houses mingle harmoniously with grand medieval churches and stately civic buildings. It's not surprising that the BBC chose the town to represent early 19th century London in their production of *Martin Chuzzlewit*. It seems, though, that word of this ancient sea-port's many treasures has not yet been widely broadcast, so most visitors to the area tend to stay on the King's Lynn bypass while making their way to the better-known attractions of the north Norfolk coast. They are missing a lot.

The best place to start an exploration of the town is at the beautiful **Church of St Margaret**, founded in 1101 and with a remarkable leaning arch of that original building still intact. The architecture is impressive, but the church is especially famous for its two outstanding 14th century brasses, generally reckoned to be the two largest and most monumental in the kingdom. Richly engraved, one shows workers in a vineyard, the other, commemorating Robert Braunche, represents the great feast which Robert hosted at King's Lynn for Edward III in 1364.

Marks on the tower doorway indicate the church's, and the town's, vulnerability to the waters of the Wash and the River Great Ouse. They show the high-water levels reached during the great floods of 11th March, 1883 (the lowest), 31st January, 1953 and 11th January, 1978.

The organist at St Margaret's in the mid 18th century was the celebrated writer on

music, Dr Charles Burney, but his daughter Fanny was perhaps even more interesting. She wrote a best-selling novel, *Evelina*, at the age of 25, became a leading light of London society, a close friend of Dr Johnson and Sir Joshua Reynolds, and at the age of 59 underwent an operation for breast cancer without anaesthetic. She only fainted once during the 20-minute operation, and went on to continue her active social life until her death at the ripe old age of 87.

Alongside the north wall of St Margaret's is the Saturday Market Place, one of the town's two market places, where visitors can explore The Old Gaol House, an experience complete with the sights and sounds of the ancient cells. A few steps further is one of the most striking sights in the town, the Guildhall of the Holy Trinity with its distinctive chequerboard design of black flint and white stone. The Guildhall was built in 1421, extended in Elizabethan times, and its Great Hall is still used today for wedding ceremonies and various civic events.

Next door to the Guildhall is the Town Hall of 1895, which in a good-neighbourly way is constructed in the same flint-and-stone pattern. The Town Hall also houses the **Museum of Lynn Life** where, along with displays telling the story of the town's 900 years, you can also admire the municipal regalia. The greatest treasure in this collection is King John's Cup, a dazzling piece of medieval workmanship with coloured enamel scenes set in gold. The Cup was supposed to be part of King John's treasure which had been lost in 1215 when his overburdened baggage train was crossing the Nene Estuary and sank into the treacherous quicksands. This venerable legend is sadly undermined by the fact that the Cup was not made until 1340,

more than a century after John's death.

A short distance from the Town Hall, standing proudly by itself on the banks of the River Purfleet, is the handsome **Custom House** of 1683, designed by the celebrated local architect Henry Bell.

There's not enough space here to list all of the town's many other important buildings, but mention must be made of the **Hanseatic Warehouse** (1428), the **South Gate** (1440), the **Greenland Fishery Building** (1605), and **St George's Guildhall**, built around 1406 and reputedly the oldest civic hall in England. The Hall was from time to time also used as a theatre; it's known that Shakespeare's travelling company played here, and it is considered highly likely that the Bard himself trod the boards. If true, his appearance would be very appropriate, since the Guildhall is now home to the **King's Lynn Arts Centre**, active all year round with events and exhibitions and since 1951 the force behind an annual Arts Festival in July with concerts, theatre and a composer in residence. Some of the concerts are held in St Nicholas' Chapel, a medieval building whose acoustics outmatch those of many a modern concert hall.

At Caithness Crystal Visitor Centre, you can watch craftsmen at close quarters as they shape and manipulate glass into beautiful objets d'art.

Around King's Lynn

CASTLE RISING
5 miles NE of King's Lynn off the A148/A149

🏛 Castle Keep

As the bells ring for Sunday morning service at Castle Rising, a group of elderly ladies leave the mellow redbrick Bede House and walk in procession to the church. They are all dressed in long scarlet cloaks, emblazoned on the left breast with a badge of the Howard family arms. Once a year, on Founder's Day, they add to their regular Sunday costume a tall-crowned hat typical of the Jacobean period, just like those worn in stereotypical pictures of broomstick-flying witches.

Castle Rising

These ladies are the residents of the almshouses founded by Henry Howard, Earl of Northampton in 1614, and their regular Sunday attendance at church was one of the conditions he imposed on the original 11 needy spinsters who were to enjoy his beneficence. Howard also required that each inmate of his 'Hospital of the Holy and Undivided Trinity' must also "be able to read, if such a one may be had, single, 56 at least, no common beggar, harlot, scold, drunkard, haunter of taverns, inns or alehouses".

The weekly *tableau vivant* of this procession to the church seems completely in keeping with this picturesque village, which rates high on any 'not to be missed' list of places to visit in Norfolk. The church to which the women make their way, St Lawrence's, is an outstanding example of Norman and Early English work, even though much of it has been reconstructed. But overshadowing everything else in this pretty village is the massive **Castle Keep** (English Heritage), its well-preserved walls rising 50 feet high, and pierced by a single entrance. The Keep's towering presence is made even more

formidable by the huge earthworks on which it stands. The Castle was built in 1150, guarding what was then the sea approach to the River Ouse. (The marshy shore is now some three miles distant and still retreating.)

Despite its fortress-like appearance, Castle Rising was much more of a residential building than a defensive one. In 1331, when Edward III found it necessary to banish his ferocious French-born mother, Isabella, to some reasonably comfortable place of safety, he chose this far-from-London castle. She was to spend some 27 years here before her death in 1358, never seeing her son again during that time. How could Edward treat his own mother in such a way? Her crime, in his view, was that the 'She-Wolf of France', as all her enemies and many of her friends called Isabella, had joined forces with her lover Mortimer against her homosexual husband Edward II (young Edward's father) and later colluded in the king's grisly murder with a red-hot poker at Berkeley Castle. For three years after that loathsome assassination, Isabella and Mortimer ruled England as Regents. The moment Edward III achieved his majority, he had Mortimer hung, drawn and quartered. His mother he despatched to a lonely retirement at Castle Rising.

Six-and-a-half centuries later, the spacious grounds around the castle provide an appropriate backdrop for an annual display by members of the White Society. Caparisoned in colourful medieval garments and armed with more-or-less authentic replicas of swords and halberds, these modern White Knights stage a battle for control of the castle.

TERRINGTON ST CLEMENT

6 miles W of King's Lynn off the A17

> 🏛 Cathedral of the Marshes
>
> 🌱 African Violet Centre

Terrington St Clement is a sizable village notable for the **Cathedral of the Marshland**, a 14th century Gothic masterwork more properly known as St Clement's church, and for the **African Violet Centre**, where some quarter of a million violets are grown each year, in a wide range of colour and species. Plants from the Centre have won many awards at the Royal Chelsea Flower Show.

WALPOLE ST PETER

10 miles W of King's Lynn off the A17/A47

> 🏛 Church

For many connoisseurs, Walpole's **Church** ranks among the finest not just in Norfolk but in the whole of England. Behind the graceful exterior the highlights include the font, the broad 17th century screen behind the nave, the chancel sanctuary and the extraordinary cobbled processional passage.

STOW BARDOLPH

8 miles S of King's Lynn off the A10

> 🏛 Holy Trinity Church

Holy Trinity Church at Stow Bardolph houses one of the oddest memorials in the country. Before her death in 1744, Sarah Hare, youngest daughter of the Lord of the Manor, Sir Thomas Hare, arranged for a life-sized effigy of herself to be made in wax. It was said to be an exceptionally good likeness: if so, Sarah appears to have been rather uncomely maiden, and afflicted with boils to boot. Her death was attributed to blood poisoning after she had pricked her finger with a needle, an act of Divine retribution,

---

EAU BRINK CACTI

Eau Brink Road, King's Lynn, Norfolk PE34 4SQ
Tel: 01558 617635

In a pleasant setting signposted off the A47 Wisbech road out of King's Lynn, **Eau Brink Cacti** is owned and run by a real expert in Derek Bowdery. Derek is an active member of the British Cactus and Succulent Society, and a frequent medal-winner at RHS shows throughout central and southern England. The sales area, in almost half an acre of glasshouses, provides space and opportunity to browse among the impressive range of plants, including specialist agaves, echeverias and ferocacti. The owner's Desert Plant Collection is a good point of reference for students or anyone wanting to learn about the thousands of different species that inhabit the world's deserts. Opening times: March to October, 10am to 5pm Sunday to Thursday. November to February – ring first.

---

apparently, for her sin of sewing on a Sunday. Sarah was then attired in a dress she had chosen herself, placed in a windowed mahogany cabinet, and the monument set up in the Hare family's chapel, a grandiose structure which is larger than the chancel of the church itself.

DOWNHAM MARKET
10 miles S of King's Lynn off the A10/A1122

Museum

Once the site for a major horse fair, this compact little market town stands at the very edge of the Fens, with the River Great Ouse and the New Bedford Drain running side by side at its western edge. Many of its houses are built in the distinctive brick and carrstone style of the area. One of the finest examples of this traditional use of local materials can be seen at Dial House in Railway Road, built in the late 1600s.

The parish church has managed to find a small hill on which to perch. It's an

unassuming building with a rather incongruously splendid glass chandelier from the 1730s. Another feature of the town, much loved by postcard manufacturers, is the elegant, riotously decorated cast-iron Clock Tower in the market place. This was erected in 1878 at a cost of £450. The tower's backdrop of attractive cottages provides a charming setting for a holiday snap.

Two great names are associated with this small town: Charles I, disguised as a clergyman, stayed at Downham Market for a night during his flight after the Battle of Naseby, and Horatio (later Lord) Nelson, son of the parson of Burnham Thorpe, was sent to the little school here.

Near Downham Bridge on the A1122 are

located Collectors World and the Magical Dickens World. The first boasts a plethora of farming and household memorabilia, carts, carriages, radios, cameras, antique and collectable dolls, Armstrong Siddeley cars and much more, with rooms dedicated to Barbara Cartland, Horatio Nelson, the 1960s and more. Dickens World offers visitors a chance to step back in time into a maze of late-19th century streets, shops, sights and sounds.

DENVER
2 miles S of Downham Market off the A10/A1122

Denver Sluice   Denver Windmill

Denver Sluice was originally built in 1651 by the Dutch engineer, Cornelius Vermuyden, as part of a scheme to drain 20,000 acres of land owned by the Duke of Bedford. Various modifications were made to the system over the years, but the principle remains the same, and the oldest surviving sluice, built in 1834, is still in use today. Running parallel with it is the modern Great Denver Sluice, opened in 1964; together these two sluices control the flow of a large complex of rivers and drainage channels, and are able to divert floodwaters into the Flood Relief Channel that runs alongside the Great Ouse.

The two great drainage cuts constructed by Vermuyden are known as the Old and New Bedford rivers, and the strip of land between them, never more than 1,000 yards wide, is called the Ouse Washes. This is deliberately allowed to flood during the winter months so that the fields on either side remain dry. The drains run side by side for more than 13 miles, to Earith in Cambridgeshire, and this has become a favourite route for walkers, with a rich variety of bird, animal and insect life to be seen along the way.

stories and anecdotes   famous people   art and craft   entertainment and sport   walks

Shouldham Warren

Distance: *3.1 miles (4.83 kilometres)*

Typical time: *90 mins*

Height gain: *10 metres*

Map: *Explorer 236*

Walk: *www.walkingworld.com ID:2108*

Contributor: *Joy & Charles Boldero*

ACCESS INFORMATION:

Norfolk Bus routes: Freecall 0500 626116
9a.m. to 5p.m. Monday to Friday to the village
of Shouldham. You can start the walk from
Point 6. However the walk starts at the free
Forestry car park at Shouldham Warren. The
village of Shouldham is situated 2 miles north
of the A1122 at Fincham which is 8 miles west
of Swaffham. To reach the Warren go north up
Eastgate Street out of the village and keep
ahead along rough track where road goes right.

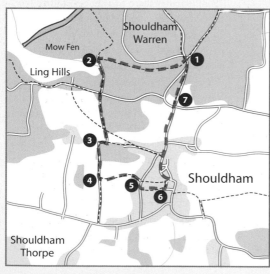

DESCRIPTION:

The outward route is through woodland to
Shouldham village and back by country lanes
through the village. There is an excellent pub,
the King's Arms, which has an extensive menu
and is open every day. The famous October
conker championships used to take place at
the King's Arms. Many centuries ago
Shouldham, was famous for the healing waters
of the Chalybeate spring, a natural mineral
water which was impregnated with iron salts.
Shouldham was also a popular place centuries
ago for its market and fair held each
autumn time.

FEATURES:

Pub, Toilets, Church, Wildlife, Birds, Flowers,
Great Views, Butterflies

WALK DIRECTIONS:

1 | From the Forestry notice board go back
along the track for a very short distance. Turn
right immediately after the flat concrete with
these markings on it. SU-WO-24 &6. Keep
the deep ditch on the left. It is
advisable in hot weather to keep dogs
to the main path as adders could be
in the bracken beside the path. The
smell of fox is quite strong along
here.

2 | Go round the barrier and turn left
over the wide earth bridge. Go along
a tree-lined path, take either path at
the fork. Cross the track and
continue along the track opposite.

3 | At a T junction of tracks turn right
with a farmhouse ahead. After about
70 paces turn left along another track.

4 | At the finger post sign turn left
along a wide grass path between

fields with houses ahead. Go through a gate, continue along a narrower path, then driveway, then track.

5 | Turn right along the village street. Opposite 'The Cottage' at the finger post sign turn left along a tarmac lane.

6 | At the T junction turn right along a lane. Turn left opposite the King's Arms in Shouldham beside the Green with an old village pump on it (You could start the walk from here). Turn left along Eastgate Street, continue along New Road and Warren Road.

7 | At the righthand bend - Spring Lane, keep straight ahead along a wide track to the start of the walk.

Denver Windmill, built in 1835 but put out of commission in 1941, when the sails were struck by lightning, re-opened in 2000. This wonderful working mill set on the edge of the Fens has been carefully restored. On-site attractions include a visitor centre, craft workshops, bakery and tea shop. Holiday accommodation is also available.

HILGAY
3 miles S of Downham Market off the A10

When the *Domesday Book* was written, Hilgay was recorded as one of only two settlements in the Norfolk Fens. It was then an island, its few houses planted on a low hill rising from the surrounding marshland. The village is scarcely any larger today, and collectors of unusual gravestones make their way to its

DENTS OF HILGAY FARM SHOP & GARDEN CENTRE

*Steels Drove, West Fen, Hilgay, Norfolk PE38 0QH
Tel: 01366 385661   e-mail: Dentsfarmshop@aol.com
Fax: 01366 385668   website: www.dentsofhilgay.co.uk*

"A haven for gardeners and lovers of fine food"

Traditionally produced food from small independent suppliers and homegrown produce is the speciality of this award winning Farm Shop. A superb selection of fresh fruit and vegetables, fresh breads are available 7 days a week together with a wonderful range of Homemade Cakes, Quality Biscuits, Free range eggs and quality locally sourced Meats. Chilled goods include a first class selection of Cheeses, Smoked Meats, Fish, Quiches and Pies . An exceptional selection of Norfolk Luxury Ice cream, irresistible Chocolate Treats,Locally brewed Beers, Juices, Wines and Ciders.

The Garden Centre offers an endless range of Plants, Shrubs, Bulbs, Seeds and Houseplants. With greenhouses a riot with Bedding Plants and ready planted Hanging Baskets during the Summer Months alongside Decorative Containers, Garden Sculptures and Water Features.

There is also a wonderful Gift area brimming with Seasonal led Decorative Items for the home, Country style décor and textiles ,Traditional Wooden Toys and French inspired Ironwork Furniture. At Christmas a stunning range of decorations sourced from around the world which rivals that of some department stores. With plenty of parking and easy access of the main A10 bypass, 4 miles South of Downham Market. Alison and Tom Dent and their staff extend a warm welcome to all visitors.

stories and anecdotes   famous people   art and craft   entertainment and sport   walks

churchyard seeking the last resting place of George William Manby. During the Napoleonic wars, Manby invented a rocket-powered life-line that could be fired to ships in distress. His gravestone is carved with a ship, an anchor, a depiction of his rocket device and an inscription that ends with the reproachful words, "The public should have paid this tribute".

OXBOROUGH
10 miles SE of Downham Market off the A134

🏛 Church of St John the Evangelist   🏛 Oxburgh Hall

How many hamlets in the country, one wonders, can boast two such different buildings of note as those to be seen at Oxborough? First there's the church of **St John the Evangelist**, remarkable for its rare brass eagle lectern of 1498 and its glorious Bedingfeld Chapel of 1525, sheltering twin monuments to Sir Edmund Bedingfeld and his wife fashioned in the then-newly popular material of terracotta.

It was Sir Edmund who built **Oxburgh Hall** (National Trust), a breathtakingly lovely moated house built of pale-rose brick and white stone. Sir Edmund's descendants still live in what a later architect, Pugin, described as "one of the noblest specimens of domestic architecture of the 15th century." Henry VII and his Queen, Elizabeth of York, visited in 1487 and lodged in the splendid State Apartments which form a bridge between the lofty gatehouse towers, and ever since have been known as the King's Room and the Queen's Room. On display here is the original Charter of 1482, affixed with Edward IV's Great Seal of England, granting Sir Edmund permission to build with 'stone, lime and sand', and to fortify the building with battlements. These rooms also house some

magnificent period furniture, a collection of royal letters to the Bedingfelds, and the huge Sheldon Tapestry Map of 1647 showing Oxfordshire and Berkshire.

Another more poignant tapestry, known as the Marian Needlework, was the joint handiwork of Elizabeth, Countess of Shrewsbury, and Mary, Queen of Scots, during the latter's captivity here in 1570. The Bedingfelds seemed always to draw the short straw when the Tudors needed someone to discharge an unpleasant or difficult task. It was an earlier Sir Edmund who was charged with the care of Henry VIII's discarded wife, Catherine of Aragon; Edmund's son, Sir Henry, was given the even more onerous task of looking after the King's official bastard, the Princess Elizabeth. After Elizabeth's accession as Queen, Sir Henry presented himself at Court, no doubt with some misgivings. Elizabeth received him civilly but, as he was leaving, tartly observed that "if we have any prisoner whom we would have hardlie and strictly kept, we will send him to you."

As staunch Catholics, the Bedingfelds were, for the next two-and-a-half centuries, consigned to the margins of English political life. Their estates dwindled as portions were sold to meet the punitive taxes imposed on adherents of the Old Faith. By the middle of the 20th century, the Bedingfelds long tenure of Oxburgh was drawing to a close. In 1951 the 9th Baronet, another Sir Edmund, sold Oxburgh to a builder, who promptly announced his intention of demolishing the house. Sir Edmund's mother, the Dowager Lady Sybil, was shocked by such vandalism and used her considerable powers of persuasion to raise sufficient funds to buy back the house. She then conveyed it into the safe keeping of the National Trust.

🏛 historic building   🏛 museum   🏛 historic site   🐾 scenic attraction   🌿 flora and fauna

The grounds at Oxburgh provide the perfect foil for the mellow old building, reflected in its broad moat. There's a wonderfully formal and colourful French garden, a walled kitchen garden, and woodland walks.

Fakenham

🏛 Museum of Gas & Local History

🐦 Pensthorpe Waterfowl Park

Fakenham is a busy and prosperous-looking market town, famous for its National Hunt Racecourse, antique and bric-a-brac markets and auctions, and as a major agricultural centre for the region. Straddling the River Wensum, this attractive country town has a number of fine late 18th and early 19th century brick buildings in and around the Market Place. And it must surely be one of the few towns in England where the former gasworks (still intact) have been turned into a **Museum of Gas & Local History**, housing an impressive historical display of domestic gas appliances of every kind. Fakenham Church also has an unusual feature, a powder room - a room over the large porch, built in 1497, used for storing gunpowder. Even older than the church is the 700-year-old hunting lodge, built for the Duchy of Lancaster, which is now part of the Crown Hotel. As an antidote to the idea that Norfolk is unremittingly flat, take the B1105 north out of Fakenham and after about half a mile take the first minor road to the left. This quiet road loops over and around the rolling hills, a 10-mile drive of wonderfully soothing countryside that ends at Wells-next-the-Sea.

Southeast of Fakenham, off the A1067, **Pensthorpe Nature Reserve and Gardens** is home to Europe's best collection of endangered and exotic waterbirds. Over 120 species of waterfowl can be seen here in their natural surroundings, a wonderful avian refuge where you may come across anything from a scarlet ibis to the more familiar oystercatcher, along with avocets and ruff. The spacious walk-through enclosures offer close contact with shy wading birds, and in the Dulverton Aviary elegant spoonbills and bearded tits vie for your attention. There are good facilities for children and visitors with disabilities, a Wildlife Brass Rubbing Centre, nature trails through 200 acres of the Wensum Valley countryside, and a restaurant and a shop.

WHICH CRAFT

19 Norwich Street, Fakenham, Norfolk NR21 9AI
Tel/Fax: 01328 855333

Since opening her **Which Craft Shop** in October 2002, Frances Neale has made this one of the very best stocked shops in its specialist field. It is a major supplier of knitting yarns, cross stitch, tapestry, card-making materials, hand-made cards, cotton, ribbons, haberdashery and general craft supplies. The window display in the delightfully old-fashioned shop front gives just a hint of the amazing range on display in the spacious, well laid-out and very colourful interior. The shop also offers an expert picture-framing service.

Around Fakenham

THURSFORD GREEN
4 miles NE of Fakenham off the A148

🏠 The Thursford Collection

About two minutes walk from Thursford Green stands what is perhaps the most unusual museum in Norfolk, **The Thursford Collection Sight and Sound Spectacular**. George Cushing began this extraordinary collection of steam-powered traction engines, fairground organs and carousels back in 1946 when 'one ton of tractor cost £1'. Perhaps the most astonishing exhibit is a 1931 Wurlitzer organ whose 1,339 pipes can produce an amazing repertoire of sounds - horses' hooves, fire engine sirens, claps of thunder, waves crashing on sand, and the toot-toot of an old railway engine are just some of the Wurlitzer's marvellous effects. There are regular live music shows when the Wurlitzer displays its virtuosity. Other attractions include a steam-powered Venetian Gondola ride, shops selling a wide variety of goods, many of them locally made, and a tearoom.

A mile or so north of the Thursford museum, in the village of Hindringham, Mill Farm Rare Breeds is home to dozens of cattle, sheep, pigs, goats, ponies, poultry and waterfowl which were once commonplace but are now very rare. These intriguing creatures have some 30 acres of lovely countryside to roam around. Children are encouraged to feed the animals and there's also an adventure playground, crazy golf course, craft & gift shop, picnic area and tearoom.

GREAT SNORING
5 miles NE of Fakenham off the A148

The names of the twin villages, Great and Little Snoring, are such a perennial source of amusement to visitors it seems almost churlish to explain that they are derived from a Saxon family called Snear. At Great Snoring the main street rises from a bridge over the River Stiffkey and climbs up to St Mary's Church.

LITTLE WALSINGHAM
5 miles N of Fakenham on the B1105

🏛 East Barsham Hall 🏛 Holy House

🏛 Shrine of Our Lady of Walsingham

🏛 Augustinian Priory 🏛 Slipper Chapel

Every year, some half a million pilgrims make their way to this little village of just over 500 souls, noted for its impressive timber-framed

---

HOLLY LODGE

1 The Street, Thursford Green, Fakenham, Norfolk NR21 0AS
Tel/Fax: 01328 878465
e-mail: info@hollylodgeguesthouse.co.uk
website: www.hollylodgeguesthouse.co.uk

Jeremy and Gillian Bolam run **Holly Lodge**, a highly individualistic guest house that is rightly considered one of the finest on the North Norfolk coast. In a former stable block next to the owners' house, three superbly restored rooms are let on a Bed & Breakfast basis, with dinner available by arrangement. Each is luxuriously appointed in individual style: Country with beams and brick and flint walls, Colonial with a Raj influence, and Claret, sumptuously decorated and furnished, with antiques, tapestries and a four-poster. Closed January.

🏛 historic building   🏠 museum   🏛 historic site   🌊 scenic attraction   🌿 flora and fauna

buildings and fine Georgian façades, to worship at the **Shrine of Our Lady of Walsingham**. In 1061 the Lady of the Manor of Walsingham, Lady Richeldis de Faverches, had a vision of the Holy Virgin in which she was instructed to build a replica of the Holy House in Nazareth, the house in which the Archangel Gabriel had told Mary

Priory Ruins, Little Walsingham

that she would be the mother of Christ. Archaeologists have located the original house erected by Lady Richeldis. It was just 13 feet by 23 feet and made of wood, later to be enclosed in stone.

These were the years of the Crusades, and the **Holy House** at Walsingham soon became a major centre of pilgrimage, because it was regarded by the pious as an authentic piece of the Holy Land. Around 1153, an **Augustinian Priory** was established to protect the shrine, now encrusted with jewels, gold and silver, and to provide accommodation for the pilgrims. The Priory is in ruins now but the largest surviving part, a stately Gatehouse on the east side of the High Street is very impressive.

For almost 500 years, Walsingham prospered. Erasmus of Rotterdam visited in 1511 and was critical of the rampant commercialisation of the Shrine with its plethora of bogus relics and religious souvenirs for sale. He was shown a gigantic bone, 'the finger-joint of St Peter' no less, and in return for a small piece of translation was

presented with a highly aromatic fragment of wood - a sliver of a bench on which the Virgin had once seated herself.

In the same year that Erasmus visited, Henry VIII also made the pilgrimage that all his royal predecessors since Richard I had undertaken. He stayed overnight at the enchanting early-Tudor mansion, **East Barsham Hall**, a glorious medley of mullioned windows, towers, turrets, and a group of 10 chimneys, each one individually carved with an amazing variety of styles. Since the King's visit the Hall has had a succession of owners over the years, among them a Hapsburg Duke who entertained his neighbours in truly Imperial style before disappearing, leaving behind some truly imperial debts, and the brothers Gibb of the pop group the Bee Gees. The Hall is today owned by a London businessman and is not open to the public, but it stands for all to see as they enter the village.

After his overnight stay at East Barsham Hall, Henry VIII, like most other pilgrims, went first to the **Slipper Chapel**, a beautiful

14th century building about a mile away in Houghton St Giles. Here he removed his shoes and completed the last stretch on foot. Despite this show of piety, some 25 years later Henry had no hesitation in closing the Priory along with all the other monastic institutions in his realm, seizing its treasures and endowments, and having its image of the Virgin publicly burnt at Chelsea.

Little Walsingham itself is an exceptionally attractive village, set in the midst of parks and woodlands, with the interesting 16th century octagonal Clink in Common Place, used in medieval times as a lock-up for petty offenders, the scanty ruins of Walsingham's Franciscan Friary of 1347, and the former Shire Hall, which is now a museum and tourist information centre.

GREAT WALSINGHAM
5 miles N of Fakenham on the B1388

🏛 St Peter's Church

English place names observe a logic of their own, so Great Walsingham is of course smaller than Little Walsingham. The two villages are very different in atmosphere and appearance, Great Walsingham displaying the typical layout of a rural Norfolk settlement, with attractive cottages set around a green watered by the River Stiffkey, and dominated by a fine 14th century church, **St Peter's**, noted for its superb window tracery, wondrously carved Norman font, and perfectly preserved 15th century carved benches.

WIGHTON
7 miles N of Fakenham on the B1105

Wighton Post Office must be one of very few in the country where you can buy a postal order and a pint at the same time. This happy state of affairs has come about because the post office desk is located in the bar of the village pub, The Carpenters Arms. The desk is open two days a week and provides all the normal post office services apart from passports and Road Tax licences. This unusual arrangement has been featured on the TV programme *Country File*.

Just outside the village, the Wells-Walsingham Light Railway trundles its way between Little Walsingham and Wells-next-the-Sea. The longest 10¼-inch narrow-gauge steam railway in the world, it runs throughout the summer along a 20-minute scenic journey through the North Norfolk countryside.

TATTERFORD
5 miles SW of Fakenham off the A148 or A1065

🏛 Houghton Hall 🌿 Tatterford Common

This tiny village is well known to botanists for **Tatterford Common**, an unspoilt tract of rough heathland with tiny ponds, some wild apple trees and the River Tat running through it to join the River Wensum about a mile away.

About four miles west of Tatterford stands **Houghton Hall**, home of the Marquess of Cholmondely and one of Norfolk's most magnificent buildings. This glorious demi-palace was built in the Palladian style during the 1720s by Sir Robert Walpole, England's first Prime Minister. The Walpoles had been gentlemen of substance here since the 14th century. With his family revenues augmented by the considerable profits Sir Robert extracted from his political office, he was in a position to spend lavishly and ostentatiously on his new house. The first step was to destroy completely the village of Houghton (it spoilt the view), and re-house the villagers a mile away at New Houghton.

Although Sir Robert deliberately cultivated

the manner of a bluff, down-to-earth Norfolk squire, the personal decisions he made regarding the design and furnishings of the house reveal a man of deep culture and refined tastes. It was he who insisted that the Hall could not be built in homely Norfolk brick, and took the expensive decision to use the exceptionally durable stone quarried at Aislaby in North Yorkshire and transport it by sea from Whitby to King's Lynn. More than two-and-a-half centuries later, the Aislaby stone is still flawless, the only sign of its age a slight weathering that has softened its colour to a creamy gold.

To decorate the interior and design the furniture, Sir Robert commissioned the versatile William Kent. Kent was at the peak of his powers - just look at the decoration in the Stone Hall, the exquisite canopied bed in the Green Velvet Bedchamber, and the finely-carved woodwork throughout which made impressive use of the newly discovered hardwood called mahogany. And then there were the paintings, an incomparable collection of Old Masters personally selected by Sir Robert. Sadly, many of them are now in the Hermitage Museum in St Petersburg, sold by his wastrel grandson to the Empress Catherine of Russia.

This grandson, George, 3rd Earl of Orford, succeeded to the title at the age of 21 and spent the next 40 years dissipating his enormous inheritance. When his uncle Horace (the 4th Earl, better known as Horace Walpole, novelist, MP and inveterate gossip) succeeded to the title he found "Houghton half a ruin ... the two great staircases exposed to all weathers; every room in the wings rotting with wet; the park half covered with nettles and weeds; mortgages swallowing the estate, and a debt of above £40,000."

Houghton's decline was arrested when the Hall passed by marriage to the Marquess of Cholmondely, Lord Great Chamberlain, in 1797. But it wasn't until 1913, when George, later the 5th Marquess, moved into the house with his new wife, Sybil Sassoon, that Houghton was fully restored to its former state of grace. The depleted collection of paintings was augmented with fine works by Sir Joshua Reynolds and others from Cholmondely Castle in Cheshire, and the Marchioness introduced new collections of exquisite French furniture and porcelain.

One of the 6th Marquess' interests was military history, and in 1928 he began the astonishing Model Soldiers Collection now on display at Houghton. More than 20,000 perfectly preserved models are deployed in meticulous reconstructions of battles such as Culloden and Waterloo, and in one exhibit, recreating the Grand Review of the British Army in 1895, no fewer than 3,000 figures are on parade. The grounds of the estate include a 450-acre deer park, home to over 600 of the famous white fallow deer and smaller groups of exotic deer.

EAST RAYNHAM
3 miles SW of Fakenham on the A1065

🏘 Raynham Hall

Raynham Hall is another superb Palladian mansion with a faultless pedigree — designed by Inigo Jones and with magnificent rooms created a century later by William Kent. The house is only open to the public by appointment since it is the private residence of the 7th Marquess of Townshend. It was his 18th century ancestor, the 2nd Viscount (better known as 'Turnip' Townshend), who revolutionised English agriculture by promoting the humble turnip as an effective

POLLYWIGGLE COTTAGE

40 The Drove, West Raynham, Nr Fakenham,
Norfolk NR21 7EU
Tel: 01603 471990   Fax: 01603 612221
e-mail: marilyn@pollywigglecottage.co.uk
website: www.pollywigglecottage.co.uk

As enchanting as the name suggest, **Pollywiggle Cottage** is a self-catering cottage that's ideally placed for exploring the Norfolk coast and countryside. The pretty brick-and-flint cottage offers abundant country comfort and character for up to eight guests, comprising five first-floor bedrooms, a beamed sitting room, dining room, well-equipped kitchen, bathroom and two WCs. There's parking for four cars and in the delightful, secluded flower garden the small pond is alive in spring with tadpoles, known as 'pollywiggles'.

means of reclaiming untended land for feeding cattle in winter, and along with wheat, barley and clover, as part of the four-year rotation of crops that provided a cycle of essential nutrients for the soil. The Townshend family have owned extensive estates in this area for centuries, and in St Mary's Church there are some fine monuments to their ancestors, the oldest and most sumptuous of which commemorates Sir Roger, who died in 1493.

Swaffham

🏛 Church of St Peter & St Paul

🏛 Swaffham Museum

🏛 Cockley Cley Iceni Village

Swaffham's one-time claim to be the 'Montpellier of England' was justified by the abundance of handsome Georgian houses that used to surround the large, wedge-shaped market place. A good number still survive, along with the Assembly Room of 1817 where the quality would foregather for concerts, balls and soirees. The central focus of the market square is the elegant Butter Cross, presented to the town by the Earl of Orford in 1783. It's not a cross at all, but a classical lead-covered

dome standing on eight columns and surmounted by a life-size statue of Ceres, the Roman goddess of agriculture - an appropriate symbol for this busy market town, from which 10 roads radiate out across the county.

From the market place an avenue of limes leads to the quite outstanding Church of **St Peter & St Paul**, a 15th century masterpiece with one of the very best double hammerbeam roofs in the county, strikingly embellished with a host of angels, their wings widespread. The unknown mason who devised the church's harmonious proportions made it 51 feet wide, 51 feet high and 102 feet long. Carved on a bench-end here is a man in medieval dress accompanied by a dog on a chain. The same two figures are incorporated in the town's coat of arms, and also appear in the elegantly designed town sign just beyond the market place. The man is 'The Pedlar of Swaffham', a certain John Chapman, who, according to legend, dreamed that if he made his way to London Bridge he would meet a stranger who would make him rich. The pedlar and his dog set off for London, and on the bridge he was eventually accosted by a stranger who asked him what he was doing there. John recounted his dream. Scoffingly, the stranger said "If I were a dreamer, I should go to Swaffham. Recently I dreamt that in Swaffham lived a man named Chapman, and in his garden, buried under a tree, lay a treasure." John hastily returned home, uprooted the only tree in his garden, and unearthed two jugs full of gold coins.

There was indeed a John Chapman who contributed generously to the building of the parish church in the late 1400s. Cynics claim that he was a wealthy merchant, and that similar tales occur in the folklore of most European countries. Whatever the truth, there's no doubt that the people of Swaffham took the story to their hearts.

John Chapman may be Swaffham's best-known character locally, but internationally the name of Howard Carter, the discoverer of Tutankhamen's tomb, is much better known. Carter was born at Swaffham in 1874; his death in 1939 was attributed by the popular press to 'the Curse of Tutankhamen'. If so, it must have been an extremely sluggish curse. Some 17 years had elapsed since Carter had knelt by a dark, underground opening, swivelled his torch and found himself the first human being in centuries to gaze upon the astonishing treasures buried in the tomb of the teenage Pharaoh.

Swaffham Museum in the Town Hall is the setting for the story of the town's past. Visitors can follow Howard Carter's road to the Valley of the Kings, see the Symonds Collection of handmade figurines, and admire the Sporle collection of locally-found artefacts.

Move on some 1,400 years from the death of Tutankhamen to Norfolk in the 1st century AD. Before a battle, members of the Iceni tribe, led by Boudicca, would squeeze the blue

Church Walk, Swaffham

sap of the woad plant onto their faces in the hope of frightening the Roman invaders (or any other of their many enemies). At **Cockley Cley Iceni Village and Museums**, three miles southwest of Swaffham off the A1065, archaeologists have reconstructed a village of Boudicca's time, complete with wooden huts, moat, drawbridge and palisades. Reconstruction though it is, the village is remarkably effective in evoking a sense of what daily life entailed more than 1,900 years ago.

A more recent addition to Swaffham's attractions is the EcoTech Centre, opened in 1998. Through intriguing interactive displays and hands-on demonstrations, visitors can discover what startling innovations current, and possible, technology may have in store for us during the next millennium.

stories and anecdotes ⚜ famous people ⚘ art and craft ⚘ entertainment and sport ⚘ walks

NAR VALLEY HOLIDAY COTTAGES

Great Ketlam Farm, Low Road, Pentney, nr King's Lynn,
Norfolk PE37 1JF
Tel: 01760 338797
e-mail: narvalley@gtketlamfarm.wanadoo.co.uk
website: www.narvalleycottagesnorfolk.com

On a superb 230-acre mixed farm with horses, ponies and other animals, **Nar Valley Holiday Cottages** provide a very high quality of self-catering accommodation in a relaxing rural setting. Gig House (two bedrooms), the Threshing Barn (three bedrooms) and Cart Lodge (three bedrooms) are all fully equipped for a self-catering holiday, and all have patio gardens with furniture and a barbecue, and ample private parking. The Threshing Barn has facilities for wheelchair users, including a wheel-in shower room. Guests have the use of an indoor heated pool.

Around Swaffham

CASTLE ACRE
4 miles N of Swaffham off the A1065

🏛 Castle Acre Priory

Set on a hill surrounded by water meadows, Castle Acre seems still to linger in the Middle Ages. William de Warenne, William the Conqueror's son-in-law, came here very soon after the Conquest and built a Castle that was one of the first, and largest, in the country to be built by the Normans. Of that vast fortress, little remains apart from the gargantuan earthworks and a squat 13th century, gateway.

Much more has survived of **Castle Acre Priory**, founded in 1090

and set in fields beside the River Nar. Its glorious West Front gives a powerful indication of how majestic a triumph of late Norman architecture the complete Priory must have been. With five apses and twin towers, the ground plan was modelled on the Cluniac

Castle Acre Priory

NARBOROUGH TROUT & COARSE LAKES

Main Road, Narborough, nr King's Lynn,
Norfolk PE32 1TE
Tel: 01760 338005
e-mail: narfish@supanet.com   website: www.narfish.co.uk

Nestling in the picturesque Nar Valley in North Norfolk, next to an old Mill, this family owned and run site is unique. Fed by the River Nar, a Site of Special Scientific Interest because of water quality, it comprises a Trout and Coarse Fish Farm and Fishery set in 27 acres of secluded woodland. The well planted fishery offers three fly lakes, a stream and two coarse lakes (one with specimen fish). Day and block tickets are available. The fishery is open all year. The shop sells tackle from leading manufacturers. Tackle hire, snacks, tuition, group and corporate entertainment are available. There is a large car park, toilets and disabled access. Guide dogs only are permitted.

   The farm grows high quality Rainbow Trout for sport in the lakes and for food. The shop sells fresh and smoked whole trout, trout fillets, smoked trout pate and smoked Norfolk chicken and duck breasts. All smoking is done on site.

   The peaceful environment is home to many forms of wildlife (over 40 species of birds have been identified). A nature walk along the Mill Stream includes views of the fish in stock ponds. Nearby are the Nar Valley Walk and Peddars way. Historic King's Lynn, Sandringham and the North Norfolk Coast are within easy reach. Holidays and fishing breaks are catered for in three well appointed en suite rooms with twin beds, kitchenette table and chairs, breakfasts provided in the conservatory.

mother church in Burgundy, where William de Warenne had stayed while making a pilgrimage to Rome. Despite the Priory's great size, it appears that perhaps as few as 25 monks lived here during the Middle Ages - and in some comfort, judging by the well-preserved Prior's House, which has its own bath and built-in wash-basin. The Priory lay on the main route to the famous Shrine at Walsingham, with which it tried to compete by offering pilgrims a rival attraction in the form of an arm of St Philip.

   Today the noble ruins of the Priory are powerfully atmospheric, a brooding scene skilfully exploited by Roger Corman when he filmed here for his screen version of Edgar Allan Poe's ghostly story, *The Tomb of Ligeia.*

   Castle Acre village is extremely picturesque, the first place in Norfolk to be designated a Conservation Area, in 1971. Most of the village, including the 15th century parish church, is built in traditional flint, with a few later houses of brick blending in remarkably happily.

LITCHAM
11 miles NE of Swaffham on the B1145

Village Museum

Small though it is, this village strung alongside the infant River Nar can boast an intriguing **Village Museum**, with displays of local artefacts from Roman times to the present, an extensive collection of photographs, some of which date back to 1865, and an underground lime kiln.

Dereham

🏚 St Withburga's Well 🐿 Dumpling Green

One of the most ancient towns in the county, Dereham has a recorded history stretching back to AD654 when St Withburga founded a Nunnery here. St Withburga was the daughter of King Anna of the East Angles and the sister of St Etheldreda, the abbess who founded the religious settlement at Ely. Her name lives on at **St Withburga's Well**, just to the west of the church. This is where she was laid to rest but, some 300 years later, the Abbot and monks of Ely robbed her grave and ensconced the precious, fundraising relic in their own Cathedral. In the saint's desecrated grave a spring suddenly bubbled forth, its waters possessed of miraculous healing properties, and St Withburga's shrine attracted even more pilgrims than before. Some still come.

In the church of St Nicholas, the second largest in Norfolk, there are features from every century from the 12th to the 16th: a magnificent lantern tower, a lofty Bell Tower, painted roofs, and a Seven Sacrament Font. This is the largest of these notable fonts, of which only 30 have survived - 28 of them in Norfolk and Suffolk.

In the northeast transept is buried a poet, some of whose lines have become embedded in the language:

'Variety's the very spice of life,
the monarch of all I survey
God made the country
and man made the town.'.

They all came from the pen of William Cowper who, despite being the author of such cheery poems as *John Gilpin*, suffered grievously from depression, a condition not improved by his association with John Newton, a former slave-trader who had repented and become 'a man of gloomy piety'. The two men collaborated on a book of hymns that included such perennial favourites as *Oh! for a closer walk with God, Hark, my soul, it is the Lord* and *God moves in a mysterious way*. Cowper spent the last four years of his life at Dereham, veering in and out of madness. In a late-flowering romance he had married the widow Mary Unwin, but the strain of caring for the deranged poet drove her in turn to insanity and death. She, too, is buried in the church.

William Cowper died four years after Mary, in 1800. Three years later, another celebrated writer was born at the quaintly named hamlet of **Dumpling Green** on the edge of the town. George Borrow was to become one of the great English travel writers, producing books full of character and colour such as *Wild Wales* and *The Bible in Spain*. In his autobiographical novel *Lavengro* he begins with a warm recollection of the town where he was born: "I love to think on thee, pretty, quiet D[ereham], thou pattern of an English market town, with thy clean but narrow streets branching out from thy modest market place, with thine old-fashioned houses, with here and there a roof of venerable thatch." The house in which George Borrow was born, Borrow's Hall, still stands in Dumpling Green.

A much less attractive character connected with Dereham is Bishop Bonner, the enthusiastic arsonist of Protestant 'heretics' during the unhappy reign of Mary Tudor. He was rector of the town before being appointed Bishop of London, and he lived in the exquisite thatched terrace now called Bishop Bonner's Cottages. The exterior is ornamented with delightful pargetting, a frieze of flower and fruit designs below the eaves, a form of decoration which is very unusual in Norfolk. The cottages now house a small museum. Dereham is at one end of the Mid-Norfolk Railway, East Anglia's longest heritage railway, linking Dereham with Wymondham. Heritage diesel services operate on most weekends during the year, and Dereham station is being restored to its appearance in the 1950s and '60s.

Around Dereham

GRESSENHALL
3 miles NW of Dereham off the B1146

Roots of Norfolk

The **Roots of Norfolk** collection is housed in an impressive late 18th century former workhouse built in rose-red brick. Gressenhall Workhouse was designed to accommodate some 700 unfortunates, so it was built on a very grand scale indeed. Now one of the UK's leading rural life museums and among Norfolk's top family attractions, there's ample room for the many exhibits illuminating the working and domestic life of Norfolk people over the last 150 years. Farming the old-fashioned way is there to be discovered on Union Farm, where heavy animals still work the fields. A stroll along the 1930s village high street takes in the grocer's, post office and schoolroom. The surrounding 50 acres of unspoilt countryside are perfect for walking. The site hosts numerous special events during the season, ranging from Steam Days to an international folk dance festival with more

PEACOCK HOUSE
Peacock Lane, Old Beetley, nr Dereham, Norfolk NR20 4DG
Tel/Fax: 01362 860371
e-mail: peacockhouse2006@aol.com
website: www.peacock-house.co.uk

Mark and Linda Stuckey are the warm, friendly hosts at **Peacock House**, a comfortable former farmhouse in a tranquil rural setting. Tastefully renovated, it retains much period character and charm, and the en suite guest rooms are prettily decorated and furnished; all have electric blankets, TVs and tea/coffee trays. Breakfast, including home-made bread and yoghurt and local produce cooked in the Rayburn, is served in the long dining room, and evening meals are available by arrangement.

There are books and games in the cosy beamed sitting room, and guests can wander round the 2½ acres of gardens, wildlife pond, orchard and meadow surrounded by lovely open farmland and woodland. Peacock House, a strictly non-smoking establishment, also offers two rather unusual amenities: a cinema with a 12ft screen and a clay pigeon shooting range. The house is located on the B1110 three miles north of Dereham.

stories and anecdotes   famous people   art and craft   entertainment and sport   walks

than 200 dancers taking part.

A mile or so south of Gressenhall, the tiny community of Dillington has great difficulty in getting itself noticed on even the most large-scale of maps. This hidden place is worth seeking out for Norfolk Herbs at Blackberry Farm, a specialist herb farm located in a beautiful wooded valley. Visitors are invited to browse through a vast collection of aromatic, culinary and medicinal herb plants, and to learn all about growing and using herbs.

BRISLEY

7 miles N of Dereham on the B1145

Brisley village is well known to local historians and naturalists for its huge expanse of heathland, some 170 acres of it. It's reckoned to be the best example of unspoilt common in Norfolk, and at its centre are scores of pits that were dug out in medieval times to provide clay for the wattle-and-daub houses of the period. Another feature of interest in the village is Gately Manor (private), an Elizabethan manor house standing within the remains of a medieval moat, and yet another moated house at Old Hall Farm in the southwest corner of the green.

NORTH ELMHAM

6 miles N of Dereham off the B1110

Near the village of North Elmham stand the sparse remains of a Saxon Cathedral. North Elmham was the seat of the Bishops of East Anglia until 1071, when they removed to Thetford (and then, 20 years later, to Norwich). Although there had been a cathedral here since the late 7th century, what has survived is mostly from the 11th century. Despite its grand title, the T-shaped ground plan reveals that the cathedral was no larger than a small parish church.

WATTON

10 miles SW of Dereham on the A1075

Wayland Wood

Watton's striking town sign depicts the 'Babes in the Wood' of the famous nursery story. The story, which was already current hereabouts in the 1500s, relates that as Arthur Truelove lay dying he decided that the only hope for his two children was to leave them in the care of their uncle. Unfortunately, the uncle decided to help himself to their inheritance and paid two men to take the children into nearby **Wayland Wood** and kill them. In a moment of unexpected compassion, one of the men decided that he could not commit the dastardly act. He disposed of his accomplice instead, and abandoned the children in the wood to suffer whatever fate might befall them. Sadly, unlike the nursery tale in which the children find their way back home and live happily ever after, this unfortunate brother and sister perished. Their ghosts are said to wander hand in hand through the woods to this day.

Wayland Wood is now owned by the Norfolk Naturalist Trust, and is believed to be one of the oldest in England; Griston Hall (private), half a mile south of the wood, is a Grade II listed building, reputedly once the home of the 'Wicked Uncle' in the real-life *Babes in the Wood* story.

Watton itself boasts an unusual Clock Tower, dated 1679, standing at the centre of its long main street.

THOMPSON

12 miles SW of Dereham off the A1075

This is a quiet village with a marshy man-made lake, Thompson Water, and a wild common. The Peddars Way long-distance footpath passes about a mile to the west and, about the same distance to the northeast, the Church is a splendid early 14th century building notable for its fine carved screen and choice 17th century fittings.

ATTLEBOROUGH
12 miles S of Dereham off the A11

🏛 Church of St Mary

The greatest glory of this pleasant market town is to be found in its **Church of St Mary**. Here, a remarkable 15th century chancel screen stretches the width of the church and is beautifully embellished with the arms of the 24 bishoprics into which England was divided at that time. The screen is generally reckoned to be one of the most outstanding in the country, a remarkable survivor of the Reformation purging of such beautiful creations from churches across the land.

Collectors of curiosities will be interested in a strange memorial in the churchyard. It takes the form of a pyramid, about six feet high, and was erected in 1929 to mark the grave of a local solicitor with the rather splendid name of Melancthon William Henry Brooke, or 'Lawyer' Brooke as he was more familiarly known. Melancthon was an amateur Egyptologist who became convinced by his studies of the Pharoahs' tombs that the only way to ensure an agreeable after-life was to be buried beneath a pyramid, precisely placed and of the correct physical dimensions. Several years before his death, he gave the most punctilious instructions as to how this assurance of his immortal existence should be

constructed and located. A few miles south of Attleborough, signposted off the a11, Snetterton Race Circuit is one of the most popular attractions in East Anglia. Highlights of the racing season include rounds of the British Superbike Championship, British Touring Car Championship and numerous classic bike and car meetings.

Thetford

🏛 Cluniac Priory 🏛 Burrell Steam Museum

🏛 Boudicca's Palace 🏛 Thetford Warren Lodge

🏛 Castle 🏛 Grimes Graves 🚶 Thetford Forest

Some 2,000 years ago, Thetford may well have been the site of **Boudicca's Palace**. In the 1980s, excavations for building development

Thomas Paine Statue, Thetford

at Gallows Hill, north of the town, revealed an Iron Age enclosure. It is so extensive it may well have been the capital of the Iceni tribe which gave the Romans so much trouble. Certainly, the town's strategic location at the meeting of the Rivers Thet and Little Ouse made it an important settlement for centuries. At the time of the *Domesday Book*, 1086, Thetford was the sixth-largest town in the country and the seat of the Bishop of East Anglia, with its own castle, mint and pottery.

Sunset Over Thetford Forest

Of the **Castle**, only the 80-foot motte remains, but it's worth climbing to the top of this mighty mound for the views across the town. An early Victorian traveller described Thetford as "An ancient and princely little town ... one of the most charming country towns in England". Despite major development all around, the heart of the town still fits that description, with a goodly number of medieval and Georgian houses presenting an attractive medley of flint and half-timbered buildings. Perhaps the most striking is the Ancient House Museum in White Hart Street, a magnificent 15th century timber-framed house with superb carved oak ceilings. It houses the Tourist Information Centre and a museum where some of the most interesting exhibits are replicas of the Thetford Treasure, a 4th century hoard of gold and silver jewellery discovered as

recently as 1979 by an amateur archaeologist with a metal detector. The originals of these sumptuous artefacts are housed in the British Museum in London.

Even older than the Ancient House is the 12th century **Cluniac Priory** (English Heritage), now mostly in ruins but with an impressive 14th century gatehouse still standing. During the Middle Ages, Thetford could boast 24 churches; today, only three remain.

Thetford's industrial heritage is vividly displayed in the **Burrell Steam Museum**, in Minstergate, which has full-size steam engines regularly 'in steam', re-created workshops and many examples of vintage agricultural machinery. The Museum tells the story of the Burrell Steam Company, which formed the backbone of the town's industry from the late

18th to the early 20th centuries, their sturdy machines famous around the world.

In King Street, the Thomas Paine Statue commemorates the town's most famous son, born here in 1737. The revolutionary philosopher, and author of *The Rights of Man* emigrated to America in 1774, where he helped formulate the American Bill of Rights. Paine's democratic views were so detested in England that even 10 years after his death in New York, the authorities refused permission for his admirer, William Cobbett, to have the remains buried in his home country. And it wasn't until the 1950s that Thetford finally got around to erecting a statue in his honour. Ironically for such a robust democrat, his statue stands in King Street and opposite The King's House, named after James I, who was a frequent visitor here between 1608 and 1618. At the Thomas Paine Hotel in White Hart Street, the room in which it is believed that Paine was born is now the Honeymoon Suite, complete with four-poster bed.

To the west of the town stretch the 90 square miles of **Thetford Forest**, the most extensive lowland forest in Britain. The Forestry Commission began planting in 1922, and although the woodland is largely given over to conifers, with Scots and Corsican Pine and Douglas Fir predominating, oak, sycamore and beech can also be seen throughout. There is a particularly varied trail leading from the Forestry Commission Information Centre which has detailed information about this and other walks through the area.

On the edge of the forest, about two miles west of Thetford, are the ruins of **Thetford Warren Lodge**, built around 1400. At that time a huge area here was preserved for farming rabbits, a major element of the medieval diet. The vast warren was owned by the Abbot of Thetford Priory, and it was he who built the Lodge for his gamekeeper.

Still in the forest, reached by a footpath from the village of Santon Downham, are **Grimes Graves** (English Heritage - see panel below), the earliest major industrial site to be discovered in Europe. At these unique Neolithic flint mines, Stone Age labourers

Grimes Graves

Nr Thetford, Norfolk IP26 5DE
Tel: 01842 810656
website: www.english-heritage.org.uk

Descend into a prehistoric flint mine. Discover the significance of over 400 pits, forming a lunar landscape amid the unique Breckland environment, famous for its unusual wildlife. These 'Devil's Holes' long confused experts: find out about their extraordinary theories, and see finds of the mysterious objects deposited by Neolithic miners. Experience an unforgettable visit to Britain's only accessible prehistoric flint mine, dug by Stone Age miners 5,000 years ago. Descend over 10 metres to the galleries where flint was mined for tools and weapons, and wonder at the courage and ingenuity of our distant ancestors.

📖 stories and anecdotes   🦢 famous people   🎨 art and craft   🎭 entertainment and sport   🚶 walks

extracted the materials for their sharp-edged axes and knives. It's a strange experience entering these 5,000 year old shafts, which descend some 30 feet to an underground chamber. (The experience is even better if you bring your own high-powered torch.)

Around Thetford

MUNDFORD
8 miles NW of Thetford on the A1065/A134

Mundford is a large Breckland village of flint-built cottages, set on the northern edge of Thetford Forest and with the River Wissey running by. If you ever watch TV,

you've almost certainly seen Lynford Hall, a mile or so northwest of Mundford. It has provided an impressive location for scenes in *Dad's Army, Allo, Allo, You Rang My Lord?* and *Love on a Branch Line*, as well as featuring in numerous TV commercials. The Hall is a superb Grade II listed mansion, built for the Lyne-Stevens family in 1885 (as a hunting-lodge, incredibly) and designed in the Jacobean Renaissance style by William Burn.

EAST HARLING
8 miles E of Thetford on the B1111

This attractive little town boasts a beautiful 15th century church in a pastoral location

THE CROWN HOTEL
Crown Road, Mundford, nr Thetford, Norfolk IP26 5HQ
Tel: 01842 878233   Fax: 01842 878982
e-mail: info@the-crown-hotel.co.uk
website: www.the-crown-hotel.co.uk

Barry Walker is the resident proprietor of the **Crown Hotel & Restaurant**, a traditional Norfolk inn that's proud to offer good old-fashioned hospitality. Dating back more than 350 years, it was once a renowned hunting inn (it's on the northern edge of Thetford Forest), and in later times the local magistrates met here. Informality is the order of the day, and owner and staff welcome guests, whether familiar faces or first-timers, as old friends; some pop in just for a drink, others for a meal, while some use the Crown as a base for touring this pleasant part of the world.

The hotel has two bars – the peaceful Squires Bar and the old-style Village Bar – and two restaurants – the Old Court with rugs on floorboards and the informal Club Dining Room at the top of a spiral staircase. Between them, the menus include traditional pub fayre, a regularly changing à la carte selection and daily specials, always interesting, with local produce to the fore. The 30 guest rooms, all en suite, include several family rooms and a four-poster room, and the very reasonable tariff includes a full English breakfast. The Crown has well-appointed function rooms, and can organise marquee hire and outside catering.

🏛 historic building   📷 museum   🏛 historic site   🌳 scenic attraction   🌿 flora and fauna

beside the River Thet. Inside, a magnificent hammerbeam roof crowns the lofty nave, there's some outstanding 15th century glass and, in the Harling Chapel, the fine marble Tomb of Robert Harling. Harling was one of Henry V's knights, who met his death at the siege of Paris in 1435. Since this was long before the days of refrigeration, the knight's body was instead stewed, then stuffed into a barrel and brought back to East Harling for a ceremonious burial.

The church houses another equally sumptuous memorial, the tomb of Sir Thomas Lovell. Sculpted in alabaster, Sir Thomas is an imposing figure, clad in armour with a long sword, his head resting on a helmet, his feet on a spray of peacock's feathers. He and his wife lie beneath a wondrously ornamented canopy, decorated with multi-coloured shields and pinnacles.

BANHAM
12 miles E of Thetford on the B1114

🦜 Banham Zoo

Banham Zoo provides the opportunity to come face to face with some of the world's rarest wildlife - many of the animals who find a home here otherwise face extinction. The Zoo, with almost 1,000 animals, is particularly concerned with monkeys and apes, but in the 25 acres of landscaped gardens you'll also come across tigers, cheetahs, lemurs, penguins and many other species. There are educational talks and displays, a children's play area, Shire Horse dray rides, and a restaurant.

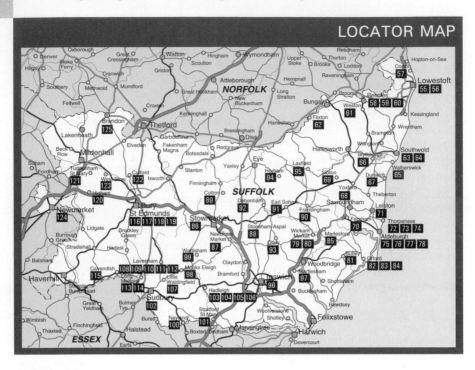

LOCATOR MAP

ADVERTISERS AND PLACES OF INTEREST

🏛 historic building   🏛 museum   🏛 historic site   ⚘ scenic attraction   🌱 flora and fauna

2 | Suffolk

Suffolk is a county with a wealth of attractions to delight the visitor: rural beauty, rivers and nature reserves, windmills and water mills, ancient wool towns and villages, churches hardly touched by the Victorian 'improvers', stately homes, thriving ports and holiday resorts, a conservation coastline standing defiant against the North Sea.

Suffolk is very much a maritime county, with over 50 miles of coastline. The whole coast is a conservation area, which the 50-mile Suffolk Coastal Path makes walkable throughout. With all the miles of meandering rivers and superb stretches of coastline, it is only natural that watery pursuits are a popular pastime, and many of the local museums also have a nautical theme; the Suffolk coast has been a source of inspiration for many of the nation's most distinguished artists, writers and composers.

📖 stories and anecdotes   ✎ famous people   🎨 art and craft   🎭 entertainment and sport   🚶 walks

The sea brings its own dangers, even in human form, and it was against the threat of a Napoleonic invasion that Martello Towers were built in southeastern Suffolk, in the tradition of Saxon and Tudor forts and the precursors of concrete pillboxes. The marshes by the coast have traditionally been a source of reeds, the raw material for the thatch

Minsmere Cliffs, Dunwich Heath

that is such a pretty sight on so many Suffolk buildings. Reed-cutting happens between December and February, the beds being drained in preparation and reflooded after the crop has been gathered. Thatching itself is a highly skilled craft, but 10 weeks of work can give a thatched roof 50 years of life.

Inland Suffolk has few peers in terms of picturesque countryside and villages, and the area of central Suffolk between the heathland and the coast is a delightful place for getting away from it all to the real countryside, with unchanged ancient villages, gently flowing rivers and rich farm land. The little market towns of Stowmarket and Needham Market are full of interest, and in this part of Suffolk some of the best-preserved windmills and watermills are to be found.

Much of Suffolk's character comes from its rivers, and in the part of the county surrounding Ipswich, the Orwell and the Stour mark the boundaries of the Shotley Peninsula. The countryside here is largely unspoilt, with wide-open spaces between scattered villages.

John Constable, England's greatest landscape painter, was born at East Bergholt in 1776 and remained at heart a Suffolk man

throughout his life. The Suffolk tradition of painting continues to this day, with many artists drawn particularly to Walberswick and what is known as 'Constable Ccountry'. Cambridgeshire, Norfolk, the A134 and the A14 frame the northern part of West Suffolk, which includes Bury St Edmunds, a pivotal player in the country's religious history, and Newmarket, one of the major centres of the horseracing world. Between and above them are picturesque villages, bustling market towns, rich farming countryside, the fens, and the expanse of sandy heath and pine forest that is Breckland. The area south and west of Bury towards the Essex border contains some of Suffolk's most attractive and peaceful countryside. The visitor will come upon a succession of picturesque villages, historic churches, remarkable stately homes, heritage centres and nature reserves. In the south, along the River Stour, stand the historic wool towns of Long Melford, Cavendish and Clare. And , of course, Sudbury, another wonderful town, the birthplace of the painter Thomas Gainsborough, the largest of the wool towns and still home to a number of weaving concerns.

Lowestoft

- Lowestoft & East Suffolk Maritime Museum
- Royal Naval Patrol Museum
- War Memorial Museum
- Lowestoft Museum
- ISCA Maritime Museum

The most easterly town in Britain had its heyday as a major fishing port during the late 19th and early 20th centuries, when it was a mighty rival to Great Yarmouth in the herring industry. That industry has been in major decline since the First World War, but Lowestoft is still a fishing port and the trawlers still chug into the harbour in the early morning with the catches of the night. Guided tours of the fish market and the harbour are available.

Lowestoft is also a popular holiday resort, the star attraction being the lovely South Beach with its golden sands, safe swimming, two piers and all the expected seaside amusements and entertainments. Claremont Pier, over 600 feet in length, was built in 1902, ready to receive day-trippers on the famous Belle steamers. The buildings in this part of town were developed in mid Victorian times by the company of Sir Samuel Morton Peto, also responsible for Nelson's Column, the statues in the Houses of Parliament, the Reform Club and Somerleyton Hall.

At the heart of the town is the old harbour, home to the Royal Norfolk & Suffolk Yacht Club and the Lifeboat Station. Further upriver is the commercial part of the port, used chiefly by ships carrying grain and timber. The

CRYSTAL WATERS TRADITIONAL SMOKEHOUSE

6 Cooke Road South, Lowestoft Industrial Estate, Lowestoft, Suffolk NR33 7NA
Tel: 01502 586866   Fax: 01502 586966
website: www.onlinefish.co.uk

Specialising in quality English and Continental seafood, **Crystal Waters Traditional Smokehouse** boasts five smokehouses on site, preparing a range of superb fish and seafood including kippers, haddock, hot-roast salmon, monkfish and prawns. The family-run business is headed by Linda Eastwood and her three sons Daniel, Simon and Matthew, all experienced fishmongers. They are well-known stockists for numerous stalls in Suffolk and Essex, including Woodbridge, Hadleigh, Saffron Walden, Chesham, Walton-on-the-Naze, Halstead, Newmarket, Manningtree, Halesworth and Bungay. Top restaurateurs and cookery schools also look to the Eastwoods for fish and seafood, not least because their traditional smoking methods bring out the very best flavours of their wares. A take-home service provides customers with leak-proof insulated cool boxes packed with ice.

World of Fish, part of this outstanding complex, has what is probably the largest selection of wet and exotic fish and shellfish in the region: Cromer crab, lobster, tiger prawns, red snapper, red mullet, tuna, swordfish, parrot fish, grouper, shark, sardines, squid and king scallops frozen or smoked.

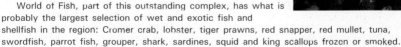

stories and anecdotes　famous people　art and craft　entertainment and sport　walks

history of Lowestoft is naturally tied up with the sea, and that heritage is remembered in a number of museums in the town. Much of that history is recorded in fascinating detail in the **Lowestoft & East Suffolk Maritime Museum** with model boats, fishing gear, a lifeboat cockpit, paintings and shipwrights' tools. The setting is a flint-built fisherman's cottage in Sparrow's Nest Gardens. The **Royal Naval Patrol Museum** nearby remembers the minesweeping service in models, photographs, documents and uniforms. On Heritage Quay, the *Mincarlo* is the last surviving fishing vessel built (including the engine) in Lowestoft. Visitors can tour the whole boat.

Lowestoft

Lowestoft had England's first lighthouse, installed in 1609. The present one dates from 1874. Also in Sparrow's Nest Gardens is the **War Memorial Museum**, dedicated to those who served during the Second World War. There's a photographic collection chronicling the bombing of the town, aircraft models and a chapel of remembrance.

St Margaret's Church, notable for its decorated ceiling and copper-covered spire, is a memorial to seafarers, and the north aisle has panels recording the names of fishermen lost at sea from 1865 to 1923.

Lowestoft also has some interesting literary and musical connections. The Elizabethan playwright, poet and pamphleteer Thomas Nash was born here in 1567. His last work, *Lenten Stuffe*, was a eulogy to the herring trade and specifically to Great Yarmouth. Joseph Conrad (Jozef Teodor Konrad Korzeniowski), working as a deckhand on a British freighter bound for Constantinople, jumped ship here

JAK 'N' ALS

192 London Road South, Lowestoft, Suffolk NR33 0BB
Tel: 01502 585835
e-mail: jaknalsantiques@aol.com

High-quality secondhand antique, reproduction and modern furniture is on display behind the double window of **Jak 'n' Als** on the main route through Lowestoft. The shop takes its name from owners Jackie and Allan Harvey, whose ever-changing stock includes general furniture, dressers, washstands, Victorian window seats, Tiffany lights, jugs, bowls, unusual gifts and anything wonderful that takes their fancy. The light-hearted name of the shop is reflected in the relaxed, friendly ambience that makes every visit a real pleasure.

🏛 historic building   🏛 museum   🏛 historic site   🏞 scenic attraction   🌿 flora and fauna

in 1878, speaking only a few words of the language in which he was to become one of the modern masters. The composer Benjamin Britten is associated with several places in Suffolk, but Lowestoft has the earliest claim, for it is here that he was born in 1913.

Just north of town, with access from the B1385, Pleasurewood Hill is the largest theme park in East Anglia.

Oulton Broad, on the western edge of Lowestoft, is a major centre of amusements afloat, with boats for hire and cruises on the Waveney. It also attracts visitors to Nicholas Everitt Park to look around **Lowestoft Museum**, housed in historic Broad House. Opened by the Queen and Prince Philip in 1985, the museum displays archaeological finds from local sites, some now lost to the sea, costumes, toys, domestic bygones, civic

regalia, paintings, radios and a fine collection of Lowestoft porcelain. (The porcelain industry lasted from about 1760 to 1800, using clay from the nearby Gunton Hall Estate. The soft-paste ware, resembling Bow porcelain, was usually decorated in white and blue.)

Lowestoft's **ISCA Maritime Museum** has a unique collection of ethnic working boats, including coracles, gondolas, junks, dhows, sampans and proas.

Around Lowestoft

BLUNDESTON
4 miles N of Lowestoft off the A12

Known chiefly as the village used by Charles Dickens as the birthplace of that writer's

THE WATERSIDE VILLAGE

The Street, Corton, nr Lowestoft, Suffolk NR32 5HS
Tel: 01502 730200   Fax: 01502 732878
e-mail: tracey.waterside@yahoo.co.uk

The **Waterside Village** is a perfect holiday site in an impressive location overlooking Corton Cliffs and the sea. The park in which the accommodation stands has recently been completely renovated and redeveloped to provide the most pleasant of surroundings for relaxing and enjoying a break.

Guests have a choice of two- and three-bedroom bungalows and a three-bedroom house, all with bathroom, kitchen, sitting area and all the expected home comforts. The bungalows have partly-covered sun patios.

Facilities in the Waterside Village include a bar and a newly refurbished restaurant serving a day-long selection of snacks and meals from its bistro-style menu. Patio doors lead from the bar to a garden overlooking the sea and a heated swimming pool and paddling pool are available during the summer months.

The Village has plenty to occupy guests of all ages, but there's an almost endless choice of places to see and things to do within an easy drive: the city of Norwich, the towns of Lowestoft and Great Yarmouth, the Broads, beaches, wildlife and theme parks, bird reserves and historic houses – and a lot more besides; there's never a dull moment in this lovely part of the world.

'favourite child', David Copperfield, the morning light shining on the sundial of Blundeston's church – which has the tallest, narrowest Saxon round tower of any in East Anglia – greeted young David as he looked out of his bedroom window in the nearby Rookery. He said of the churchyard: "There is nothing half so green that I know anywhere, as the grass of that churchyard, nothing half so shady as its trees; nothing half so quiet as its tombstones."

Blundeston has another notable literary connection: Blundeston Lodge was once the home of Norton Nichols, whose friend the poet Gray is reputed to have taken his inspiration for *An Elegy Written in a Country Church Yard* while staying there.

LOUND
5 miles N of Lowestoft off the A12

🏠 Church of St John the Baptist

Lound's parish church of **St John the Baptist**, in the very north of the county, is sometimes known as the 'golden church'. This epithet is the result of the handiwork of designer/ architect Sir Ninian Comper, seen most memorably in the gilded organ-case with two trumpeting angels, the font cover and the rood screen. The last is a very elaborate affair, with several heraldic arms displayed. The surprise package here is the modern St Christopher mural on the north wall. It includes Sir Ninian at the wheel of his Rolls Royce – and in 1976 an aeroplane was added to the scene!

SOMERLEYTON
5 miles NW of Lowestoft on the B1074

🏠 Somerleyton Hall

Somerleyton Hall, one of the grandest and most distinctive of stately homes, is a splendid Victorian mansion built in Anglo-Italian style

by Samuel Morton Peto. Its lavish architectural features are complemented by fine state rooms, magnificent wood carvings (some by Grinling Gibbons) and notable paintings. The grounds include a renowned yew-hedge maze, where people have been going round in circles since 1846, walled and sunken gardens, and a 300-foot pergola. There's also a sweet little miniature railway, and Fritton Lake Countryworld, part of the Somerleyton Estate, is a 10-minute drive away (see under Fritton in Norfolk). The Hall is open to the public on most days in summer.

Samuel Morton Peto learned his skills as a civil engineer and businessman from his uncle, and was still a young man when he put the Reform Club and Nelson's Column into his CV. The Somerleyton Hall he bought in 1843 was a Tudor and Jacobean mansion. He and his architect virtually rebuilt the place, and also built Somerleyton village, a cluster of thatched redbrick cottages. Nor was this the limit of Peto's achievements, for he ran a company which laid railways all over the world and was a Liberal MP, first for Norwich, then for Finsbury and finally for Bristol. His company foundered in 1863 and Somerleyton Hall was sold to Sir Francis Crossley, one of three brothers who made a fortune in mass-producing carpets. Crossley's son became Baron Somerleyton in 1916, and the Baron's grandson is the present Lord Somerleyton.

HERRINGFLEET
5 miles NW of Lowestoft on the B1074

🏠 Herringfleet Windmill

Standing above the River Waveney, the parish church of St Margaret is a charming sight with its Saxon round tower, thatched roof and lovely glass. **Herringfleet Windmill** is a beautiful black-tarred smock mill in working order, the last survivor of the Broadland wind pump, whose job was to assist in draining the marshes. This example was built in 1820 and worked regularly until the 1950s. It contains a fireplace and a wooden bench, providing a modicum of comfort for a millman on a cold night shift. To arrange a visit call 01473 583352.

BECCLES

9 miles W of Lowestoft on the A146

- Church of St Michael
- Beccles & District Museum
- William Clowes Museum of Print   Roos Hall

The largest town in the Waveney district at the southernmost point of the Broads, Beccles has, in its time, been home to Saxons and Vikings, and at one time the market here was a major supplier of herring (up to 60,000 a year) to the Abbey at Bury St Edmunds. At the height of its trading importance Beccles must have painted a splendidly animated picture, with wherries constantly on the move transporting goods from seaports to inland towns. The same stretch of river is still alive, but now with the yachts and pleasure boats of the holidaymakers and weekenders who fill the town in summer. The regatta in July and August is a particularly busy time.

Fire, sadly such a common part of small-town history, ravaged Beccles at various times in the 16th and 17th centuries, destroying much of the old town. For that reason the

BUTTERFLIES

4 Market Street, Beccles, Suffolk NR34 9AQ
Tel: 01502 711921
e-mail: pambonnett@talk21.com
website: www.butterfliesclothing.co.uk

On two brightly lit floors of a glass-fronted shop close to the centre of town, **Butterflies** stocks an excellent selection of smart womens' outfits for all occasions. Owner Pam Bonnett also keeps a popular range of hats and other accessories, including scarves and jewellery. Pam's policy is to stock only a small number of each main item (sometimes just one), which ensures that the choice of costume is often unique to each customer. Hats and evening wear are available to hire as well as buy. Opening hours are 9.30am to 5pm (Saturday to 4.30pm, closed Wednesday).

WILLOWS OF BECCLES

27 Smallgate, Beccles, Suffolk NR34 9AD
Tel: 01502 715545

Two floors of well-lit display space behind a small-paned shop window hold an ever-changing selection of lovely gifts and things for the home at **Willows of Beccles**. Close to the centre of town, the shop's wide-ranging stock includes silver, pewter, porcelain, glassware and jewellery, pictures and prints by local artists, turned wooden bowls (also locally made) and bespoke greetings cards. Among the many suppliers are Hot Diamond (jewellery), gifts by Pave, 2 Blue and Amber Silver Scenes, Florence figurines (art sculptures), Gleneagles crystalware, Heredities gold cast figures and Lionite Miele vanity cases.

stories and anecdotes   famous people   art and craft   entertainment and sport   walks

North Cove

Distance: *5.0 miles (8.0 kilometres)*

Typical time: *180 mins*

Height gain: *10 metres*

Map: *Outdoor Leisure 40*

Walk: *www.walkingworld.com ID:2016*

Contributor: *Joy & Charles Boldero*

ACCESS INFORMATION:

Buses: TravelLine 0545 583358.

There is parking along the 'No Thro Road' in North Cove which is situated off the A146.

At the roundabout A146/B1127 east of Beccles keep ahead along the A146 signed Lowestoft. After a very short distance, just before the North Cove sign, turn left, then right, with the pub on left, go under barrier and park.

DESCRIPTION:

This is a pleasant walk along country lanes, tracks and beside the River Waveney, that path being part of the long distance one, Angles Way. The route takes you through the Castle Marsh Nature reserve where many birds winter, flying over from Iceland and northern Europe. In summer other birds can be seen, also many butterflies and dragonflies. The Three Horse Shoes Inn is a very popular venue for food and the thatched church has 13th century wall paintings.

FEATURES:

River, Pub, Toilets, Church, Wildlife, Birds, Flowers, Great Views, Butterflies, Food Shop

WALK DIRECTIONS:

1 | Walk eastwards along the 'old' pavement with the church on the left. Turn left along Marsh Lane and keep left along it at the right hand bend. (New road to housing estate, keep along the old one of Marsh Lane.)

2 | Turn left at 'No Thro Road' sign. It ends at the railway crossing. Cross the railway and continue along a tree-lined track opposite to the end. Climb the bank.

3 | Turn right along the riverside bank with the River Waveney on the left.

4 | Turn right down the bank to a stile and the notice board of Castle Marshes Reserve. Climb the stile and keep to the right of the meadow and the 'high' bank path. Follow this around to the next stile. Continue along a grassy path, cross the railway line and continue along a path.

5 | Turn left along a country lane. At the left hand bend turn right along a track.

6 | At the lefthand bend of the track keep straight ahead along the field edge. It becomes a tree-lined path.

7 | Turn left along School Meadow road. Turn right along the pavement to a garden centre.

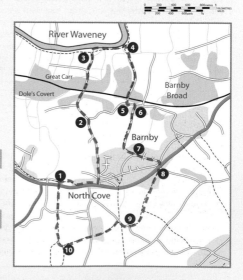

8|Turn left, signed 'Cycle and people' by the garden centre along a path. Cross the main road, turn right and cross the minor road. Go up a track by the caravan notice.

9|Turn right along a country lane. At the right-hand bend turn left along a track, signed 'By-way'. Cross the minor road and continue along a track opposite.

10|At the lefthand bend turn right along a path between the crops. Continue across a field at the sign and the next two fields, with a church in view ahead. Cross the main road and go along a short path to the start of the walk.

dwellings extant today are largely Georgian in origin, with handsome redbrick façades. One that is not is **Roos Hall**, a gabled building dating from 1583. Just outside the town, far enough away to escape the great fire of 1586,

it was built to a Dutch design, underlining the links between East Anglia and the Low Countries forged by the wool and weaving trades. Elizabeth I stayed at the Hall just after it was completed, when she visited Beccles to present the town's charter; the occasion is depicted in the town sign. One of the hall's owners was Sir John Suckling (later to become Controller of the Household to James I), one of whose descendants was Lord Nelson. Any old hall worth its salt has a ghost, and the Roos representative is a headless coachman who is said to appear on Christmas Eve.

The parish church of **St Michael** was built in the second half of the 14th century by the Abbot of Bury. Its tower stands separate, built in the 16th century, rising almost 100 feet and containing a peal of bells. An unusual feature at the north façade is an outside pulpit taking the form of a small balcony. The priest could

HEATHERLEY ANTIQUES

49 Smallgate, Beccles, Suffolk NR34 9AE
Tel/Fax: 01502 710300
e-mail: info@heatherley.net
website: www.heatherly.net

Heatherley Antiques, run by Heather Coleman, is housed in a distinguished single-storey Victorian brick building close to the town centre and a few steps east of St Michael's Church tower.

The shop specialises in fine gifts and antique jewellery, and the seasonal collections feature leading names such as Tiffany, Cartier, Piaget and Lalique. Costume jewellery also has its place here, and many of the pieces are just as beautifully designed and crafted as the more expensive big-name items. Juliana, Vendome, Hattie Carnegie and Marcel Boucher are among the leading names in this sphere. Among other stock are small items of furniture, porcelain, glass, bronze, clocks, lamps, maps, prints and other fine collectables.

Heatherley Antiques also offers expert clock and furniture restoration. The two spacious rooms, skilfully refurbished to reflect the age and style of the building, provide a comfortable, relaxing atmosphere for browsing and buying, with a real fire adding to the warmth on winter days. Opening hours are 10am to 5pm Monday to Saturday.

📖 stories and anecdotes 🕊 famous people 🎨 art and craft ✎ entertainment and sport 🚶 walks

WINTER FLORA LTD

Hall Farm, Weston, nr Beccles, Suffolk NR34 8TT
Tel: 01502 716810   Fax: 01502 717139
e-mail: info@winterflora.co.uk   website: www.winterflora.co.uk

On the A145 a mile-and-a-half south of Beccles, **Winter Flora Ltd** has since 1969 been sourcing and supplying preserved and dried flowers, foliage and home decorations. Part florist, part plant centre, part gift shop, this splendid place holds an ever-changing stock of pods, cones, gourds, mosses, reeds and rushes, grasses, barks, berries and silk flowers, garden essentials, vases, ceramics, cards and gifts. A large colour-themed garden reflects many of the natural plants for sale, and friendly staff can help with planning or creating bouquets, wreaths and seasonal decorations. Open daily from 10am to 5pm.

enter the pulpit from inside the church and preach to lepers, who were not allowed inside. Nelson's parents, the Reverend Edmund Nelson and Catherine Suckling, were married in St Michael's, as was the great Suffolk poet George Crabbe.

Another building with Dutch-style gables houses the **Beccles and District Museum**, whose contents include 19th century toys and costumes, farm implements, items from the old town gaol and memorabilia from the sailing wherries, including a wealth of old photographs. Beccles, like Bungay, is an old printing town, and has the **William Clowes Museum of Print** on the site of the Newgate works of the famed printer. Here the visitor will learn about the history of printing since the 1800s, with woodcuts, books and machinery; tours of the factory are also available.

BUNGAY

15 miles W of Lowestoft on the A144

🏚 Castle   🏚 Holy Trinity Church   🏛 Museum

An ancient fortress town on the River Waveney, the river played an important part in Bungay's fortunes until well into the 18th century, with barges laden with coal, corn, malt and timber plying the route to the coast.

The river is no longer navigable above Geldeston, but is a great attraction for anglers and yachtsmen.

Bungay is best known for its **Castle**, built in its original form by Hugh Bigod, 1st Earl of Norfolk, as a rival to Henry II's castle at Orford. In 1173 Hugh took the side of the rebellious sons of Henry, but this insurrection ended with the surrender of the castle to the King. Hugh was killed not long after this episode while on the Third Crusade; his son Roger inherited the title and the castle, but it was another Roger Bigod who came to Bungay in 1294 and built the round tower and mighty outer walls that stand today.

To the north of the castle are Bungay's two surviving churches of note (the *Domesday Book* records five). The Saxon round tower of **Holy Trinity Church** is the oldest complete structure in the town, and a brass plate on the door commemorates the church's narrow escape from the fire of 1688 that destroyed much of the town (similar disasters overtook many other towns with close-set timber-and-thatch buildings). The church of **St Mary** - now deconsecrated - was not so lucky, being more or less completely gutted. The tower survives to dominate the townscape, and points of interest in the church itself include a woodcarving of the Resurrection presented by Rider Haggard, and a monument to General Robert Kelso, who fought in the American War of Independence.

A century before the fire, the church received a visit, during a storm, from the devilish Black Shuck, a retriever-like hound who, hot from causing severe damage at Blythburgh, raced down the nave and killed two worshippers. A weather vane in the market place puts the legend into verse:

All down the church in midst of fire
The Hellish Monster Flew
And Passing onwards to the Quire
He many people slew.

Nearby is the famous octagonal Butter Cross, rebuilt after the great fire of 1688 and topped by Justice with her scales and sword. This building was once used as a prison, with a dungeon below.

Bungay Museum, housed in the Council offices in Broad Street, is home to an exhibition of local history including pictures, coins and photographs.

Norfolk & Suffolk Aviation Museum

The Street, Flixton, Nr. Bungay, Suffolk NR35 1NZ
Tel: 01986 896644
website: www.aviationmuseum.net

Founded in 1972, the **Norfolk & Suffolk Aviation Museum** was officially opened to the public in 1976. Set in the picturesque Waveney Valley, the complex covers 7½ acres, with unique undercover exhibitions, military and civil, from the pioneer days through World War I, the inter-war years, World War II right up to the present day.

The museum incorporates the Museums of the 446th Bomber Group, Royal Observer Corps, RAF Bomber Command, Air-Sea Rescue and Coastal Command. More than 25 historic aircraft are on display, along with engines, missiles, guns, bombs and ejector seats. Throughout the museum there are examples of aviation art, together with themed displays, including WWII decoy sites, Civil Defence, telephones, compasses, models and (perhaps the most fascinating of all) wreckology - the digging for the remains of aircraft in areas where they are known to have crashed.

Among the aircraft on display are an Avro Anson C19, the first aircraft acquired by the museum; a Dassault Mystère IVA, a Vampire, a Meteor, a Javelin and two Westland helicopters. The museum, officially recognised as East Anglia's Aviation Heritage Centre, is located on the B1062 off the A143 a mile west of Bungay. Admission is free, the museum relies on money put in the donation boxes or spent in the shop or NAAFI.

---

stories and anecdotes   famous people   art and craft   entertainment and sport   walks

EARSHAM
1 mile SW of Bungay off the A143

🌱 Otter Trust

All Saints Church and Earsham Hall are well worth a visit, but what brings most people here is the **Otter Trust**, on the banks of the Waveney, where the largest collection of otters in natural enclosures are bred for re-introduction into the wild. Waterfowl, herons and deer are also kept here, and there are some lovely walks by the lakes and river.

FLIXTON
2 miles SW of Bungay on the B1062

🏛 Norfolk & Suffolk Aviation Museum

Javelin, Meteor, Sea Vixen, Westland Whirlwind: names that evoke earlier days of flying, and just four of the almost 40 aircraft on show at The **Norfolk and Suffolk Aviation Museum** (see panel on page 103), on the site of a USAAF Liberator base during the Second World War. There's a lot of associated material, both civil and military, covering the period from the First World War to the present day. The site incorporates the Royal Observer Corps Museum, RAF Bomber Command Museum, the Museum and Memorial of the 446th Bomb Group – the Bungay Buckeroos – and RAF Air-Sea Rescue and Coastal Command. Exhibitions cover the story of military and civil aviation in East Anglia, and visitors can enjoy a pleasant walk on a raised boardwalk to the River Waveney. The Museum is open Sunday to Thursday in the summer; Tuesday, Wednesday and Sunday in winter.

Flixton is named after St Flik, the first Bishop of East Anglia, and he is depicted in the village sign.

MENDHAM
6 miles SW of Bungay off the A143

This pretty little village on the Waveney was the birthplace of Sir Alfred Munnings RA, who was born at Mendham Mill, where his father was the miller. Sir Alfred's painting *Charlotte and her Pony* was the inspiration for the village sign, which was unveiled by his niece Kathleen Hadingham.

CARLTON COLVILLE
3 miles SW of Lowestoft on the B1384

🏛 East Anglia Transport Museum

Many a transport enthusiast has enjoyed a grand day out at the **East Anglia Transport Museum**, where children (and grown-ups of all ages) can climb aboard to enjoy rides on buses, trams and trolleybuses (one of the resident trolleybuses was built at the Garrett Works in Leiston). The East Suffolk narrow-gauge railway (2ft) winds its way around the site behind a fleet of diesel locomotives, and there's a 1930s street with all the authentic accessories, plus lorries, vans and steamrollers.

Also in Carlton Colville is the 15th century church of St Peter, which incorporated parts of other buildings when restored in the 19th century. Carlton Marshes is Oulton Broad's nature reserve, with grazing marsh and fen, reached by the Waveney Way footpath.

KESSINGLAND
3 miles S of Lowestoft off the A12

🌱 Suffolk Wildlife Park

A small resort with a big history, Palaeolithic and Neolithic remains have come to light in Kessingland, and traces of an ancient forest have been unearthed on the sea bed. At the time of William the Conqueror, Kessingland prospered with its herring industry and was a major fishing port rivalled only by Dunwich. The estuary gradually silted up, sealing off the river with a shingle bank and cutting off the village's major source of wealth. The tower of the church of St Edmund reaches up almost 100 feet – not unusual on the coast - where it provides a conspicuous landmark for sailors and fishermen.

Most of Kessingland's maritime trappings have now disappeared: the lighthouse on the cliffs was scrapped 100 years ago, the lifeboat lasted until 1936 (having saved 144 lives), and one of the several former coastguard stations was purchased by the writer Rider Haggard as a holiday home.

The village's major tourist attraction is the **Suffolk Wildlife Park**, 100 acres of coastal parkland that are home to a wide range of wild animals, from aardvarks to zebras by way of bats, flamingos, meerkats and sitatunga. The flamingos have their own enclosure. The latest attractions include a recreation of an African savannah, complete with lions, giraffes, rhinos, cheetahs, hyenas and many other African animals and birds. Burmese pythons are used for snake-handling sessions, and there are regular birds of prey flying displays. This is very much a place for all the family, and children's amenities include an adventure play area and an under-5s soft play area.

COVEHITHE
7 miles S of Lowestoft off the A12

Leave the A12 at Wrentham and head for the tiny coastal village of Covehithe, remarkable for its 'church within a church'. The massive Church of St Andrew, partly funded by the Benedictine monks at Cluniac, was left to decline after being laid waste by Dowsing's men. The villagers could not afford a replacement on the same grand scale, so in 1672 it was decided to remove the roof and sell off some of the material. From what was left a small new church was built within the old walls. The original tower still stands, spared by Cromwell for use as a landmark for sailors.

Southwold

- Museum
- Southwold Sailors' Reading Room
- Lifeboat Museum
- Amber Museum
- Sole Bay Inn

A town full of character and interest for the holidaymaker and for the historian. Though one of the most popular resorts on the east coast, Southwold has very little of the kiss-me quick commercialism that spoils so many seaside towns. It's practically an island, bounded by creeks and marshes, the River Blyth and the North Sea, and has managed to retain the genteel atmosphere of the 19th century. There are some attractive buildings, from pink-washed cottages to elegant Georgian town houses, many of them ranged around a series of greens which were left undeveloped to act as firebreaks after much of the town was lost in the great fire of 1659.

In a seaside town whose buildings present a wide variety of styles, shapes and sizes, William Denny's Buckenham House is among the most elegant and interesting. On the face of it a classic Georgian town house, it's actually much older, dating probably from the middle of the 16th century. Richard Buckenham, a wealthy Tudor merchant, was the man who had it built and it was truly impressive in size, as can be deduced from the

THE BLACK OLIVE DELICATESSEN

80a and 80b The High Street,
Southwold, Suffolk IP18 6DP
Tel: 01502 722312

Delicatessens of outstanding range and quality are places to be treasured, and the citizens of Southwold are lucky indeed to have one of the best in the **Black Olive Delicatessen**. A magnet for food-lovers not just in Southwold but for many miles around, the Black Olive is located in the busy High Street of this marvellous town. Tracy Brown took over the premises in 2005; she knows that the people in this part of the world appreciate the good things in life, and her shop fully lives up to the promise of the sign above the entrance that offers 'a Taste of the World'.

As the name suggests, olives are here in abundance, with at least seven varieties ready to scoop: plain black or green, pitted or stuffed with garlic, almonds and sun-dried tomatoes. There are marinated mushrooms and artichokes, a tub of succulent beans, peppers stuffed with feta cheese, basil-marinated sardines, anchovies plain, with chilli, with olives (banderillas), dressed crabs, shell-on prawns, potted shrimps, lobster, scampi, cockles, mussels, samphire. Tracy's partner Sam is a fish merchant, and he provides some of the superb fish and shellfish served at the deli.

One of the cool cabinets displays a vast range of cold and cured meats, salamis and sausages, and the 40+ cheeses represent England, Wales, France, Italy, Spain, Greece and Switzerland.

There's freshly baked bread, locally made cakes and pastries, jams and preserves, pickles and chutneys (many of theses also from local producers), vinegars and oils (customers can fill their own containers with olive oil from a tap), and fruit juices, including orange juice freshly pressed to order. Tracy and her staff are happy to make up individual orders for lunches, dinners, picnics, special occasions and Christmas hampers.

Sandwiches are custom-made to order with almost any filling you can think of, and coffee comes to buy as beans, ground or in a cup to take away.

That should be enough to get the taste buds tingling, but the Black Olive Delicatessen has much, much more. Only a visit will bring the whole amazing range to life – step inside, smell the wonderful aromas, see the cornucopia of superb food, and you might decide that you never need to cook again.

dimensions of the cellar (now the Coffee House). Many fine features survive, including moulded cornices, carefully restored sash windows, Tudor brickwork and heavy timbers in the ceilings.

The town, which was granted its charter by Henry VII in 1489, once prospered, like many of its neighbours, through herring fishing, and the few remaining fishermen share the harbour on the River Blyth with pleasure craft. Also adding to the period atmosphere is the pier, though as a result of storm damage this is much shorter than in the days when steamers from London called in on their way up the east coast.

There are also bathing huts, and a brilliant white lighthouse that's over 100 years old. It stands 100 feet tall and its light can be seen 17 miles out to sea. Beneath the lighthouse stands a little Victorian pub, the **Sole Bay Inn**, whose name recalls a battle fought off Southwold in 1672 between the British and French fleets and the Dutch. This was an episode in the third Anglo-Dutch War, when the Duke of York, Lord High Admiral of England and later to be crowned James II, used Sutherland House in Southwold as his headquarters and launched his fleet (along with that of the French) from here. One distinguished victim of this battle was Edward Montagu, 1st Earl of Sandwich, great-grandfather of the man whose gambling mania did not allow him time for a formal meal. By inserting slices of meat between slices of bread, the 4th Earl ensured that his name would live on. A later Duke of York, the

---

BUCKENHAM GALLERIES

81 High Street, Southwold, Suffolk IP18 6DS
Tel: 01502 725418 Fax: 01502 722002
e-mail: becky@buckenham-galleries.co.uk
website: www.buckenham-galleries.co.uk

One of East Anglia's leading contemporary art galleries, Buckenham Galleries, offers a wide variety of paintings, ceramics, jewellery, glass work and sculpture. Situated on the High Street, the gallery is housed in one of the oldest buildings in Southwold. Richard Buckenham, after whom the house was named, was a Tudor merchant who almost certainly had the house built. Grade II listed, the Georgian fronted house retains some of its original Tudor features, such as the beams in one of the downstairs rooms, and Tudor brickwork on the walls of the cellar which has now been transformed into a warm and inviting coffee house.

After various uses, including as a vicarage, a gentleman's club and offices, Buckenham House was opened as a gallery in the summer of 1999. Situated on two floors, there are several galleries, each taking the name of a previous owner of the building. The spacious well lit rooms, with white walls, black wooden flooring and high ceilings, provide an ideal space for exhibiting art.

Buckenham Galleries have an on-going exhibition of works by Gallery Artists. In conjunction with this, there are eight major exhibitions a year where specially selected artists are invited to show their works in the upstairs rooms. With a wealth of different styles on offer, there is always something new to see.

Over the years, Buckenham Galleries has built up a first-class reputation with artists and collectors alike. Offering a relaxed and friendly atmosphere, the gallery is open every day 10am-5pm, including Bank Holidays.

📖 stories and anecdotes   🦜 famous people   🎨 art and craft   🎭 entertainment and sport   🚶 walks

one who became King George VI, visited the town from 1931 to 1938 for the Duke of york's Camp, which he founded for boys from schools and factories.

The Sole Bay Inn is one of several owned by the local brewery Adnams. One of the best known pubs is the Lord Nelson, where traces can be seen of a smugglers' passageway leading to the cliffs. Where there were smugglers, there are usually ghosts, and here it's a man in a frock coat who disappears into the cliff face. Adnams still use horse-drawn drays for local beer deliveries.

Lighthouse, Southwold

Southwold's maritime past is recorded in the **Museum** set in a Dutch-style cottage in Victoria Street. Open daily in the summer months, it records the famous battle and also features exhibits on local archaeology, geology and natural history, and the history of the Southwold railway. The **Southwold Sailors' Reading Room** contains pictures, ship models and other items, and at Gun Hill the **Southwold Lifeboat Museum** has a small collection of RNLI-related material with particular reference to Southwold. The main attraction at Gun Hill is a set of six 18-pounder guns, captured in 1746 at the Battle of Culloden and presented to the town (hitherto more or less undefended) by the Duke of Cumberland. Another museum, probably unique of its kind, is the **Amber Museum**, which traces the history of amber through millions of years.

No visitor to Southwold should leave without spending some time in the splendid church of St Edmund King and Martyr, which emerged relatively unscathed from the ravages of the Commonwealth. The lovely painted roof and wide screen are the chief glories, but the slim-stemmed 15th century pulpit and the Elizabethan Holy Table must also be seen. Inside the church there's also a splendid 'Jack o' the Clock' – a little wooden man in War of the Roses armour, holding a bell. A rope is pulled to sound the bell to mark the start of church services.

There's some great walking in the country around Southwold, both along the coast and inland. At **Wangford**, a mile or so inland, is the Perpendicular Church of St Peter and St Paul, built on the site of a Benedictine priory. Even closer to Southwold is Reydon Wood Nature Reserve.

Around Southwold

WALBERSWICK

1 mile S of Southwold on the B1387

🌱 Walberswick & Westleton Heaths

Towards the end of the 16th century, a smaller church was built within the original St Andrew's, which was by then in ruins through neglect. William Dowsing, Cromwell's Parliamentary Visitor to the churches of Suffolk, was to churches what Dr Beeching was to become to railways, and at Walberswick he destroyed 40 windows and defaced all the tombs on visits during the Civil War. The churchyard is now a nature reserve. South of the village is the bird sanctuary of **Walberswick & Westleton Heaths**.

For more than two centuries, Walberswick has been a magnet for painters, with the religious ruins, the beach and the sea being favourite subjects for visiting artists. The tradition continues unabated, and many academics have also made their homes here.

BLYTHBURGH

3 miles SW of Southwold, A1095 then A12

🏚 Holy Trinity   ⚔ Toby's Walks

Blythburgh's Church of **Holy Trinity** is one of the wonders of Suffolk, a stirring sight as it rises from the reed beds, visible for miles around and floodlit at night to spectacular effect. This 'Cathedral of the Marshes' reflects the days when Blythburgh was a prosperous port with a bustling quayside wool trade. With the silting up of the river, trade rapidly fell off and the church fell into decay. In 1577 the steeple of the 14th century tower was struck by lightning in a severe storm; it fell into the nave, shattering the font and taking two lives. The scorch marks visible to this day on the north door are said to be the claw marks of the Devil in the guise of hellhound Black Shuck, left as he sped towards Bungay to terrify the congregation of St Mary's.

Disaster struck again in 1644, when Dowsing and his men smashed windows, ornaments and statues, blasted the wooden angels in the roof with hundreds of bullets and used the nave as a stable, with tethering rings screwed into the pillars of the nave. Luckily, the bench-end carvings escaped the desecration, not being labelled idolatrous. These depict the Labours of the Months, and the Seven Deadly Sins. Blythburgh also has a Jack o'the Clock, a brother of the figure at Southwold, and the priest's chamber over the south porch has been lovingly restored

---

POTTERS WHEEL TEA ROOM

*The Green, Walberswick, nr Southwold,
Suffolk IP18 6TT
Tel: 01502 724468*

This little wooden building five minutes' walk from the beach was a pottery and gallery, before being converted into a delightful tea room. There are seats for 40 at pine tables in the brightly-painted, wood-floored **Potters Wheel Tea Room**, and plenty more in summer in the large garden. The menu runs from organic baguettes with lots of interesting fillings to ploughman's platters, jacket potatoes, hot and cold main dishes and super cream teas. Wines by the glass with meals.

📖 stories and anecdotes   🐦 famous people   🎨 art and craft   ✒ entertainment and sport   ⚔ walks

complete with an altar made with wood from *HMS Victory*. The angels may have survived, but the font was defaced to remove the signs of the sacraments.

A mile south, at the junction of the A12 and the Walberswick road, **Toby's Walks** is an ideal place for a picnic and, like so many places in Suffolk, has its own ghost story. This concerns Tobias Gill, a dragoon drummer serving with Sir Robert Rich's troop in the army of George II. He was found drunk on heathland next to the body of a Walberswick girl named Anne Blakemore. He was accused of her murder and sentenced to death by hanging in chains. His ghost is said to haunt the heath, but this should not and does not deter picnic-makers.

The Norman Gwatkin Nature Reserve is an area of marsh and fen with two hides, walkways and a willow coppice.

WENHASTON
5 miles W of Southwold off the A12

The Church of St Peter is well worth a detour. Saxon stones are embedded in its walls, but the most remarkable feature is the Doom (Last Judgement scene), said to have been painted around 1500 by a monk from Blythburgh.

HALESWORTH
8 miles W of Southwold on the A144

🏛 Halesworth & District Museum

Granted a market in 1222, Halesworth reached the peak of its trading importance

---

SOLE BAY PINE COMPANY & TEA ROOMS

Red House Farm, nr Blythburgh, Suffolk IP17 3RF
Tel: 01502 478077
e-mail: uspfurn@aol.com
website: www.solebaypine.co.uk

The name doesn't tell half the story. **Sole Bay Pine Company** is far more than just another pine shop, though it's a treasure trove of mainly locally made home and decorative pine furniture. In a farm complex just off the A12 (well signposted south of Blythburgh), a series of timber-framed showrooms also contains a wonderful array of soft furnishings, lighting, mirrors, rugs, wall hangings and many other items for house and garden in a wide variety of beautiful colours and fabrics.

Visitors looking for a break from browsing can make use of a tea room that offers a selection of cakes, pastries and light savouries (soups, burgers, home-grown vegetables from 10am to 4pm every day. An attached delicatessen sells a fine range of produce, much of it local, including preserves and pickles, oils and vinegars, home baking and ice creams. Owner Gerard Delaney manages other outlets of this splendid shop in Ipswich and Beccles.

when the River Blyth was made navigable as far as the town in 1756. A stroll around the streets reveals several buildings of architectural interest. The Market Place has a handsome Elizabethan timber-framed house, but the chief attraction for the visitor is the **Halesworth and District Museum** at the railway station, in Station Road, where exhibits on local history, railway and rural life can be seen. The station's unique moveable platforms are adjacent to the museum. Local geology and archaeology includes fossils, prehistoric and medieval finds from recent excavations.

Halesworth Gallery, at Steeple End, holds a collection of contemporary paintings, sculpture and other artwork in a converted row of 17th century almshouses.

BRAMFIELD
7 miles SW of Southwold on the A144

🏠 St Andrew's Church

The massive Norman round tower of **St Andrew's** Church is separate from the main building and was built as a defensive structure, with walls over three feet thick. Dowsing ran riot here in 1643, destroying 24 superstitious pictures, one crucifix, a picture of Christ and 12 angels on the roof. The most important monument is one to Sir Arthur Coke, sometime Lord Chief Justice, who died in 1629, and his wife Elizabeth. Arthur is kneeling, resplendent in full armour, while Elizabeth is lying on her bed with a baby in her arms. This monument is the work of Nicholas Stone, the most important English mason and sculptor of his day. The Cokes at one time occupied Bramfield Hall, and another family, in residence for 300 years, were the Rabetts, whose coat of arms in the church punningly depicts rabbits on its shield.

DUNWICH
5 miles S of Southwold off the B1105

🏠 Museum   🌿 Dunwich Forest

🏠 Dunwich Heath   🌿 Minsmere RSPB

Dunwich is the town that hardly exists, yet it's one of the most popular tourist spots along the Suffolk coast. Dunwich was once the capital of East Anglia, founded by the Burgundian Christian missionary St Felix and for several centuries a major trading port (wool and grain out; wine, timber and cloth in) and a centre of fishing and shipbuilding. St Felix opened a school here. Several Kings built ships here, and the town had a mint, a fishing fleet and eight churches. In 1286 a storm blocked the entrance to the harbour, and by the middle of the next century the merchant trade was lost, the fishermen and shipbuilders moved out, work ceased on defending the coastline and the end of Dunwich was in sight. (But it sent two MPs to Westminster until 1832 – one of the most notable was Sir George Downing, who established Downing College in Cambridge.) For the next 700 years the relentless forces of nature continued to take their toll, and all that remains now of ancient Dunwich are the ruins of a Norman leper hospital, the archways of a medieval friary and a buttress of one of the nine churches which once served the community.

Today's village comprises a 19th century church and a row of Victorian cottages, one of which houses the **Dunwich Museum**. Local residents set up the museum in 1972 to tell the Dunwich story; the historical section has displays and exhibits from Roman, Saxon and medieval times, the centrepiece being a large model of the town at its 12th century peak. There are also sections devoted to natural history, social history and the arts.

📖 stories and anecdotes   🐦 famous people   ✏ art and craft   🎭 entertainment and sport   🚶 walks

Experts have calculated that the main part of old Dunwich extended up to seven miles beyond its present boundaries, and the vengeance of the sea has thrown up inevitable stories of drama and mystery. The locals say that when a storm is threatening, the sound of submerged church bells can still be heard tolling under the waves as they shift in the currents. Other tales tell of strange lights in the ruined priory and the eerie chanting of long-gone monks.

Dunwich Forest, immediately inland from the village, is one of three – the others are further south at Tunstall and Rendlesham – named by the Forestry Commission as Aldewood Forest. Work started on these in 1920 with the planting of Scots pine, Corsican pine and some Douglas fir; oak and poplar were tried but did not thrive in the sandy soil. The three forests, which between them cover nearly 9,000 acres, were almost completely devastated in the hurricane of October 1987, Rendlesham alone losing more than a million trees. Replanting will take many years to be established.

South of the village lies **Dunwich Heath**, one of Suffolk's most important conservation areas, comprising the beach, splendid heather, a field study centre, a public hide and an information centre and restaurant in converted coastguard cottages. 1998 marked the 30th anniversary of the heath being in the care of the National Trust.

Around Dunwich Heath are the attractive villages of Westleton, Middleton, Theberton and Eastbridge.

BRIDGE NURSERIES

Dunwich, Suffolk IP17 3DZ
Tel/Fax: 01728 648850 (Tea Room 01728 648941)
e-mail: roger.collier4@btinternet.com
website: www.fiskclematis.co.uk

Bridge Nurseries are situated in the beautiful and historic coastal village of Dunwich, just a few hundred yards from the beach – but well sheltered form the buffeting North Sea breezes. They specialise in growing clematis and have hundreds of varieties available throughout the year to visitors to the nursery or by express mail order service. The plants are based on the original Jim Fisk collection and are grown on the premises. A free clematis catalogue can be had on request. The nurseries also supply a full range of unusual perennials together wild flowers and a seasonal collection of annual plants for hanging baskets and containers. Customers can purchase garden essentials from the small, well-stocked nursery shop.

A delightful extra feature here is the tearoom, which is open every day of the year – in summer, the south-facing terrace catches the sun all day. The ingredients are sourced locally, and everything is freshly made, from sandwiches, interesting salads, warming homemade soups, freshly baked cakes and locally made fruit ice creams. The Bower, a charming covered area in the clematis garden, is a lovely spot for a private party for up to 30 people. Bridge Nurseries are open seven days a week, from 10am to 5pm in summer and from 10am to 4pm in winter.

In **Westleton**, the 14th century thatched church of St Peter, built by the monks of Sibton Abbey, has twice seen the collapse of its tower. The first fell down in a hurricane in 1776; its smaller wooden replacement collapsed when a bomb fell during the Second World War. The village is also the main route of access to the RSPB-managed **Minsmere Nature Reserve**, the most important sanctuary for wading birds in eastern England. The marshland was flooded during the Second World War, and nature and this wartime emergency measure created the perfect habitat for innumerable birds. More than 100 species nest here, and a similar number of birds visit throughout the year. It is thus a birdwatcher's paradise, with many hides, and the Suffolk Coastal Path runs along the foreshore. A little way inland from Westleton lies Darsham, where another nature reserve is home to many varieties of birds and flowers.

YOXFORD
10 miles SW of Southwold on the A12

Once an important stop on the London-to-Yarmouth coaching route, Yoxford now attracts visitors with its pink-washed cottages and its arts and crafts, antiques and food shops. Look for the cast-iron signpost outside the church, with hands pointing to London, Yarmouth and Framlingham set high enough to be seen by the driver of a stagecoach.

THEBERTON
12 miles SW of Southwold on the B1122

The churchyard at Theberton contains a

SUFFOLK HOUSE ANTIQUES

High Street, Yoxford, Suffolk IP17 3EP
Tel: 01728 668122
e-mail: andrew.singleton@suffolk-house-antiques.co.uk
website: www.suffolk-house-antiques.co.uk

Situated on the junction of the A12 and A1120 roads just north of Ipswich, in the attractive Suffolk village of Yoxford, **Suffolk House Antiques** was established more than 15 years ago by Andrew Singleton. One of the country's leading dealers in early oak, walnut and country furniture, the shop boasts nine showrooms and stock stretches to more than 300 pieces.

Prices range from under £100 to over £50,000. Andrew, as a long-standing member of the British Antiques Dealers Association, has supplied pieces to many of the leading collectors of early furniture in the UK and abroad.

Most items of early furniture can be found here dressers, cupboards, chests of drawers, boxes and coffers and tables and chairs. The 'miscellaneous' collection includes stools, settles and bureaux as well as metalwork and carvings, and there is also a range of mirrors, ceramics (mostly Delftware) and tapestries. Andrew is always happy to search for particular pieces for clients. Parking is available, or clients can be collected from nearby Darsham Station. Open Monday, Tuesday, Thursday, Friday and Saturday 10am-1pm and 2.15pm - 5.15pm, or at other times by appointment.

---

reminder that this part of the coast was closely involved in warfare. In June 1917 a 600ft Zeppelin came in at Orford Ness and dropped bombs near Martlesham. It was shot down, and the 16 members of the crew who were killed are buried in Theberton churchyard.

SIBTON
12 miles SW of Southwold on the A1120

Two miles west of Yoxford, on the A1120, Sibton is known chiefly for its abbey (only the ruins remain), the only Cistercian house in Suffolk. The Church of St Peter is certainly not a ruin, however, and should be seen for its fine hammerbeam and collar roof.

SAXMUNDHAM
12 miles SW of Southwold off the A12

A little town that was granted its market charter in 1272. On the font of the church in Saxmundham is the carving of a 'woodwose' - a tree spirit or green man. He and others like him have given their name to a large number of pubs in Suffolk and elsewhere. The Town Museum is a recent addition to the visitor attractions.

BRUISYARD
4 miles NW of Saxmundham off the B1119

Just west of this village is the Bruisyard Vineyard, Winery and Herb Centre, a complex of a 10-acre vineyard with 13,000 Müller Thurgau grape vines, a wine-production

THE SIBTON WHITE HORSE INN
Halesworth Road, Sibton, nr Saxmundham,
Suffolk IP17 2JJ
Tel: 01728 660337
e-mail: info@sibtonwhitehorse.com
website: www.sibtonwhitehorse.com

The **Sibton White Horse Inn** is a delightful grade II listed free house (*rebuilt* in 1580!) serving excellent food and drink and offering comfortable guest accommodation. Neil and Gill Mason took over here in August 2005 and with several changes have created the perfect rural dining pub. The public areas never fail to amaze first time visitors with their feature inglenooks, heavy beams, old settles and vast collection of old agricultural implements.

Weekly guest ales from breweries around the country join local Adnams Bitter and Broadside, and there's also a good choice of wines and malt whiskies. Food, freshly prepared and cooked to order from mainly local ingredients, is traditional with a difference. Lunch and evening dinner is available, Sunday lunch is also served. In the summer you can enjoy a meal in the impressive gardens, whilst in the winter choose from the warm and cosy bar or elegant dining room.

The bed & breakfast accommodation, available throughout the year, comprises seven en suite rooms in a converted outbuilding. Many rooms have views over the open countryside.

FRIDAY STREET FARM SHOP & TEAROOMS

Farnham, Saxmundham, Suffolk IP17 1JX
Tel/Fax: 01728 602783

Just yards from the A12 along the A1094 Aldeburgh road, **Friday Street Farm Shop & Tearooms** is open seven days a week for the sale of a wonderful range of local produce, seasonal home-grown fruit and vegetables and pick-your-own. This spacious and always busy place has the freshest fruit, vegetables and farm produce, shelves and shelves of jams and preserves, a variety of fresh and frozen meats, smoked fish, ice cream, cheeses and other dairy products, cakes, bread, fresh flowers, crafts and much more. In season, visitors can gather their own broad beans, courgettes, sweetcorn and table-top soft fruits.

Friendly, hardworking staff are happy to create individual fruit and vegetable baskets, bouquets of flowers, suggest recipes for seasonal foods – even, at quieter times, do the shopping while the customer takes a break in the tearooms, which is open daily and can seat nearly 40 in comfort. The tempting menu includes light lunches, delicious homemade cakes and pastries, luxury desserts and cream teas. Throughout the summer the maize maze, which changes every year, is an attraction that's popular with children and grown-ups alike. Other events include tasting days, a Halloween Dungeon and seasonal competitions for all age groups.

centre, herb and water gardens, a tea shop and a picnic site.

PEASENHALL

6 miles NW of Saxmundham on the A1120

 Woolhall

A little stream runs along the side of the main street in Peasenhall, whose buildings present several styles and ages. Most distinguished is the old timbered **Woolhall**, splendidly restored to its 15th century grandeur. The oddest is certainly a hall in the style of a Swiss chalet, built for his workers by James Josiah Smyth, grandson of the founder of James Smyth & Sons. This company, renowned for its agricultural drills, was for more than two centuries the dominant industrial presence in Peasenhall. On the south side of St Michael's

churchyard stands the 1805 drill-mill where James Smyth manufactured his nonpareil seed drills, one of which is on display in Stowmarket's museum.

FRISTON

3 miles SE of Saxmundham off the A1094

Friston's post mill, the tallest in England, is a prominent sight on the Aldeburgh-Snape road, moved from Woodbridge in 1812 just after its construction. It worked by wind until 1956, then by engine until 1972. St Mary's Church dates from the 11th century.

LEISTON

4 miles E of Saxmundham off the B1119

Long Shop Museum   Abbey

The first **Leiston Abbey** was built on

Nunsmere marshes in 1182, but in 1363 the Earl of Suffolk rebuilt it on its present site. It became one of the largest and most prestigious monasteries in the country, and its wealth probably spelled its ruin, as it fell within Henry VIII's plan for the Dissolution of the Monasteries. A new abbey was built near the ruins of the old.

For 200 years the biggest name in Leiston was that of Richard Garrett, who founded an engineering works here in 1778 after starting a business in Woodbridge. In the early years ploughs, threshers, seed drills and other agricultural machinery were the main products, but the company later started one of the country's first production lines for steam machines. The Garrett works are now the **Long Shop Museum**, the factory buildings having been lovingly restored, and many of the Garrett machines are now on display, including traction engines, a steam-driven tractor and a road roller; there's also a section where the workings of steam engines are explained. During World War II the works manufactured radar equipment and sections of Mulberry Harbours. A small area of the museum recalls the USAAF's 357th fighter group, who flew from an airfield outside Leiston during the Second World War. One of their number, a Captain Chuck Yeager, was the first man to fly faster than the speed of sound.

The Garrett works closed in 1980, but what could have been a disastrous unemployment situation was alleviated to some extent by the nuclear power station at Sizewell. The coast

FIELD END GUEST HOUSE

1 Kings Road, Leiston, Suffolk IP16 4DA
Tel/Fax: 01728 833527
website: www.fieldendbedandbreakfast.co.uk
e-mail: herbert@herbertwood.wanadoo.co.uk

Opened in February 1999, **Field End Guest House** is a large, comfortable and smartly refurbished Edwardian guest house south of Leiston town centre. Two of the guest rooms have en suite facilities and the others have private bath/shower rooms. All have a hand basin, TV, radio alarm, shaver point, hairdryer and hot drinks tray. Three of the doubles are equipped with DVD players. The family room is fitted with a double and a single bed, with space for a Z-bed for a child or cot. The house is fully centrally heated and the bedrooms double glazed.

A full breakfast menu is served in the dining room, and there are games, cards and a radio in the lounge for guests' use. The bedrooms and the lounge are available all day and throughout the year. Owner Herbie Wood also offers self-catering accommodation in Hillside Cottage at nearby Aldringham, on the B1122 road to Aldeburgh. The cottage has two bedrooms, a sitting room, dining room, kitchen, bathroom and garden with patio furniture. The guest house and the cottage are both non-smoking, and no pets.

road in the centre of Leiston leads to this establishment, where visitors can take tours - on foot with access to buildings at Sizewell A or by minibus, with a guide and videos, round Sizewell B.

ALDRINGHAM

4 miles E of Saxmundham on the B1122

Craft Market

Aldringham's church is notable for its superb 15th century font, and the village inn was once a haunt of smugglers. It now helps to refresh the visitors who flock to the **Aldringham Craft Market**, founded in 1958 and extending over three galleries, with a serious selection of arts and crafts, clothes and gifts, pottery, basketry, books and cards.

THORPENESS

6 miles E of Saxmundham on the B1353

Thorpeness is a unique seaside village with a charm all of its own. Buying up a considerable packet of land called the Sizewell estate in 1910, the architect, barrister and playwright Glencairn Stuart Ogilvie created what he hoped would be a fashionable resort with cottages, some larger houses and an atmospheric and lovely 65-acre boating and pleasure lake called the Meare, which is one metre in depth throughout and fed by the River Hundred.

The 85-foot water tower, built to aid in the lake's construction, looked out of place, so Ogilvie disguised it as a house. Known ever since as the House in the Clouds, it is now available to rent as a holiday home. The neighbouring mill, moved lock, stock and millstones from Aldringham, stopped pumping in 1940 but has been restored and now houses a visitor centre.

Every August, in the week following the Aldeburgh Carnival, a regatta is held on the

THORPENESS COUNTRY CLUB APARTMENTS

Lakeside Avenue, Thorpeness, Suffolk IP16 4NH
Tel: 01728 452176 Fax: 01728 453868
e-mail: info@thorpeness.co.uk   website: www.thorpeness.co.uk

The unique holiday village of Thorpeness on the Suffolk coast is home to **Thorpeness Country Club Apartments**. The four wings of the original Edwardian Thorpeness Country Club were converted into 11 self-catering seaside apartments and houses. Individually appointed and furnished, they comprise two- and three-bedroom units, some overlooking the sea, others with sun decks looking out to the private tennis courts. Membership of the Country Club is included in the tariff, and also of the Golf Club attached to the Thorpeness Hotel (see separate entry). Rental of the apartments is usually by the week or weeks, but shorter breaks (three or four days) and winter weekend breaks are also available.

Thorpeness is a village like no other. The vision and creation of the architect, barrister and playwright Glencairn Stuart Ogilvie, a walk round the village reveals surprises at every turn: mock-Tudor houses, the House in the Clouds, and a 65-acre boating and pleasure lake known as The Meare. Rowing boats can be hired and fishing licences obtained for use on The Meare, which holds a splendid regatta complete with fireworks every August in the week following the popular Carnival at nearby Aldeburgh. The Thorpeness Country Club Apartments are part of Thorpeness & Aldeburgh Hotels Limited (see also the Thorpeness Hotel and Golf Club, the Brudenell Hotel and White Lion Hotel in Aldeburgh and the Swan at Lavenham).

THE THORPENESS HOTEL & GOLF CLUB

Lakeside Avenue, Thorpeness, Suffolk IP16 4NH
Tel: 01728 452176   Fax: 01728 453868
e-mail: info@thorpeness.co.uk   website: www.thorpeness.co.uk

In a holiday village created in the Suffolk dunes by G S Ogilive in the early 20th century, the three star **Thorpeness Hotel** is situated in a peaceful location next to the Meare and 10 minutes' walk from the beach. As soon as you arrive, you can't help but leave the stresses of everyday life behind you. Offering traditional hospitality throughout the year and operating to the highest of standards, facilities include 30 spacious and comfortable non-smoking en suite bedrooms, many of which have views of the Meare or the golf course.

The relaxing and stylish lounge overlooks the landscaped gardens leading down to the Meare boating lake and open fires in winter provide a warm and cosy feel. The hotel's bar and restaurant have been newly refurbished, introducing a warm and subtle marriage of the contemporary with the traditional.

The bright and spacious restaurant seats up to 80 guests and has marvellous views over the 3rd tee. It offers a relaxed and intimate atmosphere, ideal for couples or for mature guests.

A stylish lounge overlooks landscaped gardens that lead down to The Meare pleasure lake, where guests can hire a punt or rowing boat or enjoy a spot of fishing. Guests can also use the facilities, including the bar and the tennis courts, of the sister establishment Thorpeness Country Club along the road.

THE MEARE SHOP & TEA ROOM

Thorpeness, nr Aldeburgh, Suffolk IP16 4NW
Tel/Fax: 01728 452156
e-mail: meareshop@lycos.co.uk
website: www.meareshop.co.uk

Fresh produce on sale at **The Meare Shop & Tearoom** includes jams, chutneys, biscuits, cakes and savouries; the shop also sells paintings, gifts, cards, ornaments, books on local history and much more. Owner Elizabeth Everett is an expert on Thorpeness history; she and her friendly, helpful staff are happy to offer advice on the many items for sale. Pies and pasties are baked daily on the premises, and complement a menu bursting with delicious homemade soups, jumbo filled rolls, salads and snacks, together with a range of wonderful ice creams and puddings.

Cream teas are a speciality, served with a variety of teas, coffees, soft drinks, beers or wine. The children's menu, with things on toast, pizza and 'pirate boat' jacket potatoes, is a very popular addition to the options, and easy-to-use cutlery and mugs are available for toddlers. Set alongside The Meare, the surroundings are very attractive: there are lovely walks around the lake itself, boats can be hired, and the site is only 100 yards from the seashore and beach.

Meare, culminating in a splendid fireworks show.

ALDEBURGH

6 miles SE of Saxmundham on the A1094

Moot Hall

Aldeburgh Festival

The House in the Clouds, Thorpeness

And so down the coast road to Aldeburgh, another coastal town that once prospered as a port with major fishing and shipbuilding industries. Drake's *Greyhound* and *Pelican* were built at Slaughden, now taken by the sea, and during the 16th century some 1,500 people were engaged in fishing. Both industries declined as shipbuilding moved elsewhere and the fishing boats became too large to be hauled up the shingle. Suffolk's best-known poet, George Crabbe, was born at Slaughden in 1754 and lived through the village's hard times. He reflected the melancholy of those days when he wrote of his fellow townsmen:

Here joyless roam a wild amphibious race,
With sullen woe displayed in every face;
Who far from civil arts and social fly,
And scowl at strangers with suspicious eye.

He was equally evocative concerning the sea and the river, and the following lines written about the River Alde could apply to several others in the county:

With ceaseless motion comes and goes the tide
Flowing, it fills the channel vast and wide;
Then back to sea, with strong majestic sweep
It rolls, in ebb yet terrible and deep;
Here samphire-banks and salt-wort bound the flood
There stakes and seaweed withering on the mud;

And higher up, a ridge of all things base,
Which some strong tide has rolled upon the place.

It was Crabbe who created the character of the solitary fisherman Peter Grimes, later the subject of an opera composed by another Aldeburgh resident, Benjamin Britten.

Aldeburgh's role gradually changed into that of a holiday resort, and the Marquess of Salisbury, visiting early in the 19th century, was one of the first to be attracted by the idea of sea-bathing without the crowds. By the middle of the century the grand houses that had sprung up were joined by smaller residences, the railway had arrived, a handsome water tower was put up (1860) and Aldeburgh prospered once more. There were even plans for a pier, and construction started in 1878, but the project proved too difficult or too expensive and was halted, the rusting girders being removed some time later.

One of the town's major benefactors was

stories and anecdotes   famous people   art and craft   entertainment and sport   walks

Moot Hall, Aldeburgh

first woman doctor in England (having qualified in Paris at a time when women could not qualify here) and the first woman mayor (of Aldeburgh, in 1908). This lady married the shipowner James Skelton Anderson, who established the golf club in 1884.

If Crabbe were alive today he would have a rather less cantankerous opinion of his fellows, especially at carnival time on a Monday in August when the town celebrates with a colourful procession of floats and marchers, a fireworks display and numerous other events.

Newson Garrett, a wealthy businessman who was the first mayor under the charter of the Local Government Act of 1875. This colourful character also developed the Maltings at Snape (see under Snape), but is perhaps best remembered through his remarkable daughter Elizabeth, who was the

As for the arts, there is, of course, the **Aldeburgh Festival**, started in 1948 by Britten and others; the festival's main venue is Snape Maltings, but many performances take

MOO MOOS
144 High Street, Aldeburgh, Suffolk IP15 5AQ
Tel: 01728 454368

Following on the great success enjoyed by her first **Moo Moos** in Holt, Nerissa Brittain opened a second shop in 2005 on the High Street of the delightful coastal town of Aldeburgh. Run by her eldest daughter, this Moo Moos stocks a similar mix of stylish, elegant items for the home, for family and friends and for a special personal treat. The ever-changing, eclectic selection gathered from near and far runs from china and glassware to handbags, luggage, linen, quilts, clothes and small items of furniture. This second Moo Moos is enjoying similar success to the first, and with the stock constantly changing and evolving, every visit is guaranteed to be rewarded with something special.

⌂ historic building   ⌂ museum   ⌂ historic site   ⌂ scenic attraction   ⌂ flora and fauna

place in Aldeburgh itself.

The town's maritime connections remain very strong. There has been a lifeboat here since 1851, and down the years many acts of great heroism have been recorded. The very modern lifeboat station is one of the town's chief attractions for visitors, and there are regular practice launches from the shingle beach. It is recorded that in1843 Aldeburgh had about 200 licensed fishing boats, catching sole, lobster, sprats and herring in great numbers. Just a handful of fishermen still put out to sea from the beach, selling their catch from their little wooden huts, while a thriving yacht club is the base for sailing on the Orde and, sometimes, on the sea. On the beach at the northern edge of town is a remarkable work of art – a giant steel scallop shell designed by the renowned Suffolk-born artist Maggi Hambling. It is a monument to Benjamin Britten, and the words on its rim – 'I hear those voices that will not be drowned' – are taken from Britten's opera *Peter Grimes*. The area inland from here is a nature reserve.

At the very southern tip of the town, the Martello Tower is one of 75 hastily built on the coast between Suffolk and Sussex against the threat of a Napoleonic invasion. This one dates from 1814 and never saw action, although its four guns were manned until the middle of the 19th century. It serves as a reminder of the power of the sea: old pictures show it standing well back from the waves, but now the seaward side of the moat has disappeared and the shingle is constantly being shored up to protect it. Beyond it, a long strip

THE WENTWORTH HOTEL

Wentworth Road, Aldeburgh, Suffolk IP15 5BD
Tel: 01728 452312 Fax: 01728 454343
e-mail: stay@wentworth-aldeburgh.co.uk
website: www.wentworth-aldeburgh.com

Distinguished and impressive, the **Wentworth Hotel & Restaurant** is everything a seaside hotel should be. Spacious, gracious and very civilised, this excellent hotel in the heart of town is a happy blend of the traditional and the contemporary, and one of the main reasons for its success is the unbroken management of the Pritt family, here since 1920. Handsomely appointed and furnished throughout, the hotel has 28 bedrooms in the main building – the majority looking straight out to sea beyond the fishermen's huts – and seven rooms in Darfield House, opposite the main building, with its own secluded patio garden. Five of the bedrooms are located on the ground floor for easier access.

The spacious lounges, graced with books, paintings, sculptures and china, are perfect to unwind in comfort, reading or watching the promenaders on the seafront. The terrace bar is open every day for drinks and light lunches, and the restaurant offers diners the best in English and French cuisine served by friendly, attentive staff in elegant surroundings. Local produce is used as much as possible, including fish that simply could not be fresher.

THE BRUDENELL HOTEL

The Parade, Aldeburgh, Suffolk IP15 5BU
Tel: 01728 452071   Fax: 01728 454082
e-mail: info@brudenellhotel.co.uk   website: www.brudenellhotel.co.uk

The charm of the town and the invigorating air are among the attractions of the **Brudenell Hotel**, set right by the beach at the south end of the town, close to the Yacht Club. This large and impressive hotel, distinctive and handsome, is the perfect choice for a family holiday. The Brudenell's 42 bedrooms are all furnished to a very high standard and are decorated in a light, airy and relaxing style. Most have glorious views of the sea or the River Alde and its surrounding marshland.

Dining in The Brudenell's stylish AA Two Rosette Restaurant is truly an experience. With its amazing panoramic sea views, the Ocean Bar's sea-blue and sunshine-yellow décor brings the seaside, inside. The restaurant's emphasis is on flexibility and informality, offering constantly changing menus and a wide variety of dishes using local produce. Grills, fish and seafood are a speciality.

There is a real cosmopolitan atmosphere during the summer months when al fresco dining is available on the hotel's sea-facing terrace; what better than to savour a crab salad or 'The Bru's' popular homemade fishcakes, whilst listening to the soothing sound of waves crashing on the beach.

Two-night stays and other short breaks are available at the Brudenell, which is part of the Thorpeness & Aldeburgh Hotels Ltd Group.

THE WHITE LION HOTEL

Market Cross Place, Aldeburgh, Suffolk IP15 5BJ
Tel: 01728 452720
Fax: 01728 452986
e-mail: info@whitelion.co.uk
website: www.whitelion.co.uk

Located in the heart of Aldeburgh, just opposite the shingle beach and the fishermen's huts, The **White Lion** offers a warm Suffolk welcome. The hotel has 38 en suite bedrooms, some commanding views out to the expanse of the North Sea, some boasting four-poster beds. A stair lift provides access to first floor rooms. Attention to detail is evident in every room, and the staff are unfailingly friendly and helpful.

The hotel bar overlooks the sea, while the oak-panelled AA Rosette Restaurant 1563 – named after the year in which the hotel was built – offers elegant dining from a menu that includes seafood specials, traditional roasts and vegetarian options. During the periods of the Aldeburgh Festival and the August proms at Snape, guests can enjoy pre-concert meals or late suppers at the hotel. Hampers can also be provided during the proms.

The White Lion is part of Thorpeness & Aldeburgh Hotels Limited.

🏛 historic building   🏛 museum   🏛 historic site   ⌘ scenic attraction   🌱 flora and fauna

of marsh and shingle stretches right down to the mouth of the river at Shingle Street.

Back in town there are several interesting buildings, notably the **Moot Hall** and the parish church of St Peter and St Paul. The Moot Hall is a 16th century timber-framed building that was built in what was once the centre of town. It hasn't moved, but the sea long ago took away several houses and streets. Inside the Hall is a museum of town history and finds from the nearby Snape burial ship. Britten set the first scene of *Peter Grimes* in the Moot Hall. A sundial on the south face of the Hall proclaims, in Latin, that it only tells the time when the sun shines.

The church, which stands above the town as a very visible landmark for mariners, contains a memorial to George Crabbe and a beautiful stained-glass window, the work of John Piper, depicting three Britten parables: *Curlew River*, *The Burning Fiery Furnace* and *The Prodigal Son*. Britten is buried in the churchyard, alongside his companion Peter Pears and the musician Imogen Holst, daughter of Gustav Holst, sometime Director of the Aldeburgh Festival and for several years Britten's musical assistant. Elizabeth Garrett Anderson is buried in the family grave enclosed by wrought-iron railings. Part of the churchyard is set aside for the benefit of wildlife.

SNAPE

3 miles S of Saxmundham on the A1094

🔎 Snape Maltings

This 'boggy place' has a long and interesting history. In 1862 the remains of an Anglo-Saxon ship were discovered here, and since that time regular finds have been made, with some remarkable cases of almost perfect preservation. Snape, like Aldeburgh, has benefited over the years from the

philanthropy of the Garrett family, one of whose members built the primary school and set up the Maltings, centre of the Aldeburgh Music Festival.

The last 30-odd years have seen the development of the **Snape Maltings Riverside Centre**, a group of shops and galleries located in a complex of restored Victorian granaries and malthouses that is also the setting for the renowned Aldeburgh festival.

The Maltings began their designated task of converting grain into malt in the 1840s, and continued thus until 1965, when the pressure of modern techniques brought them to a halt. There was a real risk of the buildings being demolished, but George Gooderham, a local farmer, bought the site to expand his animal feeds business and soon saw the potential of the redundant buildings (his son Jonathan is the current owner of the site).

The Concert Hall came first, in 1967, and in 1971 the Craft Shop was established as the first conversion of the old buildings for retail premises. Conversion and expansion continue to this day, and in the numerous outlets visitors can buy anything from fudge to country-style clothing, from herbs to household furniture, silver buttons to top hats. Plants and garden accessories are also sold, and art galleries feature the work of local painters, potters and sculptors. The Centre hosts regular painting, craft and decorative art courses, and more recent expansion saw the creation of an impressive country-style store.

A short distance west of Snape, off the B1069, lies Blaxhall, famed for its growing stone. The Blaxhall Stone, which lies in the yard of Stone Farm, is reputed to have grown to its present size (five tons) from a comparative pebble the size of a football,

Iken - Snape

Distance: *5.3 miles (8.53 kilometres)*

Typical time: *150 mins*

Height gain: *12 metres*

Map: *Explorer 212*

Walk: *www.walkingworld.com ID:640*

Contributor: *Brian and Anne Sandland*

ACCESS INFORMATION:

From Woodbridge take the A1152 eastwards. When the road forks (still on the A1152) bear left towards Snape. At Tunstall, just after the right-angled bend, turn left onto the B1069 ('Snape'). After you pass through the northern end of the Tunstall Forest the road from Blaxhall comes in from the left. Ignore this, but take the next turn right (to Orford/Iken). At the next left ('Iken 2') turn left and in 150 yards look for a picnic site sign left. This takes you down a narrow track to the picnic site at Iken Cliff with glorious views over the Alde. Park here.

DESCRIPTION:

Wildlife and birds abound. There is also varied plantlife. A visit to St Botolph's Church can be included and after the walk through the forest you can see the wonderful variety of attractions at Snape Maltings. These include an internationally famous concert hall, galleries full of furniture, books, pictures, crafts, antiques and food. There is a restaurant and even a small garden centre.

FEATURES:

Toilets and tea and shops are only available if you include Snape Maltings, River, Church, Wildlife, Birds, Flowers, Great Views

WALK DIRECTIONS:

1 | Head down into the right-hand corner of the picnic site.

2 | Take the footpath which leads along the Alde to Cliff Reach. Continue close to the river finally turning away from the river to reach a road.

3 | Leave the river area by steps and walk to the road. If you want to visit the church turn left and in 75 yards left again (signed Iken Church). There are superb views along and across the Alde from the churchyard. Return to the point where you first joined the road then continue, rising slightly. Go left at the junction (signed to Sandy Lane). Pass a number of cottages and after the one named "The Drift", where the road bends sharp left, go right along a track.

4 | Follow this signposted track. At trees on the right bear right. Then go left following the edge of the trees (ignore track off left through the trees) to arrive at a broad cross-track. Go slightly right then left along another track, to continue in your original direction, this time with trees on your right. When trees on the right end, go right and then left with the track and exit carefully through bushes onto the road. Cross the road and at a broad cross-track, go right for 30 yards.

5 | Turn left at the yellow waymark. Now walk between young pine trees on either side (planted after the devastation of the hurricane of 1987). At next fork bear right along a narrower path. DO NOT follow main track with yellow waymark. In 150 yards reach another wide cross-track. Cross straight over and follow the track leading straight ahead, which is now wider than the footpath you have just left. Carry on in this direction, ignoring all turns off to the right and left until you suddenly and unexpectedly come across a house on your right (Heath Cottages). Join its

drive and walk on to a junction. Take the right turn following the direction of a sign with the number 24. (Do not take the track immediately right).

6 | Despite what the map indicates here, there is no fire tower. After 100 yards or so the broad track bears right and runs straight into the distance. Leave it and take the narrower grass track which snakes off left. A white waymark should be visible on a post at the intersection. You will soon pass through a clearing. Once again ignore tuns off to right and left and carry on to meet a road.

7 | Turn right and follow this exceedingly pleasant, narrow metalled lane, which bisects the forest, until you reach a crossroads. Cross over and continue straight ahead until you reach the picnic place sign, pointing left to your car and the start point.

8 | If you wish to visit the Maltings, with all its attractions, descend to the bottom left of the picnic site this time. Then follow the footpath left along the Alde. To return, retrace your steps. (If you have had enough walking you could, of course take your car to the Maltings. There is ample free parking).

when it first came to local attention 100 years ago. Could there be more 'Blarney' than Blaxhall at work here?

Woodbridge

🏠 Tide Mill and Buttrum's Mill 🏛 Museum

🏛 Suffolk Punch Heavy Horse Museum

Udebyge, Wicbryge, Wodebryge, Wudebrige … just some of the ways of spelling this splendid old market town since it was first mentioned in writing back in AD970. As to what the name means, it could simply be 'wooden bridge' or 'bridge by the wood', but the most likely and most interesting explanation is that it is derived from Anglo-Saxon words meaning 'Woden's (or Odin's) town'.

Standing at the head of the Deben estuary, it is a place of considerable charm with a wealth of handsome, often historic buildings and a considerable sense of history, as both a market town and a port.

The shipbuilding and allied industries flourished here, as at most towns on the Suffolk coast, and it is recorded that both Edward III, in the 14th century, and Drake in the 16th sailed in Woodbridge ships. There's still plenty of activity on and by the river, though nowadays it is all leisure-orientated. The town's greatest benefactor was Thomas Seckford, who rebuilt the abbey, paid for the chapel in the north aisle of St Mary's Church and founded the original almshouses in Seckford Street. In 1575 he gave the town the splendid Shire Hall on Market Hill. Originally used as a corn exchange, it now houses the **Suffolk Punch Heavy Horse Museum**, with an exhibition devoted to the Suffolk Punch breed of heavy working horse, the oldest such breed in the world. The history of the breed and its rescue from near-extinction in the 1960s is covered in fascinating detail, and there's a section dealing with the other famous Suffolk breeds – the Red Poll cattle, the Suffolk sheep and the Large Black pigs. Opposite the Shire Hall is **Woodbridge Museum**, a treasure trove of information on the history of the town and its more notable residents; from here it is a short stroll down the cobbled alleyway to the magnificent parish church of St Mary, where Seckford was buried in 1587.

Seckford naturally features prominently in the museum, along with the painter Thomas Churchyard, the map-maker Isaac Johnson and the poet Edward Fitzgerald. 'Old Fitz' was something of an eccentric and, for the most part, fairly reclusive. He loved Woodbridge and particularly the River Deben, where he often sailed in his little boat *Scandal*.

Woodbridge is lucky enough to have two marvellous mills, both in working order, and both great attractions for the visitor. The **Tide Mill**, on the quayside close to the town centre, dates from the late 18th century (though the site was mentioned 600 years previously) and worked by the power of the tide until 1957. It has been meticulously restored and the waterwheel still turns, fed by a recently created pond which replaced the original huge mill pond when it was turned into a marina. **Buttrum's Mill**, named after the last miller, is a tower mill standing just off the A12 bypass a mile west of the town centre. A marvellous sight, its six storeys make it the tallest surviving tower mill in Suffolk. There is a ground-floor display of the history and workings of the mill.

Many of the town's streets are traffic-free, so shopping is a real pleasure. If you should

catch the Fitzgerald mood and feel like 'a jug of wine and a loaf of bread', Woodbridge can oblige with a good variety of pubs and restaurants.

Around Woodbridge

SUTTON HOO
1 mile E of Woodbridge off the B1083

🏛 Sutton Hoo

A mile or so east of Woodbridge on the opposite bank of the Deben is **Sutton Hoo**, sometimes known as 'page one of the history of England'. A unique and fascinating place to visit, the discovery of ship rivets in an ancient burial mound in 1939 led to one of the most amazing finds in the nation's history. This, the ship burial of an Anglo-Saxon warrior king and his most treasured possessions, had lain undisturbed for more than 1,300 years. The permanent display in the special exhibition hall reveals how Anglo-Saxon nobles lived, went to war and founded a kingdom in East Anglia. Here visitors can discover how the famous helmet and exquisite gold jewellery were made and used. A second hall houses an exhibition investigating the Anglo-Saxon thirst for imported luxuries from the Mediterranean and elsewhere. Visitors can also take the short walk to the burial mounds to see for themselves the site where the ship and treasures were found. It is now believed that the ship was the burial place of Raedwald, of the Wuffinga dynasty, King of East Anglia from about 610 to 625. Access to the site is on foot from the B1083. The site's extensive facilities include a restaurant, shop, children's play area and variety of walks in the surrounding countryside. There is good access for visitors with disabilities to all the site.

BROMESWELL

3 miles NE of Woodbridge off the B1084

This quiet village occupies a scenic setting. Bromeswell's church has a 12th century archway at its entrance, a 15th century font and an unusual Flemish well. The angels in the hammerbeam roof are plastic replicas of the originals, whose wings were clipped by Cromwell's men.

UFFORD

3 miles NE of Woodbridge off the A12

🏛 Church of the Assumption

Pride of place in a village that takes its name from Uffa (or Wuffa), the founder of the leading Anglo-Saxon dynasty, goes to the 13th century **Church of the Assumption**. The font cover, which telescopes from five feet to 18 feet in height, is a masterpiece of craftsmanship, its elaborate carving crowned by a pelican. Many 15th century benches have survived, but Dowsing smashed the organ and most of the stained glass – what's there now is mainly Victorian, some of it a copy of 15th century work at All Souls College, Oxford.

Ufford is where the Suffolk Punch originated, Crisp's 404 being, in 1768, the progenitor of this distinguished breed of horses.

WICKHAM MARKET

5 miles N of Woodbridge off the A12

Places to see in this straggling village are the picturesque watermill by the River Deben and All Saints Church, whose 137-foot octagonal tower has a little roof to shelter the bell. At Boulge, a couple of miles southwest of Wickham Market, is the grave of Edward

KITTY'S HOMESTORE

46 High Street, Wickham Market, Suffolk IP13 0QS
Tel/Fax: 01728 748370
e mail: info@kittyshomestore.com
website: www.kittyshomestore.com

Kitty's Homestore is a charming place filled with tasteful and distinctive items for special treats or gifts or to grace a home or a garden. This mini-department store features home furnishings and much more: fashion accessories such as scarves, belts, handbags and jewellery, creative gift wrap, cards and wonderful gift ideas – along with everything for enhancing a home and garden. The carefully chosen items are designed to give any home those lovely little touches that make it unique and welcoming.

The staff are always polite and friendly and are happy to leave customers to browse or to offer well-informed help when it comes to choosing from among the range of tableware, crockery, candlesticks, vases, enamel bread bins, kitchen bins and canisters, and lovely linens, lamps and soft furnishings such as rugs, cushions and throws – and for the garden a delightful range of furnishings and accessories. Set in the town square, the pretty and very welcoming shop is well worth a visit for its range of traditional and modern items and its excellent customer service.

Another Kitty's is in Well Close Square, Framlingham.
Tel: 01728 723295.

VALLEY FARM

The Cottage, Valley Farm, Wickham Market,
Suffolk IP13 0ND
Tel: 01728 746916
e-mail: sarah@valleyfarmonline.co.uk
website: www.valleyfarmonline.co.uk

Valley Farm fully deserves its reputation as 'The Fun Place for Everything Equestrian'. Established in 1977 in the beautiful Deben Valley, the Farm, owned and run by the Ling family, offers the widest range of equestrian activities in the UK, catering for both fun and serious riders with around 40 horses and ponies ranging from miniatures to heavy horses. The smart purpose-built indoor school allows visitors to ride in comfort in any weather, and there are outdoor riding areas and extensive tracks around the 80 acres of farm and woodland. Other facilities include show jumps and a 'Peter Pan' cross-country course.

Individual and group lessons are available for all ages and skills in a variety of disciplines, starting with basic riding and including dressage, side-saddle, Western, show-jumping, carriage driving and musical drill. Escorted rides provide enjoyable days along the bridleways and country lanes. A wide range of events are staged throughout the year, and the Farm can arrange half or full days of fun and activities for parties and corporate groups. The centre is also famous for its collections of animals, among which are Clive the Goat, Camelot the Camel and Muffin the Mule. Valley Farm is also the home of the only breeding herd of French Camargue horses in Britain.

Fitzgerald, whose free translation of *The Rubaiyat of Omar Khayyam* is an English masterpiece. Tradition has it that on his grave is a rose bush grown from one found on Omar Khayyam's grave in Iran. Fitzgerald never left his native Suffolk in all his 74 years.

RENDLESHAM

5 miles NE of Woodbridge on the A1152

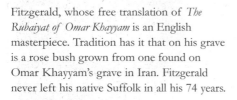
🌲 Rendlesham Forest

The church of St Gregory the Great dates from the 14th century, but there is evidence (not physical, unfortunately) of an earlier Christian presence in the shape of Raedwald's palace. Rendlesham Hall was built in 1871 but was burnt down in 1898 and demolished in 1949. A surviving part is Woodbridge Lodge, a remarkable Gothic folly

Rendlesham Forest, part of the Forest of Aldewood, was ravaged by the great hurricane of October 1987. Seven years before that, on Christmas night, another visitation had occurred. Security guards at RAF Woodbridge, at that time a front line NATO base, spotted strange lights in the forest and went to investigate. They came upon a nine-foot high triangular object with a series of lights around it. As they approached, it did what all good UFOs do and flew off before it could be photographed. The next day the guards returned to the spot where it had landed and found three depressions in the ground. The UFO was apparently sighted again two days later, and security in the area was heightened. No explanation has ever been forthcoming about the incident, but interest in it continues and from time to time guided walks to the landing site are arranged.

BUTLEY
5 miles E of Woodbridge on the B1084

Butley Priory & Staverton Thicks

At the northern edge of Rendlesham Forest, the village of Butley has a splendid 14th century gatehouse, all that remains of **Butley Priory**, an Augustinian priory founded by Ranulf de Glanville in 1171. The gatehouse is, by itself, a fairly imposing building, with some interesting flintwork on the north façade (1320) and baronial carvings. Butley's parish church is Norman, with a 14th century tower.

There are some splendid country walks here, notably by **Staverton Thicks**, which has a deer park and woods of oak and holly. The oldest trees date back more than 400 years. Butley Clumps is an avenue of beech trees planted in fours, with a pine tree at the centre of each clump – the technical term for such an arrangement is a *quincunx*. Butley was long renowned for its oysters, and the beds have recently been revived.

CHILLESFORD
6 miles E of Woodbridge on the B1084

Brick was once big business here, and while digging for clay the locals made many finds, including hundreds of varieties of molluscs and the skeleton of an enormous whale. Chillesford supplies some of the clay for Aldeburgh brickworks.

BUTLEY POTTERY, GALLERY & BARN CAFÉ

Mill Lane, Butley, Woodbridge, Suffolk IP12 3PA
Tel: 01394 450785
e-mail: honorhussey@btconnect.com

A group of sensitively converted farm buildings incorporate **Butley Pottery**, the Barn Café and a summer Artists' Gallery. The showroom displays studio pottery, individual pieces with slip or majolica designs, sculpture in various media and Dan Hussey's unique and beautiful hand-crafted range of steam bent coppiced ash furniture. There are changing exhibitions in the gallery, during the summer by contemporary artists. Self-catering bed and breakfast is also available here, in a charming apartment.

   The Barn Café (Tel: 01394 450800/382332) specialises in innovative cuisine, using locally produced meat and

vegetables, and an abundance of fresh herbs. Unusual vegetarian creations are always on the menu. Lunch bookings advisable, evening parties by arrangement. This is a delightful area of the coast, offering many hidden attractions. Cycle routes, footpaths and bird reserves abound, the river Ore and historic places such as Sutton Hoo, Orford castle and medieval woods are close by.

ORFORD
12 miles E of Woodbridge at the end of the B1084

🏛 Castle 🏛 St Bartholomew's Church

🌱 Orford Ness 🏛 Suffolk Underwater Studies

🌱 Havergate Island

Without doubt one of the most charming and interesting of all the places in Suffolk, Orford has something to please everyone. The ruins of one of the most important castles in medieval England are a most impressive sight, even though the keep is all that remains of the original building commissioned by Henry II in 1165. The walls of the keep of **Orford Castle** are 90 feet high and 10 feet deep, and behind them are many rooms and passages in a remarkable state of preservation. A climb up the spiral staircase to the top provides splendid views over the surrounding countryside and to the sea.

St Bartholomew's Church was built at the same time, though the present church dates from the 14th century. A wonderful sight at night when floodlit, the church is regularly used for the performance of concerts and recitals, and many of Benjamin Britten's works were first heard here, including *Noyes Fludde* and the trio of oratorios *Curlew River, The Burning Fiery Furnace* and *The prodigal Son*. At the east end lie the still-splendid Norman remains, all that is left of the original chancel.

These two grand buildings indicate that Orford was a very important town at one time. Indeed it was once a thriving port, but the steadily growing shingle bank of Orford Ness gradually cut it off from the sea, and

RICHARDSON'S SMOKEHOUSE
Baker's Lane, Orford, Suffolk IP12 2LH
Tel: 01394 450103

Richardson's Smokehouse is the place to find traditionally cured, meats, game, poultry and fish. Among the gastronomic delights for sale from this charming shop are molasses-coated hams, chicken, duck, pheasant, pigeon, kippers, salmon, trout, mackerel, smoked cod roe, mature English cheddar, Stilton, smoked garlic bulbs and exquisite pâtés. The art of long, slow smoking using only oak wood is the secret of their delicious, moist succulence. No preservatives, dyes or additives are used; only pure salt is added to the wholesome goodness of the food here.

Other specialities include ham roasted in cider and a range of mouth-watering sausages such as pork and garlic, pork and venison, pork and apple and chorizo. This thriving business has been going strong since 1986, and is set in a side lane off the Main Square in Orford, with a small serving area, kitchens to the rear, and the adjoining brickbuilt smoke rooms, one hot - for the game and some fish - and one cold - for the haddock, prawns, cheese and other delicacies. For a taste of high quality food at very reasonable prices, prepared in a simple and natural way, look no further.

Open: Seven days a week, 10am-4pm. Telephone orders are welcome, and there's a mail order service on request.

🏛 historic building 🏛 museum 🏛 historic site 🌀 scenic attraction 🌱 flora and fauna

down the years its appeal has changed. The sea may have gone but the river is still there, and in summer the quayside is alive with yachts and pleasure craft. On the other side of the river is **Orford Ness**, the largest vegetated shingle spit in England which is home to a variety of rare flora and fauna. The lighthouse marks the most easterly point (jointly with Lowestoft) in Britain.

Orford Harbour

THE OLD BUTCHER'S SHOP

111 Church Street, Orford, Suffolk IP12 2LL
Tel: 01394 450517   Fax: 01394 459436
e-mail: sarah@oldbutchers-orford.co.uk
website: www.oldbutchers-orford.co.uk

There's plenty for visitors to discover in Orford, and the **Old Butcher's Shop** offers a quiet, comfortable base for bed & breakfast guests in a listed building. Two of the three letting rooms have en suite showers, while the third has sole use of a bathroom. The house has a small courtyard where guests can take breakfast in the summer, and a large garden with fine views of the church. In conjunction with the B&B, owner Sarah Hollands runs a gift shop selling work by local artists and a range of cards and prints linked to the local museum.

ORFORD CRAFTS

Front Street, Orford, Suffolk IP12 2LN
Tel: 01394 450678
Fax: 01394 450323

Two very different attractions in an old brick coach house next to the 15th century church. Much of the stock in **Orford Crafts** is locally made or has a local theme, including baskets, pottery, books, jams and preserves. Also on sale are products from Isle of Arran and Crabtree & Evelyn. Owner Stuart Bacon is a noted marine archaeologist, and on the first floor **Suffolk Underwater Studies** provides a fascinating insight into the Suffolk shoreline and offshore; the centrepiece is a detailed study of the underwater site of medieval Dunwich.

THE ANTIQUES WAREHOUSE

The Old Mill, Main Road (A12), Marlesford,
Suffolk IP13 0AG
Tel: 01728 747438   Fax: 01728 747627
e-mail: antiqueswarehouse@btinternet.com
website: www.antiqueswarehouse.it

The **Antiques Warehouse**, Merchants of Antiques and Makers of Fine Furniture, is located by the A12 at Marlesford, a short drive northeast of Woodbridge. Owners John and Lesley Ball run the business, which has been making furniture and buying and selling antiques since 1989. Both are totally involved in the day-to-day affairs of the Warehouse, and their different but complementary tastes in antiques ensure that the stock covers an exceptionally wide and interesting range. Between them, they do all the buying, and John travels extensively at least twice a year to source items; they only buy pieces they like and 'can live with'.

The floors of display space contain an amazing variety of pieces small and large, old and new. There's every conceivable item of furniture, from footstools and side tables to bureaux, chests, cupboards and bedroom and dining suites. In two large workshops they make an impressive range of furniture from a variety of woods, including oak, cherry, mahogany and pine, and in a variety of finishes. Traditional designs can be copied or modified to suit individual requirements, and John's background in antiques ensures that those designs always feature strongly. The range of furniture on display extends to the garden, with a selection of stylish tables and chairs, gazebos and structures in painted steel, urns, planters and fountains. Furniture is by no means all that the Warehouse stocks, and other well-chosen pieces include silver and porcelain, mirrors, ceiling and centre lights, lanterns and rugs. John and Lesley are very knowledgeable and very approachable, and visitors are encouraged to browse at leisure, and to touch and examine any item.

Interested customers can access a particularly informative website that provides pictures and descriptions of many of the items in stock, but nothing can beat a visit in person to this outstanding enterprise. Opening hours are 9am to 5pm Monday to Saturday and 11am to 4.30pm on Sundays and Bank Holidays. The friendly approach has enabled the owners to build a large and loyal customer base, and anyone who visits the Warehouse can be sure of a warm welcome not just from the owners and staff but also from their popular five-year-old rescue dog Barnes Wallace (BaBa for short). Why Barnes Wallace? Well, he's very bouncy, and he goes down a bomb with everyone who meets him!

Access to the spit, which is in the hands of the National Trust, is by ferry from Orford quay. For many years the Ness was out of bounds to the public, being used for various military purposes, including pre-war radar research under Sir Robert Watson-Watt. Boat trips also leave Orford quay for the RSPB reserve at **Havergate Island**, haunt of avocet and tern (the former returned in 1947 after being long absent).

Dunwich Underwater Studies in Front Street features exhibits on marine archaeology, coastal erosion and more, gleaned from the exploration of the ruins of the former town of Dunwich (qv), now largely claimed by the sea.

Back in the market square are a handsome town hall, two pubs with a fair quota of smuggling tales, a well-loved restaurant serving Butley oysters and a smokehouse where kippers, salmon, trout, ham, sausages, chicken and even cheese and garlic are smoked over Suffolk oak.

CAMPSEA ASHE
6 miles NE of Woodbridge on the B1078

On towards Wickham Market the road passes through Campsea Ashe in the parish of Campsey Ashe. The 14th century church of St John the Baptist has an interesting brass showing one of its first rectors in full priestly garb.

HOLLESLEY
5 miles SE of Woodbridge off the B1083

The Deben and the Ore turn this part of Suffolk almost into a peninsula, and on the seaward side lie Hollesley and Shingle Street. The latter stands upon a shingle bank at the entrance to the Ore and comprises a row of little houses, a coastguard cottage and a Martello tower. Its very isolation is an

attraction, and the sight of the sea rushing into and out of the river is worth the journey.

Brendan Behan did not enjoy his visit. Brought here on a swimming outing from the Borstal at Hollesley, he declared that the waves had 'no limit but the rim of the world'. Looking out to the bleak North Sea, it is easy to see what he meant.

BAWDSEY
7 miles SE of Woodbridge on the B1083

The B1083 runs from Woodbridge through farming country and several attractive villages (Sutton, Shottisham, Alderton) to Bawdsey, beyond which lie the mouth of the River Deben, the end of the Sussex Coastal Path, and the ferry to Felixstowe. The late-Victorian Bawdsey Manor was taken over by the Government and became the centre for radar development when Orford Ness was deemed unsuitable. By the beginning of the Second World War there were two dozen secret radar stations in Britain, and radar HQ moved from Bawdsey to Dundee. The manor is now a leisure centre.

RAMSHOLT
7 miles SE of Woodbridge off the B1083

Ramsholt is a tiny community on the north bank of the Deben a little way up from Bawdsey. The pub is a popular port of call for yachtsmen, and half a mile from the quay, in quiet isolation, stands the Church of All Saints with its round tower. Road access to Ramsholt is from the B1083 just south of Shottisham.

Stowmarket

Museum of East Anglian Life

Gipping Valley Walk

The largest town in the heart of Suffolk,

Museum of East Anglian Life

Stowmarket, Suffolk IP14 1DL
Tel: 01449 612229 Fax: 01449 672307
website: www.eastanglianlife.org.uk

The Museum of East Anglian Life occupies a 75-acre
site in the heart of Stowmarket. Its rich collections of
social, rural and industrial history include a number of
historic buildings such as a working watermill, a
smithy, a chapel and a 13th century farmhouse. There is something for the whole family to
enjoy with a variety of farm animals, adventure playground, picnic sites, café and gift shop.
Throughout the year the museum holds special events as well as demonstrations of crafts
and engines in steam. The museum is open from April to October.

Stowmarket enjoyed a period of rapid growth
when the River Gipping was still navigable to
Ipswich and when the railway arrived. Much of
the town's history and legacy are brought
vividly to life in the splendid **Museum of East
Anglian Life** (see panel above), situated in the
centre of town to the west of the marketplace
(where markets are held twice a week), in a 70-
acre meadowland site on the old Abbot's Hall
Estate (the aisled original barn dates from the
13th century). Part of the open-air section
features several historic buildings that have
been moved from elsewhere in the region and
carefully re-erected on site. These include an
engineering workshop from the 1870s, part of
a 14th century farmhouse, a watermill from
Alton and a wind pump which was rescued in a
collapsed state at Minsmere in 1977. There's
also a collection of working steam engines,
farm animals and year-round demonstrations
of all manner of local arts and crafts, from
coopering to chandlery, from sheep shearing to
saddlery. Stowmarket's church of St Peter and
St Mary acquired a new spire in 1994, replacing
the 1715 version (itself a replacement) which
was dismantled on safety grounds in 1975.

The town certainly merits a leisurely stroll,
while for a peaceful picnic the riverbank
beckons. Serious scenic walkers should make
for the **Gipping Valley River Park** walk,
which follows the former towpath all the way
to Ipswich and incorporates a number of
nature reserves.

Around Stowmarket

ELMSWELL
7 miles NW of Stowmarket off the A14

Clearly visible from the A14, the impressive
church of St John the Baptist with its massive
flint tower stands at the entrance to the
village, facing Woolpit across the valley. A
short drive north of Elmswell lies Great
Ashfield, an unspoilt village whose now
disused airfield played a key role in both
World Wars. In the churchyard of the 13th
century All Saints is a memorial to the
Americans who died during the Second World
War, as attested to by the commemorative
altar. Some accounts say that Edmund was
buried here in AD903 after dying at the hands
of the Danes; a cross was put up in his
memory. The cross was replaced in the 19th
century and now stands in the garden of
Ashfield House.

HAUGHLEY

4 miles NW of Stowmarket off the A14

 Haughley Park

On the run into Stowmarket, Haughley once had the largest motte-and-bailey castle in Suffolk. All that now remains is a mound behind the church. **Haughley Park** is a handsome Jacobean redbrick manor house set in eight acres of gardens and surrounding woodland featuring ancient oaks and splendid magnolias. Woodland paths take the visitor past a half-mile stretch of rhododendrons, and in springtime the bluebells and lilies of the valley are a magical sight. The gardens are open on Tuesdays between May and September, the house by appointment only.

HARLESTON

4 miles NW of Stowmarket off the A14

The churches of Shelland and Harleston lie in close proximity on a minor road between Woolpit and Haughley picnic site. At Shelland, the tiny church of King Charles the Martyr is one of only four in England to be dedicated to King Charles I. The brick floor is laid in a herringbone pattern, there are high box pews and a triple-decker pulpit, but the most unusual feature is a working barrel organ dating from the early 19th century.

The church of St Augustine at Harleston stands all alone among pine trees and is reached by a track across a field. It has a thatched roof, Early English windows and a tower with a single bell.

BUXHALL

3 miles W of Stowmarket just off the B1115

The village church here is notable for its six heavy bells, but the best-known landmark in this quiet village is undoubtedly the majestic tower mill, without sails since a gale removed them in 1929 but still standing as a silent, sturdy reminder of its working days. This is good walking country, with an ancient wood and many signposted footpaths.

NEEDHAM MARKET

4 miles SE of Stowmarket off the A14

 Church of St John the Baptist

A thriving village whose greatest glory is the wonderful carvings on the ceiling of the Church of **St John the Baptist**. The church's ornate double hammerbeam roof is nothing short of remarkable, especially when bathed in light from the strategically placed skylight. The roof is massive, as high as the walls of the church itself; the renowned authority on Suffolk churches, H Munro Cautley, described the work at Needham as 'the culminating achievement of the English carpenter'. The village also boasts some excellent examples of Tudor architecture.

The River Gipping flows to the east of the High Street and its banks provide miles of walks: the towpath is a public right of way walkable all the way from Stowmarket to Ipswich. On the riverbank at Needham is a 25-acre picnic site and a nature reserve.

Monthly farmers' markets are held at Alder Carr Farm, where there is also a pottery, crafts centre and farm shop.

Nearby Barking, on the B1018 south of Needham, was once more important than its neighbour, being described in 1874 as 'a pleasant village ... including the hamlet of Needham Market'. This explains the fact that Barking's church is exceptionally large for a village house of worship: it was the mother church to Needham Market and was used for Needham's burials when Needham had no burial ground of its own.

BAYLHAM
7 miles SE of Stowmarket off the B1130

🌾 Baylham House Rare Breeds Farm

The Roman site of Combretrovium is home to **Baylham House Rare Breeds Farm**, and visitors (April-early October) will find displays and information relating to both Rome and rare animals. The farm's chief concern is the survival of rare breeds, and there are breeding groups of cattle, sheep, pigs, goats and poultry.

EARL STONHAM
5 miles E of Stowmarket on the A1120

A scattered village set around three greens in farming land, Earl Stonham's church of St Mary the Virgin boasts one of Suffolk's finest

single hammerbeam roofs, and is also notable for its Bible scene murals, the 'Doom' (Last Judgement scene) over the chancel arch and a triple hour-glass, presumably to record just how protracted were some of the sermons.

STONHAM ASPAL
6 miles E of Stowmarket on the A1120

🌾 Stonham Barns Owl Sanctuary 🌾 Redwings

On the other side of the A140 lies Stonham Aspal, where in 1962 the remains of a Roman bath-house were unearthed. The parish church has an unusual wooden top to its tower, a necessary addition to house the 10 bells that a keen campanologist insisted on installing. **Stonham Barns** is a leisure, rural pursuits and shopping complex that also houses the **Suffolk Owl Sanctuary** and the **Redwings Horse Rescue Centre**, which opened in 2003 and provides sanctuary for over 30 rescued horses, ponies and donkeys, a few of which are available for adoption.

MENDLESHAM
6 miles NE of Stowmarket off the A140

On the green in Old Market Street, Mendlesham, lies an enormous stone which is said to have been used as a preaching stone, mounted by itinerant Wesleyan preachers. In the Church of St Mary there is a collection of parish armour assembled some 400 years ago, and also some fine carvings. The least hidden local landmark is a 1,000-ft TV mast put up by the IBA in 1959.

BROCKFORD
7 Miles NE of Stowmarket off the A410

📷 Mid-Suffolk Light Railway Museum

Off the A140, Brockford is where visitors will find **Mid-Suffolk Light Railway Museum**, open on summer Sundays and

STONHAM BARNS

Pettaugh Road, Stonham Aspal, nr Stowmarket,
Suffolk IP14 6AT
Tel: 01449 711755   Fax: 01449 711174
e-mail: stonham@barns123.fsnet.co.uk
website: www.stonhambarns.co.uk

Stonham Barns is a leisure, shopping and rural pursuits complex on the A1120 at Stonham Aspal, midway between Stowmarket and Framlingham. A great day out for all ages is assured at the Barns, where the attractions include a showground, restaurant, garden centre, owl sanctuary, golf course, fishing lake, arts and crafts outlets and specialist shops. The complex has been chosen as the setting for the Mid-Suffolk Showground, a major centre for rurally-themed events; the Mid-Suffolk Annual Show in April is the most important of the many big shows staged here every year.

The Garden Centre is stocked with a wide variety of traditional and tropical plants, plus Country Feeds food for all kinds of animals and pets. The licensed restaurant is open until 4.30pm seven days a week with a daily-changing choice of freshly prepared home cooked food on a traditional British menu; light snacks are served all day, with the main menu available from noon to 2pm. A real crowd-pleaser at the Barns is the Suffolk Owl Sanctuary, home to eagles, hawks, falcons, kites and vultures as well as owls. There's also a red squirrel colony, and a rescue centre for horses, ponies and donkeys.

during school holidays. The museum includes original station buildings, a steam locomotive, railway coaches, photographs and memorabilia.

WETHERINGSETT

7 Miles NE of Stowmarket off the A410

Wetheringsett has had two well-known rectors, famous for very different reasons. Richard Hakluyt, incumbent from 1590 to 1616, is remembered for his major work *Voyages* (full title *Principal Navigation, Voyages, Traffiques and Discoveries of the English Nation*). The rector between 1858 and 1883 was a certain George Wilfrid Ellis, sometime tailor and butler, and finally a bogus clergyman. After he was unmasked as a sham, a special Act of Parliament was needed to validate the marriage ceremonies he had illegally performed, and to legitimise the issue of those marriages.

COTTON

5 miles N of Stowmarket off the B1113

Mechanical Music Museum

South of Finningham, where Yew Tree House displays some fine pargetting, and just by Bacton, a lovely village originally built around seven greens, lies the village of Cotton, which should be visited for several reasons, one of which is to see the splendid 14th century flint church of St Andrew, impressive in its dimensions and notable for its double hammerbeam roof with carved angels.

Cotton's **Mechanical Music Museum & Bygones** (see panel on page 138) has an

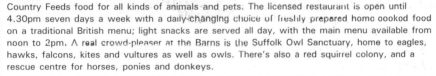

Mechanical Music Museum & Bygones

Blacksmith Road, Cotton, Nr. Stowmarket,
Suffolk IP14 4QN
Tel: 01449 613876

There are musical treasures aplenty at the **Mechanical Music Museum & Bygones**, which houses a unique collection of music boxes, polyphons, street pianos, pianolas and organs. Stars of the show include a Limonaire fairground organ dating from around 1850 and a mighty Wurlitzer theatre organ originally installed in the Stilwell Theatre, Brooklyn, in 1926.

It was later shipped to England and for many years graced London's Luxury Theatre (later the Leicester Square Theatre), which was built by the great star Jack Buchanan. The Mechanical Museum acquired the Wurlitzer in the early 1980s. The museum, which also boasts a large collection of teapots and musical memorabilia, is open on Sunday afternoons from June to September, and for an annual fair organ enthusiasts day on the first Sunday in October.

extensive collection that includes gramophones, music boxes, street pianos, fairground organs and polyphons, as well as the marvellous Wurlitzer Theatre pipe organ.

THORNHAM MAGNA & PARVA

10 miles N of Stowmarket off the A140

🚶 Thornham Walks

The **Thornham Walks and Field Centre**, with 12 miles of walks and a herb garden and nursery, caters admirably for hikers, horticulturists and lovers of the countryside. The tiny thatched church of St Mary at Thornham Parva houses a considerable treasure in the shape of an exquisite medieval altar painting, known as a *retable*, with a central panel depicting the Crucifixion and four saints on each side panel. Its origins are uncertain, but it was possibly the work of the Royal Workshops at Westminster Abbey and made for Thetford Priory, or for a nearby

Dominican monastery. Also to be admired is the 14th century octagonal font and a series of fascinating wall paintings. In the churchyard is a monument to Sir Basil Spence (1907-76), architect of Coventry Cathedral.

YAXLEY

12 miles N of Stowmarket on the A140

Yaxley's Church of St Mary offers up more treasures. One is an extremely rare sexton's wheel, which hangs above the south door and was used in medieval times to select fast days in honour of the Virgin. When a pair of iron wheels were spun on their axle, strings attached to the outer wheel would catch on the inner, stopping both and indicating the chosen day. The 17th century pulpit is one of the finest in the country, with the most glorious, sumptuous carvings. Yaxley's most famous son is Sir Frederick Ashton, who is buried in the churchyard.

Framlingham

🏰 Castle 🏰 Church of St Michael 🏛 Lanman Museum

The marvellous **Castle**, brooding on a hilltop, dominates this agreeable market town, as it has since Roger Bigod, 2nd Earl of Norfolk, built it in the 12th century (his grandfather built the first a century earlier, but this wooden construction was soon demolished). The Earls and Dukes of Norfolk, the Howards, were here for many generations before moving to Arundel in 1635. The castle is in remarkably good condition, partly because it was rarely attacked – though King John put it under siege in 1215. Its most famous occupant was Mary Tudor, who was in residence when proclaimed Queen in 1553.

During the reign of Elizabeth I it was used as a prison for defiant priests and, in the 17th century after being bequeathed to Pembroke College, Cambridge, it saw service as a home and school for local paupers. Nine of the castle's 13 towers are accessible - the climb up the spiral staircase and walk round the battlements are well worth the effort. On one side the view is of the Meres, a bird sanctuary. In the north wing is the **Lanman Museum**, devoted to agricultural, craftsman's tools and domestic memorabilia.

The castle brought considerable prestige and prosperity to Framlingham, evidence of which can be found in the splendid Church of **St Michael**, which has two wonderful works of art. One is the tomb of Henry Fitzroy, bastard son of Henry VIII, beautifully adorned with

🎭 stories and anecdotes 🍴 famous people 🎨 art and craft ✏ entertainment and sport 🚶 walks

scenes from Genesis and Exodus and in a superb state of repair. The other is the tomb of the 3rd Duke, with carvings of the apostles in shell niches. Also of note is the Carolean organ of 1674, a gift of Sir Robert Hitcham, to whom the Howards sold the estate. Cromwell and the Puritans were not in favour of organs in churches, so this instrument was lucky to have escaped the mass destruction of organs at the time of the Commonwealth. Sir Robert is buried in the church.

Around Framlingham

SAXTEAD GREEN
2 miles W of Framlingha off the A1120

🏛 Mill

One of the prettiest sights in Suffolk is the white **18th Century Mill** that stands on the marshy green in Saxtead. This is a wonderful example of a post mill, perhaps the best in the world, dating back to 1796 and first renovated in the 19th century. It worked until 1947 and has since been kept in working order, with the sails turning even though the mill no longer grinds. In summer, visitors can climb into the buck (body) of this elegant weatherboarded construction and explore its machinery.

EARL SOHAM
3 miles W of Framlingham on the A1120

Earl Soham comprises a long, winding street that was once part of a Roman road. It lies in a valley, and on the largest of its three greens the village sign is a carved wooden statue of a falconer given as a gift by the Women's

---

EAT ANGLIA

The Street, Earl Soham, nr Woodbridge, Suffolk IP13 7RT
Tel: 01728 685557
e-mail: Patrick@eatanglia.co.uk
website: www.eatanglia.co.uk

Eat Anglia has just opened in Earl Soham and it has been described as one of the region's finest delicatessens, with a relaxed style of shopping and eating. Customers can buy locally produced food, relax with a coffee, enjoy a freshly cooked, hot lunch or a sandwich (having selected something from the deli counter) and even surf the internet. 70% of the shop's produce comprises locally farmed foods or Suffolk made produce including locally farmed meats, dairy and cheeses, smoked fish, fruit and vegetables, organic and non-organic breads, even beers, with the Earl Soham Brewery handily next door. Other produce is specially selected from small local producers in areas such as Yorkshire and Cornwall and wines from a small Rhone Valley vineyard. There is also an all year round mail service and a hamper service and between May & October fresh picnics can be pre-ordered for outdoor events and trips to the coast. Visit www.eatanglia.co.uk for more details on this.

For the holiday season and second home owners Eat Anglia have just launched their Holiday Let Starter Packs. They contain all the essentials to survive the first 24 hours of the holiday but most importantly will enable visitors to reach their destination knowing that the food and drink is there, chilled and ready to enjoy.

🏛 historic building 📷 museum 🏛 historic site 💠 scenic attraction 🌿 flora and fauna

DOVE VALLEY

2 Chancery Lane, Debenham, Suffolk IP14 6RN
Tel: 01728 861258 Fax: 01728 862027
e-mail: enquiries@dovevalley.co.uk website: www.dovevalley.co.uk
Housed in a square brick building on the main street of Debenham,
Dove Valley stocks a wide range of organic vegetables and fruit and
dairy products, much of it produced on local farms. Also on sale in
the delightful little shop are Fair Trade and speciality food, organic
teas and coffees, gluten-free products, dried fruit, nuts and pulses.
Owner Dale Lawrence operates an organic vegetable and fruit box,
bag and hamper scheme for collection or delivery to houses or places
of work. Opening hours are 8am-5.30pm Monday to Saturday, 10am-4pm Sunday.

Institute in 1953. The Church of St Mary, dating from the 13th century, is well worth a visit.

DEBENHAM

6 miles W of Framlingham on the B1077

Debenham is a sizable village of architectural distinction, with a profusion of attractive timber-framed buildings dating from the 14th to the 17th centuries. The River Deben flows beside and beneath the main street and, near one of the little bridges there is a pottery centre. St Mary's Church is unusual in having an original Saxon tower, and the roof alternates hammerbeams with crested tie beams.

DENNINGTON

2 miles N of Framlingham on the B1116

Church of St Mary

The pretty little village of Dennington boasts one of the oldest post offices in the country, this one having occupied the same site since 1830. The **Church of St Mary** has some very unusual features, none more so than the hanging 'pyx' canopy above the altar. A pyx served as a receptacle for the Reserved Sacrament, which would be kept under a canopy attached to weights and pulleys so that the whole thing could be lowered when the sacrament was required for the sick and the dying.

The church also has many interesting carvings, the most remarkable being that of a skiapod, the only known representation in this county of a mythical creature of the African

Dennington

desert, humanoid but with a huge boat-shaped foot with which it could cover itself against the sun. This curious beast was 'known' to Herodotus and to Pliny, who remarked that it had 'great pertinacity in leaping'. In the chapel at the top of the south aisle stands the tomb of Lord Bardolph, who fought at Agincourt, and of his wife, their effigies carved in alabaster.

PARHAM
2 miles SE of Framlingham on the B1116

🏛 Parham Airfield

Parham Airfield is now agricultural land, but in the control tower and an adjacent hut can be found memorabilia of the 390th Bomb Group of the USAAF. Exhibits include recovered aircraft engines, parts of allied and Axis aircraft, uniforms, combat records and photographs. One of the best-known pieces is part of Joe Kennedy's Liberator bomber that exploded over Blythburgh in 1944. Also in 1944, a Flying Fortress called *Glory Ann II* crashed near the airfield, killing the crew. Here, too, is the Museum of the British Resistance Organisation, the only museum in the UK dedicated to the Auxiliary Units set up to counter the threat of invasion in 1940.

EASTON
5 miles S of Framlingham off the B1078

A scenic drive leads to the lovely village of Easton, one of the most colourful, flower-bedecked places in the county. A remarkable sight to the west of the village is the two-mile-long crinkle-crankle wall that surrounds Easton Park. This extraordinary type of wall, also known as a ribbon wall, weaves snake-like in and out and is much stronger than if it were straight. This particular wall, said to be the world's longest, was built by Lord of the Manor, the Earl of Rochford, in the 1820s.

CHARSFIELD
5 miles S of Framlingham off the B1078

A minor road runs from Framlingham through picturesque Kettleburgh and Hoo to Charsfield, best known as the inspiration for Ronald Blyth's book *Akenfield*, later memorably filmed by Sir Peter Hall. A cottage

Otley Hall

Otley, Suffolk IP6 9PA
Tel: 01473 890264
website: www.otleyhall.co.uk

Otley Hall is a stunningly beautiful 15th/16th century moated Hall. Still a family home, it is set in 10 acres of gardens in the tranquil Suffolk countryside. It is privately owned by Ian and Catherine Beaumont.

Otley Hall welcomes groups by appointment all year round for private guided tours of the house and gardens. A guide will accompany you on your tour to share interesting and intriguing knowledge and facts about Otley Hall and the Gosnold family. Richly carved beams and superb linenfold panelling can be seen, as well as 16th century wall paintings which celebrated the marriage of Robert Gosnold in 1559.

🏛 historic building   🏛 museum   🏛 historic site   🔾 scenic attraction   🌱 flora and fauna

garden in the village displays the Akenfield village sign and is open to visitors in the summer.

OTLEY
7 miles SW of Framlingham on the B1079

🏠 Moated Hall

The 15th century **Moated Hall** (see panel opposite) in Otley is open to the public at certain times of the year. Standing in 10 acres of gardens that include a canal, a nuttery and a knot garden, the hall was long associated with the Gosnold family, whose coat of arms is also that of the village. The best-known member of that family was Bartholomew Gosnold, who sailed to the New World, coined the name 'Martha's Vineyard' for the island off the coast of Massachusetts, discovered Cape Cod and founded the settlement of Jamestown, Virginia. The 13th century church of St Mary has a remarkable baptistry font measuring six feet in length and two feet eight inches in depth. Though filled with water, the font is not used and was only discovered in 1950 when the vestry floor was raised. It may have been used for adult baptisms.

HELMINGHAM
7 miles SW of Framlingham on the B1077

Another moated hall, this one a Tudor construction, stands in Helmingham. Although the house is not open to the public, on Sundays in summer the gardens can be visited; attractions include herbaceous and spring borders, many varieties of roses, safari rides and deer, Highland cattle and Soay sheep. The Tollemache family were here for many years - and one of their number founded a brewery, which, after a merger, became the Tolly Cobbold brewery, based in Ipswich.

FRAMSDEN
7 miles SW of Framlingham on the B1077

The scenery in these parts is real picture-postcard stuff, and in the village of Framsden the picture is completed by a fine Post Mill, built high on a hill in 1760, refitted and raised in 1836 and in use until 1934. The milling machinery is still in place and the mill is open for visits (at weekends, by appointment only).

CRETINGHAM
4 miles SW of Framlingham off the A1120

The village sign is the unusual item here, in that it has two different panels: one shows an everyday Anglo-Saxon farming scene, the other a group (of Danes?) sailing up the River Deben, with the locals fleeing. The signs are made from mosaic tiles.

BRANDESTON
3 miles SW of Framlingham off the A1120

A further mile to the east, through some charming countryside, Brandeston is another delightful spot, with a row of beautiful thatched cottages and the parish church of All Saints with its 13th century font. The best-known vicar of Brandeston was John Lowes (1572-1646) who was accused of witchcraft by the villagers, interrogated by witchfinder General Matthew Hopkins and hanged at Bury St Edmunds. His sad end was made even sadder by the fact that before being strung up he had to read out the burial service of a condemned witch himself, as no priest was allowed to conduct the service. Hopkins made a handsome living out of this bizarre business, preying on the superstitions of the times and using the foulest means to obtain confessions. One account of Hopkins' end is that he himself was accused of being a witch and hanged. The less satisfactory alternative is that he died of tuberculosis.

Eye

Distance: *3.5 miles (5.64 kilometres)*

Typical time: *90 mins*

Height gain: *10 metres*

Map: *Explorer 230*

Walk: *www.walkingworld.com ID:1484*

Contributor: *Joy & Charles Boldero*

For buses ring Travel Line 0545 583358. You can start this walk in Eye and point 7*. The car park at the Pennings picnic site car park is just outside the town. This is where the walk starts . The car park is situated on a country lane south of the B1117 just east of Eye. Eye is situated on the B1077 off the A140, 4 miles southeast of Diss.

ADDITIONAL INFORMATION:

Eye Town Moor Wood has a lot of unusual features in it. The pond you pass has conical structures in it and beside it a lovers seat.

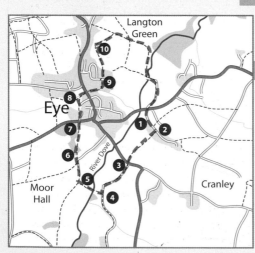

Eye has many beautiful buildings, one the 15th century Guildhall by the church, which is said to be one of the finest in the county. Near the church is the old castle. The Queen's Head has an excellent menu but does not serve food on Mondays.

At point 10 there was once a Priory, built in about 1080 by Robert Malet, Lord of Eye, in memory of his father, William, a Norman baron. There were fish ponds near by, now they are a wild life habitat, kingfishers can be seen there. To the right is the 16th century brick building, which became part of a farm complex, milling, malting and brewing beer. Opposite is the 'Abbey'. The 18th century red brick front hides a mediaeval timber farmed building in which the Prior lived.

DESCRIPTION:

This walk is mostly across meadows, along tracks and through woodland and touches the fine old town of Eye which has so many lovely and ancient buildings. The route uses part of the Mid-Suffolk designated paths.

FEATURES:

Lake, Pub, Toilets, Church, Castle, Wildlife, Birds, Flowers, Great Views, Butterflies, Food Shop

WALK DIRECTIONS:

1|From the car park turn right along the country lane.

2|Turn right at the finger post and cross meadows going over stiles.

3|Cross the road and continue along the track opposite, Park Lane. Go under a barrier where the track becomes grassy.

4|Turn right towards an iron bar and cross a stile to its left. Cross a meadow keeping a copse on the left. Go over a concrete humped bridge and climb a stile in the corner. Cross a second meadow and an earth bridge, then cross a third meadow to a stile ahead.

5 | After climbing this stile and crossing a bridge turn right along a fourth meadow keeping to its left-hand side. Climb the stile and turn right along the track.

6 | At the finger post turn left along the field edge. This path goes into the wood. Cross the bridge and take the right fork. By the pond ignore a path on the right. Keep along the main path to the notice board, ignoring all paths left off it.

7 | Turn right over the bridge and turn left along the gravel track. Turn right along the pavement. Turn left at the road junction. At the Town Hall * turn left to the Queens Head

and then turn right. By the alms houses cross the road.

8 | Turn right at the finger post along a driveway. The path keeps right by a stream over grass lawn. At the end turn left, then left again along a lane with houses.

9 | Cross the road and go along a signed path opposite. Keep on through a newish housing estate.

10 | Soon after house No. 3 turn right along a track; it becomes a grassy one. Climb the stile, cross a meadow and go through a gate. Turn left along the track. Climb a stile and continue along a track. Cross the road and continue along a driveway opposite. Turn right over the stile and cross a meadow. Climb a stile and go along a path under trees then turn right along a country lane to the car park.

Eye

🏛 Church of St Peter & St Paul

The name of this excellent little town is derived from the Saxon for an island, as Eye was once surrounded by water and marshes. The Church of **St Peter and St**

Paul stands in the shadow of a mound on which a castle once stood (the remains are worth a look and the mound offers a panoramic view of the town – almost a bird's eye view, in fact). The church's 100-foot tower was described by Pevsner as 'one of the wonders of Suffolk' and the interior is a masterpiece of restoration, with all the essential medieval features in place. The rood screen, with painted panels depicting St Edmund, St Ursula, Edward the Confessor and Henry VI, is particularly fine.

Other interesting Eye sights are the ornate redbrick Town Hall; the timbered Guildhall, with the archangel Gabriel carved on a corner post; a 'crinkle-crankle' (serpentine) wall fronting Chandos Lodge, where Sir Frederick Ashton once lived; and a

Eye

🎭 stories and anecdotes 🕊 famous people 🎨 art and craft 🖊 entertainment and sport 🚶 walks

thriving theatre, one of the smallest professional theatres in the country.

Around Eye

HOXNE
4 miles NE of Eye on the B1118

 Goldbrook Bridge

Palaeolithic remains indicate the exceptionally long history of Hoxne (pronounced Hoxon), which stands along the banks of the River Waveney near the Norfolk border. It is best known for its links with King Edmund, who was reputedly killed here, though Bradfield St Clare and Shottisham have rival claims to this distinction. The Hoxne legend is that Edmund was betrayed to the Danes by a newlywed couple who were crossing the **Goldbrook Bridge** and spotted his golden spurs reflected from his hiding place below the bridge. Edmund put a curse on all newlyweds crossing the bridge, and to this day some wedding couples take care to avoid it.

The story continues that Edmund was tied to an oak tree and killed with arrows. That same oak mysteriously fell down in 1848 while apparently in good health, and a monument at the site is a popular tourist attraction. In the church of St Peter and St Paul an oak screen (perhaps that very same oak?) depicts scenes from the martyr's life. A more cheerful event is the Harvest Breakfast on the village green that follows the annual service.

HORHAM
6 miles E of Eye on the B1117

Three distinct musical connections distinguish this dapper little village. The Norman church has had its tower strengthened for the rehanging of the peal of eight bells, which is believed to be the oldest in the world. Benjamin Britten, later associated with the Aldeburgh Festival, lived and composed in Horham for a time, and on a famous day during the Second World War, Glenn Miller brought his band here to celebrate the 200th flying mission to set out from the American aerodrome.

WORLINGWORTH
8 miles SE of Eye off the B1118

It's well worth taking the country road to Worlingworth, a long, straggling village whose church of St Mary has a remarkable font cover reaching up about 30 feet. It is brilliantly coloured and intricately carved, and near the

---

LOG CABIN HOLIDAYS

Athelington Hall, Horham, nr Eye, Suffolk IP21 5EJ
Tel: 01728 628233 Fax: 01728 384491
e-mail: peter@logcabinholidays.co.uk
website: www.logcabinholidays.co.uk

Log Cabin Holidays are based in picturesque rural Suffolk, with many of the county's top country and coastal attractions within an easy drive. In the grounds of Athelington Hall, Peter and Sally Havers have five immaculate two-bedroom lodges offering everything for a carefree self-catering holiday, including a fully equipped kitchen, additional sleeping for two in the lounge and a veranda with garden furniture. Among the facilities in the grounds are an outside covered heated swimming pool, a jacuzzi hot tub, a games room and fishing in the moat.

🏠 historic building   🏛 museum   🏚 historic site   ⚜ scenic attraction   🌱 flora and fauna

top is an inscription in Greek which translates as 'wash my sin and not my body only'. Note, too, the Carolean box pews, the carved pulpit and an oil painting of Worlingworth's Great Feast of 1810 to celebrate George III's jubilee.

LAXFIELD
12 miles E of Eye on the B1117

🏠 Heveningham Hall   🏛 Museum

Laxfield & District Museum, on the first floor of the 15th century Guildhall, gives a fine insight into bygone ages with geology and natural history exhibits, agricultural and domestic tools, a Victorian kitchen, a village shop and a costume room. The museum is open on Saturday and Sunday afternoons in summer.

All Saints Church is distinguished by some wonderful flint 'flushwork' (stonework) on its tower, roof and nave. In the 1808 Baptist church is a plaque remembering John Noyes, burnt at the stake in 1557 for refusing to take Catholic vows. History relates that the villagers - with a single exception - dowsed their fires in protest. The one remaining fire, however, was all that was needed to light the stake.

A couple of miles east of Laxfield, **Heveningham Hall** is a fine Georgian mansion, a model of classical elegance designed by James Wyatt with lovely grounds by Capability Brown. As it runs through the grounds, the River Blyth widens into a lake.

WINGFIELD
6 miles NE of Eye off the B1118

🏠 Wingfield Old College

Wingfield Old College is one of the country's most historic seats of learning, founded in 1362 as a college for priests with a bequest from Sir John de Wingfield, Chief Staff Officer to the Black Prince. Sir John's wealth came from ransoming a French nobleman at the Battle of Poitiers in 1356. Surrendered to Henry VIII at the time of the Dissolution, the college became a farmhouse and is now in private hands. The façade is now Georgian, but the original medieval Great Hall still stands, and the college and its three acres of gardens are open to the public at weekends in summer. Attractions include regular artistic events and printing demonstrations.

The church of St Andrew was built as the collegiate church and has an extra-large chancel to accommodate the college choir. The church contains three really fine monuments: to Sir John (in stone); to Michael de la Pole, 2nd Earl of Suffolk (in wood); and

---

MEADOW COTTAGE LAXFIELD

Quinton House, Gorhams Mill Lane, Laxfield, Suffolk IP13 8DN
Tel: 01986 798345
e-mail: will.ayers@btinternet.com

The 19th century **Meadow Cottage** offers home-from-from comfort in the heart of this pretty village. Sympathetically refurbished in 2002 it has three bedrooms – a double, a twin and a single – and provides a lovely quiet base for exploring the area or for unwinding. The kitchen, which overlooks the garden and meadow beyond, provides plenty of room for the family to eat together and includes a wide range of modern amenities. The lounge, with its wood-burning stove, is the perfect place to relax after enjoying the delights of the Suffolk countryside, and in the summer the meadow provides a beautiful backdrop for a garden barbecue.

📖 stories and anecdotes   🐦 famous people   🎨 art and craft   ✍ entertainment and sport   🚶 walks

to John de la Pole, Duke of Suffolk (in alabaster). In the churchyard there is a 'hudd' – a shelter for the priest for use at the graveside in bad weather. On a hill outside the village are the imposing remains of a castle built by the 1st Earl.

FRESSINGFIELD
10 miles NE of Eye on the B1116

🏠 Ufford Hall

Fressingfield's first spiritual centre was the church of St Peter and St Paul. It has a superb hammerbeam roof and a lovely stone bell tower that was built in the 14th century. On one of the pews the initials A P are carved. These are believed to be the work of Alice de la Pole, Duchess of Norfolk and grand-daughter of Geoffrey Chaucer. Was this a work of art or a bout of vandalism brought on by a dull sermon?

At nearby **Ufford Hall** lived the Sancroft family, one of whom became Archbishop of Canterbury. He led the revolt of the bishops against James II and was imprisoned in the Tower of London. Released by William IV and sacked for refusing to swear the oath of allegiance, he returned home and is entombed by the south porch of the church. The village sign is a pilgrim and a donkey, recording that Fressingfield was a stopping place on the pilgrim route from Dunwich to Bury St Edmunds.

Ipswich

🏠 Christchurch Mansion   🏛 Ipswich Museum

🏛 Ipswich Transport Museum

🌿 Orwell Country Park

History highlights Ipswich as the birthplace of Cardinal Wolsey, but the story of Suffolk's county town starts very much earlier than that. It has been a port since the time of the Roman occupation, and by the 7th century the Anglo-Saxons had expanded it into the largest port in the country. King John granted a civic charter in 1200, confirming the townspeople's right to their own laws and administration, and for several centuries the town prospered as a port, exporting wool, textiles and agricultural products.

Thomas Wolsey arrived on the scene in 1475, the son of a wealthy butcher. Educated at Magdalen College, Oxford, he was ordained a priest in 1498 and rose quickly in influence, becoming chaplain to Henry VII and then Archbishop of York, a cardinal, and Lord Chancellor under Henry VIII. He

Christchurch Mansion, Ipswich

🏠 historic building   🏛 museum   🏛 historic site   🌿 scenic attraction   🌿 flora and fauna

was quite indispensable to the king and had charge of foreign policy as well as powerful sway over judicial institutions. He also managed to amass enormous wealth, enabling him to found a grammar school in Ipswich and Cardinal's College (later Christ Church) in Oxford. Wolsey had long been hated by certain nobles for his low birth and arrogance, and they were easily able to turn Henry against him when his attempts to secure an annulment from the Pope of the king's marriage to Catherine of Aragon met with failure. Stripped of most of his offices following a charge of overstepping his authority as a legate, he was later charged with treason, but died while travelling from York to London to face the king. His death put an end to his plans for the grammar school - all that remains now is a red-brick gateway.

When the cloth market fell into decline in the 17th century, a respite followed in the following century, when the town was a food-distribution port during the Napoleonic Wars. At the beginning of the 19th century the risk from silting was becoming acute at a time when trade was improving and industries were springing up. The Wet Dock, constructed in 1842, solved the silting problem and, with the railway arriving shortly after, Ipswich could once more look forward to a safe future. The Victorians were responsible for considerable development: symbols of their civic pride include the handsome Old Custom House by the Wet Dock, the Town Hall, and the splendid Tolly Cobbold brewery, rebuilt at the end of the 19th century, 150 years after

SALTHOUSE HARBOUR HOTEL

No 1 Neptune Quay, Ipswich, Suffolk IP4 1AX
Tel: 01473 226789 Fax: 01473 226927
e-mail: staying@salthouseharbour.co.uk
website: www.salthouseharbour.co.uk

Ipswich's **Salthouse Harbour Hotel** is an exciting four-star boutique townhouse hotel which has been converted from a Victorian warehouse. It has brought together the most up-to-date designers and artists to create 21st-century chic while retaining the building's traditional charm and character.

There are 43 spacious en suite guest bedrooms, including two glass fronted penthouse suites situated on the sixth-floor, which feature a separate seating area and stunning views across the marina and beyond. The design is a creative marriage of old and new, Eastern and Western.

The hotel also houses a wonderful art collection, with over 70 images – paintings, prints and photographs - by a selection of local and international artists which have already become a great talking point for visitors and guests. The décor and artwork evoke images of the building's distinguished past, when it was the first stop for goods making their way from exotic lands.

🎬 stories and anecdotes 🦆 famous people 🎨 art and craft 🎭 entertainment and sport 🚶 walks

brewing started on the site. Victorian enterprise depleted some of the older buildings, but a number survive, notably the house where Wolsey was born, the Ancient House with its wonderful pargetting, and the fine former Tudor merchants' houses which grace the town's historic waterfront, such as Isaac Lord's and The Neptune (the latter was once home of Thomas Eldred, who circumnavigated the world with Thomas Cavendish shortly after Drake). A dozen medieval churches remain, of which St Margaret's is the finest, boasting some very splendid flintwork and a double hammerbeam roof. Another, St Stephen's, today houses the town's Tourist Information Centre.

Christchurch Mansion is a beautiful Tudor home standing in 65 acres of attractive parkland, a short walk from the town centre. Furnished as an English country house, it contains a major collection of works by Constable and Gainsborough, as well as many other paintings, prints and sculptures by Suffolk artists from the 17th century onwards, and pottery, porcelain and fine period furniture.

Wolsey Art Gallery is a purpose-built space entered through Christchurch Mansion which features changing displays including touring and national exhibitions.

Ipswich Museum is in a Victorian building in the High Street. Displays include a natural history gallery, a wildlife gallery complete with a model of a mammoth, a reconstruction of a Roman villa, and replicas of Sutton Hoo treasures. A recent addition is a display of elaborately carved timbers from the homes of wealthy 17th century merchants. There is also a rolling programme of exciting temporary exhibitions, events and displays.

In a former trolleybus depot on Cobham Road is the **Ipswich Transport Museum**, a fascinating collection of vehicles, from prams to fire engines, all made or used around Ipswich. Among the more unusual exhibits are a monorail for transporting spoil, a road sweeper converted from a Morris car and the oldest trolleybus in the world (Ipswich no.2, built by Railless in 1923).

Ipswich's position at the head of the River Orwell has always influenced the town's fortunes; today, a stroll along the waterfront should be included in any visit. Tudor houses and medieval churches stand alongside stylish new apartments which overlook the new marinas. An art gallery and choice of eateries enhance the experience, and there are regular pub cruises, leaving the Ipswich waterfront and travelling the Orwell (recently voted one of the prettiest rivers in England) as far as Felixstowe harbour.

On the outskirts of town, signposted from Nacton Road, is **Orwell Country Park**, a 150-acre site of wood, heath and reedbeds by the Orwell estuary. At this point the river is crossed by the imposing Orwell Bridge, a graceful construction in pre-stressed concrete that was completed in 1982 and is not far short of a mile in length. Local nature reserves have been established around Ipswich and all the way up the Gipping Valley as far as Stowmarket.

Notables from the world of the arts with Ipswich connections include Thomas Gainsborough, who got his first major commissions here to paint portraits of local people; David Garrick, the renowned actor-manager, who made his debut here in 1741 as Aboan in Thomas Southerne's *Oroonoko*; and the peripatetic Charles Dickens, who stayed at the Great White Horse while still a young reporter with the *Morning Chronicle*. Soon afterwards, he featured the tavern in *The Pickwick Papers* as the place where Mr Pickwick wanders inadvertently into a lady's bedroom. Sir V S Pritchett was born in Ipswich, while Enid Blyton trained as a kindergarten teacher at Ipswich High School.

Around Ipswich

BRAMFORD
1 mile NW of Ipswich off the A14

Bramford has a pretty little church, St Mary's, with a 13th century stone screen. Elizabeth Mee, who played the church's first organ for 35 years, overcame the disability of being born blind. Bramford was once an important spot on the river route, when barges from Ipswich stopped to unload corn; the walls of the old lock are still visible. In the vicinity is Suffolk Water Park, where the lake welcomes canoeists and windsurfers.

NACTON
4 miles SE of Ipswich off the A14

🏠 Orwell Park House 🦆 Nacton Picnic Site

South of Nacton's medieval church lies **Orwell Park House**, which was built in the 18th century by Admiral Edward Vernon, sometime Member of Parliament for Ipswich. The admiral, who had won an important victory over the Spanish in the War of Jenkins Ear, was known to his men as 'Old Grog' because of his habit of wearing a cloak of coarse grogram cloth. His nickname passed into the language when he ordered that the rum ration dished out daily to sailors should be diluted with water to combat the

drunkenness that was rife in the service. That was in 1740, but this allotted ration of 'grog' was officially issued to sailors right up until 1970.

George Tomline bought Orwell Park House in 1857 and made it even more splendid, adding a conservatory, a ballroom and towers. He also changed the façade along handsome Georgian lines. The house became the setting for some of the grandest shooting parties ever seen in this part of the world, and such was the power of the Tomlines that they were able to move the village away from the house to its present site.

Nacton Picnic Site in Shore Lane (signposted from the village) commands wonderful views of the Orwell and is a prime spot in winter for birdwatchers. The birds feed very well off the mud flats

LEVINGTON
5 miles SE of Ipswich off the A14

A pretty village on the banks of the Orwell. Fisons established a factory here in 1956, and developed the now famous Levington Compost. On the foreshore below the village is an extensive marina which has brought a bustling air to the area. The coastal footpath along the bank of the Orwell leads across the nature reserve of Trimley Marshes and on to Felixstowe.

TRIMLEY ST MARY & TRIMLEY ST MARTIN
6 miles SE of Ipswich off the A14

🦆 Trimley Marshes

Twin villages with two churches in the same churchyard, famous Trimley residents have included the Cavendish family, whose best-known member was the adventurer Thomas

Cavendish. In 1590 he became the second man to sail round the world. Two years later he died while embarked on another voyage. He is depicted on the village sign. **Trimley Marshes** were created from farmland and comprise grazing marsh, reed beds and wetland that's home to an abundance of interesting plant life and many species of wildfowl, waders and migrant birds. Access is on foot from Trimley St Mary.

NEWBOURNE
7 miles E of Ipswich off the A12

A small miracle occurred here on the night of the hurricane of October 1987. One wall of the ancient St Mary's Church was blown out, and with it the stained glass, which shattered into fragments. One piece, showing the face of Christ, was found undamaged and was later incorporated into the rebuilt wall.

Two remarkable inhabitants of Newbourne were the Page brothers, who both stood over seven feet tall; they enjoyed a career touring the fairs, and are buried in Newbourne churchyard.

WALDRINGFIELD
7 miles E of Ipswich off the A12

Waldringfield lies on a particularly beautiful stretch of the Deben estuary, and the waterfront is largely given over to leisure boating and cruising. The quay was once busy with barges, many of them laden with coprolite. This fossilised dung, the forerunner of today's fertilisers, was found in great abundance in and around Waldringfield, and a number of exhausted pits can still be seen.

FELIXSTOWE
12 miles SE of Ipswich off the A14

Felixstowe Museum   Landguard Point

Until the early 17th century, Felixstowe was a little-known village - but it was the good Colonel Tomline of Orwell Park who put it on the map by creating a port to rival its near neighbour Harwich. He also started work on the Ipswich-Felixstowe railway (with a stop at Nacton for the guests of his grand parties), and 1887 saw the completion of both projects. Tomline also developed the resort aspects of Felixstowe, rivalling the amenities of Dovercourt, and when he died in 1887 most of his dreams had become reality. (He was, incidentally, cremated, one of the first in the county to be so disposed of in the modern era.) What he didn't live to see was the pier, opened in 1904 and still in use.

The town has suffered a number of ups and downs since that time, but continues to thrive as one of England's busiest ports, having been

MEMORIES – THE CARD & GIFT SHOP
The Square, Martlesham Heath, nr Ipswich, Suffolk IP5 3SL
Tel: 01473 626888

Memories – The Card & Gift Shop occupies a modern brick building on the Square at Martlesham Heath, on the A12 between Ipswich and Woodbridge. Owner Pamela Gale stocks a range of cards for all occasions and all ages – some 15,000 or so, probably the best selection in the whole of Suffolk. Shoppers will also find an array of gifts and soft toys (many with an animal theme), photo frames, locally made pottery, kitchenware, therapy oils and much, much more.

historic building   museum   historic site   scenic attraction   flora and fauna

much extended in the 1960s. The resort is strung out round a wide, gently curving bay, where the long seafront road is made even prettier with trim lawns and gardens.

The Martello tower is a noted landmark, as is the Pier, which was once long enough to merit an electric tramway. It was shortened as a security measure during the Second World War. All kinds of attractions are provided for holidaymakers, including one very unusual one. This is the Felixstowe Water Clock, a curious piece assembled from dozens of industrial bits and pieces.

The original fishing hamlet from which the Victorian resort was developed lies beyond a golf course north of the town. This is Felixstowe Ferry, a cluster of holiday homes, an inn, a boatyard, fishing sheds and a Martello tower. The sailing club is involved mainly with dinghy racing, and the whole place becomes a hive of activity during the class meetings. A ferry takes foot passengers (plus bicycles) across to Bawdsey.

At the southernmost tip of the peninsula is **Landguard Point**, where a nature reserve supports rare plants and migrating birds.

Just north on this shingle bank is Landguard Fort, built in 1718 (replacing an earlier construction) to protect Harwich harbour. It is now home to **Felixstowe Museum**. The museum is actually housed in the Ravelin Block (1878), which was used as a mine storage depot by the army when a mine barrier was laid across the Orwell during the First World War. A fascinating variety of exhibits includes local history, model aircraft and model paddle steamers, Roman coins and the history of the fort itself, which was the scene of the last invasion of English soil, by the Dutch in 1667. Beyond the fort is an excellent viewing point for watching the comings and goings of the ships.

FRESTON
3 miles S of Ipswich off the B1080

Freston is an ancient village on the south bank of the Orwell, worth visiting for some fine old buildings and some curiosities. The most curious and best known of these buildings is the six-storey Tudor tower by the river in Freston Park (it's actually best viewed from across the river). This red-brick house, built around 1570, has just six rooms, one per storey. It might be a folly, but it was probably put up as a lookout tower to warn of enemies sailing up the river. The nicest theory is that it was built for Ellen, daughter of Lord Freston, to study a different subject each day, progressing floor by floor up the tower: charity on the ground floor, then tapestry weaving, music, ancient languages, English literature, painting and astrology (and with Sundays off presumably). A 4,000-year-old archaeological site at Freston was revealed by aerial photography.

WOOLVERSTONE
4 miles S of Ipswich on the B1456

Dating back to the Bronze Age, Woolverstone has a large marina along the banks of the Orwell. One of the buildings in the complex is Cat House, where it is said that a stuffed white cat placed in the window would be the all-clear sign for smugglers. Woolverstone House was originally St Peter's Home for 'Fallen Women', run by nuns. It was designed by Sir Edwin Lutyens and has its own chapel and bell tower.

TATTINGSTONE
4 miles S of Ipswich off the A137

🎭 Tattingstone Wonder

The Tattingstone Wonder, visible from the A137 road between Tattingstone and Stutton,

Tattingstone Wonder

destroyed by a flying bomb in 1944. In the same parish is the tiny riverside community of **Pin Mill**, a well-known beauty spot and sailing centre. The river views are particularly lovely at this point, and it's also a favourite place for woodland and heathland walks. Pin Mill was once a major manufacturer of barges, and those imposing craft can still be seen, sharing the river with sailing boats and pleasure craft. Each year veteran barges

looks like a church from the front, but it isn't. It was built by Edward White, a local landowner, to provide accommodation for estate workers. He presumably preferred to look at a church from his mansion than some plain little cottages. Tattingstone lies at the western edge of Alton Water, a vast man-made lake created as a reservoir in the late 1970s. A footpath runs round the perimeter, and there's a wildlife sanctuary. On the water itself all sorts of leisure activities are on offer, including angling, sailing and windsurfing.

gather for a race that starts here, at Buttermans Bay, and ends at Harwich. Arthur Ransome, author of *Swallows and Amazons*, stayed here and had boats built to his specifications. His *We Didn't Mean to Go to Sea* starts aboard a yacht mooring here.

The local hostelry is the 17th century Butt & Oyster, much visited, much painted and one of the best-known pubs in the county. To the east of the Quay is Cliff Plantation, an ancient coppiced wood of alder and oak.

CHELMONDISTON
5 miles S of Ipswich on the B1456

🦢 Pin Mill

The church here is modern, but incorporates some parts of the original, which was

STUTTON
6 miles S of Ipswich on the B1080

The elongated village of Stutton lies on the southern edge of Alton Water. The *Domesday Book* records six manor houses standing here, and there are still some grand properties down

🏠 historic building   🏛 museum   🏚 historic site   🦢 scenic attraction   🌱 flora and fauna by the Stour. St Peter's Church stands isolated overlooking Holbrook Bay, and a footpath from the church leads all the way along the river to Shotley Gate. A little way north, on the B1080, Holbrook is a large village with a brook at the bottom of the hill. Water from the brook once powered Alton Mill, a weatherboarded edifice on a site occupied by watermills for more than 900 years. The mill is now a restaurant.

ERWARTON
6 miles S of Ipswich off the B1456

Erwarton Hall

An impressive red-brick Jacobean gatehouse with a rounded arch, buttresses and pinnacles is part of **Erwarton Hall**, the family home of the Calthorpes. Anne Boleyn was the niece of Philip Calthorpe, and visited as a child and as queen. Just before her execution Anne apparently requested that her heart be buried in the

family vault at St Mary's Church. A casket in the shape of a heart was found there in 1836, but when opened contained only dust that could not be positively identified. The casket was resealed and laid in the Lady Chapel.

SHOTLEY
8 miles S of Ipswich on the B1456

Right at the end of the peninsula, with the Orwell on one side and the Stour on the other, Shotley is best known as the home of *HMS Ganges*, where generations of sailors received their training. The main feature is the 142-foot mast, up which trainees would shin at the passing-out ceremony. A small museum records the history of the establishment from 1905 to 1976, when it became a police academy. At the very tip of the peninsula is a large marina where a classic boat festival is an annual occasion.

HINTLESHAM
7 miles W of Ipswich on the A1071

Hintlesham's glory is a magnificent hall dating from the 1570s, when it was the home of the Timperley family. It was considerably altered during the 18th century, when it acquired its splendid Georgian façade. For some years the hall was owned by the celebrated chef Robert Carrier, who developed it into the county's leading restaurant. It still functions as a high-class hotel and restaurant.

MONKS ELEIGH
16 miles W of Ipswich on the A1141

The setting of thatched cottages, a 14th century church and a pump on the village green is so traditional that Monks

Village Pump, Monks Eleigh

stories and anecdotes   famous people   art and craft   entertainment and sport   walks

CORNCRAFT GIFT SHOP & TEA ROOM

Monks Eleigh, nr Hadleigh, Suffolk IP7 7AY
Tel: 01449 740456 Fax: 01449 741665
e-mail: rwgage@lineone.net
website: www.corncraft.co.uk

Some of the talented and creative artists and craftspeople display their wares at **Corncraft**, which occupies farm buildings converted after farming activities ceased 20 years ago.

The two shops are filled with a wonderful array of gifts and homeware that includes stationery and cards, leather purses, bags and belts, pottery and ceramics, cosmetics, scented and plain wax candles, preserves, traditional corn dollies and dried and silk flowers.

In the bright, airy and spotless pine-furnished tea room, a selection of cakes, biscuits and hot and cold meals is served seven days a week.

Home-cured Suffolk ham, quiches, pasta bakes and chilli are just some of the most popular dishes. Monks Eleigh, with its thatched cottages, 14th century church and old pump on the village green, is a charming place to visit, and the presence of Corncraft must be added to the places not to be missed on a visit here.

Eleigh was regularly used on railway posters as a lure to this wonderful part of the country.

BILDESTON

14 miles W of Ipswich on the B1115

More fine old buildings here, including timber-framed cottages with overhanging upper floors. The Church of St Mary has a superb carved door and a splendid hammerbeam roof.

A tablet inside the church commemorates Captain Edward Rotherham, Commander of the *Royal Sovereign* at the Battle of Trafalgar. He died in Bildeston while staying with a friend, and is buried in the churchyard.

WATTISHAM HALL HOLIDAY COTTAGES

The Green, Wattisham, nr Stowmarket, Suffolk IP7 7JX
Tel: 01449 740240 Fax: 01449 744535
e-mail: jhsquirr@farming.co.uk website: www.wattishamhall.co.uk

On a 350-acre working arable farm in a quiet but accessible setting, the Squirrell family offer an excellent base for tourists and holidaymakers. **Wattisham Hall Holiday Cottages** comprise beautifully renovated beamed barns tucked away in a quiet courtyard behind Wattisham Hall. The three self-catering cottages, sleeping 4, 7 and 8 guests, combine traditional structure and ambience with modern comfort and amenities. Shared facilities include a laundry room, games room and children's play area. The cottages are non-smoking. Shooting and photographic breaks can be arranged.

 historic building   museum   historic site  scenic attraction flora and fauna

Constable Country

England's greatest landscape painter was born at East Bergholt in 1776 and remained at heart a Suffolk man throughout his life. His father, Golding Constable, was a wealthy man who owned both Flatford Mill and Dedham Mill, the latter on the Essex side of the Stour. The river was a major source of inspiration to the young John Constable, and his constant involvement in country matters gave him an expert knowledge of the elements and a keen eye for the details of nature.

Flatford Mill

He was later to declare 'I associate my careless boyhood with all that lies on the banks of the Stour. Those scenes made me a painter and I am grateful.' His interest in painting developed early and was fostered by his friendship with John Dunthorne, a local plumber and amateur artist. Constable became a probationer at the Royal Academy Schools in 1799, and over the following years developed the technical skills to match his powers of observation. He painted the occasional portrait and even attempted a couple of religious works, but he concentrated almost entirely on the scenes that he knew and loved as a boy.

The most significant works of the earlier years were the numerous sketches in oil which were forerunners of the major paintings of Constable's mature years. He had exhibited at the Royal Academy every year since 1802, but it was not until 1817 that the first of his important canvases, *Flatford Mill on the River Stour*, was hung. This was succeeded by the six large paintings which became his best-known

works. These were all set on a short stretch of the Stour, and all except *The Hay Wain* show barges at work. These broad, flat-bottomed craft were displayed in scenes remarkable for the realism of the colours, the effects of light and water and, above all, the beautiful depiction of clouds. His fellow-artist Fuseli declared that whenever he saw a Constable painting he felt the need to reach for his coat and umbrella. Though more realistic than anything that preceded them, Constable's paintings were never lacking soul, and his work was much admired by the painters of the French Romantic School.

Two quotations from the man himself reveal much about his aims and philosophy:

"In a landscape I want to give one brief moment caught from fleeting time a lasting and sober existence."
"I never saw any ugly thing in my life; in fact, whatever may be the shape of an object, light, shade or perspective can always make it beautiful."

At the time of his death in 1837, Constable's reputation at home was relatively modest, though he had many followers and admirers in France. Awareness and understanding of his unique talent grew only in the ensuing years, so that, today, his place as England's foremost landscape painter is rarely disputed.

Suffolk has produced many other painters of distinction. Thomas Gainsborough, born in Sudbury in 1727, was an artist of great versatility, innovative and instinctive, and equally at home with portraits and landscapes. He earned his living for a while from portrait painting in Ipswich before making a real name for himself in Bath. His relations with the Royal Academy were often stormy, however, culminating, in 1784, in a major dispute over the height at which a painting should be hung. He withdrew his intended hangings from the exhibition and never again showed at the Royal Academy.

A man of equally indomitable spirit was Sir Alfred Munnings, born at Mendham in the north of Suffolk in 1878. The last of the great sporting painters in the tradition of Stubbs and Marshall, Munnings was outspoken in his opinions on modern art. In 1949, as outgoing President of the Royal Academy, he launched an animated attack on modern art as 'silly daubs' and 'violent blows at nothing'. The occasion was broadcast on the radio; in response many listeners complained about the 'strong language' Munnings had used. In 1956, Munnings jolted the art world again by describing that year's Summer Exhibition as 'bits of nonsense' hung on the wall.

Mary Beale, born at Barrow in 1633, was a noted portrait painter and copyist; some of her work has been attributed to Lely and Kneller, and it was rumoured that Lely was in love with her.

Philip Wilson Steer (1860-1942) was among the most distinguished of the many painters who were attracted to Walberswick. He studied in Paris and acquired the reputation of being the best of the English impressionist painters.

The Suffolk tradition of painting continues to this day, with many artists drawn to this part of the county. While nowadays crowds congregate throughout the Stour valley at summer weekends, at other times the tranquillity and loveliness are just as unmatched as they were in Constable's day.

CAPEL ST MARY
6 miles SW of Ipswich on the A12

Constable sketched here, but modern building has more or less overrun the old. A feature of the Church of St Mary is the 'weeping chancel' - a slight kink between the nave and the chancel that is meant to signify Christ's head leaning to the right on the cross.

BRANTHAM
8 miles SW of Ipswich on the A137

 Cattawade Picnic Site

Also known as 'Burnt Village' – possibly because it was sacked during a Danish invasion 1,000 years ago – Brantham's Church of St Michael owns one of the only two known religious paintings by Constable, *Christ Blessing the Children*, which he executed in the style of the American painter Benjamin West. It is kept in safety in Ipswich Museum. Just off the junction of the A137 and the B1070 is **Cattawade Picnic Site**, a small area on the edge of the Stour estuary. It's a good spot for birdwatching, and redshanks, lapwings and oystercatchers all breed on the well-known Cattawade Marshes. Fishing and canoeing are available, and there are public footpaths to Flatford Mill.

 historic building   museum   historic site   scenic attraction   flora and fauna

EAST BERGHOLT

8 miles SW of Ipswich on the B1070

- Stour House
- Flatford Mill
- Willy Lot's Cottage
- St Mary's Church
- Constable Country Trail

Narrow lanes lead to this picturesque and much visited little village. The **Constable Country Trail** starts here, where the painter was born, and passes through Flatford Mill and on to Dedham in Essex. The actual house where he was born no longer stands, but the site is marked by a plaque on the fence of its successor, a private house called Constables. A little further along Church Street is Moss Cottage, which Constable once used as his studio. **St Mary's** is one of the many grand churches built with the wealth brought by the wool trade. This one should have been even grander, with a tower to rival that of Dedham across the river.

The story goes that Cardinal Wolsey pledged the money to build the tower, but fell from grace before the funds were forthcoming. The tower got no further than did his college in Ipswich, and a bellcage constructed in the churchyard as a temporary house for the bells became their permanent home, which it remains to this day. In this unique timber-framed structure the massive bells hang upside down and are rung by hand by pulling on the wooden shoulder stocks - an arduous task, as the five bells are among the heaviest in England, weighing in at over four tons.

The church is naturally something of a shrine to Constable, his family and his friends. There are memorial windows to the artist and to his beloved wife Maria Bicknell, who bore him seven children and whose early death was an enormous blow to him. His parents, to whom he was clearly devoted, and his old friend Willy Lot, whose cottage is featured famously in *The Hay Wain*, are buried in the churchyard.

East Bergholt has an interesting mix of houses, some dating back as far as the 14th century. One of the grandest is **Stour House**, once the home of Randolph Churchill. Its gardens are open to the public, as is East Bergholt Place Garden on the B1070.

A leafy lane leads south from the village to the Stour, where two of Constable's favourite subjects, **Flatford Mill** and **Willy Lot's Cottage**, both looking much as they did when he painted them, are to be found. Neither is open to the public, and the brick watermill is

Willy Lot's Cottage

run as a residential field study centre.

Nearby, Bridge Cottage at Flatford is a restored 16th century building housing a Constable display, a tea room and a shop. There's also a restored dry dock, and the whole area is a delight for walkers; it is easy to see how Constable drew constant inspiration from the wonderful riverside setting.

NAYLAND
14 miles SW of Ipswich on the B1087

On a particularly beautiful stretch of the Stour in Dedham Vale, Nayland has charming colour-washed cottages in narrow, winding streets, as well as two very fine 15th century buildings in Alston Court and the Guildhall. Abels Bridge, originally built of wood in the 15th century by wealthy merchant John Abel, divides Suffolk from Essex. In the 16th

century a hump bridge replaced it, allowing barges to pass beneath. The current bridge carries the original keystone, bearing the initial A. In the Church of St James stands an altarpiece by Constable entitled *Christ Blessing the Bread and Wine*.

One mile west of Nayland, at the end of a track off the Bures road, stands the Norman Church of St Mary at Wissington. The church has a number of remarkable features, including several 13th century wall paintings, a finely carved 12th century doorway and a tiebeam and crown post roof.

STRATFORD ST MARY
10 miles SW of Ipswich off the A12

🏠 Ancient House and the Priest's House

Another of Constable's favourite locations, Stratford St Mary is the most southerly village

---

JOSÉPHINE

3 High Street, Nayland, Suffolk CO6 4JE
Tel: 01206 263350　Fax: 01206 263277
e-mail: frances@josephine.uk.com
website: www.josephineinteriors.co.uk

In elegant period premises on the main street of Nayland, **Joséphine** specialises in French and French-themed products, drawing its main inspiration from the life and exquisite taste in décor and fashion of Napoleon's wife Joséphine. The collection assembled by owner Frances Lamb captures the elegance and simplicity of that age. Quality is paramount throughout a carefully sourced range that includes timeless furniture and fabrics that look equally at home in a contemporary or classical setting, home accessories, faience country china, face and body preparations, home fragrances and jewellery. Several designs were developed exclusively by Frances, including printed and plain linens, striking florals and natural textures.

Joséphine is one of the few outlets in the UK to stock paints from the Belgian Flamant Company. A large in-house curtain department produces handmade curtains and blinds; curtain designs for period properties are a speciality, and Joséphine has dressed many houses in the UK and overseas. Tiebacks and poles come at prices to suit all pockets, along with finials based on ideas found in French chateaux. A curtain design and fitting service is available.

🏠 historic building　　🏛 museum　　🏛 historic site　　♨ scenic attraction　　🌿 flora and fauna

HALL FARM SHOP & CAFÉ-RESTAURANT

Stratford St Mary, Suffolk CO7 6LS
Tel: 01206 322572
website: www.hallfarmshop.co.uk

The Barrie family have farmed at Stratford St Mary for three generations and **Hall Farm Shop** was opened in 2003 primarily to sell home produced beef, lamb and potatoes. This mini food hall now also sells other local meat and poultry, fresh fruit and vegetables, pies and pastries, fresh bread and dairy produce. An excellent deli section sells English and Continental cheeses, fish, and a dozen types of olives. Of course there are jams and preserves, pickles and sauces, homemade cakes, and desserts. A variety of fine wines and local beers and ciders are also available along with local chocolates, unusual gifts and greeting cards. A real farm with real food as their logo promises. Well worth a visit.

A café-restaurant is due to open in Summer 2006. It will serve a range of snacks and light meals incorporating home-produced and local ingredients. There will be a farm courtyard where animals will be on view.

in Suffolk. *The Young Waltonians* and *A House in Water Lane* (the house still stands today) are the best known of his works set in this picturesque spot. The village church is typically large and imposing, with parts dating back to 1200. At the top of the village are two splendid half-timbered cottages called the **Ancient House** and the **Priest's House**. Stratford was once on the main coaching route to London, and the largest of the four pubs had stabling for 200 horses. It is claimed that Henry Williamson, author of *Tarka the Otter*, saw his first otter here.

STOKE BY NAYLAND

12 miles SW of Ipswich on the B1087

🏠 Church of St Mary

The drive from Nayland reveals quite stunning

views, and the village itself has a large number of listed buildings. The magnificent **Church of St Mary**, with its 120-foot tower, dominates the scene from its hilltop position. This church also appears in more than one Constable painting, the most famous showing the church lit up by a rainbow. William Dowsing destroyed 100 'superstitious pictures' here in his Puritan purges, but plenty of fine work is still to be seen, including several monumental brasses.

The Guildhall is another very fine building, now private residences but in the 16th century a busy centre of trade and commerce. When the wool trade declined, so did the importance of the Guildhall, and for a time this noble building saw service as a workhouse.

The decline of the cloth trade in East

St Mary's Church, Stoke by Nayland

a stone spire and the very early bricks used in its construction. The builders used not only these bricks, but also tiles and tufa, a soft, porous stone much used in Italy. In the grounds of the hall stand the remains of a 'Gospel Oak' said to have been 1,300 years old when it collapsed in 1953. Legend has it that Saxon missionaries preached beneath it in the 7th century; an open-air service is still held here annually. The rectory is said to be one of the most haunted, with phenomena including a presence in the attic and a voice calling 'John'. A former rector is said to drive around the village in a carriage drawn by a headless horse.

Anglia had several causes. Fierce competition came from the northern and western weaving industries, which generally had easier access to water supplies for fulling; the wars on the continent of Europe led to the closure of some trading routes and markets; and East Anglia had no supplies of the coal that was used to drive the new steam-powered machinery. In some cases, as at Sudbury, weaving or silk took over as smaller industries.

POLSTEAD
11 miles SW of Ipswich off the B1068

Polstead is a very pretty village set in wooded, hilly countryside, with thatched, colour-washed cottages around the green and a wide duck pond at the bottom of the hill. Standing on a rise above the pond are Polstead Hall, a handsome Georgian mansion, and the 12th century Church of St Mary. The church has two features not found elsewhere in Suffolk –

Polstead has two other claims to fame. One is for Polstead Blacks, a particularly tasty variety of cherry which was cultivated in orchards around the village and which used to be honoured with an annual fair. The other is much less agreeable, for it was here that the notorious Red Barn murder hit the headlines in 1827. A young girl called Maria Marten, daughter of the local molecatcher, disappeared with William Corder, a farmer's son who was the girl's lover and father of her child. It was at first thought that they had eloped, but Maria's stepmother dreamt three times that she had been murdered and buried in a red barn. A search of the barn soon revealed this to be true. Corder was tracked down to Middlesex, tried and found guilty of Maria's murder and hanged. His skin was used to bind a copy of the trial proceedings and this, together with his scalp, is on display at Moyse's Hall in Bury St Edmunds. The incident aroused a great deal of interest; today's visitors to the village will still find reminders of the ghastly deed: the thatched cottage where Maria lived stands, in what is now called Marten's Lane, as does the farm where the murderer lived, now called Corder's Farm.

BOXFORD
12 miles W of Ipswich on the A1071

A gloriously unspoilt weaving village, surrounded by the peaceful water meadows of the River Box, Boxford's St Mary's Church dates back to the 14th century. Its wooden north porch is one of the oldest of its kind in the country. In the church is a touching brass in memory of David Byrde, son of the rector, who died a baby in 1606. At the other end of

the continuum is Elizabeth Hyam, four times a widow, who died in her 113th year.

EDWARDSTONE
14 miles W of Ipswich off the A1071

Just to the north of Boxford and close to Edwardstone Hall and the Temple Bar Gate House, Edwardstone is now a 700-acre estate originally home to the Winthrop family. Winthrop was born in Edwardstone and emigrated to the New World, eventually becoming Governor of Massachusetts.

BURES
17 miles W of Ipswich on the B1508

At this point the River Stour turns sharply to the east, creating a natural boundary between Suffolk and Essex. The little village of Bures straddles the river, lying partly in each county. Bures St Mary in Suffolk is where the church

is, overlooked by houses of brick and half-timbering.

Bures wrote itself very early into the history books when on Christmas Day AD855 it is thought that Edmund the Martyr, the Saxon king, was crowned at the age of 15 in the Chapel of St Stephen. For some time after that momentous occasion, Bures was the capital seat of the East Anglian kings.

Bures also has a long connection with the Waldegrave family, possibly from as far back

Bures Mill

as Chaucer's day. One of the Waldegrave memorials shows graphically the results of a visitation by Dowsing and the Puritan iconoclasts: all the figures of the kneeling children have had their hands cut off.

Sudbury

🏠 Gainsborough's House

Sudbury is another wonderful town, the largest of the 'wool towns' and still home to a number of weaving concerns. Unlike Lavenham, Sudbury kept its industry because it was a port, and the result is a much more varied architectural picture. The surrounding countryside is some of the loveliest in Suffolk, and the River Stour is a further plus, with launch trips and fishing available.

Sudbury boasts three medieval churches, but what most visitors make a beeline for is **Gainsborough's House** on Gainsborough Street. The painter Thomas Gainsborough was born here in 1727 in the house built by his father John. More of the artist's work is displayed in this Georgian-fronted house than in any other gallery, and there is also assorted 18th century memorabilia and furnishings. A changing programme of contemporary art exhibitions includes fine art, photography and sculpture, highlighting East Anglian artists in particular. A bronze statue of Gainsborough stands in the square.

About those churches: All Saints dates from the 15th century and has a glorious carved tracery pulpit and screens; 14th century St Gregory's is notable for a wonderful medieval

PLAIN JANE

17 North Street, Sudbury, Suffolk CO10 1RB
Tel: 01787 313759 Fax: 01787 466837
website: www.plainjaneinteriors.co.uk

Owner Jane Thompson has been involved in interior design for 15 years and opened her shop in Sudbury in 2004. **Plain Jane** is a selected outlet for the popular Kath Kidston range of interior accessories, part of the extensive and wide-ranging stock displayed to excellent effect in the brightly lit shop. A comprehensive selection of giftware from Sweden, France, Holland and Denmark is backed up by many other ideas for gifts or the home, including colourful pottery from Gabriella Miller, Arran Aromatic toiletries, Maxwell & Williams all-white porcelain tableware and greeting cards handmade by Jane herself.

Among larger items are Scandinavian-style tables, chairs, chests and cupboards. Jane has recently opened a dedicated interior design area within the shop. A public car park, with the first three hours free, is a couple of minutes' walk from the shop, so Plain Jane's customers have plenty of time to browse at leisure.

🏠 historic building   🏛 museum   🏚 historic site   ⚘ scenic attraction   🌱 flora and fauna

font; and St Peter's has some marvellous painted screen panels and a piece of 15th century embroidered velvet.

Other buildings of interest are the Victorian Corn Exchange, now a library, Salter's Hall, a 15th century timbered house, and the Quay Theatre, a thriving centre for the arts.

Around Sudbury

HADLEIGH
12 miles E of Sudbury on the A1071

🏛 Guildhall

The old and not-so-old blend harmoniously in a variety of architectural styles in Hadleigh. Timber-framed buildings, often with elaborate

plasterwork, stand in the long main street as a reminder of the prosperity generated by the wool trade in the 14th to 16th centuries, and there are also some fine houses from the Regency and Victorian periods. The 15th century **Guildhall** has two overhanging storeys, and together with the Deanery Tower and the church, makes for a magnificent trio of huge appeal and contrasting construction – timber for the Guildhall, brick for the tower and flint for the church.

Guthrun, the Danish leader who was captured by Alfred and pardoned on condition that he became a Christian, made Hadleigh his HQ and lived here for 12 years. He was buried in the church, then a wooden construction but subsequently twice rebuilt. In the south chapel

---

CINNAMON STUDIOS - VINTAGE ART

Hadleigh, Suffolk IP7 5RZ
Tel: 01473 823683
e-mail: niki@cinnamonstudios.com
website: www.lovevintageart.com

Cinnamon Studios is the brainchild of artist and writer Niki Jackson, who does most of her business online. Working from home, she specialises in hand-crafted country and vintage home décor, and among the most sought after lines are vintage greeting cards, framed paintings on calico, notepaper sets with original hand-drawn designs, art and sketch books and a wonderful selection of pot-pourri, including cinnamon, spiced orange and vanilla nut.

THE ORANGERIE

Victoria House, Market Place, Hadleigh,
Suffolk IP7 5DL
Tel: 01473 823600

On the market place in Hadleigh, **The Orangerie** is an attractive café open throughout the day seven days a week. Contemporary in décor and furnishings, it offers a traditional range of dishes including home-made cakes, pastries and puddings and hot and cold savouries on a daily changing menu. Owner Tony Haynes sources most of the ingredients locally, some from Hadleigh's Friday market. Excellent Italian coffee and speciality teas accompany the food.

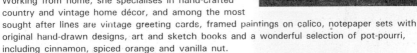

🎭 stories and anecdotes   🕊 famous people   ✎ art and craft   ✐ entertainment and sport   🚶 walks

AMERICAN PINE & HARDWOOD FURNITURE CO. LTD.

Buyright, Hadleigh, Suffolk IP7 5EW
Tel/Fax: 01473 828668
website: www.americanpine.co.uk

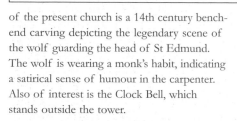

A brightly lit space inside the Buyright Superstore is the sales area for the **American Pine & Hardwood Furniture Co.Ltd.** A wide selection of high-quality pine and hardwood furniture includes an unusual and attractive range of tables, chairs and occasional furniture in a choice of colours. Pine pieces can also be made to measure. The display also includes a full range of solid oak furniture, including cabinets, desks, mirrors and carved wooden figures.

of the present church is a 14th century bench-end carving depicting the legendary scene of the wolf guarding the head of St Edmund. The wolf is wearing a monk's habit, indicating a satirical sense of humour in the carpenter. Also of interest is the Clock Bell, which stands outside the tower.

A famous resident of Hadleigh was the rector Dr Rowland Taylor, who was burnt at the stake on Aldham Common for refusing to hold a mass. A large stone, inscribed and dated 1555, marks the spot.

There are two good walks from Hadleigh, the first being along the Brett with access over

VINTAGE 2 VOGUE

White Horse House, Stone Street, Hadleigh,
Suffolk IP7 6DN
Tel/Fax: 01473 823234
e-mail: info@vintage2vogue.co.uk
website: www.vintage2vogue.co.uk

Vintage 2 Vogue is a unique interiors shop a short drive north of Hadleigh on the A1141 Lavenham road. Kate Bolton put her background in antiques to excellent use when she opened the shop in 2005. V2V sells both antiques and modern designer furniture under one roof, sharing the common qualities of beauty, fine design and first-class workmanship. **Vintage** is based in a 17th century former inn, which provides the perfect backdrop for a full range of antiques from 17th century oak to Victorian and Edwardian furniture. The shop also specialises in fossils, from pocket money shark's teeth to large collector's pieces.

Other items include coffee tables, vases and candleholders made from fossilised stone, artwork, cushions, lamps, jewellery and kitchenware....the list is almost endless. **Vogue** stocks contemporary designs displayed in a stunning modern setting. V2V is one of the few UK distributors of Venetian glass chandeliers, which can be made to order in any size, colour and shape. Everyone, from private house-owners to commercial designers, will find something of interest at V2V, which is open from 10am to 5pm on Tuesday, Thursday, Friday and Saturday.

🏛 historic building   🏛 museum   🏛 historic site   🐍 scenic attraction   🌿 flora and fauna

medieval Toppesfield Bridge. The other is a walk along the disused railway line between Hadleigh and Raydon through peaceful, picturesque countryside.

At Raydon a few buildings survive from the wartime base of the 353rd, 357th and 358th Fighter Groups of the USAAF.

Two miles east of Hadleigh is Wolves Wood, an RSPB reserve with woodland nature trails - and no wolves!

KERSEY

11 miles E of Sudbury off the A1141

Water Splash

The ultimate Suffolk picture-postcard village, Kersey boasts a wonderful collection of timbered merchants' houses and weavers' cottages with paint and thatch. The main street has a **Water Splash**, which, along with the 700-year-old Bell Inn, has featured in many films and travelogues. The Church of St Mary, which overlooks the village from its hilltop position, is of massive proportions, testimony to the wealth that came with the wool and cloth industry. Kersey's speciality was a coarse twill broadcloth much favoured for greatcoats and army uniforms. Headless angels and mutilated carvings are reminders of the Puritans' visit to the church, though some treasures survive, including the ornate flintwork of the 15th century south porch.

Traditional craftsmanship can still be seen in practice at the Kersey Pottery, which sells

Kersey Watersplash

many items of stoneware plus paintings by Suffolk artists.

CHELSWORTH

10 miles NE of Sudbury off the A1141

Chelsworth is an unspoilt delight in the lovely valley of the River Brett, which is crossed by a little double hump-backed bridge. The timbered houses and thatched cottages look much the same as when they were built, and every year the villagers open their gardens to the public.

BRENT ELEIGH

8 miles NE of Sudbury off the A1141

The church at Brent Eleigh, on a side road off

The Waldingfields

Distance: *3.1 miles (4.83 kilometres)*

Typical time: *60 mins*

Height gain: *15 metres*

Map: *Explorer 196*

Walk: *www.walkingworld.com   ID:1876*

Contributor: *Brian and Anne Sandland*

To reach the church at Great Waldingfield turn south east off the B1115.

DESCRIPTION:

This walk visits two churches and quaint old Suffolk villages. There are picturesque cottages and excellent paths, tracks and lanes on the way. The walk can be combined with another which starts from Great Waldingfield Church and visits Acton as well as reaching the outskirts of Little Waldingfield.

FEATURES:

Pub, Church, Wildlife, Birds, Flowers, Great Views, Butterflies, Woodland

WALK DIRECTIONS:

1 | Starting from the church take the road signposted No through road - Footpath to Little Waldingfield. After a descent on the track to Hole Farm look for a signposted footpath on the right just before the farm.

2 | Turn right and before long follow a stream beside a wood (left), then take a signposted footpath left over a bridge and through the wood.

3 | After the wood cross a footbridge, then continue beside a very large field (on your left). When you reach a lane by the road to Archers Farm turn left along it. Pass the church at Little Waldingfield then turn left at the T-junction with the B 1115 (past the Swan Inn).

4 | Just beyond the thatched cottage The Grange (left) take the right hand of two signposted footpaths off left. At the far end of the field cross a footbridge, then follow signs (and a concrete roadway) around Hole Farm before reaching the lane you used at the start of your walk and ascending it to reach Great Waldingfield church again.

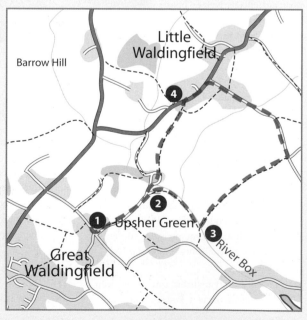

NEWMANS HALL FARM

Monks Eleigh Road, Little Waldingfield, nr Sudbury,
Suffolk CO10 0SY
Tel: 01787 249111 Fax: 01787 210125
e-mail: microplant@btclick.com

Reached down a private drive off the B1115, **Newmans Hall Farm** provides high-quality bed & breakfast accommodation in a quiet rural setting. The architect-designed house, which was built in 1963, is run by resident owners Anne Miller and her son Charles, whose family has lived in the area for more than 50 years.

The three guest bedrooms are notably warm and comfortable, and like the residents' lounge, are decorated and furnished to a very high standard. The house has a non-smoking policy.

Guests have the use of a tennis court and an indoor heated swimming pool, and the gardens and grounds are pleasant spots for a gentle stroll. This is great walking country, and a scenic three-mile marked walk takes in two churches, picturesque cottages and the villages of Little Waldingfield and Great Waldingfield. The area is also rich in history, and the towns of Long Melford, Lavenham, Hadleigh and Sudbury areall within an easy drive of Newmans Hall Farm.

---

the A1141, is remarkable for a number of quite beautiful ancient wall paintings, discovered during maintenance work as recently as 1960. The most striking and moving of the paintings is one of the Crucifixion.

LAVENHAM

6 miles N of Sudbury on the A1141

🏛 Guildhall 🏛 Little Hall 🏛 Priory

🏛 Church of St Peter & St Paul

An absolute gem of a town, the most complete and original of the medieval 'wool towns', with crooked timbered and whitewashed buildings lining the narrow streets. From the 14th to the 16th centuries Lavenham flourished as one of the leading wool and cloth-making centres in the land. With the decline of that industry, however, the

prosperous times soon came to an end. It is largely due to the fact that Lavenham found no replacement industry that so much of its medieval character remains: there was simply not enough money for the rebuilding and development programmes that changed many other towns, often for the worse. The medieval street pattern still exists, complete with market place and market cross.

More than 300 of Lavenham's buildings are officially listed as being of architectural and historical interest, and none of them is finer than the **Guildhall**. This superb 16th century timbered building was originally the meeting place of the Guild of Corpus Christi, an organisation that regulated the production of wool. It now houses exhibitions of local history and the wool trade, and has a walled garden with a special area devoted to dye plants. **Little Hall** is hardly less remarkable, a

THE WILDLIFE ART GALLERY

97 High Street, Lavenham,
Suffolk CO10 9PZ
Tel: 01787 248562
e-mail: wildlifeartgallery@btinternet.com
website: www.wildlifeartgallery.com

The Wildlife Art Gallery is situated in the heart of the village of Lavenham and is approached by a small courtyard, which then leads into one of the biggest art galleries in Suffolk. The Gallery's main focus is wildlife art and it has work by some of the very best artists from both the UK and Europe. Established in 1988 it has built up a reputation for showing the full spectrum of work from fine detail to loose impressionism, both wooden and bronze sculptures, and original prints, watercolours and oils.

The gallery concentrates on work from initial sketches to finished paintings by leading wildlife artists past and present who have been inspired by nature. With several major exhibitions a year, the feel of the Gallery is regularly changing. Occasionally it will hold exhibitions on a rural theme by both contemporary artists and past masters such as Harry Becker and George Soper.

The gallery, not only sells but publishes, books on wildlife art. Planned publications to accompany major exhibitions of their work are on artists Terance James Bond and Ralph Thompson.

Details of all the exhibitions, events and books for sale at the gallery are available on request or by visiting the website.

🏠 historic building   🏛 museum   🏚 historic site   🍃 scenic attraction   🌸 flora and fauna

THE SWAN AT LAVENHAM

High Street, Lavenham, Suffolk CO10 9QA
Tel: 01787 247477 Fax: 01787 248286
e-mail: info@theswanatlavenham.co.uk
website: www.theswanatlavenham.co.uk

Lavenham is a wonderful Tudor market town with, for its size, an almost unsurpassed array of old and listed buildings. One of the undoubted jewels in its crown is The **Swan at Lavenham**, a superb hotel and restaurant and a quintessential English country retreat that combines the appeal of its 14th century origins with up-to-date comfort, service and facilities. The outstanding guest accommodation comprises 51 en suite rooms, each named after a village in the surrounding area, featuring top-quality linen, rich fabrics and TVs; some boast splendid four-poster beds.

The Old Bar, serving Adnams ales and light dishes, is a favourite meeting place for local residents as well as tourists, with an unusual talking point of a collection of World War II airmen's signatures and cap badges. The Garden Bar is a light, summery restaurant, while the AA Two Rosette Gallery Restaurant provides an elegant setting for savouring the delights of the Swan's two or three-course dinners. Daily changing menus feature high quality Suffolk and Norfolk produce, expertly prepared in dishes that combine traditional skills with contemporary flair. In the summer, the herb garden provides a delightful alfresco alternative for a drink or a meal.

15th century hall house with a superb crown post roof. It was restored by the Gayer Anderson brothers, and has a fine collection of their furniture. The **Church of St Peter and St Paul** dominates the town from its elevated position. It's a building of great distinction, perhaps the greatest of all the 'wool churches' and declared by the 19th century architect August Pugin to be the finest example of Late Perpendicular style in the world. It was built, with generous help from wealthy local families (notably the Spryngs

TIMBERS ANTIQUES

High Street, Lavenham, Sudbury, Suffolk CO10 9PT
Tel: 01787 247218
e-mail: jeni@upstarts.co.uk

Jeni and Tom White are owners and partners in **Timbers Antiques**, where an ever-changing range of high-quality antiques and collectables is provided by over 30 dealers. The stock includes items large and small, from books and postcards to brass and china, jewellery and watches, linens and furniture. The High Street premises, which date from the 15th century, house seven showrooms, and friendly, well-informed dealers are always on hand with advice for shoppers. Timber Antiques is open seven days a week including bank holidays.

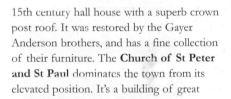

ELIZABETH GASH KNITWEAR

36 Market Place, Lavenham, Suffolk CO10 9QZ
Tel: 01787 248561   e-mail: lizgash.knit@tinyworld.co.uk

Knitwear designer Elizabeth Gash sold to shops, in galleries and at fairs and shows before opening her own shop, first in the High Street, and in 2001 here in Market Place opposite the imposing Guildhall. **Elizabeth Gash Knitwear** stocks her own beautiful designs in Scottish yarn, silks and lamb's wool, as well as other leading British designers including Lorry Marshall, Bill Baber and Sophies Wild Woollens, and textile designers Shirley Pinder, Karen Miknas and Caroline Hall. In summer the range is extended to include linen clothes with ranges by Noa Noa, Flax, Cut Loose and Natural Wave. Personal attention is a key feature here, and a made-to-measure service is available for much of the knitwear.

and the de Veres) in the late 15th and early 16th centuries to celebrate the end of the Wars of the Roses. Its flint tower is a mighty 140 feet in height, and it's possible to climb to the top to take in the glorious views over Lavenham and the surrounding countryside.

Richly carved screens and fine (Victorian) stained glass are eye-catching features within.

The Priory originated in the 13th century as a home for Benedictine monks; the beautiful timber-framed house on the site dates from about 1600. In the original hall, at

THE AVOCET COLLECTION

16a High Street, Lavenham, Suffolk   CO10 9PT
Tel: 01787 247347
e-mail: avocet@lavenham16.fsworld.co.uk
website: www.avocetcollection.co.uk

Set in the charming village of Lavenham, The Avocet Collection is an absolute must for anyone looking for that special something. Selling beautiful gifts and decorative accessories, this friendly family-run business opened in 2003 and has established an enviable reputation where reasonable prices combine with high quality.

The Collection has a diverse array of items ranging from designer jewellery to well crafted furniture. There is an extensive selection of leather products including quality names such as Radley, Tula, Hidesign and Smith & Canova. Jean Paul Gautier umbrellas sit aside lavish modern pearl jewellery from Claudia Bradby. There is a display of unusual culinary pewter pieces by South African designer, Carrol Boyes and ceramic collectables from Dresden and Limoge. The garden showroom boasts

beautiful wrought iron furniture along with inspiring picnic and barbecue wear from Picnic At Ascot. This large shop also features a selection of limited edition prints, a variety of amusing books, greeting cards and much more. The atmosphere is always relaxed and informal, and the staff informed, welcoming and helpful. Customers will not leave disappointed and there are gift vouchers or wish lists available for future visits.

🏚 historic building   🏛 museum   🏚 historic site   ♤ scenic attraction   🐦 flora and fauna

the centre of the building, is an important collection of paintings and stained glass. The extensive grounds include a kitchen garden, a herb garden and a pond.

John Constable went to school in Lavenham, where one of his friends was Jane Taylor, who wrote the words to *Twinkle Twinkle Little Star.*

LONG MELFORD
2 miles N of Sudbury off the A134

🏛 Melford Hall 🏛 Holy Trinity Church

🏛 Kentwell Hall

The heart of this atmospheric wool town is its very long and, in stretches, fairly broad main street, set on an ancient Roman site in a particularly beautiful part of south Suffolk. In Roman times the Stour was a navigable river, and trade flourished. Various Roman finds have been unearthed, notably a blue glass vase which is now on display in the British Museum in London. The street is filled with antiques shops, book shops and art galleries, and is a favourite place for collectors and browsers. Some of the houses are washed in the characteristic Suffolk pink, which might originally have been achieved by mixing ox blood or sloe juice into the plaster.

Holy Trinity Church, on a 14-acre green at the north end of Hall Street, is a typically exuberant manifestation of the wealth of the wool and textile trade. It's big enough to be a cathedral, but served (and still serves) comparatively few parishioners. John Clopton, grown rich in the woollen business, was

largely responsible for this magnificent Perpendicular-style edifice, which has a 180-foot nave and chancel and half timbers, flint 'flushwork' (stonework) of the highest quality, and 100 large windows to give a marvellous sense of light and space. Medieval glass in the north aisle depicts religious scenes and the womenfolk of the Clopton family. There are many interesting monuments and brasses, and in the chantry entrance is a bas relief of the Three Wise Men, the Virgin and Child, and St Joseph. In the Lady Chapel, reached by way of the churchyard, a children's multiplication table written on one wall is a reminder that the chapel served as the village school for a long period after the Reformation.

John Clopton's largesse is recorded rather modestly in inscriptions on the roof parapets.

Kentwell Hall

Long Melford, Suffolk CO10 9BA
Tel: 01787 310207   Fax: 01787 379318
e-mail: info@kentwell.co.uk
website: www.kentwell.co.uk

Kentwell Hall, a romantic, mellow, moated redbrick Tudor mansion in a tranquil parkland setting, has a great deal to offer the visitor. The house was built by the Clopton family in the first half of the 16th century with wealth accrued from the wool trade, and the exterior has changed little down the centuries. After the Cloptons, the house saw a succession of owners and tenants before being requisitioned by the Army in the Second World War. It was in a poor state of repair when acquired by the present owner Patrick Phillips in 1970, since when he and his wife Judith have been lovingly restoring the house and its gardens.

Visitors can enjoy the Tudor service rooms such as the Great Kitchen and the Wardrobe Privy in the main house and the Bakehouse, Brewhouse and Dairy in the separate 15th century service building. Hopper's Gothic Great Hall and Dining Room and a series of classical 18th century rooms should also be seen, along with the State Bedroom, the Chinese Room, the brick-paved Tudor Rose Maze Courtyard and some very fine early heraldic stained glass. The owners have created a rare breeds farm in the superb grounds, where other features include a restored working ice house, a rose garden, a fern stumpery, a coppice walk, a living sundial and the largest carved tree in England, representing the Tower of Babel.

Kentwell is famous for its recreations of Tudor domestic life and of wartime Britain, when it saw service as a transit camp. These events take place on Bank Holidays and selected weekends throughout the year, and in the summer a series of open-air entertainment, from jazz to Shakespeare, is invariably well attended. The Hall was the setting for the film version of *Toad of Toad Hall*.

His tower was struck by lightning in the early 18th century; the present brick construction dates from around 1900. The detail of this great church is of endless fascination, but it's the overall impression that stays in the memory, and the sight of the building floodlit at night is truly spectacular. The distinguished 20th century poet Edmund Blunden spent his last years in Long Melford and is buried in the churchyard. The inscription on his gravestone reads 'I live still to love still things quiet and unconcerned.'

Melford Hall, east of town beyond an imposing 16th century gateway, was built around 1570 by Sir William Cordell on the site of an earlier hall that served as a country retreat, before the Dissolution of the Monasteries, for the monks of St Edmundsbury Abbey. There exists an account of Cordell entertaining Queen Elizabeth I at the Hall in 1578, when she was welcomed by '200 young gentlemen in white velvet, 300 in black and 1,500 serving men'. Much of the fine work of Sir William (whose body lies in Holy Trinity Church) has been altered in restoration, but the pepperpot topped towers are original, as is the panelled banqueting hall. The rooms are in various styles, some with ornate walnut furniture, and there's a notable collection of Chinese porcelain on show. Most delightful of all is the Beatrix Potter room, with some of her watercolours, first editions of her books and, among the toys, the original of Jemima Puddleduck. She was a frequent visitor here (her cousins, the Hyde Parkers, were then the owners), bringing small animals to draw. The Jeremy Fisher illustrations were mostly drawn at Melford Hall's fishponds, and the book is dedicated to Stephanie Hyde Parker. The Hall, which is a National Trust property, stands in a lovely garden with some distinguished clipped box hedges. William Cordell was also responsible for the red-brick almshouses, built in 1593 for '12 poor men', which stand near Holy Trinity. On the green near the Hall is a handsome brick conduit built to supply water to the Hall and the village along wooden pipes.

Kentwell Hall (see panel opposite) is a red-brick Tudor moated mansion approached by a long avenue of limes. Its grounds include a unique Tudor rose maze, and are set out to illustrate and re-create Tudor times, with a walled garden, a bakery, a dairy and several varieties of rare-breed farm animals. The buildings include a handsome 14th century aisle barn. The Hall was the setting for a film version of *Toad of Toad Hall.*

Long Melford is a great place for leisurely strolls, and for the slightly more energetic there's a scenic three-mile walk along a disused railway track and farm tracks that leads straight into Lavenham.

GLEMSFORD
5 miles NW of Cavendish on the B1065

Driving into Glemsford, the old Church of St Mary makes an impressive sight on what, for Suffolk, is quite a considerable hill. Textiles and weaving have long played a prominent part in Glemsford's history, and thread from the silk factory, which opened in 1824 and is still going strong, has been woven into dresses and robes for various members of the royal family, including the late Princess Diana's wedding dress. During the last century several factories produced matting from coconut fibres, and in 1906 Glemsford was responsible for the largest carpet in the world, used to cover the floor at London's Olympia. To this day one factory processes horse hair for use in judges' wigs, sporrans and busbies.

EMBLETON HOUSE

Melford Road, Cavendish, nr Sudbury,
Suffolk CO10 8AA
Tel: 01787 280447   Fax: 01787 282396
e-mail: silverned@aol.com
website: www.embletonhouse.co.uk

Edward Silver and his parents John and Rosemary look forward to welcoming you. Opened in August 2000 they have an excellent reputation for their friendly welcome, delicious local breakfasts, and comfortable relaxing rooms. **Embleton House** was built in 1932 for the village Doctor on this 1.6 acre plot which he purchased from a local farmer. He had his dream house built with the provision of a waiting room and a surgery on the ground floor, which are now used for two en-suite rooms.

The house is set well back from the road and with the help of many of the mature specimen trees and shrubs, some planted in the 1930s, it is secluded and peaceful. In addition to the beautiful gardens, there is a hard tennis court and a well heated outdoor swimming pool for guests to use by arrangement in the summer months. There are five large en-suite rooms in total, all carefully designed with comfort and relaxation in mind. Two large double/twins are on the ground floor, one with wheelchair access and both with their own entrances and parking spaces right outside, enabling guests to come and go with ease. Two doubles upstairs have beautiful Stour Valley views, and a wonderful superior room in the former games room has huge bay windows, a dressing area and luxury bathroom. Wake up in one of these to the sound of bird song and wander into the guests' lounge with French doors to the garden or a roaring log fire to welcome you in winter.

Make your choice from Embleton's famous full Suffolk breakfast, with lots of local produce slowly griddled for a fuller flavour - farmers market 100% pork sausages, Long Melford dry cure bacon, mushrooms, potatoes, English tomatoes and fresh free range eggs from Willow Farm Shop, one mile down the road. Along with bread from Clare Bakery and a wide selection of homemade jams and jellies from the garden.

Whether in Suffolk on business, touring by car, cycling or simply visiting friends and family, Embleton is the perfect base to relax and enjoy this special part of Suffolk. When you return, you will find a flask of fresh milk on your tea tray and some of Rosemary's homemade shortbread to tide you over until supper. When you want to eat there are two excellent places in Cavendish, both within a 10 minute walk, and many more a short drive away. Whatever your plans Edward can supply you with extra information to make your visit more enjoyable; route maps, suggested restaurants and pubs, garden tours etc.

Embleton has four stars and a Silver Award from the English Tourism Council and has been recommended by *Which?* for four years. Edward and his parents really love what they do and this really shows through with their attention to detail and with all the extra little touches they will leave for you to discover.

CAVENDISH

5 miles W of Sudbury on the A1092

A most attractive village, where the Romans stayed awhile - the odd remains have been unearthed - and the Saxons settled. Cavendish is splendidly traditional, with its church, thatched cottages, almshouses, and the 16th century rectory

Cavendish

Nether Hall, now the headquarters of Cavendish Vineyards. The Sue Ryder Foundation Museum is now closed, but the shop is still open. In the Church of St Mary, whose tower has a pointed bellcote and a room inside complete with fireplace and shuttered windows, look for the two handsome lecterns, one with a brass eagle (15th century), the other with two chained books; and for the Flemish and Italian statues. In 1381 Wat Tyler, leader of the Peasants' Revolt, was killed at Smithfield, in London, by John Cavendish, son of Sir John Cavendish, then lord of the manor and Chief Justice of England. Sir John was then hounded by the peasants, who caught him and killed him near Bury St Edmunds. He managed en route to hide some valuables in the belfry of St Mary's here in Cavendish, and bequeathed to the church £40, sufficient to restore the chancel. A later Cavendish – Thomas – sailed round the world in the 1580s and perished on a later voyage. In the shadow of the church, on the edge of the village green, is a cluster of immaculate thatched cottages at a spot known as Hyde Park Corner. Pink-washed and pretty as a picture, they look almost too good to be true – and they almost are, having been rebuilt twice since the Second World War due to unhappy forces that included fires and dilapidation.

CLARE

7 miles W of Sudbury on the A1092

🏠 Ancient House 🏠 Clare Castle

🎋 Clare Castle Country Park

A medieval wool town of great importance, Clare repays a visit today with its fine old buildings and some distinguished old ruins. Perhaps the most renowned tourist attraction is **Ancient House**, a timber-framed building dated 1473 and remarkable for its pargeting. This is the decorative treatment of external plasterwork, usually by dividing the surface into rectangles and decorating each panel. It was very much a Suffolk speciality, particularly in the 16th and 17th centuries, with some examples also being found in Cambridgeshire and Essex. The decoration could be simple brushes of a comb, scrolls or squiggles, or more elaborate, with religious motifs, guild signs or family crests. Some pargeting is incised, but the best is in relief – pressing moulds into wet plaster or shaping it by hand. Ancient House sports some splendid entwined flowers and branches, and a representation of two figures holding a shield. The best-known workers in this unique skill had their own distinctive styles, and the expert eye could spot the particular 'trademarks' of each man (the same is the case with the master thatchers). Ancient House is now a museum, open during the summer months and housing an exhibition on local history.

Another place of historical significance is Nethergate House, once the workplace of dyers, weavers and spinners. The Swan Inn, in the High Street, has a sign which lays claim to being the oldest in the land. Ten feet in length and carved from a solid piece of wood, it portrays the arms of England and France. **Clare Castle** was a motte-and-bailey fortress that sheltered a household of 250. **Clare Castle Country Park**, with a visitor centre in the goods shed of a disused railway line, contains the remains of the castle and the moat, the latter now a series of ponds and home to varied wild life.

At the Prior's House, the original cellar and infirmary are still in use. Established in 1248 by Augustine friars and used by them until the Dissolution of 1538, the priory was handed back to that order in 1953 and remains their property.

A mile or so west of Clare on the A1092 lies Stoke-by-Clare, a pretty village on one of the region's most picturesque routes. It once housed a Benedictine priory, whose remains are now in the grounds of a school. There's a fine 15th century church and a vineyard: Boyton Vineyards at Hill Farm, Boyton End, is open early April-October for a tour, a talk and a taste.

KEDINGTON
12 miles W of Sudbury on the B1061

🏠 Church of St Peter & St Paul

Haverhill intrudes somewhat, but the heart of the old village of Kedington gains in appeal by the presence of the River Stour. Known to many as the 'Cathedral of West Suffolk', the Church of **St Peter and St Paul** is the village's chief attraction. Almost 150 feet in length, it stands on a ridge overlooking the Stour Valley. It has several interesting features, including a 15th century font, a Saxon cross in the chancel window, a triple-decker pulpit (with a clerk's desk and a reading desk) and a sermon-timer, looking rather like a grand egg-timer. The foundations of a Roman building have been found beneath the floorboards.

The Bardiston family, one of the oldest in Suffolk, had strong links with the village and many of the family tombs are in the church. In the church grounds is a row of 10 elm trees, each, the legend says, with a knight buried beneath its roots.

Following the Stour along the B1061, the visitor will find a number of interesting little villages. In Little Wratting, Holy Trinity Church has a shingled oak-framed steeple (a feature more usually associated with Essex churches). John Sainsbury was a local resident, while in Great Wratting another magnate, W H Smith, financed the restoration of St Mary's Church in 1887. This church boasts some diverting topiary in the shape of a church, a cross and – somewhat comically - an armchair.

HAVERHILL
14 miles W of Sudbury on the A604

🏠 Anne of Cleves House   🧍 East Town Park

Notable for its fine Victorian architecture, Haverhill also boasts one fine Tudor gem.

Although many of Haverhill's buildings were destroyed by fire in 1665, the **Anne of Cleves House** was restored and is well worth a visit. Anne was the fourth wife of Henry VIII and, after a brief political marriage, she was given an allowance and spent the remainder of her days at Haverhill and Richmond. Haverhill Local History Centre, in the Town Hall, has an interesting collection of memorabilia, photographs and archive material.

East Town Park is an attractive and relatively new country park on the east side of Haverhill.

GREAT AND LITTLE THURLOW
15 miles W of Sudbury on the B1061

Great and Little Thurlow form a continuous village on the west bank of the River Stour a few miles north of Haverhill. Largely undamaged thanks to being in a conservation area, together they boast many 17th century cottages and a Georgian manor house. In the main street is a schoolhouse built in 1614 by Sir Stephen Soame, one-time Lord Mayor of London, whose family are commemorated in the village church.

A short distance further up the B1061 stands the village of Great Bradley, divided in two by the River Stour, which rises just outside the village boundary. Chief points of note in the tranquil parish church are a fine Norman doorway sheltering a Tudor brick porch and some beautiful stained glass poignantly depicting a soldier in the trenches during the First World War. The three bells in the tower include one cast in the 14th century, among the oldest in Suffolk.

Bury St Edmunds

🏛 St Mary's Church 🏛 Cathedral 🎨 Art Gallery

🏛 Theatre Royal 🏛 Manor House Museum

🏛 Moyse's Hall Museum 🌱 Mowton Park

🏛 Greene king Brewery Museum 🏛 Abbey Ruins

A gem among Suffolk towns, rich in archaeological treasures and places of religious and historical interest, Bury St Edmunds takes its name from St Edmund, who was born in Nuremberg in AD841 and came here as a teenager to become the last King of East Anglia. He was a staunch Christian, and his refusal to deny his faith caused him to be tortured and killed by the Danes in AD870. Legend has it that although his body was recovered, his head (cut off by the Danes) could not be found. His men searched for it for 40 days, then heard his voice directing them to it from the depths of a wood, where they discovered it lying protected between the paws of a wolf. The head and the body were seamlessly united and, to commemorate the wolf's deed, the crest of

Abbey Ruins, Bury St Edmunds

🎬 stories and anecdotes   🕊 famous people   🎨 art and craft   ⚽ entertainment and sport   🚶 walks

COPELAND INTERIORS

17 St John's Street, Bury St Edmunds,
Suffolk IP33 1SJ
Tel: 01284 754388 Fax: 01284 752105
e-mail: info@copelandinteriors.co.uk

Copeland Interiors is a family business that has been based in the same Bury premises for almost 130 years. Clare Hindle and her staff offer clients a full interior design service, and on show in the atmospheric 14th century building is a wide range of top-quality upholstery, curtains and blinds, furniture and fabrics. Copeland is able to source individual products to match customers' individual needs, and the personal approach has earned the shop an excellent reputation throughout East Anglia and beyond.

the town's armorial bearings depicts a wolf with a man's head.

Edmund was possibly buried first at Hoxne, the site of his murder, but when he was canonised in about AD910 his remains were moved to the monastery at Beodricsworth, which changed its name to St Edmundsbury.

A shrine was built in his honour, later incorporated into the Norman Abbey Church after the monastery was granted abbey status by King Canute in 1032. The town soon became a place of pilgrimage, and for many years St Edmund was the patron saint of England, until replaced by St George.

CANDLE & BLUE

66 St John's Street, Bury St Edmunds, Suffolk IP33 1SJ
Tel: 01284 765522
e-mail: info@candleandblue.co.uk
website: www.candleandblue.co.uk

Bury St Edmunds is a prosperous and historic market town serving a large rural area in the heart of East Anglia. Take the time to walk around Bury where there are many beautiful buildings dating from the 17th and 18th centuries.

St John's Street, just off the market square and one of the main streets in Bury St Edmunds, is renowned for its rich and diverse range of independent shops and a must see, whether you intend to shop or just to sight-see.

Candle & Blue, a lifestyle boutique, offers an ever changing and exciting collection of gifts, jewellery, top quality homecare and outdoor living products, along with a range of children's accessories.

Natalie Rice, the owner, has a passion for unique and interesting products which has led her to source products from home and abroad.

At Candle & Blue they are keen for the boutique to stay fresh and exciting, so sourcing new and exclusive items is their hallmark.

So when looking for something contemporary or traditional for your home, garden and family or a treat for yourself, take time to stop at Candle & Blue which takes its place among the town's many interesting shops.

🏛 historic building   🏛 museum   🏛 historic site   🌳 scenic attraction   🌿 flora and fauna

Growing rapidly around the great abbey, which became one of the largest and most influential in the land, Bury prospered as a centre of trade and commerce, thanks notably to the cloth industry.

The next historical landmark was reached in 1214, when on St Edmund's Feast Day the then Archbishop of Canterbury, Simon Langton, met with the Barons of England at the high altar of the Abbey and swore that they would force King John to honour the proposals of the Magna Carta. The twin elements of Edmund's canonisation and the resolution of the Barons explain the motto on the town's crest: *sacrarium regis, cunabula legis* – 'shrine of a king, cradle of the law'.

Rebuilt in the 15th century, the Abbey was largely dismantled after its Dissolution by Henry VIII, but imposing ruins remain in the colourful Abbey Gardens beyond the splendid Abbey Gate and Norman Tower. **St Edmundsbury Cathedral** was originally the Church of St James, built in the 15th/16th centuries and accorded cathedral status (alone in Suffolk) in 1914. The original building has been much extended over the years (notably when being adapted for its role as a cathedral) and outstanding features include a magnificent hammerbeam roof, whose 38 beams are decorated with angels bearing the emblems of St James, St Edmund and St George. The monumental Bishop's throne depicts wolves guarding the crowned head of St Edmund, and there's a fascinating collection of 1,000 embroidered kneelers.

St Mary's Church, in the same complex, is also well worth a visit: an equally impressive hammerbeam roof, the detached tower

OUNCE HOUSE HOTEL

Northgate Street, Bury St Edmunds,
Suffolk IP33 1HP
Tel: 01284 761779 Fax: 01284 768315
e-mail: enquiries@ouncehouse.co.uk
website: www.ouncehouse.co.uk

Bury St Edmunds is one of the most interesting of all the towns in East Anglia, and the latest addition to its many attractions is the cathedral lantern tower, a recently completed Millennium project. One of the very best places for visitors to stay is **Ounce House Hotel**, a charming and gracious Victorian house set in the centre of Bury at the high point of one of its finest residential streets. Elegant, quiet and civilised, Jenny and Simon Pott's home, accurately described as a 'country town hotel', has five individually decorated and furnished bedrooms, all with big beds, chairs, desks and en suite bathrooms with pampering toiletries.

The day starts with an excellent breakfast featuring local produce. Guests have the use of a lovely drawing room with an honesty bar, a perfect spot for meeting other guests or planning the day's activities. Ounce House, a non-smoking establishment, has a lovely garden and private off-road parking.

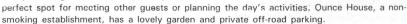
stories and anecdotes   famous people   art and craft   entertainment and sport   walks

standing much as Abbot Anselm built it in the 12th century, and several interesting monuments, the most important commemorating Mary Tudor, sister of Henry VIII, Queen of France and Duchess of Suffolk. Her remains were moved here when the Abbey was suppressed; a window in the Lady Chapel recording this fact was the gift of Queen Victoria.

The **Abbey Gardens**, laid out in 1831, have as their central feature a great circle of flower beds following the pattern of the Royal Botanical Gardens in Brussels. Some of the original ornamental trees can still be seen, and other - later - features include an Old English rose garden, a water garden and a garden for the blind where fragrance counts for all. Ducks and geese live by the little River Lark, and there are tennis courts, putting and bowls greens and children's play equipment.

Bury is full of fine non-ecclesiastical buildings, many with Georgian frontages concealing medieval interiors. Among the most interesting are the handsome **Manor House Museum** with its collection of clocks, paintings, furniture, costumes and objets d'art; the Victorian Corn Exchange with its imposing colonnade; the Athenaeum, hub of social life since Regency times and scene of Charles Dickens's public readings; Cupola House, where Daniel Defoe once stayed; the Angel Hotel, where Dickens and his marvellous creation Mr Pickwick stayed; and the Nutshell, owned by Greene King Brewery and a contender for the title of the smallest pub in the country. The **Theatre Royal**, now in the care of the National Trust, was built in 1819 by William Wilkins, who was also

---

THE ANGEL HOTEL

Angel Hill, Bury St Edmunds, Suffolk IP33 1LT
Tel: 01284 714000 Fax: 01284 714001
e-mail: sales@theangel.co.uk
website: www.theangel.co.uk

The Angel Hotel is situated in the town of Bury St Edmunds, which was voted "Best Little Town in the World" two years running by Nations in Bloom. The Angel, opposite the magnificent Cathedral with its Millennium Tower, the award-winning Abbey Gardens (voted best park in East Anglia), the ruins of the former Abbey of St Edmund and the historic Norman Tower.

Steeped in history, this quintessentially English Hotel offers a warm and personal service. It has 75 bedrooms, all different in style including four-posters, suites, traditional, contemporary, some with air-conditioning and all serviced by a guest lift.

There are two restaurants, the atmospheric Vaults Brasserie, which dates back to the 12th century - totally unique, and the Abbeygate Restaurant, overlooking the beautiful Georgian square. Both serve award-winning two AA rosette food - you will be spoilt for choice.

With so many interesting local places to visit, including Newmarket (horseracing), Cambridge (exploring the heritage of this stunning city, leaving time for a leisurely 'punt'), the breathtaking Suffolk villages of Lavenham and Long Melford (famous for its abundance of antique shops - Lovejoy country) to name but a few, you will almost certainly want to return.

🏛 historic building   🏛 museum   🏛 historic site   🏞 scenic attraction   🌿 flora and fauna

responsible for the National Gallery in London. It once staged the premiere of *Charley's Aunt*, and still operates as a working theatre.

One of Bury's oldest residents and newest attractions is the **Greene King Brewery Museum and Shop**. Greene King has been brewed here in Bury since 1799; the museum's informative storyboards, artefacts, illustrations and audio displays bring the history and art of brewing to life. Brewery tours include a look round the museum and beer-tasting. The shop sells a variety of memorabilia, souvenirs, gifts and clothing – as well, of course, as bottles and cans of the frothy stuff.

The **Bury St Edmunds Art Gallery** is housed in one of Bury's noblest buildings, built to a Robert Adam design in 1774. It has filled many roles down the years, and was rescued from decline in the 1960s to be restored to Adam's original plans. It is now one of the county's premier art galleries, with eight exhibitions each year and a thriving craft shop.

Perhaps the most fascinating building of all is **Moyse's Hall Museum**, located at one end of the Buttermarket. Built of flint and limestone about 1180, it has claims to being the oldest stone domestic building in England. Originally a rich man's residence, it later saw service as a tavern, gaol, police station and railway parcels office, but since 1899 it has been a museum, and has recently undergone total refurbishment. It houses some 10,000 items, including many important archaeological collections, from a Bronze Age hoard, Roman pottery and Anglo-Saxon jewellery to a 19th century doll's house and relics of the notorious Red Barn murder. A new wing contains the Suffolk Regiment collection and education room.

Outside the Spread Eagle pub on the western edge of town is a horse trough erected to the memory of the Victorian romantic novelist 'Ouida' (Maria Louisa Ramee, 1839-1908).

Steeped though it is in history, Bury also moves with the times, and its sporting, entertainment and leisure facilities are impressive. A mile-and-a-half outside town on the A14 (just off the East Exit) is **Nowton Park**, 172 acres of countryside landscaped in Victorian style and supporting a wealth of flora and fauna; the avenue of limes, carpeted with daffodils in the spring, is a particular delight. There's also a play area and a ranger centre.

Bury's disciplined network of streets (the layout was devised in the 11th century) provides long, alluring views. A great fire destroyed much of Bury in 1608, but it was rebuilt using traditional timber-framing techniques. Arriving here in 1698, Celia Fiennes, the inveterate traveller and architecture critic, was uncharacteristically favourable in her remarks about Cupola House, which had just been completed at the time of her visit. William Cobbett (1763-1835), a visitor when chronicling his Rural Rides, did not disagree with the view that Bury St Edmunds was 'the nicest town in the world' - a view which would be endorsed by many of today's inhabitants and by many of the millions of visitors who have been charmed by this jewel in Suffolk's crown.

Around Bury St Edmunds

ICKLINGHAM
8 miles NW of Bury St Edmunds on the A1101

The village of Icklingham boasts not one but

THE LIGHTING GALLERY

The Old Station, Higham, nr Bury St Edmunds,
Suffolk IP28 6NL
Tel: 01284 810569   Fax: 01284 811101
e-mail: info@lightinggallery.co.uk
website: www.lightinggallery.co.uk

When Dr Beeching took his axe to England's rural railway network in the 1960s, he left behind many redundant railway buildings, many of which have been put to a variety of new uses. Higham Station became the headquarters of a business making and selling lamp stands and lampshades, a business which was taken over in 1989 by the present directors Peter Jackson and Neil Pettit. In 1999 the retail company the **Lighting Gallery** was born, and in 2000 Peter and Neil expanded the showroom by opening up the main station building, a former goods shed.

The old arches and brickwork were superbly restored to create a really splendid showroom where lighting products from all over the world are on display, the principal manufacturers being based in the UK, Spain, Italy, Germany and the Far East. Designs ranging from period through traditional to contemporary and futuristic are all available to transform customers' homes. An adjacent building is now the Lighting Gallery's offices and workshops. Personal service and years of expertise ensure that qualified staff are always on hand to discuss options to suit each customer's individual lighting plans and to solve lighting problems.

LONGWOOD ORGANIC FARM SHOP

Longwood Farm, Tuddenham St Mary,
nr Bury St Edmunds, Suffolk IP28 6TB
Tel: 01638 717120   Fax: 01638 711168
e-mail: longwoodorganic@hotmail.com
website: www.longwoodfarm.co.uk

Shoppers looking for a great, totally organic shopping experience should make tracks for **Longwood Organic Farm Shop**, signposted in the village of Tuddenham St Mary. Owners Louise and Matthew Unwin started in 1990 with the simple idea of producing and selling great-tasting organic meat, and constant demand has led to moving the shop into an empty farm building closer to the road.

The animals raised on the farm have the freedom to graze in meadows with acres of space to move around, and are butchered on site to the highest standards.

Lamb, beef, pork and poultry are all of the very best quality, and other foodstuffs on sale in the shop include fruit and vegetables from local farms, dairy products, bread, biscuits, preserves, oils, flour, rice, beans, sugar, dried fruit and nuts. Among the range of other goods are cards and stationery, bird tables and bird feed, baby care products, household cleaning products and educational gifts.

🏛 historic building   🏠 museum   🏚 historic site   🍃 scenic attraction   🌿 flora and fauna

two churches - the parish church of St James (mentioned in the *Domesday Book*) and the deconsecrated thatched-roofed All Saints, with medieval tiles on the chancels and beautiful east windows in the south aisle. At the point where the Icknield Way crosses the River Lark, Icklingham has a long history, brought to light in frequent archaeological finds, from pagan bronzes to Roman coins. The place abounds in tales of the supernatural, notably of the white rabbit who is seen at dusk in the company of a witch, causing – it is said - horses to bolt and men to die.

Just south of Icklingham, at the A1101, is Rampart Field picnic site, where pleasant walks through gorse-filled gravel workings reveal the varied plant life of a typical Breckland heath.

WEST STOW
4 miles NW of Bury St Edmunds off the A1101

🏠 Anglo-Saxon Village 🌳 Country Park

The villages of West Stow, Culford, Ingham, Timworth and Wordwell were for several centuries part of a single estate covering almost 10,000 acres. Half the estate was sold to the Forestry Commission in 1935 and was renamed the King's Forest in honour of King George V's Jubilee in that year.

An Anglo-Saxon cemetery was discovered in the village in 1849; subsequent years have revealed traces of Roman settlements and the actual layout of the original **Anglo-Saxon Village** (see panel on page 187). A trust was established to investigate further the Anglo-Saxon way of life and their building and farming techniques. Several buildings were constructed using, as accurately as could be achieved, the tools and methods of the 5th century. The undertaking has become a major tourist attraction, with assistance from guides

both human (in Anglo-Saxon costume) and in the form of taped cassettes. There are pigs and hens, growing crops, craft courses, a Saxon market at Easter, a festival in August and special events all year round. This fascinating village, which is entered through the Visitor Centre, is part of **West Stow Country Park**, a large part of which is designated a Site of Special Scientific Interest (SSSI). Over 120 species of birds and 25 species of animals have been sighted in this Breckland setting, and a well-marked five-mile nature trail links this nature reserve with the woods, a large lake and the River Lark.

HENGRAVE
3 miles NW of Bury St Edmunds on the A1101

🏠 Hengrave Hall

A captivating old world village of flint and thatch, excavations and aerial photography indicate that there has been a settlement at Hengrave since Neolithic times. Those parts of the village that are of archaeological interest are now protected. The chief attraction is **Hengrave Hall**, a rambling Tudor mansion built partly of Northamptonshire limestone and partly of yellow brick by Sir Thomas Kytson, a wool merchant. A notable visitor in the early days was Elizabeth I, who brought her court here in 1578.

Several generations of the Gage family were later the owners of Hengrave Hall - one of them, with a particular interest in horticulture, imported various kinds of plum trees from France. Most of the bundles were properly labelled with their names, but one had lost its label. When it produced its first crop of luscious green fruit, someone had the bright idea of calling it the green Gage.

The name stuck, and the descendants of these trees, planted in 1724, are still at the

CULFORD FARM COTTAGES

Culford, nr Bury St Edmunds,
Suffolk IP28 6DS
Tel/Fax: 01284 728334
e-mail: enquiries@homefarmculford.co.uk

Two hundred and fifty acres of tranquil, attractive farmland are the setting for **Culford Farm Cottages**, located less than three miles from Bury St Edmunds. Three comfortable cottages, stylishly and skilfully converted from period buildings, provide everything needed for a self-contained, stress-free self-catering holiday. Each has its own particular charm and character, and guests enjoy shared use of a sheltered swimming pool for the summer.

The Dairy, converted from a Victorian dairy building, stands next to the owners' handsome Tudor farmhouse. It has two bedrooms, one on the ground floor, the other overlooking the sitting room. French doors lead to the enclosed garden and the hot tub.

The Smoke House, also with two bedrooms, both en suite, is a charming conversion which also has an enclosed garden and a hot tub (situated in the secluded swimming pool garden area). Piglet's Place, an imaginative single-storey conversion, has doors and full-length windows opening onto a quiet courtyard garden – and a hot tub. It has a double bedroom with en suite shower and two twin-bedded rooms, one with zip and link beds. This property is accessible to wheelchairs users. All the cottages have oil-fired central heating, TV with a video/DVD library, radio, microwave, fridge-freezer, hairdryer and garden furniture.

The grounds of Culford Farm Cottages offer guests the chance to stroll along the banks of the River Lark, enjoying the fresh air, the scenery and the varied birdlife. Charolais cattle and horses graze in the meadows. One dog is allowed in The Dairy and The Smokehouse, but not in Piglet's Place. The cottages are well placed for touring all the many sights of the area. The Abbey and its gardens, the Cathedral and the Theatre Royal are among the attractions in nearby Bury, and Thetford Forest, Melford Hall, West Stow Anglo-Saxon Village and Ickworth House are all within an easy drive.

West Stow Anglo-Saxon Village

The Visitor Centre, Icklingham Road, West Stow,
Bury St Edmunds, Suffolk IP28 6HG
Tel: 01284 728718 Fax: 01284 728277
website: www.stedmundsbury.gov.uk/weststow.htm

Between 1965 and 1972 the low hill by the River Lark in Suffolk was excavated to reveal several periods of occupation, but in particular, over 70 buildings from an early Anglo-Saxon village. There was also information from about 100 graves in the nearby cemetery. It was decided that such extensive evidence about these people should be used to carry out a practical experiment to test ideas about the buildings that formed the elements of the original village.

Part of the Anglo Saxon Village has been reconstructed on the site where the original (inhabited from around 420-650 AD) was excavated. The reconstructions have been built over a period of more than 20 years. Each of the eight buildings is different, to test different ideas, and each has been built using the tools and techniques available to the early Anglo-Saxons. Exploring the houses is an excellent way of finding out about the Anglo-Saxons who lived at West Stow. Costumed "Anglo-Saxons" bring the village to life at certain times, especially at Easter and during August. The new Anglo-Saxon Centre is an exciting addition to the site, housing the original objects found there and at other local sites. Many of the objects have never been seen by the public before. The displays show aspects of village life and the focal point is a series of life size reconstructions of costume, based upon the grave finds

West Stow Anglo-Saxon Village lies in the middle of a beautiful 125-acre Country Park, part of which is a Site of Special Scientific Interest. The park has a number of different habitats, including woodland, heathland, a lake and a river. There is a play area, a bird feeding area and bird hides. The Park is open daily all year, from 9am-5pm in winter, 9am-8pm in summer. Entry to the park is free.

Hall, which may be visited by appointment. In the grounds stands a lovely little church with a round Saxon tower and a wealth of interesting monuments. The church was for some time a family mausoleum; restored by Sir John Wood, it became a private chapel and now hosts services of various denominations.

FLEMPTON

4 miles NW of Bury St Edmunds on the A1101

🦌 Lark Valley Park

An interesting walk from this village just

north of the A1101 follows the **Lark Valley Park** through Culford Park, providing a good view of Culford Hall, which has been a school since 1935. A handsome cast-iron bridge dating from the early 19th century - and recently brought to light from amongst the reeds - crosses a lake in the park.

LACKFORD

6 miles NW of Bury St Edmunds on the A1101

More interest here for the wildlife enthusiast. Restored gravel pits have been turned into a

🎬 stories and anecdotes 🦜 famous people 🎨 art and craft 🎵 entertainment and sport 🦌 walks

reserve for wildfowl and waders. Two hides are available.

EUSTON
9 miles N of Bury St Edmunds on the A1088

🏠 Euston Hall

Euston Hall, on the A1088, has been the seat of the Dukes of Grafton for 300 years. It's open to the public on Thursday afternoons and is well worth a visit, not least for its portraits of Charles II and its paintings by Van Dyck, Lely and Stubbs. In the colourful landscaped grounds is an ice-house disguised as an Italianate temple, the distinguished work of John Evelyn and William Kent.

Euston's church, in the grounds of the Hall, is the only one in the county dedicated to St Genevieve. It's also one of only two Classical designs in the county, being rebuilt in 1676 on part of the original structure. The interior is richly decorated, with beautiful carving on the hexagonal pulpit, panelling around the walls and a carved panel of the Last Supper. Parts of this lovely wood carving are attributed by some to Grinling Gibbons. Behind the family pew is a marble memorial to Lord Arlington, who built the church.

Euston's watermill was built in the 1670s and rebuilt in 1730 as a Gothic church.

PAKENHAM
4 miles NE of Bury St Edmunds off the A143

🏠 Nether Hall 🏠 Newe House

🏚 Watermill and Windmill

On a side road just off the A143 (turn right just north of Great Barton) lies the village of Pakenham, whose long history has been unearthed in the shape of a Bronze Age barrow and kiln, and another kiln from Roman times.

Elsewhere in Pakenham are the 17th century **Nether Hall**, from whose lake in the park the

village stream flows through the fen into the millpond. From the same period dates **Newe House**, a handsome Jacobean building with Dutch gables and a two-storey porch. The Church of St Mary has an impressive carved Perpendicular font, and in its adjacent vicarage is the famous Whistler Window - a painting by Rex Whistler of an 18th century parish priest. The fens were an important source of reeds, and many of Pakenham's buildings show off the thatcher's art.

Pakenham's current unique claim to fame is in being the last parish in England to have a working watermill *and* windmill, a fact proclaimed on the village sign. The **Watermill** was built around 1814 on a site mentioned in the *Domesday Book* (the Roman excavations suggest that there could have been a mill here as far back as the 1st century AD). The mill, which is fed from Pakenham fen, has many interesting features, including the Blackstone oil engine, dating from around 1900, and the Tattersall Midget rollermill from 1913, a brave but ultimately unsuccessful attempt to compete with the larger roller mills in the production of flour. The mill and the neighbouring recreation park are well worth a visit.

No less remarkable is the **Windmill**, one of the most famous in Suffolk. The black-tarred tower was built in 1831 and was in regular use until the 1950s. One of the best preserved mills in the county, it survived a lightning strike in 1971. Both mills lie on the village's circular walks, and fresh flour is available from both.

IXWORTH
5 miles NE of Bury St Edmunds on the A143

Ixworth played its part as one of the Iceni tribe's major settlements, with important Roman connections and, in the 12th century, the site of an Augustinian priory. The remains of the priory were incorporated into a

Georgian house known as Ixworth Abbey, which stands among trees by the River Blackbourne. The village has many 14th century timber-framed dwellings, and the Church of St Mary dates from the same period, though with many later additions.

A variety of circular walks take in lovely parts of the village, which is also the staring point of the Miller's Trail cycle route.

A little way north of the village, on the A1088, are a nature trail and bird reserve at Ixworth Thorpe Farm. At this point a brief diversion northwards up the A1088 is very worth while.

BARDWELL
7 miles NE of Bury St Edmunds just off the A1088

Bardwell offers another tower windmill. This one dates from the 1820s and was worked by wind for 100 years, then by an oil engine until 1941. It was restored in the 1980s, only to suffer severe damage in the great storm of October 1987, when its sails were torn off. Stoneground flour is still produced by an auxiliary engine.

Also in this delightful village are a 16th century inn and the Church of St Peter and St Paul, known particularly for its medieval stained glass.

HONINGTON
7 miles NE of Bury St Edmunds on the A1088

Back on the A1088, the little village of Honington was the birthplace of the pastoral poet Robert Bloomfield (1766-1823), whose best known work is *The Farmer's Boy*. The house where he was born is now divided, one part called Bloomfield Cottage, the other Bloomfield Farmhouse. A brass plaque to his memory can be seen in All Saints Church, in the graveyard of which his parents are buried.

BARNINGHAM
8 miles NE of Bury St Edmunds on the B1111

Knettishall Heath Country Park

Near the Norfolk border, Barningham was the first home of the firm of Fisons, which started in the late 18th century. Starting with a couple of windmills, they later installed one of the earliest steam mills in existence. The engine saw service for nearly 100 years and is now in an American museum; the mill building exists to this day, supplying animal feed.

This is marvellous walking country, and **Knettishall Heath Country Park**, on 400 acres of prime Breckland terrain, is the official starting place of the Peddars Way National Trail to Holme-next-Sea and of the Angles Way Regional Path that stretches 77 miles to Great Yarmouth by way of the Little Ouse and Waveney valleys.

STANTON
7 miles NE of Bury St Edmunds on the A143

Stanton is mentioned in the *Domesday Book*; before that, the Romans were here. A double ration of medieval churches - All Saints and St John the Baptist - will satisfy the ecclesiastical scholar, while for more worldly indulgences Wyken Vineyards will have a strong appeal. Four acres of gardens - herb, knot, rose, kitchen and woodland - are on the same site, and the complex also includes an Elizabethan manor house, a 16th century barn, a country shop and a café. There's also a splendid woodland walk.

WALSHAM-LE-WILLOWS
9 miles NE of Bury St Edmunds off the A143

St Mary's Church

A pretty name for a pretty village, with weatherboarded and timber-framed cottages along the willow-banked river which flows throughout its length. **St Mary's** church is no less pleasing to the eye, with its sturdy western tower and handsome windows in the Perpendicular style. Of particular interest inside is the superb tie and hammerbeam roof of the nave, and (unique in Suffolk, and very rare elsewhere) a tiny circular medallion which hangs suspended from the nave wall, known as a 'Maiden's Garland' or 'Virgin's Crant'. These marked the pew seats of unmarried girls who had passed away, and the old custom was for the young men of the village to hang garlands of flowers from them on the anniversary of a girl's death. This particular example celebrates the virginity of one Mary Boyce, who died (so the inscription says) of a broken heart in 1685, just 20 years old. There is also a carving on the rood screen which looks rather like the face of a wolf: this may well be a reference to the benevolent creature that plays such an important role in the legend

of St Edmund. A museum by the church has changing exhibitions of local history.

REDGRAVE
13 miles NE of Bury St Edmunds on the B1113

Arachnophobes beware! Redgrave and Lopham Fens form a 360-acre reserve of reed and sedge beds where one of the most interesting inhabitants is the Great Raft Spider. The village is the source of the Little Ouse and Waveney rivers, which rise on either side of the B1113 and set off on their seaward journeys in opposite directions.

THELNETHAM
12 miles NE of Bury St Edmunds off the B111

West of Redgrave between the B1113 and the B1111 lies Thelnetham – which boasts a windmill of its own. This one is a tower mill, built in 1819 to replace a post mill on the same site, and worked for 100 years. It has now been lovingly restored. Stoneground flour is produced and sold at the mill. If you wish to visit you should set sail on a summer Sunday or Bank Holiday Monday; other times by appointment.

Thelnetham Windmill

RICKINGHALL
12 miles NE of Bury St Edmunds on the A143

More timber-framed buildings, some thatched, are dotted along the streets of the two villages, Superior and Inferior, which follow an underground stream running right through them. Each has a church dedicated to St Mary and featuring fine flintwork and tracery. The upper church, now closed, was used as a school for London evacuees during the Second World War.

HESSETT

4 miles E of Bury St Edmunds off the A14

Dedicated to St Ethelbert, King of East Anglia, Hessett's church has many remarkable features, particularly some beautiful 16th century glass and wall paintings, both of which somehow escaped the Puritan wave of destruction. Ethelbert was unlucky enough to get on the wrong side of the mighty Offa, King of the Mercians, and was killed by him at Hereford in AD794.

WOOLPIT

6 miles E of Bury St Edmunds on the A14

Museum Lady's Well Woolpit Legend

The church of St Mary the Virgin is Woolpit's crowning glory, with a marvellous porch and one of the most magnificent double hammerbeam roofs in the county.

Voted winner of Suffolk Village of the Year in 2000, the village was long famous for its brick industry, and the majority of the old buildings are faced with 'Woolpit Whites'. This yellowish-white brick looked very much like more expensive stone, and for several centuries was widely exported. Some was used in the building of the Senate wing of the Capitol Building in Washington DC. Red bricks were also produced, and the village **Museum**, open in summer, has a brick-making display and also tells the story of the evolution of the village. Woolpit also hosts an annual music festival.

Nearby is a moated site known as **Lady's Well**, a place of pilgrimage in the Middle Ages. The water from the spring was reputed to have healing properties, most efficacious in curing eye troubles.

A favourite Woolpit legend concerns the **Green Children**, a brother and sister with green complexions who appeared one day in a field, apparently attracted by the church bells. Though hungry, they would eat nothing until some green beans were produced. Given shelter by the lord of the manor, they learned to speak English and said that they came from a place called St Martin. The boy survived for only a short time, but the girl thrived, lost her green colour, was baptised and married a man from King's Lynn – no doubt leaving many a Suffolk man green with envy!

THE BRADFIELDS

7 miles SE of Bury St Edmunds off the A134

Bradfield Woods

The Bradfields - St George, St Clare and Combust - and Cockfield thread their way through a delightful part of the countryside and are well worth a little exploration, not only to see the picturesque villages themselves but for a stroll in the historic **Bradfield Woods**. These woods stand on the eastern edge of the parish of Bradfield St George and have been turned into an outstanding nature reserve, tended and coppiced in the same way for more than 700 years, and home to a wide variety of flora and fauna. They once belonged to the Abbey of St Edmundsbury, and one area is still today called Monk's Park Wood.

Coppicing involves cutting a tree back down to the ground every 10 years or so. Woodlands were managed in this way to provide an annual crop of timber for local use and fast regrowth. After coppicing, as the root is already strongly established, regrowth is quick. Willow and hazel are the trees most commonly coppiced. Willow is often also pollarded, a less drastic form of coppicing where the trees are cut far enough from the ground to stop grazing animals having a free lunch.

Bradfield St Clare, the central of the three

Bradfields, has a rival claim to that of Hoxne as the site of the martyrdom of St Edmund. The St Clare family arrived with the Normans and added their name to the village, and to the church, which was originally All Saints but was then rededicated to St Clare; it is the only church in England dedicated to her. Bradfield Combust, where the pretty River Lark rises, probably takes it curious name from the fact that the local hall was burnt to the ground during the 14th century riots against the Abbot of St Edmundsbury's

War Memorial, Cockfield

crippling tax demands. Arthur Young (1741-1820), the noted writer on social, economic and agricultural subjects, is buried in the village churchyard.

COCKFIELD
8 miles SE of Bury St Edmunds off the A1141

Cockfield is perhaps the most widely spread village in all Suffolk, its little thatched cottages scattered around and between no fewer than nine greens. Great Green is the largest, with two football pitches and other recreation areas, while Parsonage Green has a literary connection: the Old Rectory was once home to a Dr Babbington, whose nephew Robert Louis Stephenson was a frequent visitor and who is said to have written *Treasure Island* while staying there.

Cockfield also shelters one of the last windmills to have been built in Suffolk (1891).

Its working life was very short but the tower still stands, now in use as a private residence.

THORPE MORIEUX
9 miles SE of Bury St Edmunds off the B1071

St Mary's Church in Thorpe Morieux is situated in as pleasant a setting as anyone could wish to find. With water meadows, ponds, a stream and a fine Tudor farmhouse to set it off, this 14th century church presents a memorable picture of old England. Look at the church, then take the time to wander round the peaceful churchyard with its profusion of springtime aconites, followed by the colourful flowering of limes and chestnuts in summer.

GREAT WELNETHAM
2 miles S of Bury St Edmunds off the A134

One of the many surviving Suffolk windmills

is to be found here, just south of the village. The sails were lost in a gale 80 years ago, but the tower and a neighbouring old barn make an attractive sight.

HAWKEDON

9 miles S of Bury St Edmunds off the A143

Hawkedon is designated a place of outstanding natural beauty. Here the Church of St Mary is located atypically in the middle of the village green. The pews and intricately carved bench-ends take the eye here, along with a canopied stoup (a recess for holding holy water) and a Norman font. There is a wide variety of carved animals, many on the bench-ends but some also on the roof cornice. One of the stalls is decorated with the carving of a crane holding a stone in its claw: legend has it that if the crane were on watch and should fell asleep, the stone would drop and the noise would wake it.

WICKHAMBROOK

9 miles S of Bury St Edmunds on the B1063

Wickhambrook is a series of tiny hamlets with no fewer than 11 greens and three manor houses. The greens have unusual names - Genesis, Nunnery, Meeting, Coltsfoot - whose origins keep local historians busy. One of the two pubs has the distinction of being officially half in Wickhambrook and half in Denston.

ALPHETON

10 miles S of Bury St Edmunds on the A134

There are several points of interest in this little village straddling the main road. It was first settled in AD991 and its name means 'the farm of Aefflaed'. That lady was the wife of Ealdorman Beorhtnoth of Essex, who was killed resisting the Danes at the Battle of Maldon and is buried in Ely Minster.

The hall, the farm and the church stand in a quiet location away from the main road and about a mile from the village. This remoteness is not unusual: some attribute it to the villagers moving during times of plague, but the more likely explanation is simply that the scattered cottages, originally in several tiny hamlets, centred on a more convenient site than that of the church. Equally possible is that the church was located here to suit the local landed family (who desired to have the church next door to their home). The main features at the church of St Peter and St Paul are the flintwork around the parapet, the carefully restored 15th century porch and some traces of an ancient wall painting of St Christopher with the Christ Child. All in all, it's a typical country church of unpretentious dignity and well worth a short detour from the busy main roads.

Back in the village, two oak trees were planted and a pump installed in 1887, to commemorate Queen Victoria's 50th year on the throne. Another of the village's claims to fame is that its American airfield was used as the setting for the classic film *Twelve o'Clock High*, in which Gregory Peck memorably plays a Second World War flight commander cracking under the strain of countless missions. Incidentally, one of the reasons for constructing the A134 was to help in the development of the airfield. The A134 continues south to Long Melford. An alternative road from Bury to Long Melford is the B1066, quieter and more scenic, with a number of pleasant places to visit en route.

SHIMPLING

9 miles S of Bury St Edmunds off the B1066

Shimpling is a peaceful farming community whose church, St George's, is approached by a lime avenue. It is notable for Victorian stained glass and a Norman font, and in the churchyard is the Faint House, a small stone building where ladies overcome by the tightness of their stays could decently retreat from the service. The banker Thomas Hallifax built many of Shimpling's cottages, as well as the village school and Chadacre Hall, which Lord Iveagh later turned into an agricultural college (a role it ceased to hold in 1989 - the Hall is today again in private hands).

LAWSHALL
8 miles S of Bury St Edmunds off the A134

A spread-out village first documented in AD972 but regularly giving up evidence of earlier occupation, Lawshall was the site where a Bronze Age sword dated at around 600BC was found (the sword is now in Bury Museum). The Church of All Saints, Perpendicular with some Early English features, stands on one of the highest points in Suffolk. Next to it is Lawshall Hall, whose owners once entertained Queen Elizabeth I. Another interesting site in Lawshall is the Wishing Well, a well-cover on the green put up in memory of Charles Tyrwhitt Drake, who worked for the Royal Geographic Society and was killed in Jerusalem.

HARTEST
9 miles S of Bury St Edmunds on the B1066

🏛 Gifford's Hall   🏛 Hartest Stone

Hartest, which has a history as long as Alpheton's, celebrated its millennium in 1990 with the erection of a village sign (the hart, or stag). It's an agreeable spot in the valley, with colour-washed houses and chestnut trees on the green. Also on the green are All Saints Church (mentioned in the *Domesday Book*) and a large glacial stone, the **Hartest Stone**, which was dragged by a team of 45 horses from

where it was found in a field in neighbouring Somerton. From 1789 until the 1930s, Hartest staged a St George's Day Fair, an annual event celebrating King George III's recovery from one of his spells of illness. Just outside the village is **Gifford's Hall**, a smallholding which includes 14 acres of nearly 12,000 grapevines, as well as a winery producing white and rosé wines and fruit liqueurs. There are also organic vegetable gardens, wildflower meadows, black St Kilda sheep, black Berkshire pigs, goats and free-range fowl, together with a trailer ride ('The Grape Express') and children's play area. The Hall is particularly famous for its sweet peas and roses, and an annual festival is held on the last weekend in June. Open from Easter to the end of October.

HORRINGER
3 miles SW of Bury St Edmunds on the A143

🏛 Ickworth House

Rejoining the A143 by Chedburgh, the motorist will soon arrive at Horringer, whose village green is dominated by the flintstone Church of St Leonard. Beside the church are the gates of one of the country's most extraordinary and fascinating houses, now run by the National Trust. **Ickworth House** was the brainchild of Frederick Augustus Hervey, the eccentric 4th Earl of Bristol and Bishop of Derry, a collector of art treasures and an inveterate traveller (witness the many Bristol Hotels scattered around Europe). His inspiration was Belle Isle, a house built on an island in Lake Windermere, and the massive structure is a central rotunda linking two semi-circular wings. It was designed as a treasure house for his art collection, and work started in 1795. In 1798 Hervey was taken prisoner in Italy by Napoleonic troops and his first collection confiscated. Hervey died of stomach gout in 1803 and his son, after some hesitation, saw the work through to completion in 1829. Its chief glories are some marvellous paintings by Titian, Gainsborough, Hogarth, Velasquez, Reynolds and Kauffman, but there's a great deal more to enthral the visitor: late Regency and 18th century French furniture, a notable collection of Georgian silver, friezes and sculptures by John Flaxman, frescoes copied from wall paintings discovered at the Villa Negroni in Rome in 1777. The Italian garden, where Mediterranean species

Ickworth House, Horringer

have been bred to withstand a distinctly non-Mediterranean climate, should not be missed, with its hidden glades, orangery and temple rose garden, and in the park landscaped by Capability Brown there are designated walks and cycle routes, bird hides, a deer enclosure and play areas. More recent attractions include the vineyard and plant centre. The House is open from Easter until the end of October, while the park and gardens are open throughout the year.

Arable land surrounds Horringer, with a large annual crop of sugar beet grown for processing at the factory in Bury, the largest of its kind in Europe.

Newmarket

🏠 National Horseracing Museum 🏛 Palace House

On the western edge of Suffolk, Newmarket is home to some 16,000 human and 3,000 equine inhabitants. The historic centre of British racing lives and breathes horses, with 60 training establishments, 50 stud farms, the top annual thoroughbred sales and two racecourses (the only two in Suffolk). Thousands of the population are involved in the trade, and racing art and artefacts fill the shops, galleries and museums; one of the oldest established saddlers even has a preserved horse on display - 'Robert the Devil', runner-up in the Derby in 1880.

History records that Queen Boudicca of the Iceni, to whom the six-mile Devil's Dyke stands as a memorial, thundered around these parts in her lethal chariot behind her shaggy-haired horses. She is said to have established the first stud here. In medieval times the chalk heathland was a popular arena for riders to display their skills. In 1605, James I paused on a journey northwards to enjoy a spot of hare

🎞 stories and anecdotes 🐦 famous people 🎨 art and craft 🏅 entertainment and sport 🚶 walks

coursing. He enjoyed the place and said he would be back. By moving the royal court to his Newmarket headquarters, he began the royal patronage which has remained strong throughout the years. James' son, Charles I, maintained the royal connection, but it was Charles II who really put the place on the map when he, too, moved the Royal court here in the spring and autumn of each year. He initiated the Town Plate, a race which he himself won twice as a rider and which, in a modified form, still exists.

One of the racecourses, the Rowley Mile, takes its name from Old Rowley, a favourite horse of the Merry Monarch. Here the first two classics of the season, the 1,000 and 2,000 Guineas, are run, together with important autumn events including the Cambridgeshire and the Cesarewich. There are some 18 race days at this track, while on the leafy July course, with its delightful garden-party atmosphere, a similar number of race days take in all the important summer fixtures.

The visitor to Newmarket can learn almost all there is to know about flat racing and racehorses by making the grand tour of the several establishments open to the public (sometimes by appointment only). The Jockey Club, which was the first governing body of the sport and, until recently, its ultimate authority, was formed in the mid-18th century and occupies an imposing building which was restored and rebuilt in Georgian style in the 1930s. Originally a social club for rich gentlemen with an interest in the turf, it soon became the all-powerful regulator of British racing, owning all the racing and training land. When holding an enquiry the stewards sit round a horseshoe-shaped table while the jockey or trainer under scrutiny faces them on a strip of carpet by the door - hence the expression 'on the mat'.

Next to the Jockey Club in the High Street is the **National Horseracing Museum**. Opened by the Queen in 1983, its five galleries chronicle the history of the Sport of Kings from its royal beginnings through to the top trainers and jockeys of today. Visitors can ride a mechanical horse, try on racing silks, record a race commentary, ask questions and enjoy a snack in the café, whose walls are hung with murals of racing personalities. The chief treasures among the art collection are equine paintings by Alfred Munnings, while the most famous item is probably the skeleton of the mighty Eclipse, whose superiority over his contemporaries gave rise to the saying 'Eclipse first, the rest nowhere'.

A few steps away is **Palace House**, which contains the remains of Charles II's palace and which, as funds allow, has been restored over the years for use as a visitor centre and museum. In the same street is Nell Gwynn's House, which some say was connected by an underground passage beneath the street to the palace. The diarist John Evelyn spent a night in (or on?) the town during a royal visit, and declared the occasion to be 'more resembling a luxurious and abandoned rout than a Christian court'. The palace is the setting for the Newmarket Tourist Information Centre.

Racehorses Excercising, Newmarket

Other must-sees on the racing enthusiast's tour are Tattersalls, where leading thoroughbred sales take place from April to December; the British Racing School, where top jockeys are taught the ropes; the National Stud, open from March till the end of September (plus race days in October - booking essential); and the Animal Health Trust based at Lanwades Hall, where there's an informative Visitor Centre. The National Stud at one time housed no fewer than three Derby winners - Blakeney, Mill Reef, and Grundy.

Horses aren't all about racing, however. One type of horse you won't see in Newmarket is the wonderful Suffolk Punch, a massive yet elegant working horse which can still be seen at work at Rede Hall Park Farm near Bury St Edmunds and at Kentwell Hall in Long Melford. All Punches descend from Crisp's horse, foaled in 1768. The Punch is part of the Hallowed Trinity of animals at the very centre of Suffolk's agricultural history; the others being the Suffolk Sheep and the Red Poll Cow. It is entirely appropriate that the last railway station to employ a horse for shunting wagons should have been at Newmarket. That hardworking one-horse-power shunter retired in 1967.

Newmarket also has things to offer the tourist outside the equine world, including the churches of St Mary and All Saints and St Agnes, and a landmark at each end of the High Street - a Memorial Fountain in honour of Sir Daniel Cooper and the Jubilee Clock Tower commemorating Queen Victoria's Golden Jubilee.

Around Newmarket

EXNING
2 miles NW of Newmarket on the A14

A pause is certainly in order at this ancient village, whether on your way from Newmarket or arriving from Cambridgeshire on the A14. Anglo-Saxons, Romans, the Iceni and the Normans were all here, and the *Domesday Book* records the village under the name of Esselinga. The village was stricken by plague during the Iceni occupation, so its market was moved to the next village along - thus Newmarket acquired its name.

Exning's written history begins when Henry II granted the manor to the Count of Boulogne, who divided it between four of his knights. References to them and to subsequent Lords of the Manor are to be found in the little Church of St Martin, which might well have been founded by the Burgundian Christian missionary monk St Felix in the 7th century. Water from the well used by that saint to baptise members of the Saxon royal family is still used for baptisms by the current vicar.

KENTFORD
5 miles E of Newmarket by the A14

🎋 Gypsy Boy's Grave

At the old junction of the Newmarket-Bury road stands the grave of Joseph the Gypsy Boy, a shepherd boy who hanged himself after being accused of sheep-stealing. Suicides were refused burial in a churchyard, and it was a well-established superstition that suicides be buried at a crossroads to prevent their spirits from wandering. Flowers are still sometimes laid at the **Gypsy Boy's Grave**, sometimes by punters hoping for good luck at Newmarket races.

MOULTON
4 miles E of Newmarket on the B1085

This most delightful village lies in wonderful countryside on chalky downland in farming country; its proximity to Newmarket is apparent from the racehorses which are often to be seen on the large green. The River Kennett flows through the green before running north to the Lark, a tributary of the Ouse. Flint walls are a feature of many of the buildings, but the main point of interest is the 15th century four-arch Packhorse Bridge on the way to the church.

DALHAM
5 miles E of Newmarket on the B1063

🏠 Dalham Hall   🎋 St Mary's Church

Eighty per cent of the buildings in Dalham are thatched (the highest proportion in Suffolk) and there are many other attractions in this pretty village. Above the village on one of the county's highest spots stands **St Mary's** Church, which dates from the 14th century. Its spire toppled over during the gales which swept the land on the night that Cromwell died, and was replaced by a tower in 1627. Sir Martin Stutteville was the

Packhorse Bridge, Moulton

leading light behind this reconstruction; an inscription at the back of the church notes that the cost was £400. That worthy's grandfather was Thomas Stutteville, whose memorial near the altar declares that, 'he saw the New World with Francis Drake'. (Drake did not survive that journey - his third to South America.) Thomas' grandson died in the fullness of his years (62 wasn't bad for those times) while hosting a jolly evening at The Angel Hotel in Bury St Edmunds.

Dalham Hall was constructed in the first years of the 18th century at the order of the Bishop of Ely, who decreed that it should be built up until Ely Cathedral could be seen across the fens on a clear day. That view was sadly cut off in 1957 when a fire shortened the hall to only two storeys high. Wellington lived here for some years, and much later it was bought by Cecil Rhodes, who unfortunately died before taking up residence. His brother Francis erected the village hall in the adventurer's memory, and he himself is buried in the churchyard.

All in all, Dalham is a place of charm and interest - clearly no longer resembling the place described in *The Times* in the 1880s as full of ruffians and drunks, where the vicar felt obliged to give all the village children boxing lessons to increase their chances of survival.

MILDENHALL
8 miles NE of Newmarket off the A11

🏛 Church of St Mary 🏛 Museum

On the edge of the Fens and Breckland, Mildenhall is a town which has many links with the past. It was once a port for the hinterlands of West Suffolk, though the River Lark has long ceased to be a trade route. Most of the town's heritage is recorded in the

excellent **Mildenhall & District Museum** in King Street. Here will be found exhibits of local history (including the distinguished RAF and USAAF base), crafts and domestic skills, the natural history of the Fens and Breckland and, perhaps most famously, the chronicle of the 'Mildenhall Treasure'. This was a cache of 34 pieces of 4th century Roman silverware - dishes, goblets and spoons - found by a ploughman in 1946 at Thistley Green and now on display in the British Museum in London, while a replica makes its home here where it was found. There is evidence of much earlier occupation than the Roman era, with flint tools and other artefacts being unearthed in 1988 on the site of an ancient lake.

The parish of Mildenhall is the largest in Suffolk, so it is perhaps fitting that it should boast so magnificent a parish church as **St Mary's**, built of Barnack stone; it dominates the heart of the town and indeed its west tower commands the flat surrounding countryside. Above the splendid north porch (the largest in Suffolk) are the arms of Edward the Confessor and of St Edmund. The chancel, dating back to the 13th century, is a marvellous work of architecture, but pride of place goes to the east window, divided into seven vertical lights. Off the south aisle is the Chapel of St Margaret, whose altar, itself modern, contains a medieval altar stone. At the west end, the font, dating from the 15th century, bears the arms of Sir Henry Barton, who was twice Lord Mayor of London and whose tomb is located on the south side of the tower. Above the nave and aisles is a particularly fine hammerbeam roof whose outstanding feature is the carved angels. Efforts of the Puritans to destroy the angels failed, though traces of buckshot and arrowheads remain and have been found embedded in the woodwork.

Sir Henry North built a manor house on the north side of the church in the 17th century. His successors included a dynasty of the Bunbury family, who were Lords of the Manor from 1747 to 1933. Sir Henry Edward Bunbury was the man chosen to let Napoleon Bonaparte know of his exile to St Helena, but the best-known member of the family is Sir Thomas, who in 1780 tossed a coin with Lord Derby to see whose name should be borne by a race to be inaugurated at Epsom. Lord Derby won, but Sir Thomas had the satisfaction of winning the first running of the race with his colt, Diomed.

The other focal point in Mildenhall is the Market Place, with its 16th century timbered cross.

WORLINGTON
2 miles W of Mildenhall on the B1102

Worlington is a small village near the River Lark, known chiefly as the location of Wamil Hall, an Elizabethan mansion which stands on the riverbank. Popular lore has it that a person called Lady Rainbow haunts the place, though the spot she once favoured for appearances, a flight of stairs, was destroyed in one of the many fires the mansion has suffered. Cricket is very much part of the village scene (there's a splendid village green), and has been since the early days of the 19th century.

BRANDON
9 miles NE of Mildenhall on the A1065

🏛 Heritage Centre	🏛 Grime's Garves
🌲 Breckland	🌲 Thetford Forest
🌲 Brandon Country Park	

On the edge of **Thetford Forest** by the Little Ouse, Brandon was long ago a thriving port, but flint is what really put it on the map. The

town itself is built mainly of flint, and flint was mined from early Neolithic times to make arrowheads and other implements and weapons of war. The gun flint industry brought with it substantial wealth, and a good flint-knapper could produce up to 300 gun flints in an hour. The invention of the percussion cap killed off much of the need for this type of work, however, so they turned to shaping flints for church buildings and ornamental purposes. **Brandon Heritage Centre**, in a former fire station in George Street, provides visitors with a splendid insight into this industry, while for an even more tangible feel, a visit to **Grime's Graves**, just over the Norfolk border, reveals an amazing site covering 35 acres and 300 pits (one of the shafts is open to visitors). With the close proximity of numerous warrens and their rabbit population, the fur trade also flourished here, and that, too, along with forestry, is brought to life in the Heritage Centre.

The whole of this northwestern corner of Suffolk, known as **Breckland**, offers almost unlimited opportunities for touring by car, cycling or walking. A mile south of town on the B1106 is **Brandon Country Park** (see panel opposite), a 30-acre landscaped site with a tree trail, forest walks, a walled garden and a visitor centre. There's also an orienteering route leading on into Thetford Forest, Britain's largest lowland pine forest. The High Lodge Forest Centre, near Santon Downham (off the B1107), also attracts with walks, cycle trails and adventure facilities.

ELVEDEN
8 miles NE of Mildenhall on the A11

| 🏛 Elvedon Hall |

Elveden Hall became more remarkable than its builders intended when Prince Duleep Singh, the last Maharajah of Punjab and a noted

Brandon Country Park

Bury Road, Brandon, Suffolk IP27 0SU
Tel: 01842 810185

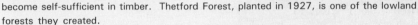

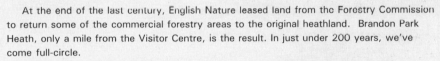

For thousands of years the area where the Park is now was an open, sandy, windswept heath. Until 1942, when Lakenheath airbase was built, it was Europe's largest inland sand dune system.

Edward Bliss, a businessman, bought over a thousand hectares of the Brecks in 1820 to create a wooded park and arboretum. By the end of World WarI, the park had fallen into neglect. As a result of the economic depression caused by the war, the Government was determined to become self-sufficient in timber. Thetford Forest, planted in 1927, is one of the lowland forests they created.

At the end of the last century, English Nature leased land from the Forestry Commission to return some of the commercial forestry areas to the original heathland. Brandon Park Heath, only a mile from the Visitor Centre, is the result. In just under 200 years, we've come full-circle.

When you and your family want to enjoy nature, and learn about the environment and its history, visit Brandon Country Park. At Brandon, you can stroll and picnic in the charming walled garden. You can also head further afield, following the invigorating walks and cycle trails that guide you through the arboretum, commercial forest and restored heathland.

sportsman, crack shot and the man who handed over the Koh-I-Noor diamond to Queen Victoria, arrived on the scene. Exiled to England with a handsome pension, he bought the Georgian house in 1863 and commissioned John Norton to transform it into a palace modelled on those in Lahore and Delhi. Although it is stated that in private Duleep Singh referred to Queen Victoria as 'Mrs Fagin … receiver of stolen goods', he kept close contact with the royal household and the Queen became his son's godmother. The Guinness family (Lord Iveagh) later took the

Hall over and joined in the fun, adding even more exotic adornments including a replica Taj Mahal, while at the same time creating the largest arable farm in the whole of the country. In recent times, Stanley Kubrick's last film, *Eyes Wide Shut*, was shot here, as was *Tomb Raider*. The Elveden Memorial is a grand 100ft Corinthian column erected in 1921 and dedicated to the memory of local soldiers from the three parishes of Elveden, Eriswell and Icklingham who died in action in World War I. Their names are inscribed on the base, and a shorter list was added after World War II.

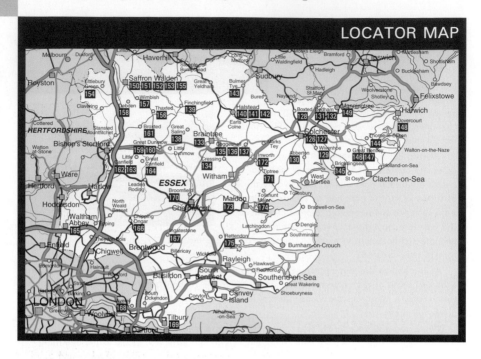

LOCATOR MAP

ADVERTISERS AND PLACES OF INTEREST

  historic building   museum   historic site   scenic attraction   flora and fauna

3|Essex

Bordering the north bank of the River Thames, Essex has long been a gateway to London, and while it contains much heavy industry and urban development, it also encompasses some lovely countryside, coastal attractions and important wildlife habitats. Northeast Essex has the true feel of East Anglia, particularly around the outstanding villages of the Stour Valley - which has come to be known as Constable Country, a title it shares with neighbouring Suffolk. The inland villages and small towns here are notably historic and picturesque, offering very good touring and walking opportunities. A plethora of half-timbered medieval buildings, farms and churches mark this region out as of particular historical interest. Monuments to engineering feats past and present include Hedingham Castle, Chappel Viaduct and the Post Mill at Bocking Church Street. There are also many lovely gardens to visit, and the region's principal town, Colchester, is a mine of interesting sights and experiences.

The north Essex coast has a distinguished history and a strong maritime heritage, as exemplified in towns like Harwich, Manningtree and Mistley. Further examples are the fine Martello Towers - circular brick edifices built to provide a coastal defence against Napoleon's armies - along the Tendring coast at Walton, Clacton, Jaywick and Point Clear. The Tendring Coast contains an interesting mix of extensive tidal inlets, sandy beaches and low cliffs, and the Tendring District Council publishes a series of Tendring Trails beginning at Mistley, Manningtree, Debenham, Ardleigh and other places along the North Essex Coast.

The Stour Estuary, Hamford Water and Colne Estuary are all renowned for seabirds and other wildlife. Many areas are protected nature reserves. In the part of the county known as 'the sunshine holiday coast' resorts, both boisterous and more tranquil, dot the landscape here: Clacton-on-Sea, Frinton-on-Sea and Walton-on-the-Naze offer many opportunities for relaxation and recreation.

The small northwest Essex towns of Saffron Walden, Thaxted, Great Dunmow and Stansted Mountfichet are among the most

🎬 stories and anecdotes   🦅 famous people   🎨 art and craft   🎭 entertainment and sport   🚶 walks

beautiful and interesting in the nation. This area is also home to a wealth of picturesque villages boasting weatherboarded houses and pargetting. This area also retains three beautiful and historic windmills, at Stansted Mountfichet, Aythorpe Roding and Thaxted. Visitors to southwest Essex and the Epping Forest will find a treasure-trove of woodland, nature reserves, superb gardens and rural delights. Epping Forest dominates much of the far western corner, but all this part of Essex is rich in countryside, forests and parks. Southwest Essex also has major attractions in Audley End House and Waltham Abbey.

Mountnessing Mill

The borough of Thurrock includes huge swathes of greenbelt country, and along its 18 miles of Thames frontage there are many important marshland wildlife habitats. History, too, abounds in this part of the county. Henry VIII built riverside block houses at East and West Tilbury, which later became Coalhouse Fort and Tilbury Fort. It was at West Tilbury that Queen Elizabeth I gave her most famous speech to her troops, gathered to meet the Spanish Armada threat. At the extreme southeast of the county, Southend is a popular and friendly seaside resort with a wealth of

sights and amenities. There are also smaller seaside communities which repay a visit. The area surrounding the Rivers Blackwater and Crouch contains a wealth of ancient woodland and other natural beauties, particularly along the estuaries and the Chelmer and Blackwater Canal.

There are hundreds of acres of ancient woodland, much of it coppiced, which is the traditional woodland-management technique which encourages a vast array of natural flora and fauna. This stretch of Essex affords some marvellous walking, cycling, birdwatching and other treats for everyone who loves the great outdoors.

Colchester

- 🏛 Castle 🏛 Castle Museum
- 🏛 Hollytrees Museum 🏛 Natural History Museum
- 🏛 Tymperleys Clock Museum 🏛 St Botolph's priory
- 🏛 Bourne Mill 🎨 Colchester Arts Centre
- 🎨 First Site 🐾 Zoo 🐾 High Woods Country Park

This ancient market town and garrison stands in the midst of rolling East Anglian countryside. England's oldest recorded town, it has over almost 3,000 years of history, much of it there to be discovered by visitors. It was first established during the 7th century BC, and to the west of town are the remains of the massive earthworks built to protect it in pre-Roman times. During the 1st century, Colchester's prime location made it an obvious target for invading Romans. The Roman Emperor Claudius accepted the surrender of 11 British Kings in Colchester (Camolodunum). In AD60, Queen Boudicca helped to establish her place in history by taking revenge on the Romans and burning the town to the ground, before going on to destroy London and St Albans. Here in this town that was once capital of Roman Britain, Roman walls - the oldest in Britain - still surround the oldest part of town. Balkerne Gate, west gate of the original Roman town, is the largest surviving Roman gateway in the country, and remains magnificent to this day.

Today the town is presided over by its lofty town hall and enormous Victorian water tower, nicknamed 'Jumbo' after London Zoo's first African elephant, an animal sold to P T

🎭 stories and anecdotes　🦅 famous people　🎨 art and craft　🎭 entertainment and sport　🚶 walks

Barnum (causing some controversy) in 1882. The tower has four massive pillars made up of one-and-a-quarter million bricks, 369 tons of stone and 142 tons of iron, all working to support the 230,000-gallon tank.

The town affords plenty to see and explore. There are many guided town walks available, as well as bus tours. The local Visitor Information Centre on Queen Street has details of the many places to visit. Market days in this thriving town are Friday and Saturday.

A good place to start any exploration of the town is **Colchester Castle** itself and its museum. When the Normans arrived, Colchester (a name given the town by the Saxons) was an important borough. The Normans built their castle on the foundations of the Roman temple of Claudius. Having used many of the Roman bricks in its construction, it boasts the largest Norman keep ever built in Europe - the only part still left standing. The keep houses the **Castle Museum**, one of the most exciting hands-on

Hollytrees Museum

High Street, Colchester, Essex CO1 1UG
Tel: 01206 282940
website: www.colchestermuseums.org.uk

Hollytrees is a beautiful Georgian town house in the grounds of the award-winning Castle Park. Built in 1718 it has been owned by some of the wealthiest families in Colchester and is now a fascinating museum for all to enjoy and explore.

History is told at this vibrant museum with humour and fun in mind, making it an ideal venue for families. Visit the childhood gallery with its a large playroom with snakes and ladders incorporated into the floor. There is a crawling tunnel, toy bins, toddler 'time out' area and exciting displays celebrating Colchester's famous nursery rhymes *Old King Cole* and *Twinkle, Twinkle Little Star*.

Meet the many different characters from the past and find out what life was like for them living and working in a house like Hollytrees. Experience Colchester's fascinating past through audio, hands-on activities and stories, and be transported back to the days before washing machines, to try out a dolly peg, dress up as a servant, make your own Victorian silhouette and experience the miniature world of the Hollytrees dolls house.

Join in with many special events and changing exhibitions throughout the year that bring history to life the fun way, and don't forget to visit the museum shop to find that perfect gift.

The museum has free admission so you can enjoy it and visit time and time again.

🏛 historic building   🏛 museum   🏛 historic site   🏞 scenic attraction   🌿 flora and fauna

Balkerne Gate, Colchester

historical attractions in the country. Its fascinating collection of Iron Age, Roman and medieval relics is one of the most important in the country. There are tombstones carved in intricate detail and exquisite examples of Roman glass and jewellery. Visitors can try on Roman togas and helmets, touch some of the 2,000-year-old pottery unearthed nearby, and experience the town's murkier past by visiting the castle prisons, where witches were interrogated by the notorious witchfinder General Matthew Hopkins. A key can be obtained at the Museum to St Martin's Church, a redundant 14th century church with recycled Roman brickwork in its fabric. **Hollytrees Museum** (see panel opposite) in the High Street is located in a fine Georgian home dating back to 1718. This award-winning museum can be found on the edge of Castle Park and houses a wonderful collection of toys, costumes, curios and antiquities from the last two centuries, and a number of fine paintings including a view of Colchester by Pissarro. Also nearby, housed in the former All Saints' Church, is the **Natural History Museum**, with exhibits and many hands-on displays illustrating the natural history of Essex from the Ice Age right up to the present day.

Housed in the Minories Art Gallery, **First Site** (see advertisement) is a recent addition to Colchester's fine choice of art institutes, and features changing exhibitions of contemporary visual art, housed in a converted Georgian town house with beautiful walled garden. An arch in Trinity Street leads to **Tymperleys Clock Museum**, the 15th century timber-framed home of William Gilberd, who entertained Elizabeth I with experiments in electricity. Today this fine example of architectural splendour houses a magnificent collection of 18th and 19th century Colchester-made clocks. The **Colchester Arts Centre**, not far from Balkerne Gate, features a regular programme of visual arts, drama, music, poetry and dance; the Mercury Theatre is the town's premier site for stage dramas, comedies and musical theatre.

Dutch Protestants arrived in Colchester in the 16th century, fleeing Spanish rule in the Netherlands, and revitalised the local cloth industry. The houses of these Flemish weavers in the Dutch Quarter to the west of the castle, and the Civil War scars on the walls of Siege House in East Street, bear testimony to their place in the town's history. The Dutch

Quarter west of the castle remains a charming and relatively quiet corner of this bustling town.

Close to the railway station are the ruins of **St Botolph's Priory**, the oldest Augustinian priory in the country. Its remains are a potent reminder of the bitterness of Civil War times, as it was here that Royalists held out for 11 weeks during the siege of Colchester, before finally being starved into submission.

On Bourne Road, south of the town centre just off the B1025, there's a striking stepped-and-curved gabled building known as **Bourne Mill**, now owned by the National Trust. Built in 1591 from stone taken from the nearby St John's Abbeygate, this delightful restored building near a lovely millpond was originally a fishing lodge, later converted (in the 19th

century) into a mill - and still in working order.

Colchester Zoo, just off the A12 outside the town, stands in the 40-acre park of Stanway Hall, with its 16th century mansion and church dating from the 14th century. Founded in 1963, the Zoo has a wide and exciting variety of attractions. The Zoo has gained a well-deserved reputation as one of the best in Europe. Its award-winning enclosures allow visitors closer to the animals and provide naturalistic environments for the 170 species. There are 15 unique daily displays including opportunities to feed an African elephant, bear, chimp or alligator, stroke a snake and watch a penguin parade. Among major new attractions are the sea lion pool with an underwater tunnel and 'Tiger Taiga' for the endangered Siberian tiger.

Colchester has been famous in its time for

CARTER'S VINEYARDS

Green Lane, Boxted, nr Colchester, Essex CO4 5TS
Tel: 01206 271136   Fax: 01206 273625
e-mail: enquiries@cartersvineyards.co.uk
website: www.cartersvineyards.co.uk

Carter's Vineyards extend to seven acres of planted vines and, with over 40 acres of wildflower meadows, lakes and woodland, provide a glorious setting in the picturesque Stour Valley. The vines produce a number of award-winning wines that appeal to a variety of tastes:-

Sparkling: Lovejoy and Colchester Sparkling Rosé
Red: King Coel and Boudicca
Aromatic Dry White: Carter's Bacchus
Crisp Dry White: Orion
Medium Dry: St Helena and Colchester Rosé

Visitors can tour the vineyards and take advantage of the various attractions of owner Ben Bunting's enterprise. The modest entrance fee includes a video show and a self-guided tour of the vines and winery usually accompanied by the owners friendly dogs! Nature trails lead round the lakes and through woodland and meadows abounding in wildlife – lucky visitors might spot the family of kingfishers in residence. Evening visits, including light supper and guided tour, can be arranged. One of the most interesting features of this fascinating place is the alternative energy project that harnesses wind and sun to produce electricity to run the whole enterprise. Carter's Vineyards are open between 11am and 5pm from Easter Monday to the end of October.

🏨 historic building   🏛 museum   🏚 historic site   🐟 scenic attraction   🌱 flora and fauna

both oysters and roses. Colchester oysters are still cultivated on beds in the lower reaches of the River Colne, which skirts the northern edge of town. A visit to the Oyster Fisheries on Mersea Island is a fascinating experience, and the tour includes complimentary fresh oysters and a glass of wine.

Just north of the centre of town, **High Woods Country Park** offers 330 acres of woodland, grassland, scrub and farmland. A central lake is fed by a small tributary of the River Colne. The land originated as three ancient farms, and forms part of a Royal hunting forest. Large numbers of musket balls dating from the Civil War period have been unearthed, indicating that the woods served as a base for the Roundheads.

Wivenhoe

Around Colchester

WIVENHOE
4 miles SE of Colchester off the A133

This riverside town on the banks of the River Colne was once renowned as a smugglers' haunt, and its pretty quayside is steeped in maritime history. There are still strong connections with the sea, with boat-building having replaced fishing as the main industry. The lovely church, with its distinctive cupola atop a sturdy tower, stands on the site of the former Saxon church and retains some impressive 16th century brasses.

The small streets lead into each other and end at the picturesque waterfront, where fishing boats and small sailing craft bob at their moorings. On the Quay visitors will find the Nottage Institute, the River Colne's nautical academy; classes here teach students about knots, skippering and even

---

THE VILLAGE DELICATESSEN

4 High Street, Wivenhoe, nr Colchester, Essex CO7 9BJ
Tel: 01206 822824

Behind the smart frontage of a 16th century building by the Church of St Mary the Virgin, the **Village Delicatessen** is a magnet for the food-lovers of Wivenhoe and the surrounding area. It's owned by Katharine Lilley and Michael Foreman who also have the Dedham Gourmet, and the range of top-quality foodstuffs is similar: a fine selection of cheeses, locally made preserves and pickles, daily deliveries of bread and cakes, free range Suffolk ham and bacon, and loose teas and coffees. There are also interesting wines and quality local and imported beers.

---

how to build a boat. It is open to visitors on Sundays in summer. The Wivenhoe Trail, by the river, is an interesting cycle track starting at the railway station and continuing along the river to Colchester Hythe. Wivenhoe Woods is dotted with grassy glades set with tables, the perfect place for a picnic.

East of the Quay, the public footpath takes visitors to the Tidal Surge Barrier, one of only two in the country. Volunteers run a ferry service operating across the River Colne between the Quay at Wivenhoe, Fingringhoe and Rowhedge. Nearby Wivenhoe Park has been the site of the campus for the University of Essex since 1962. Visitors are welcome to stroll around the grounds.

ABBERTON

3 miles S of Colchester off the B1026

🐦 Abberton Reservoir Nature Reserve

🐦 Fingringhoe Wick Nature Reserve

Two natural beauties are within reach of this village. **Abberton Reservoir Nature Reserve** is a 1,200-acre reservoir and wildlife

centre, ideal for birdwatching. A site of international importance, home to goldeneye, wigeon, gadwall and shovellers, as well as a resting colony of cormorants, the site features a conservation room, shop, toilets and hides.

Four miles further east, **Fingringhoe Wick Nature Reserve** offers visitors 125 acres of woodland and lakes by the Colne estuary. Bird watchers and nature lovers will happily explore the grassland, heathland, estuarine and freshwater habitats. Open all year round except on Mondays, the reserve hosts a full programme of events including children's activity days.

COPFORD

3½ miles SW of Colchester off the B1022

🏛 Church of St Michael & All Angels

Copford is home to the wonderful Norman Church of **St Michael and All Angels**, with its magnificent, well-restored medieval wall paintings, while Copford Green is a lovely and peaceful village. The Church of St Mary the Virgin also repays a visit.

🏛 historic building   📷 museum   🏛 historic site   🔎 scenic attraction   🐦 flora and fauna

LAYER BRETON

5½ miles SW of Colchester off the B1026

On the right side of Layer Breton Heath is Stamps and Crows, a must for gardening enthusiasts. Two-and-a-half acres of moated garden surrounding a 15th century farmhouse. The farmhouse is not open to the public, but the gardens boast herbaceous borders, mixed shrubs, old roses and good ground cover. There is also a recently created bog garden and dovecote.

LAYER MARNEY

6 miles SW of Colchester off the B1022

🏛 Layer Marney Tower

🏛 Church of St Mary

The palace, which was planned to rival Hampton Court, was never completed, but its massive eight-storey Tudor gatehouse, known as **Layer Marney Tower**, is very impressive. Built between 1515 and 1525, it is one of the most striking examples of 16th century architecture in Britain. Its magnificent four red brick towers, covered in 16th century Italianate design, were built by Lord Marney, Henry VIII's Lord Privy Seal. As well as spectacular views from the top of the towers, they are surrounded by formal gardens designed at the turn of the century, with lovely roses, yew hedges and herbaceous borders. There is also on site a rare breeds farm, farm shop and tea room. The **Church of St Mary** that was built behind the site of the palace is one of the finest in the county, with a chapel and many monuments to the Marney family and a charming mural of St Christopher.

Off the B1026 a couple of miles southwest of Layer Marney is the village of Great Wigborough, which saw an early visit from a German airship. Zeppelin L33, which was hit over Bromley, crashed here in September 1916; a contemporary record of the event is in St Stephen's Church, framed by aluminium taken from the wreck.

ALDHAM

4 miles W of Colchester off the A604

This picturesque village was, for a time, home to the famous Essex historian Philip Morant,

Layer Marney Tower

Layer Breton

Distance: *4.0 miles (6.44 kilometres)*

Typical time: *90 mins*

Height gain: *10 metres*

Map: *Explorer 184*

Walk: *www.walkingworld.com ID:1458*

Contributor: *Brian and Anne Sandland*

ACCESS INFORMATION:

The walk starts in the car park of Layer Breton church.

ADDITIONAL INFORMATION:

Layer Marney Tower was built around 1520 by Henry VIII's Privy Seal. It is the tallest Tudor tower and has a magnificent residence, farm and gardens attached.

DESCRIPTION:

Following field paths and country lanes this walk takes you through three small, out-of-the-way settlements, past two churches, a deer compound and a magnificent tower.

FEATURES:

Toilets, Museum, Play Area, Church, Wildlife, Birds, Flowers, Butterflies, Good for Kids, Mostly Flat, Ancient Monument

WALK DIRECTIONS:

1 | From Layer Breton church car park take the road south then the first road right (signposted Layer Marney and Tiptree). Follow Shatters Road past a pond and then a junction left. Where the road goes sharp right take a signposted footpath left.

2 | Follow the path, which bends right then follows the right hand edge of a field and heads in a dead straight line to the right of Layer Marney Tower and church. When you reach a road go left. At the entrance to Layer Marney Tower car park go right.

3 | Pass the entrance to the Tower, then the church (right) and continue on a broad grass track which bends left then right (signposted) beside a deer compound, carrying on ahead when the wire fence bends left to pass through a hedge and cross a ditch by a footbridge. Continue along the right hand edge of another huge field to a gap in the hedge (right), then pass a garage (left) and use the drive of a house to reach the road at a junction where you go right.

4 | Just after the road bends right and before houses on the right take a footpath left.

5 | Cross the stile and head straight across the field to a gap in the hedge between two telegraph poles. Bear half right to head for a stile next to a gate with houses beyond. At the road go right then continue ahead (signposted Messing, Kelvedon and Colchester). Continue to a path off right through trees where the road begins a sharp left hand bend.

6 | Follow the path to the B1022 and turn right. When this road goes sharp left take a

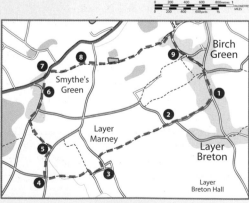

signposted footpath right (through a lay-by) to keep a hedge on your right.

7 | Continue to a stile through the hedge on the right. Cross this, turn left and carry on to another stile, which you cross to reach a road.

8 | Cross the road and take a signposted footpath over a stile. Cross a small field and another signposted stile and footbridge, and follow a clear path ahead to a track on a bend where you continue ahead passing a reservoir on your left . Ignore a track off left. Your track passes two lonely oak trees then heads towards houses. Just beyond Briar Cottage turn right on a tarmac lane past housing on both sides.

9 | You pass houses on your left and trees and a tall hedge right, then when you reach another road you turn right to return to the church car park at Layer Breton.

who held the post of vicar here. He is buried in the local churchyard. Old Hill House in Aldham is a one-acre garden with mixed shrubs, herbaceous borders and formal herb garden for year-round interest.

CHAPPEL
5 miles W of Colchester off the A604

East Anglian Railway Museum   Chappel Viaduct

Here, on a four-acre site beside Chappel and Wakes Colne Station, is the **East Anglian Railway Museum**, a comprehensive collection spanning 150 years of railway history, with period railway architecture, engineering and memorabilia in beautifully restored station buildings. For every railway buff, young or old, this is the place to try your hand at being a signalman and admire the handsome restored engines and carriages. There is also a delightful miniature railway. Special steam days and other events are held throughout the year.

The dramatic 32-arched **Chappel Viaduct** standing 75 feet above the Colne Valley, a designated European Monument, was begun in 1846 and opened in 1849.

ARDLEIGH
3 miles NE of Colchester off the A137

The westernmost village in the district known as Tendring comprises an attractive group of 16th and 17th century cottages grouped around the fine 15th century Butterfield Church. Spring Valley Mill, a now privately owned 18th century timber-framed and weatherboarded edifice, was once a working watermill, later adapted to steam. Day and half-day canoeing and sailing lessons can be taken at the Ardleigh Outdoor Education Centre.

Nearby is Ardleigh Reservoir, offering up many opportunities for water sports and trout fishing.

DEDHAM
6 miles NE of Colchester off the A14

Toy Museum   Bridge Cottage
Sir Alfred Munnings Art Museum
Dedham Vale Family Farm

This is true Constable country, along the border with Suffolk, the county's prettiest area. The village has several fine old buildings, especially the 15th century flint church, its pinnacled tower familiar from so many Constable paintings. There's also the school Constable went to, and good walks through the protected riverside meadows of Dedham Vale to **Flatford**, where **Bridge Cottage** is a restored thatched 16th century building housing a display about Constable, who featured this cottage in several of his paintings (his father's mill is across the river lock in Dedham).

Dedham Vale Family Farm on Mill Street

MILSOM HOTELS

Gun Hill, Dedham, nr Colchester, Essex CO7 6HP
Tel: 01206 321125   Fax: 01206 323689
e-mail: sue@milsomhotels.com   website: www.milsomhotels.com

The above are the head office details. Contact: Sue Bunting, Sales & Marketing Manager

In 1952, Gerald Milsom discovered a tea room in a beautiful setting by the River Stour. The delightful timber-framed Le Talbooth was the start of a company that has expanded under the Milsom family to comprise three properties within half a mile of each other in Dedham and another in the historic port of Harwich.

Le Talbooth, which retains much of the atmosphere of its 16th century origins, is an acclaimed restaurant where the chefs add flair and individuality to classic and contemporary cuisine. The freshest ingredients, many of them locally sourced, guarantee a memorable dining experience, and the stock in the wine cellar reflects and complements the quality of the cooking; the immaculate gardens and grounds add another delightful dimension. **Maison Talbooth**, a splendid Victorian country house, is the hotel sister to Le Talbooth, located a short distance along the river, with dedicated transport available between the two. The 10 superb bedrooms combine a comfortable contemporary style and up-to-date amenities with a great respect for the original features. Each room has a style and character all its own, and the undoubted stars of the show are the principal suites, Shakespeare and Keats, with Mulberry fabrics, Bang & Olufsen TVs and hot tubs on private terraces. **milsoms** is a lively gastrobar that's open throughout the day, an ideal choice for meeting friends or entertaining business clients, and a great place to unwind with a glass of wine at the end of the working day. In the dining area the chefs produce an extensive range of dishes with British, European and Asian influences. At most times of the year a drink or a meal can be enjoyed on the terrace with its huge sail-style canopy and patio heaters. milsoms also has 15 stylish, well-equipped bedrooms. Standing on the quay in Harwich, **The Pier** has two restaurants and 14 bedrooms. Sparkling fresh seafood is the speciality in the first-floor Harbourside Restaurant, much of it landed at Harwich harbour. The ground-floor Ha'penny Pier offers similar quality in a relaxed brasserie-style setting. Natural fabrics and muted colours give an understated elegance to the bedrooms, which include a suite with panoramic views – and a telescope to enjoy them.

The Milsom establishments offer a variety of meeting and function facilities, and Talbooth Catering can plan off-site banquets and functions for almost any numbers.

Le Talbooth Restaurant, Gun Hill, Dedham CO7 6HP
Tel: 01206 323150 Fax: 01206 322309 e-mail: talbooth@milsomhotels.com
Maison Talbooth, Stratford Road, Dedham
Tel: 01206 322367 Fax: 01206 322752 e-mail: maison@milsomhotels.com
milsoms, Stratford Road, Dedham
Tel: 01206 322795 Fax: 01206 323689 e-mail: milsoms@milsomhotels.com
The Pier at Harwich, The Quay, Harwich CO12 3HH
Tel: 01255 241212 Fax: 01255 551922

🏛 historic building   🏛 museum   🏛 historic site   🜨 scenic attraction   🌱 flora and fauna

THE DEDHAM GOURMET

High Street, Dedham, Essex CO7 6HA
Tel: 01206 323623

A lifelong passion for good food led Katharine Lilley several years ago to buy the **Dedham Gourmet** in the High Street. Now situated in a handsome corner property, the Gourmet specialises in British cheeses and locally made products such as jams, pickles, mustards and dressings. There is also charcuterie, including free range Suffolk ham, daily bread and cake deliveries from a local baker, filled rolls made to order, fresh coffee and Christmas puddings made by Katharine's mum. The range of wines is small but interesting and varied. Katherine and her husband Michael Foreman also own the Village Delicatessen at Wivenhoe.

is a traditional 16-acre farm boasting a comprehensive collection of British farm animals, including many different breeds of livestock such as pigs, sheep, cattle, Suffolk horses, goats and poultry. Children may enter some of the paddocks to stroke and feed the animals (bags of feed provided).

The Art & Craft Centre on Dedham's High Street is well worth a visit. Marlborough Head, a wool merchant's house dating back to 1475, is now a pub. The **Toy Museum** has a fascinating collection of dolls, teddies, toys, games, doll houses and other artefacts of childhoods past.

At Castle House, approximately three-quarters of a mile from the village centre on the corner of East Lane and Castle Hill, The **Sir Alfred Munnings Art Museum** is housed in the former home, studios and grounds of the famous painter, who lived here between 1898 and 1920. The museum prides itself on the diversity of paintings and sculptures on view. The house itself is a mixture of Tudor and Georgian periods, carefully restored. Munnings' original furniture is still in place. The spacious grounds boast well-maintained gardens.

Braintree

 Museum

The twin towns of Braintree and Bocking are sited at the crossroads of two Roman roads and Braintree in particular was a Roman market town with evidence of metal industries and farming. However, it is the establishment of the wool industry in the 14th century, with many of the original timber framed buildings from this era still surviving in Bradford Street, which led to the spreading fame

River Stour, Dedham

📖 stories and anecdotes   🐿 famous people   🎨 art and craft   ✐ entertainment and sport   🚶 walks

of the towns. Flemish weavers settled in the District bringing their weaving skills and by the 17th century the bay cloth trade was well established. It was the sudden demise of the wool trade at the end of the 18th century which attracted the Huguenot family of Courtauld to settle in the District and establish a silk weaving industry. Courtaulds developed mechanised weaving of silk and by the 1860's employed over 3,000 local workers. The Company became a worldwide success after the artificial silk industry revolutionised fashion and houseold textiles in the 20th century.

The **Braintree District Museum** (see panel below) housed in a Victorian school on Manor Street tell the story of the fascinating industrial heritage of the District and the Warner Textile Archive, part of the Museum's collection, is housed in the Warner's Mills in Silks Way, Samuel Courtauld's original Mill which was sold to Daniel Walters and later Warner & Son. The Warner Textile Collection is the second largest archive in Britain and has examples of the many leading 19th and 20th century designers who worked for the Company.

The magnificent Town Hall Centre is one of the many Courtauld legacies in the town. It was built in 1928 with panelled walls, murals by Grieffenhagen showing scenes of local history, and a grand central tower with a striking clock. Another fascinating reminder of the Courtaulds generosity is the 1930's bronze fountain portraying a young boy with dolphins, near St Michaels Church, which itself was founded in 1199.

A Market Charter was awarded by King John, also in 1199, and a colourful street market

BRAINTREE DISTRICT MUSEUM

The Town Hall Centre, Market Place, Braintree, Essex CM7 3YG
Tel: 01376 328868   Fax: 01376 344345
e-mail: museum@braintree.gov.uk
website: www.enjoybraintreedistrict.co.uk

In the historic market square (market days Wednesday and Saturday), **Braintree District Museum** is housed in a beautifully converted Victorian school. Visitors are assured of a warm welcome at this award-winning museum, whose elegant exhibition areas are in contrast to the somewhat stern Victorian façade; the exception to this is the faithfully re-created Victorian classroom, where nostalgia lovers will be in their element and where role-play lessons are provided for schools on a daily basis.

Braintree was the centre of the medieval wool trade in north Essex and gained international fame when Courtaulds evolved their revolutionary silk industry in the town. The permanent galleries tell the fascinating story of this industry and also of the development of engineering design - Braintree was also the home of Crittalls. Country crafts such as straw plaiting are featured, along with the rural artists who made their home in Great Barfield and became pivotal in the development of fine and decorative arts in the 1950s and 1960s. John Ray, often considered the father of English natural history, has a dedicated gallery to his ground-breaking research in the 17th century.

A feature of the museum is the programme of changing exhibitions, often with a craft base such as ceramics, decorative arts and particularly textiles. Friendly staff are pleased to welcome visitors with a free Soundalive audio tour and explain the wide range of craft items available in the shop.

🏠 historic building   🏛 museum   🏛 historic site   ♔ scenic attraction   ❦ flora and fauna

Cressing Temple Barns

Witham Road, Braintree, Essex CM7 8PD
Tel: 01376 584903
website: www.cressingtemple.org.uk

The 13th century wheat and barley barns at Cressing Temple are of unequalled national and international importance being the finest remaining pair of medieval barns in Europe.

The Manor of Cressing was granted to the Order of the Knights Templar in 1137 by Matilda, wife of King Stephen, and the barns were built during this period. In 1312 the Knights Templar were disbanded and the manor of Cressing was given to another religious order, the Knights Hospitaller.

In 1381, during the Peasants' Revolt, Cressing Temple was attacked and the buildings pulled down, but the barns were not touched. The estate was then leased to John Edmondes in 1515 and later to Sir John Smyth. He probably built the great house that was once on the site. This was demolished in the 16th century although the Tudor granary and walled garden still remain.

An exhibition located in one half of the wheat barn explains the history of the manor and the Templars, how the barns were built and how the other buildings fit into the wider context of the regional timber-framed building tradition.

A Tudor garden has been recreated in the 16th century walled garden. The garden features knot gardens, a flowery mead, a nosegay garden and physic plant area. Special attractions include a fount, a pool watered by a rill, an arbour and a viewing platform set at the same height as the original Tudor terrace. A new visitor centre houses a shop and restaurant.

is still held to this day every Wednesday and Saturday. Gants, perculiar to the town, trace the original layout of the medieval market.

Around Braintree

FAIRSTEAD
4 miles S of Braintree off the A131

🏠 Church of St Mary & St Peter

Fairstead (or Fairsted) is an undulating parish about three miles east of the A131, some four miles northwest of Witham. The **Church of St Mary and St Peter** is an ancient building of flint, in the Norman style, consisting of

chancel, nave, north porch and a western tower with a lofty shingled spire with four bells, one of which dates back to before the Reformation. During restoration in the late 1800s various handsome mural paintings were discovered, including, over the chancel arch, those entitled *Our Lord's Triumphal Entry into Jerusalem, The Last Supper, The Betrayal, Our Lord being crowned with thorns, and Incidents on the way to Calvary.*

CRESSING
4 miles SE of Braintree off the B1018

🏠 Cressing Temple Barns

Cressing Temple Barns (see panel above), set in the centre of an ancient farmstead, are

BAUMANNS BRASSERIE

4-6 Stoneham Street, Coggeshall, Essex CO6 1TT
Tel: 01376 561453 Fax: 01376 563762
e-mail: food@baumannsbrasserie.co.uk
website: www.baumannsbrasserie.co.uk

Situated in the historic and picturesque market town of Coggeshall, Baumanns Brasserie is an absolute must for food lovers. Guests can dine on anything from pan-fried medallions of venison with sweet and sour leeks, to caviar and chips. Meanwhile, regular jazz evenings are held in the intimate half-timbered dining room.

Owned by internationally acclaimed Master Chef, Mark Baumann, this bright 16th century brasserie offers a truly relaxed dining experience. Former chef at Langan's Brasserie, Coggeshall, Mark took over the restaurant following the tragic death of eccentric Irish entrepreneur Peter Langan in 1988. While the brasserie has retained all its original charm and character, it is the restaurant's fine cuisine that has earned it such a wide acclaim.

Featured in every major food guide in Great Britain, Baumanns Brasserie is famous for its innovative cuisine and a la carte menu. Trained at the Royal Champagne (France) owned by Moet & Chandon, Mark applies the same attention to detail when cooking for patrons of his brasserie as when he has cooked for royalty.

Tourists can have a light lunch following a visit to nearby Marks Hall Estate and Arboretum, one of a number of country parks in the surrounding area. After lunch a short trip to Colchester Castle, a stroll round the many local antiques shops and boutiques, or a walk along the awesome and varied Essex coastline might conclude the perfect day out. A former location for the BBC series *Lovejoy*, Coggeshall is steeped in English history and is home to several National Trust properties.

Mark Baumann

Mark recently received global acclaim with an inclusion in *The International Who's Who of Chefs*. He is among just under 3,000 chefs from 70 countries to make the list, sharing the limelight with notables including Michel Roux of Le Gavroche in London; Alan Bird head chef at The Ivy Restaurant in London; Raymond Blanc of Le Manoir aux Quat'Saisons in Great Milton, Oxford; Jamie Oliver of Fifteen in London; and John Williams executive chef at Claridges Hotel, London.

Mark has notched up a number of TV appearances, both with his own ITV Anglia series *Baumann Goes to Market* and as a guest presenter of UKTV Food's flagship programme *Great Food Live*. Diners can view footage of Mark's TV appearances via the restaurant website.

🏠 historic building   🏛 museum   🏛 historic site   ⚘ scenic attraction   🌿 flora and fauna

two splendid medieval timber barns commissioned in the 12th century by the Knights Templar. They contain the timber of over 1,000 oak trees; an interpretive exhibition explains to visitors how the barns were made, as a special viewing platform brings visitors up into the roof of the magnificent Wheat Barn for a closer look. There's also a beautiful walled garden re-creating the Tudor style, with an arbour, fount and physic garden. Special events are held throughout the year.

COGGESHALL

5 miles E of Braintree on the A120

🏠 Paycocke's House 🏠 Grange Barn

📖 Marks Hall

This medieval hamlet, a pleasant old cloth and lace town, has some very fine timbered buildings. **Paycocke's House** on West Street, a delightful timber-framed medieval merchant's home dating from about 1500, boasts unusually rich panelling and wood carvings, and is owned by the National Trust. Inside there's a superb carved ceiling and a display of Coggeshall lace. Outdoors there's a lovely garden. The village also has some good antique shops and a working pottery.

Located in Stoneham Street, Coggeshall

Heritage Centre displays items of local interest and features changing exhibitions on themes relating to the past of this historic wool town. There's an authentic, working wool loom on site.

The National Trust also owns the restored **Coggeshall Grange Barn**, which dates from around 1140 and is the oldest surviving timber-framed barn in Europe. Built for the monks of the nearby Cistercian Abbey, it is a magnificent example of this type of architecture.

Marks Hall is an historic estate and arboretum that began life in Saxon times, and is mentioned in the *Domesday Book*. In the 15th century, then-owner Sir Thomas Honywood was a leading Parliamentarian who commanded the Essex Regiment during the Civil War. Local legend has it that the two artificial lakes on the grounds were dug by Parliamentary troops during the siege of Colchester in 1648. One of his successors, General Philip Honywood, in 1758 forbade (under the terms of his will) any of his successors to fell timber - thus his lasting legacy of avenues of mature oaks, limes and horse chestnuts, surrounded by one of the largest continuous areas of ancient woodland in the county.

📖 stories and anecdotes   🍴 famous people   🎨 art and craft   🎭 entertainment and sport   🚶 walks

OUT OF THE BLUE

20a Church Street, Coggeshall,
Essex CO6 1TX
Tel/Fax: 01376 564229

A collection of beautiful bags, evening wear, casual clothing, accessories, jewellery and much more can be found at **Out of the Blue**, a delightful emporium of unusual fashion in late-19 th century premises a short walk from the town centre. Anyone looking for something out of the ordinary and completely original should visit this gem of a place, where owner Henrietta Lyttelton showcases the work of some of the country's top emerging designers. Exquisite beaded dresses, tops and skirts, luxurious chenilles and velvets, handmade bags, suede skirts and coats, silk scarves, jewellery made with freshwater pearls, semi-precious stones and fashions from Out of Xile, Cazz, Flax, Rene Derhy, Patric Casey and After Shock.

The interior of the shop is custom designed and fitted, while retaining some fine old beams, and the overall effect is of a fresh modern ambience that is spot on for a contemporary fashion shop. Customers looking for an outfit that is both fashionable and distinctive need look no further than Out of the Blue.

The estate fell on hard times in the 19th and early 20th century, but owner Thomas Phillips Price began an association with Kew Gardens and left the estate to be held and used for 'advancement in the National interest of Agriculture, Aboriculture and Forestry'. The Thomas Phillips Price Trust was formed and registered as a charity in 1971, and a major programme of revitalisation and restoration began. The estate now flourishes with native plants and wildlife, ornamental lakes, a 17th century walled garden, cascades, Coach House and Information Centre. This last is housed in a painstakingly refurbished 15th century barn, and features informative displays as well as a gift shop and tea room.

Plans for the on-site arboretum were first drawn up in the late 1980s, to cover 120 acres. Still being established, it will contain a collection of trees from all over the world, laid out in geographical themes - Europe, Asia, America, and the southern hemisphere.

FEERING
6 miles E of Braintree off the A12

Feeringbury Manor near Feering has a fine, extensive riverside garden with ponds, streams, a little waterwheel, old-fashioned plants and bog gardens, and fascinating sculpture by artist Ben Coode-Adams.

BLAKE END
3 miles W of Braintree off the A120

🏵 Craft centre   🕴 The Great Maze

The Great Maze at Blake End is one of the most challenging in the world. Set in over 10 acres of lovely North Essex farmland, it is

THE WHITE HART INN

The Street, Great Saling, nr Braintree, Essex CM7 5DT
Tel: 01371 850341

The **White Hart Inn** is a 16th century country pub with good food at reasonable prices, real ales and comfortable accommodation. The Euston family – Brian, Rhoda and daughter Kathy – are the friendliest of hosts, and the beamed bar is a perfect spot to meet old friends and make new ones over a glass of beer. The White Hart enjoys a fine reputation for the quality of its cooking, and in the atmospheric Gallery restaurant classic British dishes, including super fish specials, keep the customers happy. For visitors exploring the local countryside and quaint Essex villages, the pub offers luxurious self-contained B&B accommodation with en suite facilities and Sky TV.

grown every year from over half a million individual maize and sunflower seeds, and is open every summer. Continuing innovations bring with them extra twists and turns, making this wonderful maze, with more than five miles of pathways, even more of a brain teaser. A viewing platform makes it easy to help anyone hopelessly lost! Ten per cent of all profits go to the Essex Air Ambulance service.

Blake House Craft Centre comprises carefully preserved farm buildings centred round a courtyard. One of the county's prettiest craft centres, visitors will find a fine array of craft shops and a restaurant serving breakfast and morning coffee, lunch and afternoon tea.

GREAT SALING
4 miles NW of Braintree off the A120

Saling Hall Garden is a 12-acre garden including a walled garden dating from 1698. The small park boasts a collection of fine trees, and there are ponds, a water garden and an extensive collection of unusual plants with an emphasis on rare trees.

WETHERSFIELD
5 miles NW of Braintree on the B1053

Boydells Dairy Farm is a working farm where visitors are welcome to join in with tasks such as milking, feeding and more. A guided tour mixes fun with education, and all questions are most welcome. From bees to llamas, just about every kind of farm animal can be found here. Goat rides and donkey cart rides, a lovely picnic area and refreshments made on site make for a most enjoyable day out. Open to the public April to September.

FINCHINGFIELD
6 miles NW of Braintree off the B1053

🏠 Church of St John the Baptist 🏠 Guildhall

This charming village is graced with thatched cottages spread generously around a sloping village green that dips to a stream and duck pond at the centre of the village. Nearby stands an attractive small 18th century Post Mill with one pair of stones and tailpole winding. Extensively restored, today's visitors can climb up the first two floors.

Just up the hill, visitors will find the Norman church of **St John the Baptist**, and the **Guildhall** (mentioned in the *Domesday Book*), which has a small museum open Sundays and also houses a local heritage centre with displays of artwork, paintings, pottery, sewing and weaving.

📖 stories and anecdotes   🎭 famous people   🎨 art and craft   🎵 entertainment and sport   🚶 walks

MALLARDS

The Green, Finchingfield, Essex CM7 4JS
Tel: 01371 811188   mob: 07960 469251
e-mail: jacquie@mallardsoffinchingfield.co.uk
website: www.mallardsoffinchingfield.co.uk

Next to the pond in the village where ducks take priority over cars, **Mallards** is a place where customers can set their imaginations free. The warm, inviting interior of the 100-year-old premises is full of beautiful, stylish and unusual items to make a house special, and what the pictures, lamps, ornaments, furniture, throws and bedding, glassware and jewellery have in common is their originality.

Owners Alan and Jacquie Pirrie have taken various themes, including French and English country style and displayed them on beautiful antique pine furniture in this wonderful shop in one of the prettiest villages in England. The owners and their friendly, helpful staff are on hand with help and advice, and the peaceful, relaxed atmosphere, the variety of the stock and the very realistic prices make any visit here an occasion to savour. Mallards has another feather in its cap in the shape of a party plan – home visits can be arranged.

Finchingfield is easily one of the most picturesque and most photographed villages in Essex, featured in many TV programmes and the home of the series *Lovejoy*. Here visitors will also find the privately owned Tudor stately home, Spains Hall, which has a lovely flower garden containing a huge Cedar of Lebanon planted in 1670 and an Adams sundial. Many good roses surround the kitchen garden, which contains an ancient Paulonia tree and a bougainvillea in the greenhouse. The garden is generally open on Sunday afternoons in summer.

Finchingfield also has an easily followed path along the Finchingfield Brook leading from the village to Great Bardfield.

Finchingfield

🏠 historic building   🏛 museum   🏚 historic site   🦢 scenic attraction   🌿 flora and fauna

GREAT BARDFIELD
6 miles NW of Braintree off the B1053

 Museum

This old market town on a hill above the River Pant is a pleasant mixture of cottages and shops, nicely complemented by the 14th century Church of St Mary the Virgin. Perhaps Great Bardfield's most notable feature is, however, a restored windmill that goes by the unusual name of 'Gibraltar'.

Here in one of the prettiest villages in all of Essex, the **Great Bardfield Museum** occupies a 16th century charity cottage and 19th century village lockup, and features exhibits of mainly 19th and 20th century domestic and agricultural artefacts and some fine examples of rural crafts such as corn-dollies and straw-plaiting.

GOSFIELD
4 miles N of Braintree off the A1017

Gosfield Lake Leisure Resort

Gosfield Lake Leisure Resort, the county's largest freshwater lake, lies in the grounds of Gosfield Hall. This Tudor mansion was remodelled in the 19th century by its owner Samuel Courtauld. He also built the attractive mock-Tudor houses in the village.

Halstead

Townsford Mill

The name 'Halstead' comes from the Anglo-Saxon for *healthy place*. Like Braintree and Coggeshall, Halstead was an important weaving centre. **Townsford Mill** is certainly

HEAD STREET GALLERY

1 Head Street, Halstead, Essex CO9 2AT
Tel: 01787 472705
e-mail: information@headstreetgallery.co.uk

Head Street Gallery is relaxed, affordable and accessible, with friendly staff offering a wide range of fine art and hand-crafted gifts to suit all tastes and budgets. Visitors are encouraged to take time to browse around the three gallery rooms and enjoy the quality and variety of works on offer.

Combining paintings and sculpture with furniture, ceramics, glass, jewellery, toys, cards and handmade gifts, an impressive selection of work is always on display. Exhibitions of paintings change every eight weeks throughout the year.

With a coffee bar serving freshly ground coffee and other beverages, why not browse through the gallery's art library, or take advantage of the gift wrapping service to make a special gift even more special.

Head Street Gallery is situated on the A131 just beyond the top of Halstead High Street, directly opposite St Andrew's Church. It is open daily, excluding Wednesdays, Sundays and Bank Holidays from 9am to 5.30pm.

stories and anecdotes   famous people   art and craft   entertainment and sport   walks

EVANS

14 High Street, Halstead, Essex CO9 2AP
Tel/Fax: 01787 472799
e-mail: huderrick@aol.com

Hugh and Sue Derrick own and run **Evans**, a home
fashion and accessories shop in 1830s premises on the
main street of Halstead. One of the most important
ranges is SIA Inspiration home fashion, ranging from silk
flowers and table linen to china, glass, picture frames,
mirrors and garden furniture. The owners travel
extensively to source new stock, which includes lovely
painted furniture from France and a variety of other
furniture. Sheets and quilts, pillows and cushions come
from England, Ireland, France and Italy, and there's a
large selection of wicker baskets for many purposes –
linen, washing, bread, logs and dogs.

  Among the smaller items on display are lamps and
lampshades, white china, candles, soaps, pictures,
prints and greeting cards. Hugh and Sue and their staff
are particularly friendly and helpful, making browsing
and shopping at Evans a real pleasure, and with the stock constantly changing, every visit is
certain to reveal something new and desirable, whether it's something for the home or for a
special gift. A second Evans has recently opened in Great Bentley.

HIWAY UK LTD

Unit 8, 2nd Avenue, Halstead, Essex CO9 2SU
Tel/Fax: 01787 475665
e-mail: sales@hiwaycraft.co.uk
website: www.hiwaycrafts.co.uk

Tim Jenkins spent much of his working life as a print
supplier to the paper industry, so it was a natural
progression that led him, in 2002, to open Hiway UK,
the on-line offshoot of Hiway Crafts, a hobby and craft
centre featuring the top names in card-making supplies.
The shop, located on the Bluebridge Estate a short drive
from the centre of Halstead, is stocked with an amazing
range of arts and crafts items, including all forms of
card-making, rubber stamps, stencils, pens and pencils,
water, oil and acrylic paints, brushes, sketch pads scrap
books, beads, threads and tapes, cross-stitch kits,
modelling clay, inkjet paper........and a great deal more.

  A comfortable seating area, where customers can
take a break and enjoy free tea or coffee, is also used
for the classes that Tim runs on a regular basis. One-
hour, two-hour and all day courses cover a variety of
craft topics, including absolutely everything to do with card-making. Spring 2006 saw the
addition of a craft, gift and picture gallery at the showroom.

the most picturesque reminder of Halstead's industrial heritage. Built in the 1700s, it remains one of the most handsome buildings in a town with a number of historic buildings. This white, weatherboarded three-storey mill across the River Colne at the Causeway was once a landmark site for the Courtauld empire, producing both the famous funerary crepe and rayon. Today the Mill is an antiques centre, one of the largest in Essex, with thousands of items of furniture, porcelain, collectables, stamps, coins, books, dolls, postcards, costume, paintings, glass and ceramics, old lace and clocks.

There are several historic buildings in the shopping centre of Halstead, which is part of a designated conservation area.

Though it may now seem somewhat improbable, Halstead's most famous product was once mechanical elephants. Life-sized and weighing half a ton, they were built by one W Hunwicks. Each one consisted of 9,000 parts and could carry a load of eight adults and four children at speeds of up to 12 miles per hour. Rather less unusual is the Tortoise Foundry Company, remembered for its warm 'tortoise stoves'

Around Halstead

CASTLE HEDINGHAM
3 miles NW of Halstead off the B1058

🏰 Castle 🏛 Colne Valley Railway Museum

🐾 Colne Valley Farm Park

This town is named after its Norman **Castle**, which dominates the landscape. One of England's strongest fortresses in the 11th century, even now it is impossible not to sense its power and strength. The impressive stone keep is one of the tallest in Europe, with four floors and rising over 100 feet, with 12ft thick walls. The banqueting hall and minstrels' gallery can still be seen. It was owned by the Earls of Oxford, the powerful de Veres family, one of whom was among the barons who forced King John to accept the Magna Carta. Amongst those entertained at the castle were Henry VII and Elizabeth I.

The village itself is a maze of narrow streets radiating from Falcon Square, named after the half-timbered Falcon Inn.

Castle Hedingham

🎭 stories and anecdotes   🐦 famous people   🎨 art and craft   🖉 entertainment and sport   🚶 walks

THE BULMER BRICK & TILE CO LTD

Bulmer, Near Sudbury, Suffolk CO10 7EF
Tel: 01787 269232   Fax: 01787 269040
e-mail: bbt@bulmerbrickandtile.co.uk

A brickworks has stood on the site of **Bulmer Brick & Tile Co Lt**d since the 15th century. Today it is a family business run by Peter Minter and his two sons, Tony and David. Peter's father Lawrence moved to Bulmer in 1936 when looking to start a business of his own, having trained and worked for many years for F.G.Minters, a large and successful building firm in London.

The Second World War came soon afterwards, and many of the staff were called up for military service. Peter's early knowledge came from the older men too old for call up. This, in years to come, proved invaluable when, after Laurie's death in 1974, Peter was asked to speak at a conference that was looking at the heritage of the trade for the first time. It became clear that people had lost many of the old skills, skills that Bulmer Brick still used and took for granted. Peter began re-learning old techniques, and remembering what the old craftsmen had said.

Today, almost all the production is made to order. Responding to the needs of buildings country wide, exploiting the wonderful natural resource of London bed clay that matches so well buildings such as Hampton Court Palace and the exciting development of St Pancras Station, or the old windmill at Moulton, standing close by The Wash. A collection of some 5,000 moulds, many over 100 years old, adds to the continuity of brick, terracotta, tiles and red rubbers that are the hallmark of Bulmer.

Attractive buildings include many Georgian and 15th century houses comfortably vying for space, and the Church of St Nicholas, built by the de Veres, which avoided Victorian 'restoration' and is virtually completely Norman, with grand masonry and interestingly carved choir seats. There is a working pottery in St James' Street.

At the **Colne Valley Railway and Museum**, a mile of the Colne Valley and Halstead line between Castle Hedingham and Great Yeldham has been restored and now runs steam trains operated by enthusiasts. These lovingly restored Victorian railway buildings feature a collection of vintage engines and carriages; short steam train trips are available. **Colne Valley Farm Park**, set in 30 acres of traditional river meadows, is open from April to September.

The B1058 towards Sudbury, then left through Gestingthorpe and the Belchamps, makes for a pleasant excursion.

SIBLE HEDINGHAM
3 miles NW of Halstead off the A1017

Mentioned in the *Domesday Book* as the largest parish in England, Sible Hedingham was the birthplace of Sir John Hawkwood, one of the 14th century's most famous soldiers of fortune. He led a band of mercenaries to Italy, where he was paid to defend Florence and where he also died. Hawkwood was buried in Florence Cathedral, where he is commemorated with a fresco by Uccello. It is thought that his body was returned to Essex and lies beneath the monument to him in Sible Hedingham's Church of St Stephen, decorated with hawks and various other beasts.

Swan Street is the main artery of this charming village, boasting several delightful establishments devoted to providing visitors and natives of the town with places to shop, dine, enjoy a quiet drink and even stay for the night.

GESTINGTHORP
5 miles N of Halstead off the A131

🏛 Church of St Mary the Virgin

The Church of **St Mary the Virgin** in Gestingthorp is distinctive in many respects. Witness to centuries of Christian worship, the *Domesday Book* of 1086 tells that 'Ghestingetorp' was held by Ledmer the priest before 1066. The oldest part extant of the existing building is the blocked-up lancet window in the north wall of the chancel, which dates back to the 1200s. Apart from this, most of the chancel, nave and south aisle dates from the 14th century. The tower, constructed in about 1500, is 66 feet high. Of the six bells hung in the tower, four were cast in 1658-9 by Miles Gray, a Colchester bellfounder. The 16th century fifth and sixth bells were cast in Bury St Edmunds, and recast in 1901. The west door, set in a stepped brick arch, is the original. The unusual tracery in the East window consists of arches placed atop the apexes of the arches beneath them. The late 15th century/early 16th century nave roof is of the double hammer-beam type, and one of the finest in Essex. The font is late 14th century. One of the church's handsome memorials commemorates Captain L E G Oates, who died in an attempt to save the lives of his companions on an ill-fated expedition to the Antarctic in 1912.

The North Essex Coast

The Essex Sunshine Coast has 36 miles of clean, sandy beaches, including two European Blue Flag beaches (Brightlingsea and Dovercourt Bay) and five Seaside award winning beaches at Clacton, Frinton, Walton, Brightlingsea and Dovercourt Bay.

CLACTON-ON-SEA
16 miles SE of Colchester on the A133

🏖 Jaywick Sands

Clacton is a traditional sun-and-sand family resort with a south-facing, long sandy beach, lovely gardens on the seafront and a wide variety of shops and places to explore. It also boasts a wide variety of special events and entertainments taking place throughout the year.

Settled by hunters during the Stone Age - which is borne witness to by the wealth of flint implements and the fossilised bones of the cave lion, straight-tusked elephant and wild ox unearthed on the Clacton foreshore and at Lion Point - the town grew over the centuries from a small village into a prosperous seaside resort in the 1800s, when the craze for the health benefits of coastal air and bathing was at its peak. The Pier was constructed in 1871; at first paddle steamers provided the only mode of transport to the resort, the railway arriving in 1882. The Pier was widened from 30 to over 300 feet in the 1930s. On the pier, apart from the traditional sideshows, big wheel, restaurants and fairground rides, there is the fascinating Seaquarium and Reptile Safari.

Amusement centres include the arcades and Clacton Pavilion. The two theatres, Princes Theatre and West Cliff, are open all year. Clacton Pavilion boasts a range of attractions, including crazy golf, dodgems and a rock & roll Fun House. The Clifftop Public Gardens also repay a visit.

Great Clacton is the oldest part of town,

comprising an attractive grouping of shops, pubs and restaurants within the shadow of the 12th century parish church.

A walk round the town rewards the visitor with some very handsome sights. There are three Martello Towers along this bit of the Essex coast. Just south of the town, **Jaywick Sands** is the ideal spot for a picnic by the sea, boasting one of the finest natural sandy beaches in the county.

LITTLE CLACTON
3 miles NW of Clacton off the A133

Church of St James

Though it shares its name with its near neighbour, this is a town apart. Quiet and secluded, multiple-winner of the Best Kept Village Award, Little Clacton features a lovely Jubilee Oak, planted to celebrate Victoria's 50th year on the throne.

The fine **Church of St James** has been described as one of the most beautiful medieval churches in Essex, and sits at the heart of the village

Oakwood Crafts Resource Centre in Little Clacton provides an environment for people with learning disabilities to learn and develop work skills, motivation, responsibility, team spirit, self-esteem and confidence through horticulture, woodwork, ceramics, crafts and catering. Set in three acres of land, it opened in 1975 and, as a horticultural centre, sells a wide range of bedding plants, shrubs and hanging baskets seasonally, along with a selection of wooden garden implements, furnishings and other items, and ceramics. Teas and coffees are available.

WEELEY
5 miles NW of Clacton off the A133

St Andrew's is the handsome parish church just south of the centre of this picturesque village. There is a lovely tree-lined path that passes Weeleyhall Wood and Weeley Lodge, with its beautifully kept gardens. Here visitors will also pass a navigational beacon that forms part of Aircraft Flight Operations for both civil and military flights.

A mile south, off the B1411, Weeley Heath is a small and attractive community boasting a lovely village green and stunning surrounding countryside.

TENDRING
7 miles NW of Clacton off the A133

This village that gives its name to both the peninsula and the district council contains the handsome Church of St Edmund with its elegant spire which can be seen for miles around. The church is dedicated to the last King of independent East Anglia, martyred by the Danes in the 9th century.

BEAUMONT-CUM-MOZE
7 miles NW of Clacton off the B114

This small village once had a quay originally constructed for loading and unloading the vessels plying the Walton backwaters. The disused Trading Quay was rebuilt in 1832 using stone from the old London Bridge. The 11th century parish Church of St Leonard contains the grave of Viscount Byng of Vimy, one-time Governor General of Canada.

HOLLAND-ON-SEA
1½ miles NE of Clacton off the B1032

Holland Haven Country Park

This attractive community is home to **Holland Haven Country Park**, 100 acres of open space near the seashore, ideal for watching the marine birds and other wildlife of the region. Throughout the area there are a number of attractive walks which take full

EPICURIOUS DELI

The Old Shop, High Street, Thorpe-le-Soken,
nr Frinton-on-Sea, Essex CO16 0EY
Tel: 01255 860707

On the main street of Thorpe-le-Soken, a short drive inland from Frinton-on-Sea, **Epicurious Deli** is the younger sibling of the long-established Manningtree Deli in High Street Manningtree. The range and quality of the speciality foods on offer are similar, with the finest bacon, sausages and patés, seafood, oils, vinegars, preserves and pickles, pasta, herbs and spices, fresh-bakes bread, cakes and pastries, luxury chocolates, speciality teas and coffees and an impressive range of wines, ports and whiskies. Open 8.30am to 5.30pm Monday to Saturday.

advantage of the varied coastal scenery.

FRINTON-ON-SEA

3 miles NE of Clacton off the B1032

Once a quiet fishing village, this town was developed as a select resort by Sir Richard Cooper, and expanded in the 1880s to the genteel family resort it is today. Situated on a long stretch of sandy beach, Frinton remains peaceful and unspoilt. The tree-lined residential avenues sweep elegantly down to the Esplanade and extensive clifftop greensward. Along its main shopping street in Connaught Avenue, the 'Bond Street' of the East Coast, shopkeepers maintain a tradition of friendly and courteous service. Summer theatre and other open-air events take place throughout the season, and there are also some excellent tennis and golf clubs in the town. The grace and elegance of this sophisticated resort is evidenced all round, as are hints of its distinguished past: Victorian beach huts still dot the extensive beach.

The area south of Frinton Gates has a unique local character, being laid out with detached houses set along broad tree-lined avenues.

The Church of Old St Mary in the town contains some panels of stained glass in the East window designed by the Pre-Raphaelite artist Burne Jones.

A good example of 20th century English vernacular architecture is The Homestead at the corner of Second Avenue and Holland Road, built in 1905 by C F Voysey.

KIRBY-LE-SOKEN

5 miles NE of Clacton off the B1034

There is a footpath in this attractive village which begins to the west of the 14th century Ship Inn and affords views of the backwaters of Hamford Water, with views of Horsey and Hedge End Islands in the middle distance.

WALTON-ON-THE-NAZE

8 miles NE of Clacton on the B1034

Old Lifeboat House Museum The Naze

Walton is all the fun of the fair. It is a cheerful, traditional resort which focuses on the pier and all its attractions, including a 10-pin bowling alley. The gardens at the seafront are colourful and the beach has good sand. The Backwaters to the rear of Walton are made up of a series of small harbours and saltings, which lead into Harwich harbour. Walton has an outstanding sandy beach. The town's seafront was developed in 1825 and provides a fine insight into the character of an early

Victorian seaside resort. The charming narrow streets of the town contain numerous shops, restaurants and pubs overlooking the second longest pier in the country. Marine Parade, originally called The Crescent, was built in 1832. The Pier, first built in 1830, was originally constructed of wood and measured 330 feet in length. It was extended to its present length of 2,610 feet in 1898.

Walton-on-the-Naze

The wind-blown expanse of **The Naze** just north of Walton is an extensive coastal recreation and picnic area, pleasant for walking, especially out of season when the visitor is unlikely to have to share the 150 acres, with great views out over the water. The shape of the Naze is constantly changing, eroded by wind, water and tide.

The year 1796 saw the demise of the medieval church, and somewhere beyond the 800-foot pier lies medieval Walton. The sandstone cliffs are internationally important for their shell fossil deposits. Inhabitants have been enjoying the bracing sea air at Walton since before Neolithic times: flint-shaping instruments have been found here, and the fossil teeth and the ears of sharks and whales have been discovered in the Naze's red crag cliffs. The Naze Tower is brickbuilt and octagonal in shape, originally built as a beacon in 1720 to warn seamen of the West Rocks off shore. A nature trail has been created nearby, and the Essex Skipper butterfly and Emperor moth can be seen here. The John

Weston Nature Reserve provides important habitats for migrant birds.

The **Old Lifeboat House Museum** at East Terrace, in a building over 100 years old, houses an interpretive museum of local history and development, rural and maritime, covering Walton, Frinton and the Sokens.

BRIGHTLINGSEA
7 miles W of Clacton on the B1029

🏚 All Saints Church 🏚 Jacobes Hall 🏛 Museum

Brightlingsea enjoys a long tradition of shipbuilding and seafaring. In 1347, 51 men and five ships were sent to the siege of Calais. Among the crew members of Sir Francis Drake's fleet which vanquished the Spanish Armada was one William of Brightlingsea. Brightlingsea has the distinction of being the only limb of the Cinque Ports outside Kent and Sussex.

🏚 historic building   🏛 museum   🏛 historic site   🔱 scenic attraction   🐦 flora and fauna

CORNFLOWER WHOLEFOODS

49 High Street, Brightlingsea, Essex CO7 0AQ
Tel/Fax: 01206 306679

Cornflower Wholefoods was established here in Brightlingsea's High Street in the 1980s and bought by Alice and Ray Davies in February 2006. The 200-year-old premises have a delightful period look, providing a charming ambience in which to tarry while deciding on which particular goodies to buy. And that can be quite a problem, as everything is top-quality and

really appetising, with locally sourced organic products a speciality and everything geared to promoting healthy, wholesome eating and living. There's an excellent array of delicatessen items in the chilled display cabinets, along with super preserves and chutneys, bread, eggs, dried pulses and legumes, fruit, nuts, rice, flour, fruit juices, herbs and spices. The shop also stocks a range of specialist foods, including gluten-free and dairy-free, and a range of herbal and homeopathic remedies.

Alice has another shop, the nearby dress agency **Chrysalis** at 2 Osbornes Court. Tel: 01206 303106.

The 13th century **Jacobes Hall** in the town centre is one of the oldest occupied buildings in Essex. It is timber-framed with an undulating tile roof and an external staircase. Used as a meeting hall during the reign of Henry III, its name originates from its first owner, Edmund, Vicar of Brightlingsea, who was known locally as Jacob le Clerk.

All Saints Church, which occupies the highest point of the town on a hill about a mile from the centre, is mainly 13th century. Here are to be found some Roman brickwork and a frieze of ceramic tiles commemorating local

All Saints Church, Brightlingsea

CARPENTERS FARM SHOP

*Carpenters Farm, St Mary's Road, Aingers Green,
Great Bentley, nr Colchester, Essex CO7 8NJ
Tel/Fax: 01206 250221
e-mail: fiona.morton@carpentersfarmshop.co.uk
website: www.carpentersfarmshop.co.uk*

Carpenters Farm Shop and PYO Fruit is a treasure waiting to be discovered. Its attractive displays and well stocked shelves are full of farm-fresh, local and regional foods and drinks. The shop, now in its 15th year, sells an array of fresh and frozen produce including free-range, organic, vegetarian and gluten-free options. The display includes meat, poultry, fish, bread, deli items, icecreams, cakes and pies, preserves and honeys, confectionery, plants and food-related gifts. The shop is one mile south of Great Bentley railway station and opens seven days a week. Visa, Mastercard and Amex are accepted.

EVANS

The Green, Great Bentley, Essex CO7 8PJ

Having established their first **Evans** on Halstead's High Street, Hugh and Sue Derrick have opened a second branch on the Green at Great Bentley. The shop stocks a wide range of items to enhance the home, including the SIA Inspiration range of home fashion that runs from silk flowers, table linen and glassware to garden furniture. Also on display are French painted furniture, bedding, lamps, candles, soaps, white china, cards, prints and wicker baskets to hold bread, linen, logs or dogs.

residents whose lives were lost at sea. Its 97-foot tower can be seen from 17 miles out to sea. A light was once placed in the tower to guide the town's fishermen home.

The Town Hard is where you can see all the waterfront comings and goings, including the activities of the Colne Smack Preservation Society, which maintains a seagoing link with the past.

Brightlingsea Museum in Duke Street offers an insight into the lives, customs and traditions of the area, housing a collection of exhibits relating to the town's maritime connections and the oyster industry.

There are plenty of superb walks along Brightlingsea Creek and the River Colne,

which offer a chance to watch the birdlife on the saltings and the plethora of boats on the water. Today the town is a haven for the yachting fraternity and is the home of national and international sailing championships, with one of the best stretches of sailing on the East Coast. Day and half-day sailing and canoeing sessions are held at the Brightlingsea Outdoor Education Centre. A foot ferry service operates between Brightlingsea, St Ostyh and East Mersea.

GREAT BENTLEY

4 miles N of Brightlingsea off the A133

Reputed to have the largest village green in England, this lovely village has a number of shops, a pub with a restaurant, a beautiful church and a chapel.

ELMSTEAD MARKET
6 miles N of Brightlingsea off the A120

🌿 Beth Chatto Gardens

The Church of St Anne and St Lawrence to the north of this village has a rare carved oak, recumbent effigy of a knight in armour.

Elmstead Market is perhaps best known as the location of **Beth Chatto Gardens**, at White Barn House, renowned the world over. Here visitors will find five acres of landscaped gardens including extensive water gardens, shady walks and a Mediterranean-style gravel garden where aromatic drought loving plants thrive. The adjoining nursery contains a wide variety of plants for sale. Close by is the Rolts Nursery Butterfly Farm.

THORRINGTON
3 miles NW of Brightlingsea off the AB1027

Thorrington Tide Mill, built in the early 19th century, is the only remaining Tide Mill in Essex, and one of very few left in East Anglia. It has been fully restored, and although no longer in use, the Wheel can be run for guided groups. There is a public footpath which runs along the creek.

China Maroc Bonsai is a specialist nursery, part of which is devoted to a peaceful Japanese garden with a waterfall and pool, where one can enjoy the tranquil atmosphere and the many fascinating outdoor bonsai. Crossing the bridge over the pool, one enters a tropical tunnel containing hundreds of indoor bonsai, many of which are imported from the hotter regions of the world, as well as bonsai and seedlings grown and cultivated on the premises.

POINT CLEAR
2 miles SE of Brightlingsea off the B1027

🏛 East Essex Aviation Society & Museum

The **East Essex Aviation Society & Museum**, located in the Martello Tower at Point Clear, not only retains its original flooring and roof, but today contains interesting displays of wartime aviation, military and naval photographs, uniforms and other memorabilia with local and US Air Force connections. There are artefacts on show from the crash sites of wartime aircraft in the Tendring area, including the engine and fuselage section of a recovered P51D Mustang fighter. The museum also explores civil and military history from both World Wars. There are very good views from the tower over the Colne Estuary and Brightlingsea.

ST OSYTH
3 miles SE of Brightlingsea off the B1027

🏛 Priory

This pretty little village has a fascinating history and centres around its Norman church and the ancient ruins of **St Osyth Priory**, founded in the 12th century. The village and Priory were named by Augustinian Canons after St Osytha, martyred daughter of Frithenwald, first Christian King of the East Angles, who was beheaded by Diceian pirates in AD 653. Little of the original Priory remains, except for the magnificent late 15th century flint gatehouse, complete with battlements.

The village is centred on a crossroads and contains an attractive group of shops and restaurants. The Church of St Peter and St Paul in the village centre has unusual internal red brick piers and arches. The nearby creek has a small boatyard and water-skiing lake.

MERSEA ISLAND
2 miles SW of Brightlingsea off the B1025

🏛 Mersea Island Museum   🍃 Nature Reserve

🍃 Cudmore Grove Country Park

Much of this island is a **National Nature Reserve**, home to its teeming shorelife. The island is linked to the mainland by a narrow causeway which is covered over at high tide. The towns of both East and West Mersea have excellent facilities for sailing enthusiasts. On the High Street, West Mersea, **Mersea Island Museum** has exhibits of Mersea's social and natural history, archaeology and the fishing industry, including a fisherman's cottage display. Visitors to Mersea Island Vineyard at East Mersea can take a conducted tour followed by wine tasting and a seafood platter. East Mersea is also a haven for birdwatchers.

Cudmore Grove Country Park on Bromans Lane, East Mersea, boasts fine views across the Colne and Blackwater estuaries.

Grassland adjoining a sandy beach, it's an ideal spot for shore walks and picnics. A pathway on the sea wall leads to a birdwatching hide.

Harwich

🏛 Maritime Museum   🏛 Lifeboat Museum

🏛 National Museum of Wireless and Television

🏛 The Redoubt

Harwich's name probably originates from the time of King Alfred, when 'hare' meant army, and 'wic' a camp. This attractive old town was built in the 13th century by the Earls of Norfolk to exploit its strategic position on the Stour and Orwell estuary; the town has an important and fascinating maritime history, the legacy of which continues into the present.

During the 14th and 15th century French campaigns, Harwich was an important naval base. The famous Elizabethan seafarers Hawkins, Frobisher and Drake sailed from Harwich on various expeditions; in 1561 Queen Elizabeth I visited the town, describing it 'a pretty place and want[ing] for nothing'. Christopher Newport, leader of the *Goodspeed* expedition which founded Jamestown, Virginia, in 1607, and Christopher Jones, master of the Pilgrim ship *The Mayflower*, lived in Harwich (the latter just off the quay in

Old Thames Barge at Harwich

🏛 historic building   🏛 museum   🎟 historic site   🜄 scenic attraction   🍃 flora and fauna

King's Head Street), as did Jones' kinsman John Alden, who sailed to America in 1620. The diarist Samuel Pepys was MP for the town in the 1660s, at a time when it was the headquarters for the King's Navy. Charles II took the first pleasure cruise from Harwich's shores. Other notable visitors included Lord Nelson and Lady Hamilton, who are reputed to have stayed at The Three Cups in Church Street.

Harwich remains popular as a vantage point for watching incoming and outgoing shipping in the harbour and across the waters to Felixstowe. Nowadays, lightships, buoys and miles of strong chain are stored along the front, and passengers arriving on North Sea ferries at Harwich International Port see the 90-foot high, six-sided High Lighthouse as the first landmark. Now housing the **National Museum of Wireless & Television**, it was built in 1818 along with the Low Lighthouse. When the two lighthouses were in line they could indicate a safe shipping channel into the harbour. Each had replaced earlier wooden structures, and were themselves replaced by cast iron structures (both of which still stand on the front in nearby Dovercourt) in 1863 when the shifting sandbanks altered the channel. Shipping now relies on light buoys to find its way. The Low lighthouse is now the town's **Maritime Museum**, with specialist displays on the Royal Navy and commercial shipping.

Two other worthwhile museums in the town are the **Lifeboat Museum** off Wellington Road, which contains the last Clacton offshore 34-foot lifeboat and a history of the lifeboat service in Harwich, and the Ha'penny Pier Visitor Centre on the Quay, with information on everything in Harwich

and a small heritage exhibition. Throughout the summer, there are guided walking tours starting at the visitor centre.

The Treadwheel Crane now stands on Harwich Green, but for over 250 years it was sited in the Naval Shipyard. It is worked by two people walking in two 16-foot diameter wheels, and is the only known British example of its kind. Amazingly, it was operational up until the 1920s. Another fascinating piece of the town's history is the Electric Palace Cinema, built in 1911 and now the oldest unaltered purpose-built cinema in Britain. It was restored by a trust and re-opened in 1981.

The importance of Harwich's port during the 19th century is confirmed by **The Redoubt**, a huge grey fort built between 1808 and 1810. Its design is an enlarged version of the Martello towers which dotted the English coast, awaiting a Napoleonic invasion that never came (some of these towers, of course, still exist). Today the Harwich Society has largely restored it and opened it as a small museum.

The old town also contains many ancient buildings, including the Guildhall, which was rebuilt in 1769 and is located in Church Street. The Council chamber, Mayor's Parlour and other rooms may be viewed. The former gaol contains unique graffiti of ships, probably carved by prisoners, and is well worth putting aside a morning to explore (by appointment only).

Around Harwich

DOVERCOURT
1 mile S of Harwich off the A120

This residential and holiday suburb of

ROWLES OF DOVERCOURT

280-282 High Street, Dovercourt, Essex CO12 3PD
Tel: 01255 503636

Rowles of Dovercourt is two shops side by side in a single high-street building, one specialising in jewellery, the other in quality gifts. The business is owned and run by Janet Chapman and Julie Pratt, who took over the premises in 1998 when George and Betty Rowles retired.

The impressive window display offers glimpse of the lovely things inside, and Janet and Julie regularly attend trade fairs to ensure that the stock includes the latest fashions and 'must-have' items.

The jewellery section includes an excellent selection of rings, necklaces, bracelets, chains and earrings, as well as costume jewellery and a good range of watches. The gift shop, reached through the first, is filled with displays of lovely things for the home, including picture frames, clocks, jewellery boxes, Tiffany and Florence lamps, Willow Tree figurines, Royal Brierley, Aynsley china, Poole Pottery, vases by Franz and Disney characters from Enesco.

Rowles is open five days a week – closed Wednesday and Sunday.

Harwich has Market Day on Fridays. With its attractive cliffs and beach, it also boasts the Iron Lighthouse or 'Leading Lights' located just off lower Marine Parade. The town has been settled from prehistoric times, as attested to by the late Bronze Age axe-heads found here (now in Colchester Museum). The Romans found the town a useful source of the stone 'Septaria', taken from the cliffs and used in building. The town that visitors see today developed primarily in Victorian times as a fashionable resort.

MISTLEY

7 miles W of Harwich off the B1352

🏛 Mistley Towers   🌳 Mistley Place Park

✒ Mistley Quay Workshops

Here at the gateway to Constable Country,

local 18th century landowner and MP Richard Rigby had grand designs to develop Mistley into a fashionable spa to rival Harrogate and Bath, adopting the swan as its symbol. Sadly, all that remains of Rigby's ambitious scheme is the Swan Fountain, a small number of attractive Georgian houses and **Mistley Towers**, the remains of a church (otherwise demolished in 1870) designed by the flamboyant architect Robert Adams. From the waterfront, noted for its colony of swans, there are very pleasant views across the estuary to Suffolk. Mistley was once an important port and shipbuilding centre – Nelson's huge flagship *Amphian* was built here. Traditional crafts are still carried on in **Mistley Quay Workshops**, including a pottery workshop, lute/cello maker, harpsichord maker, wood worker, bookbinder, and stained-glass window maker and restorer. There is also a tea-shop on the premises (the key to Mistley Towers can be obtained from the Workshops).

Mistley Place Park Animal Rescue Centre is 25 acres of parkland affording country walks, wildlife habitats, lake, farm animals and great views across the Stour Estuary. Over 2,000 rescued animals, including rabbits, Vietnamese pigs and horses, roam freely.

MANNINGTREE

9 miles W of Harwich off the B1352

Museum   The Walls

The Walls, on the approach to Manningtree along the B1352, offer unrivalled views of the Stour estuary and the Suffolk coast, and the swans for which the area is famous. Lying on the River Stour amid beautiful rolling countryside, the scene has oft been depicted by artists over the centuries.

Back in Tudor times, Manningtree was the centre of the cloth trade, and later a port filled with barges carrying their various cargoes along the coast to London. Water still dominates today and the town is a centre of leisure sailing.

Manningtree has been a market town since 1238, and is still a busy shopping centre. It is the smallest town in Britain, and a stroll through the streets reveals the diversity of its past. There are still traditional (and mainly Georgian) restaurants, pubs and shops, as well as handcraft and specialist outlets. The views over the river are well known to birdspotters, sailors and ramblers. The town has an intriguing past - as a river crossing, market, smugglers' haven and home of Matthew Hopkins, the reviled and self-styled Witchfinder General who struck terror into the local community during the 17th century. Some of his victims were hanged on Manningtree's small village green.

It is believed that the reference in Shakespeare's *Henry IV* to Falstaff as 'that roasted Manningtree ox' relates to the practice of roasting an entire ox, as was known at that time to be done at the town's annual fair.

Manningtree Museum in the High Street opened in the late 1980s and mounts two exhibitions a year, together with permanent photographs and pieces relating to the heritage of Manningtree, Lawford, Mistley and the district.

Saffron Walden

🏚 Audley End house	🏛 Museum
🏛 War Memorial	
🏞 Common 🎨 Fry Public Art Gallery	

Named after the Saffron crocus - grown in the area to make dyestuffs and fulfil a variety of other uses in the Middle Ages - Saffron Walden has retained much of its original street plan, as well as hundreds of fine old buildings, many of which are timbered and have overhanging upper floors and decorative plastering (also known as pargetting). Gog and Magog (or, in some versions, folk-hero Tom Hickathrift and the Wisbech Giant) battle forever in plaster on the gable of the Old Sun Inn, where, legend has it, Oliver Cromwell and General Fairfax both lodged during the Civil War.

A typical market town, Saffron Walden's centrepiece is its magnificent church. At the **Saffron Walden Museum**, as well as the gloves worn by Mary Queen of Scots on the day she died is a piece of human skin which once coated the church door at Hadstock. The museum first opened to the public at its present location in 1835, and was founded 'to gratify the inclination of all who value natural history'. It remains faithful to this credo, while widening the museum's scope in the ensuing years. The museum has won numerous awards, including joint winner of the Museum of the Year Award for best museum of Industrial or Social History in 1997. At this friendly, family-sized museum visitors can try their hand at corn grinding with a Romano-British quern, see how a medieval timber house would have been built, admire the displays of Native American and West African embroidery, and come face to face with Wallace the Lion, the museum's faithful guardian. Over two floors, exhibits focus on town and country (with a wealth of wooden ploughs and other agricultural artefacts), furniture and woodwork, costumes, ancient Egyptian and Roman artefacts, geology exhibits, and ceramics and glass. In the Ages of Man gallery, the history of northwest Essex is traced from the Ice Age to the Middle Ages. The ruins of historic Walden Castle are also on-site.

On the local **Common**, once known as Castle Green, is the largest surviving Turf Maze in England. Only eight ancient turf mazes survive in England: though there were many more in the Middle Ages, if they are not looked after they soon become overgrown and are lost. This one is believed to be some 800 years old.

DISH

13a King Street, Saffron Walden, Essex CB10 1HE
Tel: 01799 513300
website: www.dishrestaurant.co.uk

Brother-and-sister owners Spencer and Emma have the services of an excellent chef in Robert Carroll at **Dish**, a light, airy, first-floor restaurant in 17th century premises in the centre of town. In surroundings that stylishly combine original and modern elements, diners enjoy freshly prepared dishes on menus typified by sautéed scallops with a truffle and cauliflower purée and roasted spiced pears; superb fillet steak; and cannelloni filled with spinach, artichokes and mozzarella. Jazz-themed paintings by Spencer and Emma's father adorn the walls of this Dish, and the sister Dish in Great Dunmow.

🏚 historic building 🏛 museum 🏛 historic site 🏞 scenic attraction 🌿 flora and fauna

Though many miles from the sea, it was here that Henry Winstanley - inventor, engineer and engraver, and designer of the first Eddystone Lighthouse at Plymouth - was born in 1644. He is said to have held 'lighthouse trials' with a wooden lantern in the lavishly decorated 15th to 16th century church. The Lighthouse, and Winstanley with it, were swept away in a fierce storm in 1703.

The town was also famous for its resident Cockatrice, which was reputed to have hatched from a cock's egg by a toad or serpent and could, it was said, kill its victims with a glance. The Cockatrice was blamed for any inexplicable disaster in the town. Like Perseus and Medusa the Gorgon, a Cockatrice could be destroyed by making it see its own reflection, thereby turning it to stone. The Saffron Walden Cockatrice's slayer was said to be a knight in a coat of 'cristal glass'.

To the north of the town are the Bridge End Gardens, a wonderfully restored example of early Victorian gardens, complete with the unique Hedge Maze, which is open only by appointment (which can be made at the TIC). A viewing platform was reinstated in 2000 to enhance visitors' enjoyment of these lovely gardens.

Next to the gardens is the **Fry Public Art Gallery**, with a unique collection of work by 20th century artists and designers who lived in and around Saffron Walden, such as Edward Bawden, Michael Rothenstein, Eric Ravilious, Kenneth Rowntree, Michael Ayrton, John Aldridge and Sheila Robinson. It also exhibits work by contemporary artists working in Essex today, demonstrating the area's continuing artistic tradition. The gallery was

📖 stories and anecdotes   🕊 famous people   🎨 art and craft   🎭 entertainment and sport   🚶 walks

purpose-designed and opened in 1856 to house the collection of Francis Gibson, a Quaker banker and sometime Mayor of Saffron Walden. The gallery also houses the Lewis George Fry RBA, RWA (1860-1933) Collection, which is exhibited each summer, along with works by Robert Fry (1866-1934) and Anthony Fry.

Close to Bridge End is the **Anglo-American War Memorial** dedicated by Field Marshal the Viscount Montgomery of Alamein in 1953 to the memory of all the American flyers of the 65th Fighter Wing who lost their lives in the Second World War.

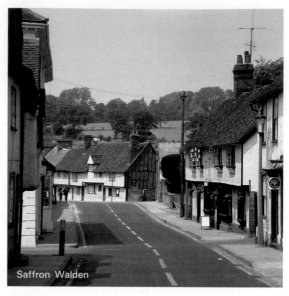

Saffron Walden

BETTER THAN CHOCOLATE

4 The Cockpit, Emson Close, Saffron Walden, Essex CB10 1HL
Tel/Fax: 01799 523533

Think of something that most women like and some can't live without. Chocolate. Think of something even better, even more essential to living. The answer might well be shopping for clothes, especially in a shop like **Better Than Chocolate**.

This friendly shop on two floors of a centuries-old building specialises in 'ladies lingerie and more....', the more including swimwear, nightwear and hosiery. On display is a wide range of all these items, everyday, unusual and exotic, and owners Jean and Aileen and their staff are always on hand to help and advise.

Lingerie suppliers include Prima Donna, Marie-Jo, Aubade, Fantasie, Charnos and Chantelle; swimwear – Maryan, Mehlhorn, Lidea, Charmline, Christina, Eda and Moontide; nightwear – Repose, Rossella, Arianne, Verde Veronica and Miss Elaine. Historical note: the cellar was used during the Civil War by Cromwell's men, but of course that was long before there was any lingerie to try on!

Audley End House

Saffron Walden, Essex CB11 4JF
Tel: 01799 522399

The beautiful interior of Audely End House remains largely unaltered since the early 1820s, reflecting many generations of style changes. Elaborately decorated rooms range from small and intimate dressing rooms, bedrooms and sitting rooms, to the magnificent Great Apartment. Some are decorated in Robert Adam's trademark Neo Classical style, while others retain their original Jacobean appearance. Paintings by masters such as Holbein, Lely and Canaletto can be admired throughout. Audley End's gift shop offers a wonderful range of interesting souvenirs, and refreshments are available. An artificial lake created with water from the River Cam runs through delightful 18th century pastoral parkland, designed by Capability Brown. The Classical Temple of Concorde, built in 1790 in honour of George III, and the restored 19th-century formal parterre garden, with its elaborately designed flowerbeds, dominate the views from the back of the house. A thriving walled Victorian kitchen garden, cultivating organic produce originally grown on the estate, and a magnificent 170 foot-long vine house, are highlights of any visit to Audley End House and Gardens.

THE CHAFF HOUSE

Ash Grove Barns, Littlebury Green,
Saffron Walden, Essex CB11 4XB
Tel: 01763 836278
e-mail: dianaduke@btopenworld.com

For a true taste of traditional country farmhouse living, **The Chaff House** offers guests a beautifully-appointed bedroom with exposed beamwork and an enormous bed. Light, bright and airy, it is tastefully and comfortably furnished. In addition there are two more guest bedrooms in a separate building which includes a kitchen and can therefore also be used for self-catering accommodation.

Set in a courtyard, there is patio seating and a lovely selection of plants in pots and tubs, making for a charming outdoor space.

Owner Diana Duke lives next door, and takes pride in providing her guests with the very best – everything from the linen and towels to the excellent food is of the very highest quality. This warm and comfortable, sympathetically restored barn conversion is set in 900 acres of beautiful countryside. Convenient for the M11, Stansted, Cambridge and other sights and attractions, it makes an excellent touring base. Dinner available by prior arrangement Monday to Friday.

Audley End House (see panel on page 241) was, at one time, home of the first Earl of Suffolk, and at one time home of Charles II. The original early 17th century house, with its two large courtyards, had a magnificence claimed to match that of Hampton Court. Remodelled in the 18th century by Robert Adam, unfortunately the subsequent earls lacked their forebears' financial acumen, and much of the house was demolished as it fell into disrepair. Nevertheless it remains today one of England's most impressive Jacobean mansions; its distinguished stone façade set off perfectly by Capability Brown's lake. The remaining state rooms retain their palatial magnificence and the exquisite state bed in the Neville Room is hung with the original embroidered drapes. The silver, the Dolls' House, the Jacobean Screen and Robert Adam's painted Drawing Room are just among the many sights to marvel at. The natural history collection features more than 1,000 stuffed animals and birds. To complement this, there are paintings by Holbein, Lely and Canaletto. Fascinating introductory talks help visitors get the most from any visit to this, one of the most magnificent houses in England. This jewel also has a kitchen garden and grounds landscaped by Capability Brown, including the Temple of Concord which Brown dedicated to George III. There is a lovely parterre, lake and Pond Garden. Circular walks help visitors make the most of all there is to see. The organic kitchen garden was recently opened to the public for the first time in 250 years. The gardens are managed by the Henry Doubleday Research Association, who grow and sell a wide range of organic produce in the shop, which also features a restaurant. The Audley End Miniature Railway (separate admission charge) is 1.5 miles long and takes visitors along Lord Braybrooke's private 10¼

inch gauge railway through the beautiful private woods of the house.

Within the rolling parkland of the grounds there are several elegant outbuildings, some of which were designed by Robert Adam. Among these are an icehouse, a circular temple and a Springwood Column.

Around Saffron Walden

HADSTOCK
4 miles N of Saffron Walden off the B1052

As well as claiming to have the oldest church door in England, at the parish Church of St Botolph, Hadstock also has a macabre tale to tell. The church's north door was once covered with a piece of human skin, now to be seen in Saffron Walden Museum. Local legend says it is a 'Daneskin', from a Viking flayed alive.

Lining doors with animal leather was common in the Middle Ages, and many so-called 'Daneskins' are just that. However, the skins at Hadstock - and at Copford, in northeast Essex - are almost certainly human, the poor wretch at Hadstock undoubtedly having his hide nailed there as a warning to others. The door itself is Saxon, as are the 11th century carvings, windows and arches, rare survivors that predate the Norman Conquest.

Linton Zoo near the village is a privately owned collection of wild animals set in 10½ acres of gardens. There is a free car park, children's play area, picnic areas and a café on site.

RADWINTER
4 miles E of Saffron Walden off the B1053

Radwinter boasts a fine church, which was largely renovated and rebuilt in the 19th

SOMETHING ELEGANT

PO Box 155, Saffron Walden, Essex CB10 2WW
Tel: 01799 516669
e-mail: sales@something-elegant.co.uk
website: www.something-elegant.co.uk

Contemporary jewellery is the main stock in trade of **Something Elegant**, which was founded by and is owned and run by Richard Ketteridge. Following the successful launch of a website specialising in modern silverware, he has now opened a retail outlet. The well-named Something Elegant offers high-quality jewellery and gifts such as photo frames in sterling silver, and visitors to the retail outlet are welcome to make a leisurely choice in a relaxed atmosphere. If time is short, customers can use the website to order for themselves or for someone special a gift-wrapped treat to treasure.

century by architect Eden Nesfield and has a fine 14th century porch. The village also has cottages and almshouses designed by Nesfield.

HEMPSTEAD
5 miles E of Saffron Walden off the B1054

🍺 The Bell Inn

The highwayman, Dick Turpin, was born here in 1705. His parents kept **The Bell Inn**, later renamed the Rose & Crown and more recently known as Turpin's Tavern. Gilt letters announce that, *'It is the Landlord's great desire that no one stands before the fire'* over the wide hearth where logs still burn; pictures all around celebrate the infamy of the former innkeeper's son. The young Dick trained as a butcher in Whitechapel before turning to cattle stealing, smuggling and robbery at the head of his gang. When capture seemed imminent he fled to Yorkshire, where he continued his life of crime under the name of John Palmer. He was eventually caught while horse stealing and was hanged in York in 1739.

Inside the 14th to 15th century village church, an impressively life-like bust carved by Edward Marshall recalls the town's rather worthier son, William Harvey (1578-1657). Harvey was chief physician to Charles I and the discoverer of the circulation of blood, as

recorded in his *De Motu Cordis* of 1628.

Like many other villages, Hempstead once boasted a village cockpit; its faint outline can still be traced, though the steep banks are now crowned with trees.

THAXTED
7 miles SE of Saffron Walden on the B184

🏛 Church of St. John the Baptist

🏛 Guildhall 🏛 Tower Windmill

This small country town has a recorded history that dates back to before the *Domesday Book*. Originally a Saxon settlement, it developed around a Roman road. The town's many beautiful old buildings contribute to its unique character and charm. To its credit Thaxted has no need of artificial tourist attractions, and is today what is has been for the last 10 centuries: a thriving and beautiful town.

Thaxted has numerous attractively pargetted and timber-framed houses, and a magnificent **Guildhall**, built as a meeting-place for cutlers around 1390. The demise of the cutlery industry in this part of Essex in the 1500s led it to becoming the administrative centre of the town. Restored in Georgian times, it became the town's Grammar School, as well as remaining a centre of administration. Once more restored

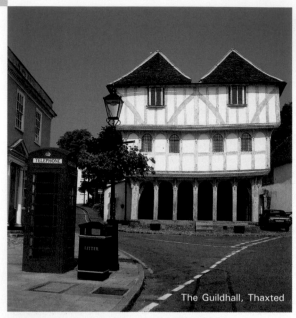
The Guildhall, Thaxted

in 1975, it houses a permanent exhibition of old photographs and objects relating to the history of Thaxted.

The town's famous **Tower Windmill** was built in 1804 by John Webb, a local farmer. In working order until 1907, it had fallen into disuse and disrepair but has now been returned to full working order. It contains a rural life museum, well worth a visit (open 2pm to 6pm Saturday and Sunday and summer Bank Holidays). Close to the windmill are the town's Almshouses, which continued to provide homes for the elderly 250 years after they were built for that purpose.

THE DAIRY B&B

Sibleys Green, Thaxted, nr Dunmow,
Essex CM6 2NU
Tel/Fax: 01371 830401
e-mail: enquiries@thedairybandb.co.uk
website: www.thedairybandb.co.uk

The Dairy B&B is a large, modern and very well appointed house in a quiet setting just off the B184 two miles south of historic Thaxted and seven miles from Stansted Airport. Run by farmer Richard Yeldham and his Australian-born wife Margaret, the house has three letting rooms – a single en suite, a double en suite and a twin with a private bathroom. All rooms are decorated and furnished to a very high standard, with efficient central heating, hot drinks tray and TV (wireless networking also available), and the day starts with a full English breakfast served in the dining room.

Guests have the use of a very comfortable lounge with a log fire and TV/DVD player, and the spacious patio and garden are delightful for a stroll or planning the day's activities. Though conveniently close to the airport, The Dairy is well clear of the flight path, and with the A120 and M11 a short drive away, access is easy to all the local villages, towns and places of interest.

🏠 historic building   🏛 museum   🏚 historic site   🐾 scenic attraction   🌿 flora and fauna

The Church of St John the Baptist stands on a hill and soars cathedral-like over the town's streets. Begun in 1340 and completed some 170 years later, it has been described as the finest parish church in the country and, though many towns may protest long and loud at this claim, it certainly is magnificent. It was also the somewhat unlikely setting for a pitched battle in 1921. The rather colourful vicar and secretary of the Church Socialist League, one Conrad Noel, hoisted the red flag of communism and the Sinn Fein flag in the church. Incensed Cambridge students tore them down and put up the Union Jack; Noel in turn ripped that down and, with his friends, slashed the tyres of the students' cars and motorbikes. A fine bronze in the church celebrates this adventurous man of the cloth.

Conrad Noel's wife is remembered for encouraging Morris dancing in the town. Today, the famous Morris Ring is held annually (usually on the Spring Bank Holiday), attracting over 300 dancers from all over the country, who dance through the streets. Dancing can also be seen around the town on most Bank Holiday Mondays, usually in the vicinity of a pub!

The composer Gustav Holst, best known for his *Planets Suite*, lived in Thaxted from 1914 to 1925, and often played the church organ. To celebrate his connection with the town a summer music festival attracts performers of international repute.

In Park Street, at Aldborough Lodge, the Thaxted Garden for Butterflies is an unprepossessing garden that has been developed with a view to pleasing birds,

THE WHITE HART RESTAURANT & BAR

Howlett End, Wimbish, nr Saffron Walden, Essex CB10 2UZ
Tel/Fax: 01799 599030
e-mail: whitehartwimbish@btconnect.com

A pair of 1/th century cottages with an ale house attached were converted long ago into the **White Hart Restaurant & Bar**, the only pub in the village of Wimbish off the B184 mid way between Thaxted and Saffron Walden.

Tenants Phil Todd and Leigh Cross recently began a major programme of refurbishment and redecoration, and the sympathetically modernised interior is a delightful place to meet for a chat, to say hello to Buster the golden retriever and to enjoy a glass of Greene King IPA or Courage Best. Seating includes leather upholstered bar stools and leather easy chairs as well as leather dining chairs, and a collection of box-framed local photographs is a point of interest.

The White Hart is also a popular restaurant, and the menu includes pub classics such as beer-battered cod or steak & Guinness pie and more elaborate main courses like pan-fried duck breast with rösti and blackcurrant jus, or fillet of sea bass with a white wine, prawn and mushroom sauce. An extensive wine list complements the excellent food, and the regular themed food evenings are always popular occasions.

DEBDEN ANTIQUES

Elder Street, Debden, nr Saffron Walden,
Essex CB11 3JY
Tel: 01799 543007 Fax: 01799 542482
e-mail: info@debden-antiques.co.uk
website: www.debden-antiques.co.uk

A stylishly converted 17th century Essex barn is the home of **Debden Antiques** providing a wonderfully relaxed setting to browse the large selection of furniture and accessories for the home and garden. Amongst the period oak, fine mahogany and victorian pine, are many Persian rugs and oil paintings.To compliment the antiques there is an array of modern accessories, from lamps and candlesticks, to mirrors and glass.

Stuck for a present? There are always many interesting things to choose from.

Outside is the **Courtyard Garden**, filled with statues, urns, wrought iron furniture and ornamental stone. For that unusual feature look no further.

The stock is constantly changing, ensuring that every visit will unearth something new and different. Debden Antiques is situated between Saffron Walden and Thaxted, just follow the brown signs.

Open Tuesday to Saturday, 10am till 5.30pm. Sundays and Bank Holidays, 11am till 4pm.

---

butterflies and other wildlife species - including humans. Displays depict the 22 native wild butterfly species that have visited the garden since its inception in 1988.

WIDDINGTON
4 miles S of Saffron Walden off the B1383

🦋 Mole Hall Wildlife Park

Covering over 20 acres of grounds and deer meadow, **Mole Hall Wildlife Park** offers visitors the chance to come close to a range of wild and domesticated animals. With the private fully-moated 13th century manor house as a backdrop, the wide variety of animals in this excellent park include South American llamas, flamingos, Formosa sika deer (which are extinct in the wild), chimpanzees, muntjac, Arctic fox, wallabies,

red squirrels and much more. Mole Hall is also home to two species of North American otter: short-clawed and North American. Domesticated animals such as guinea pigs, rabbits, goats, pigs and sheep can also be seen. The Butterfly Pavilion offers a tropical experience where brilliantly coloured butterflies flit about freely. Within the tropical pavilion you can also find lovebirds and small monkeys, along with a variety of snakes, spiders and insects (safe behind glass). The pools are inhabited by goldfish, toads and terrapins among other creatures.

Widdington is also home to Priors Hall Barn, one of the finest surviving medieval 'aisled' barns in all of southeast England, and owned by English Heritage.

🏭 historic building   🏛 museum   🏚 historic site   🦆 scenic attraction   🦋 flora and fauna

STANSTED MOUNTFITCHET
8 miles SW of Saffron Walden off the B1383

Castle   House on the Hill   Norman Village

Though rather close to Stansted Airport, there are plenty of reasons to visit this village. Certainly pilots approaching the airport may be surprised at the sight of a **Norman Village**, complete with domestic animals and the reconstructed motte-and-bailey **Mountfitchet Castle**, standing just two miles from the end of the runway. The original castle was built after 1066 by the Duke of Boulogne, a cousin of the Conqueror. Siege weapons on show include two giant catapults. Voted Essex attraction of the year in 2002 by the *Good Britain Guide*, visitors can take a trip to the top of the siege tower and tiptoe into the baron's bed chamber while he sleeps!

Next door to the castle is **The House on the Hill Museum Adventure**, where there are three museums for the price of one. The Toy Museum is the largest of its kind in the world, with some 80,000 items on show, and children of every age are treated to a unique and nostalgic display.

There is every toy imaginable here, many of them now highly prized collectors' items.

There is a shop selling new toys and a collectors' shop with many old toys and books to choose from. The Rock 'n' Roll, Film and Theatre Experience and the End-of-the-Pier Amusement machine displays also contribute to a grand day out here in Stansted Mountfichet.

Stansted Windmill is one of the best-preserved tower mills in the country. Dating back to 1787 and in use until 1910, most of the original machinery has survived. It is open on the first Sunday of each month from April to October; every Sunday in August, and on Bank Holiday Mondays.

BARTLOW
5 miles NE of Saffron Walden off the B1052

Bartlow Hills

Bartlow Hills are reputed to be the largest burial mounds in Europe dating from Roman times. Fifteen metres high, they date back to the 2nd century.

Great Dunmow

Great Dunmow Maltings   Flitch Way

The town is famous for the 'Flitch of Bacon', an ancient ceremony which dates back as far

---

DISH

15 High Street, Great Dunmow, Essex CM6 1AB
Tel: 01371 859922 Fax: 01371 859888
website: www.dishrestaurant.co.uk

Dish: the name is very much to the point, and point is simple – excellent food, served in an agreeable and relaxing ambience. Behind the frontage of one of the oldest buildings in Great Dunmow, brother and sister owners Spencer and Emma have created smart contemporary surroundings for enjoying smart contemporary cooking (by Spencer) of delectable dishes such as king prawn tempura, grilled hake on creamy mash, and a delectable passion fruit cheesecake. Jazz-themed paintings by the owners' father adorn the walls of this Dish, and the other Dish in Saffron Walden.

---

 stories and anecdotes   famous people   art and craft   entertainment and sport   walks

Stansted Mountfitchet

Distance: *3.1 miles (4.83 kilometres)*

Typical time: *60 mins*

Height gain: *15 metres*

Map: *Explorer 195*

Walk: *www.walkingworld.com ID:1835*

Contributor: *Brian and Anne Sandland*

ACCESS INFORMATION:

Stansted Mountfitchet is close to the M11, the A120 and Stansted Airport. To reach the car park from which the walk begins follow signs for Mountfitchet castle - or use the train; the station is adjacent to the car park.

DESCRIPTION:

This walk starts from the car park serving the station and visitors to the castle. It takes in one of the main streets of Stansted Mountfitchet before emerging into field paths and continuing to Ugley Green (which certainly deserves a better name!) The return is on more field and farmland paths via Aubrey Buxton (which was once the pleasure park to Norman House). This delightful woodland section passes a number of small lakes before rejoining the outward route.

FEATURES:

Lake/Loch, Pub, Toilets, Play Area, Castle, Wildlife, Birds, Flowers, Great Views, Butterflies, Food Shop, Woodland

WALK DIRECTIONS:

1 | From the car park head right past the Queen's head (left). Take a left fork (signposted Quendon and Saffron Walden) then a right fork by the Dog and Duck and continue along Gall End. Take the path to the left of North End House.

2 | Continue following the left edge of a field. Bear right then go left through the hedge.

3 | Continue on the left of another field, climbing briefly to enter and follow the right edge of another field reaching a road. Turn right then at a signposted footpath turn left over a stile.

4 | Continue in the same general direction bearing right and left through a gate.

5 | Cross a track then bear one-third right across a field. Pass through a hedge at the far side (signpost) then cross the field ahead to reach a gate. Follow the path to the right of a thatched cottage then, using its drive, arrive at a road and turn right. Bear left at a junction then take a signposted footpath right.

6 | At the far side of the first field go through a gap then right and left through a metal hurdle barrier. Continue between a hedge left

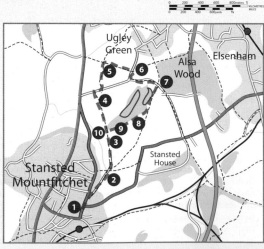

and a wire fence right, then cross a stile and continue ahead, ignoring a signposted footpath left and another right. Soon the path bears right and left to a narrow lane. Go right and left to reach the edge of Aubrey Buxton.

7 | Pass through the gate and follow the earth track, passing lakes on either side, ignoring turns off and bearing right, left and right again. Ignore a way out left into a field and turn right, (slightly downhill).

8 | Join another path and turn left past tall willows then clumps of bamboo (right). Cross a stream, climb slightly, then go left to leave the woodland through a wooden fence.

9 | Follow the left-hand edge of the field, left and right to a T-junction with another path.

10 | Turn left on this path (which is part of your outward route) and retrace your steps back to your car.

as the early 12th century. A prize of a flitch, or side, of bacon was awarded to the local man who, in the words of then Lord Mayor Robert Fitzwalter;

"does not repent of his marriage nor quarrel, differ or dispute with his wife within a year and a day after the marriage".

Amidst great ceremony, the winning couple would be seated and presented with their prize. The first recorded winner was Richard Wright in 1445, the last (genuine) in 1751 were Thomas and Anne Shakeshaft. The custom had lapsed on the Dissolution of the Monasteries, was briefly revived in the 18th century, and became established again after 1885. 'Trials' to test the truth are all in good fun, and carried out every leap year. The successful couple are carried through the streets on chairs and then presented with the Flitch. The 'bacon chair' can be seen in Little Dunmow parish church.

Other places of historical interest include the parish church of St Mary at Church End, Great Dunmow, dating back to 1322. The Clock House, a private residence built in 1589, was the home of St Anne Line, martyred for sheltering a Jesuit priest. The **Great Dunmow Maltings**, opened to the public in 2000 after restoration costing £750,000, is the most complete example of a medieval timber-framed building of its type in the United Kingdom, and a focal point for local history in the shape of Great Dunmow Museum, with changing displays illustrating the history of the town from Roman times to the present day. H G Wells lived at Brick House in Great

Church End, Great Dunmow

DELICIOUS DELICATESSEN

9 High Street, Great Dunmow, Essex CM6 1AB
Tel: 01371 859955   Fax: 01371 878050
e-mail: sales@2delicious.co.uk
website: www.2delicious.co.uk

Melton Mowbray has its pork pies, Stilton has its cheese, Bakewell has its tarts and many other towns and villages throughout the British Isles can boast a specific food connection. For many centuries the name of Great Dunmow has been associated with the famous 'flitch', or side of bacon, awarded to a couple who have not argued during the first year of their marriage. But Great Dunmow has another attraction that's available for all lovers of good food. **Delicious Delicatessen** is truly a deli with a difference, stocked with a wide range of wonderful comestibles, many of them not to be found elsewhere.

Among the mouthwatering selection are local smoked and unsmoked ham, cured meats, pies and pastries including the Dunmow 'flitch' pasty, olives and olive oils, balsamic vinegars, chutneys and preserves, sauces and marinades, British, French and Italian cheeses, gourmet breads, organic crisps, Wessex Mill flours, organic rice, chocolate, coffees and teas. This outstanding deli is owned and run by Monica Borg, who takes justifiable pride in bringing luxurious food to this wonderful corner of Essex.

Dunmow, overlooking the Doctor's Pond, where in 1784 Lionel Lukin is reputed to have tested the first unsinkable lifeboat.

The Flitch Way is a 15-mile country walk along the former Bishop's Stortford-to-Braintree railway, taking in Victorian stations, impressive views, and a wealth of woodland wildlife.

Around Great Dunmow

CHICKNEY
6 miles NW of Great Dunmow off the B1051

Here can be found the rustic and remote little Saxon Church of St Mary's, with 1,000 years of history. Delightfully unspoilt inside, it retains its 14th century tower with pyramid spire. Craftsmanship on display includes the rare pre-Reformation altar.

BROXTED
6 miles NW of Great Dunmow off the B1051

🏠 Parish Church

🔎 Church Hall Farm Antique & Craft Centre

The parish **Church of St Mary the Virgin** here in the handsome village of Broxted has two remarkably lovely stained glass windows commemorating the captivity and release of John McCarthy and the other Beirut hostages, dedicated in January 1993. Though just a few minutes' drive from Stansted Airport off the M11, it is a welcoming haven of rural tranquillity.

Church Hall Farm Antique and Craft Centre in Broxted is housed in a magnificent

🏠 historic building   📷 museum   🏛 historic site   🐸 scenic attraction   🌱 flora and fauna

THE GRANARY

Moor End Farm, Broxted, nr Great Dunmow,
Essex CM6 2EL
Tel: 01371 870821   Fax: 01371 870170
e-mail: moorendfarm@btconnect.com
website: www.moorendfarm.com

Dating from Victorian times, The Granary at Moor End Farm has been sympathetically converted into spacious, comfortable self-catering cottages. Tastefully furnished and decorated, and centrally heated throughout, each has a double and twin bedroom and a bathroom upstairs, while the open-plan downstairs floor has dining, sitting and fully fitted kitchen areas. Outside, there's ample car parking space and a large communal garden with tables, chairs and a barbecue.

The Arches (sleeps four) takes its name from the three floor-to-ceiling windows that make up one wall of the downstairs area. The Willows is named after the family connection with the manufacture of cricket bats; slightly larger than The Arches, it can sleep six using a sofa bed. Moor End is a 420 acre arable farm which has been in the Burton family since 1935. In an area of Special Landscape Value, the farm is at the centre of an extensive network of paths and trails, and it also provides an ideal base for exploring East Anglia.

Grade II listed barn flanked by a willow-lined pond with its own resident ducks! The building itself is a miracle of medieval craftsmanship, located just a few yards from Broxted parish church.

LITTLE EASTON
2 miles NW of Great Dunmow off the B184

🏠 Church

The charming 12th century **Church** in this small village is rich in historic features. Its Maynard Chapel features some outstanding marble monuments of the family that gives the chapel its name, as well as some famous brasses. The church's oldest treasures are, however, a well-preserved and priceless 12th century wall painting and several 15th century frescoes. Two more recent additions, a pair of stained glass windows, were unveiled in 1990. The Window of the Crusaders and the Window of Friendship and Peace are a lasting memorial to the American 386th Bomb Group. Known as The Marauders, they were stationed nearby for 13 months and lost over 200 of their number in battle overseas during that short time.

Little Easton Manor boasts extensive gardens, lakes and fountains. The ancient Barn Theatre at Little Easton Manor is one of the finest and oldest tithe barns in the country, with magnificent oak timbers and ancient tiled roof. Host to performances by many of the most distinguished names over the years - including Ellen Terry, Hermione Baddeley, Charlie Chaplin, George Formby and many others - the sympathetic restoration of the

THE LION & LAMB

Stortford Road, Little Canfield, nr Takeley, Dunmow, Essex CM6 1SR
Tel: 01279 870257   Fax: 01279 870423
e-mail: info@lionandlambtakeley.co.uk
website: www.lionandlambtakeley.co.uk

Hospitality comes naturally to everyone concerned with the **Lion & Lamb**, which stands on the B1256 (previously the A120) at Little Canfield. The new road has taken away much of the passing traffic, giving a tranquil feel to this picture-postcard inn. This lovely old hostelry, which started life as a coaching stop in the 18th century, is run by Mike Shields, whose strong commitment to traditional pub values, and the passing on of that commitment to the staff has been central to the great success of the Lion & Lamb. The immaculate interior has a delightful old-world appeal, with masses of oak beams, open fires, red brick features and rustic furniture. In this cosy, inviting ambience, a good well kept selection of real ales, and an outstanding selection of wines from around the world, can

be enjoyed on their own or as an ideal complement to the food. The full menu is served throughout the day, seven days a week, and an excellent head chef ensures that the standard of the cooking matches all the other aspects of this truly outstanding inn. Prime seasonal produce, much of it sourced locally, is the basis of a splendid choice of dishes to cater for all appetites: salads and quiches for light, wholesome meals, pasta with a variety of sauces, daily changing fish specials, meat dishes both plain and sauced including both familiar classics and more exotic options. The centrepiece of the popular Sunday menu is a choice of roasts, a fish dish and a vegetarian dish flanked by a selection of starters and desserts. A self-contained room with access to the garden is an ideal venue for a private party. The inn has a large car park, and there are plenty of seats in the garden for enjoying a drink or a meal in the open air.

The Lion & Lamb is easy to find: leave the new A120 Stansted Airport- Braintree road at Dunmow West junction and drive for about a mile on the B1256 towards Takeley. The inn is on the right. In Takeley itself, Mike owns the **White House** at Smiths Green, Dunmow Road, which complements the amenities of the Lion & Lamb by providing first-class guest accommodation. The three bedrooms at this 15th century Grade II listed building offer space, comfort, thoughtful touches of luxury and state-of-the-art facilities such as high-speed wireless internet connection. The White House has been awarded 4 AA Res Diamonds and is recognised by Condé Nast Johansens.

facilities has meant its continued use as a setting for special events. Both the Barn Theatre and the Turkey Barn within the grounds are available for private hire. Day-ticket angling can also be arranged.

GREAT EASTON

3 miles NW of Great Dunmow off the B184

Great Easton boasts a wealth of cottages and farmhouses with ornamental plasterwork, clustered Tudor chimneys and half-timbering. Great Easton's well known and very popular Green Man pub occupies a handsome building dating back to the 15th century.

TAKELEY

4 miles W of Great Dunmow off the A120

The village is built on the line of the old Roman Stane Street. There are plenty of pretty 17th century timbered houses and barns to be seen in the village, and the church still has many of its original Norman features along with some Roman masonry. Rather unusually, it has a modern font that is surrounded by a six-foot-high medieval cover.

HATFIELD BROAD OAK

3 miles SW of Great Dunmow off the B184

🏃 Hatfield Forest

This very pretty village has many notable buildings for visitors to enjoy, including a church dating from Norman times, some delightful 18th century almshouses and several distinctive Georgian houses.

Nearby **Hatfield Forest** is a rare surviving example of a medieval Royal hunting forest. It

LANGTHORNS PLANTERY

Little Canfield, nr Dunmow,
Essex CM6 1TD
Tel: 01371 872611
Fax: 08716 614093
e-mail: info@langthorns.com
website: www.langthorns.com

Langthorns Plantery in Little Canfield was created by the present owner Edward Cannon's parents more than 20 years ago. Trained at the Cannington College of Horticulture, Edward has worked at wholesale nurseries in Hampshire and the Netherlands, and also as head gardener at West Wratting Park in Cambridgeshire. His vast experience and unfailing attention to detail are apparent everywhere at the Plantery, where in addition to the wealth of plants on sale he can offer advice on all aspects of garden design.

The impressive and still expanding range of plants, shrubs and trees includes salvias, penstemons, hostas, viburnum, roses, ornamental trees such as variegated sweet chestnuts, magnolias, and conservatory plants, grasses and bamboos. Plants for hot sunny spots, shade, different soils, ground cover, hedging, winter interest and every colour in the rainbow – it's all here, and much more. The fully trained, knowledgeable and friendly staff are ready with expert advice on all aspects of plants and gardening. The multi-award-winning Plantery is open seven days a week.

BURY FARM COTTAGES

Bury Drive, Great Canfield, Essex CM6 1JS
Tel: 01371 873403
e-mail: sandjclarke@buryfarmcottages.co.uk
website: www.buryfarmcottages.co.uk

Bury Farm Cottages provide the perfect opportunity to discover the 'real' Essex from the peaceful village of Great Canfield, a short drive south of Great Dunmow. The Clarke family's 300-acre farm is a quiet, rural setting in which it's easy to relax and unwind. Former bakehouses and stables were renovated in 2004 into high-quality self-catering accommodation combining period features with up-to-the-minute facilities. Each is named after a particular feature. In Bakers Cottage (sleeps two), a Victorian flour store was discovered in a space in the eaves; an old bread oven discovered during the conversion of Bread Cottage (sleeps four, plus a sofa bed); and Pudding (sleeps four) takes its name from the pudding (cooking) stones that are now incorporated in the approach ramps.

The cottages have vaulted ceilings, exposed beams, oak flooring and doors, and two have retained the original fireplaces. The living areas in the cottages are provided with TV, video players and mini hi-fi systems, and the kitchens are fitted with dishwashers, fridge-freezers, electric hobs and microwave ovens. Patio doors open on to a private terrace overlooking meadowland. Shared amenities include a games room with a snooker table, and a laundry room.

has wonderful 400-year-old pollarded trees, two lakes (fishing for pike, tench, roach, rudd, perch and carp) and an 18th century shell house built as a rustic grotto. Guided tours can be arranged. Once covering a great deal more land, the remaining 400 hectares are now protected by the National Trust and offer splendid woodland walks along with good chases and rides.

AYTHORPE RODING
4 miles SW of Great Dunmow off the B184

Aythorpe Roding Windmill is the largest remaining post mill in Essex. Four storeys high, it was built around 1760 and remained in use up until 1935. It was fitted in the 1800s with a fantail which kept the sails pointing into the wind. It is open to the public on the last Sunday of each month from April to September, 2-5 p.m.

PLESHEY
5 miles SE of Great Dunmow off the A130

Pleshey, midway between Chelmsford and Great Dunmow, is surrounded by a mile-long earthen rampart protecting the remains of its castle, of which only the motte with its moat and two baileys survive. There are good views from the mound, which – although only 60 feet high – is one of the highest points in Essex. The village is truly delightful, with a number of thatched cottages, and the area is excellent for walkers and ramblers.

Waltham Abbey

🏚 Waltham Abbey	⚓ Lee Navigation Canal
📷 Epping Forest District Museum	
🏛 Royal Gunpowder Mills	🌿 Dragonfly Sanctuary
🌿 Myddleton House Gardens	

🏚 historic building   📷 museum   🏛 historic site   🌊 scenic attraction   🌿 flora and fauna

Waltham Abbey

Waltham to be buried in his church. The church that exists today was built in the first quarter of the 12th century. It was once three times its present length, and incorporated an Augustinian Abbey, built in 1177 by Henry II. The town became known as **Waltham Abbey**, as the Abbey was one of the largest in the country and the last to be the victim of Henry VIII's Dissolution of the Monasteries, in 1540.

The Abbey's Crypt Centre houses an interesting exhibition explaining the history of both the Abbey and the town, highlighting the religious significance of the site. Some visible remains of the Augustinian Abbey include the chapter house and precinct walls, cloister entry and gateway in the surrounding Abbey Gardens. The Abbey Gardens are also host to a Sensory Trail exploring the highlights of hundreds of years of the site's history; there's also a delightful Rose Garden.

Along the Cornhill Stream, crossed by the impressive stone bridge, the town's **Dragonfly Sanctuary** is home to over half the native British species of dragonflies and damselflies. It is noted as the best single site for seeing these species in Greater London, Essex and Hertfordshire.

A Tudor timber-framed house forms part of the **Epping Forest District Museum** in Sun Street. The wide range of displays

Lee Valley Regional Park

The town of Waltham began as a small Roman settlement on the site of the present-day Market Square. The early Saxon kings maintained a hunting lodge here; a town formed round this, and the first church was built in the 6th century. By the 8th, during the reign of Cnut, the town had a stone minster church with a great stone crucifix that had been brought from Somerset, were it had been found buried in land owned by Tovi, a trusted servant of the king. This cross became the focus of pilgrims seeking healing. One of those cured of a serious illness, Harold Godwinsson, built a new church, the third on the site, which was dedicated in 1060 - and it was this self-same Harold who became king and was killed in the battle of Hastings six years on. Harold's body was brought back to

includes exhibits covering the history of the Epping Forest District from the Stone Age to the present day. Tudor and Victorian times are particularly well represented, with some magnificent oak panelling dating from the reign of Henry VIII, and re-creations of Victorian rooms and shops. There is also an archaeological display and temporary exhibitions covering such subjects as contemporary arts and crafts. The museum has several hands-on displays which help to bring history to life, and features special events and adult workshops throughout the year.

Sun Street is the town's main thoroughfare, and it is pedestrianised. It contains many buildings from the 16th century onwards. The Greenwich Meridian (0 degrees longitude) runs through the street, marked out on the pavement and through the Abbey Gardens.

In spite of its proximity to London and more recent development, the town retains a peaceful, traditional character, with its timber-framed buildings and small traditional market which has been held here since the early 12th century (now every Tuesday and Saturday – there is also a Farmers' Market held every third Thursday of the month, when farm-fresh produce is the order of the day). The whole of the town centre has been designated a conservation area. The Market Square boasts many fine and interesting buildings such as the Lych-gate and The Welsh Harp, dating from the 17th and 16th centuries respectively.

The Town Hall offers a fine example of Art Nouveau design, and houses the Waltham

Royal Gunpowder Mills

Beaulieu Drive, Waltham Abbey, Essex EN9 1JY
Tel: 01992 707370 Fax: 01992 707372
website: www.royalgunpowdermills.com

The **Royal Gunpowder Mills** in Waltham Abbey is open to the general public after a 300 year history. Thanks to funding from the Heritage Lottery Fund and Ministry of Defence, this secret site which was home to gunpowder and explosive production and research for more than three centuries, has been developed to offer visitors a truly unique day out.

Gunpowder production began at Waltham Abbey in the mid 1660s on the site of a late medieval fulling mill. The Gunpowder Mills remained in private hands until 1787, when they were purchased by the Crown. From this date, the Royal Gunpowder Mills developed into the pre-eminent powder works in Britain and one of the most important in Europe.

Set in 175 acres of natural parkland and boasting 21 important historic buildings the regenerated site will offer visitors a unique mixture of fascinating history, exciting science and beautiful surroundings. Approximately 70 acres of the site, containing some of the oldest buildings and much of the canal network, will be open for visitors to explore freely. The remaining area of the site including the largest heronry in Essex has been designated as a Site of Special Scientific Interest and will be accessible to the public by way of special guided tours. Open April to September.

🏠 historic building   🏛 museum   🏚 historic site   🌳 scenic attraction   🌿 flora and fauna

Abbey Town Council Offices and Epping Forest District Council Information Desk. The Tourist Information Centre is in Highbridge Street, opposite the entrance to the Abbey Church.

To the west of town, the **Lee Navigation Canal** offers opportunities for anglers, walkers, birdwatching and pleasure craft. Once used for transporting corn and other commercial goods to the growing City of London, and having associations with the town's important gunpowder industry for centuries, the canal remains a vital part of town life.

Gunpowder production became established in Waltham as early as the 1660s; by the 19th century the **Royal Gunpowder Mills** (see panel opposite) employed 500 workers, and production did not cease until 1943, after which time the factory became a research facility. In the spring of 2000, however, all this changed and the site was opened to the public for the first time. Of the 175 acres the site occupies, approximately 80 have been designated a Site of Special Scientific Interest, as the ecology of the site offers a rare opportunity for study. With two-thirds of the site a Scheduled Ancient Monument, there are some 21 listed buildings to be found here, some of which date from the Napoleonic Wars. The site also contains some of the finest examples of industrial archaeology in the world. Regular events and activities include costumed living history.

Lee Valley Regional Park is a leisure area stretching for 26 miles along the River Lea (sometimes also spelled Lee) from East India Dock Basin, on the north bank of the River Thames in East London, to Hertfordshire. There's a range of facilities ideal for anglers, walkers and birdwatchers. The Lee Valley is an important area of high biodiversity, sustaining a large range of wildlife and birds. Two hundred species of birds, including internationally important populations of Gadwall and Shoveler ducks, can be seen each year on the wetlands and water bodies along the Lea. The Information Centre in the Abbey Gardens provides displays and information on a range of countryside pursuits and interests, sport, leisure and heritage facilities and special events. Of national importance for overwintering waterbirds including rare species of bittern and smew, this fine park makes an ideal place for a picnic. Guided tours by appointment.

At the southern end of Lee Valley Park, The House Mill, one of two tidal mills still standing at this site, has been restored by the River Lea Tidal Mill Trust. It was built in 1776 in the Dutch style, and was used to grind grain for gin distilling.

Lee Valley Park Farms, along Stubbins Hall Lane, boasts two farms on site: Hayes Hill and Holyfield Hall. At Hayes Hill Farm, visitors can interact with the animals and enjoy a picnic or the children's adventure playground. This traditional farm also boasts old-fashioned tools and equipment, an exhibition in the medieval barn and occasional craft demonstrations. The entry fee to Hayes Hill Farm also covers a visit to Holyfield Hall Farm, a working farm and dairy where visitors can see milking and learn about modern farming methods. Seasonal events such as sheep-shearing and harvesting are held, and there's an attractive farm tea room and a toy shop. A farm trail is another of the site's attractions, offering wonderful views of the Lea Valley, an expanse of open countryside dotted with lakes and wildflower meadows attracting a wide range of wildlife including otters, bats, dragonfly, kingfisher, great-crested grebe and little-ringed plover. The area is ideal for walking or fishing, and the bird hides are open to all at weekends; permits available for daily access. Guided tours by arrangement.

Myddleton House Gardens within Lee Valley Park is the place to see the work of the famous plantsman who created them - E.A. Bowles, the greatest amateur gardener of his time. Breathtaking colours and interesting plantings - such as the National Collection of award-winning bearded iris, the Tulip Terrace and the Lunatic Asylum (home to unusual plants) - are offset by a beautiful carp lake, two conservatories and a rock garden.

Epping Forest

Around Waltham Abbey

EPPING
4 miles E of Waltham Abbey off the B182

Just off the B1391, on the outskirts of Epping town centre towards Waltham Abbey, this town's handsome St John's Church was designed over 100 years ago by G F Bodley.

LOUGHTON
5 miles SE of Waltham Abbey off the A121

🦌 Epping Forest

Corbett Theatre in Rectory Lane in Loughton is a beautiful Grade I listed converted medieval tithe barn, where classical, modern and musical theatre productions are performed. The theatre is set in a five-acre site with lovely gardens.

Loughton borders **Epping Forest**, a magnificent and expansive tract of ancient hornbeam coppice, mainly tucked between the M25 and London. There are miles of leafy walks and rides (horses can be hired locally), with some rough grazing and occasional distant views.

ABRIDGE
7 miles SE of Waltham Abbey off the A113

The BBC Essex Garden at Crowther Nurseries, Ongar Road, is a working garden consisting of a vegetable plot, two small greenhouses, lawns and herbaceous and shrub borders. Sheila Chapman, clematis expert, is also on site, as the garden boasts 600 varieties of clematis. The garden is also home to a range of farmyard animals which visitors are welcome to see and interact with, and there's a delightful tea shop filled with homemade cakes.

🏛 historic building   🏛 museum   🏛 historic site   🪴 scenic attraction   🌿 flora and fauna

CHIGWELL
8 miles SE of Waltham Abbey off the A113

🌿 Hainault Forest Country Park

Hainault Forest Country Park is an ancient woodland covering 600 acres, with a lake and rare breeds farm, managed by the London Borough of Redbridge and the Woodland Trust for Essex County Council.

CHINGFORD
6 miles S of Waltham Abbey off the A11

🏠 Queen Elizabeth Hunting Lodge

Queen Elizabeth Hunting Lodge in Rangers Road, Chingford, is a timber-framed hunting grandstand first built for Henry VIII. This unique Tudor-era survivor boasts exceptional carpentry, and is situated in a beautiful part of Epping Forest with ancient oaks and fine views. At one time the Lodge was the destination for hundreds of day-trippers who came by bus from the East End and other parts of London to spend a day enjoying the open spaces and the fresh air.

BROXBOURNE
5 miles NW of Waltham Abbey off the A10

At Broxbourne Old Mill and Millpool, the remains of the old watermill can be seen, the waterwheel of which has been restored to working order.

HODDESDON
6 miles NW of Waltham Abbey off the A10

🏠 Rye House Gatehouse

Rye House Gatehouse in Rye Road was built by Sir Andre Ogard, a Danish nobleman, in 1443. It is a moated building and a fine example of early English brickwork. Now restored, visitors can climb up to the battlements. A permanent exhibition covers the architecture and history of the Rye House Plot to assassinate Charles II in 1683. Guided tours by prior arrangement. The building lies adjacent to a Royal Society for the Protection of Birds reserve. Other features include an information centre, shop, and circular walks around the site.

HARLOW
10 miles NE of Waltham Abbey on the A414

🏛 Museum 🌿 Gibberd Gardens

🎨 Gibberd Collection

🌿 Parndon Wood Nature Reserve

The New Town of Harlow sometimes gets short shrift, but it is in fact a lively and vibrant place with a great deal more than excellent shopping facilities. There are some very good museums and several sites of historic interest. The **Gibberd Collection** in Harlow Town Hall offers a delightful collection of British watercolours featuring works by Elizabeth Blackadder, Sutherland, Frink, Nash and Sir Frederick Gibberd, Harlow's master planner and the founder of the collection.

The Museum of Harlow occupies a Georgian manor house set in picturesque gardens which includes a lovely pond and is home to several species of butterfly. The museum has extensive and important Roman, post-medieval and early 20th century collections, as well as a full programme of temporary exhibitions.

Mark Hall Cycle Museum and Gardens in Muskham Road offers a unique collection of cycles and cycling accessories illustrating the history of the bicycle from 1818 to the present day, including one made of plastic, one that folds, and one where the seat tips forward and throws its rider over the handlebars if the brakes are applied too hard.

Harlow Mill

barn and 13th century church. The site has displays outlining the story of Harlow New Town.

Parndon Wood Nature Reserve, Parndon Wood Road, is an ancient woodland with a fine variety of birds, mammals and insects. Facilities include two nature trails with hides for observing wildlife, and a study centre.

CHIPPING ONGAR
8 miles SE of Harlow on the A414

🏚 Church of St Martin of Tours

Today firmly gripped in the commuter belt of London, Chipping Ongar began as a Saxon market town protected beneath the walls of a Norman castle. The motte and bailey were built by Richard de Lucy in 1155. Indeed, the town's name comes from 'cheaping', meaning market. Only the mound and moat of the castle remain, but the contemporary **Church of St Martin of Tours** still stands. Built in 1080, it has fine Norman flint walls and an anchorite's recess. There are several other interesting buildings in the town, some dating from Elizabethan times.

Explorer David Livingstone was a pupil pastor of the town's 19th century United Reform Church, and lived in what are now called Livingstone Cottages before his missionary work in Africa began.

The museum is housed in a converted stable block within Mark Hall manor. Adjacent to the museum are three period walled gardens.

Gibberd Gardens, on the eastern outskirts of Harlow in Marsh Lane, Gilden Way, is well worth a visit, reflecting as it does the taste of Sir Frederick Gibberd, the famous architect. This seven-acre garden was designed by Sir Frederick on the side of a small valley, with terraces, wild garden, landscaped vistas, pools and streams and some 80 sculptures. Marsh Lane is a turning off the B183.

Harlow Study and Visitors Centre in Netteswellbury Farm is set in a medieval tithe

JOSEPH KING

199-201 High Street, Ongar, Essex CM5 9JG
Tel: 01277 365557

A passion for English interiors led Marilyn Hornsby to open her shop **Joseph King**. Furniture is the main speciality – tables, chairs, cupboards, cabinets and other pieces in rosewood, acacia, teak, mahogany, oak and cherrywood, as well as glass and steel, all on display on the ground floor. But the stock in this marvellous place extends far beyond furniture.

Three separate rooms on the first floor are given over to three different themes: the Oriental Room, with wooden carvings, screens, fans, cushions, lamps, dolls and a treasure trove of lovely gift ideas; The Retro Room, with Art Deco lamps, brass and chrome objects, glass-topped tables, vases, jugs, mirrors, statues and amusing figures (Tom & Jerry, cowboys), pictures and prints; and the Medieval Room with woven tapestries, leather bags, candlesticks and candle holders, and solid medieval objects. Other items in stock include clocks, chandeliers, jewellery and a section devoted to baby goods, and there's even more to browse and buy in a large barn and the garden. The shop occupies part of a row of 17th century cottages that bear the name of Joseph King, a notable local benefactor.

BOBBINGWORTH

2 miles NW of Chipping Ongar off the A414

Blake Hall Gardens at Bobbingworth near Chipping Ongar incorporate a Tropical House, an Ice House, Bog garden, wild gardens, herbaceous borders, rose garden, sunken garden, duck pond and an ornamental wood. The south wing of Blake Hall itself houses the Airscene Aviation Museum run by local RAF enthusiasts.

FYFIELD

2 miles N of Chipping Ongar off the B184

🏠 Fyfield Hall

The name 'Fyfield' means five river meadows. Originally a Saxon enclave, the village church of St Nicholas is Norman. There's a beautiful

mill house with flood gates in the village.
Fyfield Hall, opposite the church, is said to be the oldest inhabited timber frame building in England (it dates from AD870).

HIGH LAVER

3 miles N of Chipping Ongar off the B184

The philosopher John Locke (1632-1704) is buried in the churchyard of All Saints, and an inscription that he himself wrote is set in the inner south wall.

WILLINGALE

3 miles NE of Chipping Ongar off the B184

St Christopher's and St Andrew's, churches of the respective parishes of Willingale Doe and Willingale Spain, stand side by side in the same churchyard in the heart of this lovely village. St Andrew's is the older, dating back to the 12th century; it is protected by the Churches Conservation Trust.

BEAUCHAMP RODING
3 miles NE of Chipping Ongar off the B184

One of the eight Rodings, it was at Beauchamp Roding that a local farm labourer, Isaac Mead, worked and saved enough to become a farmer himself in 1882. To show his gratitude to the land that made him his fortune, he had a corner of the field consecrated as an eternal resting place for himself and his family. Their graves can still be seen in the undergrowth.

Beauchamp's Church of St Botolph stands alone in the fields, marked by a tall 15th century tower and reached by a track off the B184. Inside, the raised pews at the west end have clever space-saving wooden steps, pulled out of slots by means of iron rings.

GOOD EASTER AND HIGH EASTER
5 miles NE of Chipping Ongar off the B184

A quiet farming village, now in the commuter belt for London, Good Easter's claim to fame is the making of a world-record daisy chain (6,980 feet 7 inches) in 1985. The village's interesting name is probably derived from 'Easter', the Old English for 'sheepfolds' and 'Good' from a Saxon lady named Godiva.

Close to Good Easter, and thus named because it stands on higher ground than its neighbour, High Easter is a quiet and very picturesque village not far from the impressive Aythorpe Post Mill.

KELVEDON HATCH
4 miles S of Chipping Ongar off the A128

🏛 Secret Bunker

A bungalow in the rural Essex village of

Kelvedon Hatch is the deceptively simple exterior for the **Kelvedon Hatch Secret Nuclear Bunker**.

In 1952, 40,000 tons of concrete were used to create a base some 80 feet underground for up to 600 top government and civilian personnel in the event of nuclear war. Visitors can explore room after room to see communications equipment, a BBC studio, sick bay, massive kitchens and dormitories, power and filtration plant, government administration room and the scientists' room, where nuclear fall-out patterns would have been measured.

GREENSTED
1½ miles SW of Chipping Ongar off the A414

🏛 St Andrew's Church

St Andrew's Church in Greensted is said to be the world's oldest wooden church, dating from the 9th to 11th centuries, with a later Tudor chancel. It is famous as the only surviving example of a Saxon log church extant in the world, built from split oak logs held together with dowells. Over the centuries the church has been enlarged and restored; later additions include the simple weatherboarded tower, Norman flint walls, the Tudor tiled roof, Victorian stone coping, porch and stained glass windows. The body of King Edmund (later canonised a saint) is believed to have rested here in 1013.

The village also has associations with the Tolpuddle Martyrs - six Dorset farm labourers who were taken to court on a legal technicality because they agitated for better conditions and wages, and formed a Trade Union. After their conviction in 1834 they were condemned to transportation to Australia for seven years. There was a public outcry for their release, and their sentences were commuted in 1837.

🏛 historic building   📷 museum   🏛 historic site   🍃 scenic attraction   �____ flora and fauna

Greensted Church

also a video exhibit recounting a day-to-day account of North Weald history. Guided tours of the airfield can be arranged for large groups.

Brentwood

🏛 Cathedral   📷 Museum

🌱 Thorndon Country Park

Brentwood is a very pleasant shopping and entertainment centre, with quite a distinguished past. It was on the old pilgrim and coaching routes to and from London.

Brentwood Cathedral on Ingrave Road was built in 1991. This classically-styled church incorporates the original Victorian church that stood on this spot. It was designed by the much-admired architect Quinlan Terry, with roundels by Raphael Maklouf (who also created the relief of the Queen's head used on current coins).

Brentwood Centre on Doddinghurst Road is one of the top entertainment venues in the UK, with an extensive programme of concerts, shows, bands and top comedy names. Sport and fitness facilities include pool, health suite and sunbeds.

Brentwood Museum at Cemetery Lode in Lorne Road, in the Watley Hill area of Brentwood, is a small and picturesque cottage museum concentrating on local and social interests during the late 19th and early 20th centuries. It is set in an attractive disused cemetery, which is in itself of unique interest and is open on the first Sunday of every month from 2.30pm

Unable to return to Dorset, they were granted tenancies in Greensted and High Laver.

One of the martyrs, James Brine, of New House Farm (now Tudor Cottage, on Greensted Green), married Elizabeth Standfield, daughter of one of his fellow victims - the record of their marriage in 1839 can be seen in the parish register.

NORTH WEALD
3 miles W of Chipping Ongar off the A414

📷 Airfield Museum

North Weald Airfield Museum and Memorial at Ad Astra House, Hurricane Way, North Weald Bassett is a small, meticulously detailed 'House of Memories' displaying the history of the famous airfield and all who served at RAF North Weald from 1916 to the present. Collections of photos and artefacts such as uniforms and the detailed records of all flying operations are on display. There is

Thorndon Country Park, Brentwood

to 4.30pm and throughout the summer months.

Thorndon Country Park boasts historic parkland, lakes and woods. The site, formerly a Royal deer park, also features a wildlife exhibition and attractive gift shop. Fishing is also available.

Around Brentwood

MOUNTNESSING
6 miles SE of Chipping Ongar off the A12

This village has a beautifully restored early 19th century windmill as its main landmark, though the isolated church also has a massive beamed belfry. Mountnessing Post Mill in Roman Road is open to the public. This traditional weatherboarded post mill was built

in 1807 and restored to working order in 1983. Visitors can see the huge wooden and iron gears; a pair of stones have been opened up for viewing.

INGATESTONE
6 miles E of Chipping Ongar off the B1002

🏠 Ingatestone Hall

Ingatestone Hall (see panel opposite) on Hall Lane is a 16th century mansion set in 11 acres of grounds. It was built by Sir William Petre, Secretary of State to four monarchs, whose family continue to reside here. Open to the public in summer, the Hall contains family portraits, furniture and memorabilia accumulated over the centuries. Guided tours by prior arrangement.

BILLERICAY
6 miles E of Brentwood off the A129

🏠 Chantry House 🏛 Barleylands Farm

🧍 Norsey Wood

There was a settlement here as far back as the Bronze Age, though there is to date no conclusive explanation of Billericay's name. There is no question about the attraction of the High Street, though, with its timber weatherboarding and Georgian brick. **The Chantry House**, built in 1510, was the home of Christopher Martin, treasurer to the Pilgrim Fathers.

The Peasants' Revolt of 1381 saw the massacre of hundreds of rebels just northeast of the town, at **Norsey Wood**. Today this

Ingatestone Hall

Ingatestone, Essex CM4 9NR
Tel: 01277 353010 Fax: 01245 248979

Ingatestone Hall is a 16th century mansion and grounds, built by Sir William Petre, Secretary of State to four Tudor monarchs, and still occupied by his descendants. The house substantially retains its original form and appearance (including two priests' hiding places) and contains furniture, pictures and family memorabilia accumulated over the centuries.

A programme of special events is available on request and there is a gift shop and a tea room in the grounds. A picnic area is sited in Car Park Meadow. The house and/or grounds are available to hire for a variety of events uncluding fairs, exhibitions, concerts, lectures and location filming. Open Saturday, Sunday and Bank Holiday afternoons from Easter to the end of September, plus Wednesdays, Thursdays and Fridays in the school summer holidays.

Steam Lorry at Barleylands Farm, Billericay

area of ancient woodland is a country park, managed by coppicing (the traditional way of ensuring the timber supply), which also encourages plant- and birdlife.

Barleylands Farm Museum and Visitors' Centre features a glass-blowing studio, blacksmith's and other craft shops, a wealth of farm animals, chick hatchery, duck pond and one of the largest collections of vintage farm machinery in the country, together with a play area, picnic area and, on Sunday afternoons, a steam railway.

📖 stories and anecdotes   🦅 famous people   🎨 art and craft   ✎ entertainment and sport   🚶 walks

STOCK
6 miles NE of Brentwood off the B1007

Stock boasts a fine early 19th century tower windmill on five floors, with superb late 19th century machinery that has been restored to working order.

Stock's delightful church has a traditional Essex-style wooden belfry and spire, lending character to this pleasant village of well-kept houses.

GREAT WARLEY
1 mile S of Brentwood on the B186

Warley Place was formerly home to one of the most famous women gardeners, Ellen Willmott, who died in 1934. She introduced to Warley - and to Britain - many exotic plants. A trail takes visitors through what is now Warley Place Nature Reserve, with 16 acres of what was once domesticated garden but has now reverted to woodland. A fascinating selection of trees, shrubs and wildlife make this well worth a visit.

SOUTH WEALD
2 miles W of Brentwood off the A12

🏛 Museum

🌱 Old Macdonald's Educational Farm Park

This very attractive village has, at its outskirts, Weald Country Park, a former estate with medieval deer park, partially landscaped in the 1700s. Featuring lake and woodland, visitors' centre, landscapes exhibition and gift shop, with facilities for fishing and horse-riding, there are guided events and activities programmes held throughout the year.

Another good day out in the open air can be had at **Old Macdonald's Educational Farm Park**, where visitors can see the largest selection of pure-bred British farm animals

and poultry in the southeast of England. Specialising in native rare-breeds, with nine breeds of pig, 23 of sheep, six of cattle, 30 of poultry and 30 of rabbit to see and learn about, as well as shire horses, deer, owls, otters, goats, ferrets, red squirrels and much more. The farm boasts informative breed labelling and excellent facilities.

GRAYS
4 miles E of Brentwood off the M25

🏛 Thurrock Museum

Thurrock Museum is in the Thameside Complex in Grays. It collects, conserves and displays items of archaeology and local history from prehistoric times to the end of the 20th century. The archaeological items include flint and metal tools of people who lived in prehistoric Thurrock and pottery, jewellery and coins from the Roman and Saxon period.

WEST THURROCK
1½ miles SW of Grays off the A13

Immortalised by the film *Four Weddings and a Funeral*, little St Clement's Church occupies a striking location and is one of a number of picturesque ancient churches in the borough. Although this 12th century church is now deconsecrated, it was in its day a stopping point for pilgrims; visitors can see the remains of its original round tower. There is also a mass grave to the boys of the reformatory ship *Cornwall* who were drowned in an accident off Purfleet.

Arena Essex Raceway is the chief venue for motorsports in the area. Regular 'banger racing' takes place at the track in West Thurrock, near Lakeside Shopping Centre and Retail Park. The Centre attracts many millions of visitors a year, and boasts over 300 shops, a food court and multiplex cinema. The Retail Park features more shops, as well as restaurants, a cinema, a leisure bingo complex and a watersports centre at the lake.

PURFLEET
3 miles W of Grays off the M25/A13

Heritage Military Centre

Fans of Bram Stoker's novel *Dracula* will know that in this book the famous vampire buys a house called 'Carfax' in Purfleet. The town's esteemed Royal Hotel, by the Thames, is said to have played host to Edward VII, while still Prince of Wales in the 1880s and 1890s, at which time the hotel was called Wingrove's. The **Purfleet Heritage and Military Centre** is a heritage and military museum featuring displays of many items of interest and memorabilia in the setting of the No 5 Gunpowder Magazine on Centurion Way. This

Belhus Wood Country Park

Romford Road, Aveley, Essex RM15 4XJ
Tel: 01708 865628

Belhus Woods Country Park has a diverse landscape of woodlands, grasslands and lakes. You can fish, play games, fly kites, have a picnic or ride your horse here. You may prefer to just sit by tranquil waters feeding the birds or, in spring, to quietly wander through a woodland carpet of bluebells.

The estate was once owned by the Barrett-Lennard family. Capability Brown and Richard Woods laid out an 18th century park for Lord Dacre over earlier more formal gardens. The Shrubbery and Long Pond were created by Woods in 1770 and are now cut by the M25.

A 'stench pipe' disguised as a Tudor chimney also survives in the south of the Park. The ancient wood-lands have changed little in shape and size since their mapping in 1777 by Chapman and Andre, although there has been significant extra planting since.

The woodlands are home to rich communities of wildlife. An observant bird-watcher may see green, greater or lesser spotted wood-peckers and numerous creepy crawlies can be spotted by an enthusiastic child.

The Ranger Service manages the woods according to their timber content and wildlife value. Timber from Running Water Wood is used for thatching and hurdle making, with the hazel plots cut on a regular eight year cycle. This traditional management practice, called coppicing, benefits the wildlife by increasing light penetration allowing seeds to germinate and plants to thrive. You can now experience the splendour of plants, once common in traditional coppiced woodlands, such as early purple orchids and graceful ragged robins in a sea of bluebells.

The Visitors' Centre has a shop and education facilities where light refreshments, gifts and information can be obtained. The Essex Ranger Service also offers guided walks, volunteer tasks, assisted school visits and a variety of events throughout the year.

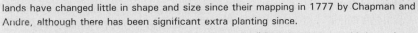
stories and anecdotes   famous people   art and craft   entertainment and sport   walks

remaining magazine was built in the 1770s for testing and issuing gun powder to the army and navy.

Purfleet Conservation Area includes several buildings which were part of a planned village built by the one-time owners of the chalk quarry, the Whitbread family.

AVELEY
3 miles NW of Grays off the M25/A13

🍀 Mardyke Valley

Mardyke Valley is an important wildlife corridor running from Ship Lane in Aveley to Orsett Fen. Many pleasant views can be had along the seven-mile stretch along footpaths and bridleways. Davy Down within Mardyke Valley consists of riverside meadows, ponds and wetland. The Visitors' Centre is in the well-preserved water pumping station on the B186 near South Ockendon. Aveley's 12th century St Michael's Church features many Flemish brasses and other items of historical interest.

SOUTH OCKENDON
3 miles N of Grays off the A13/A1306

🍀 Belhus Woods Country Park

🍀 Grangewater Country Park

Belhus Woods Country Park (see panel on page 267) covers approximately 250 acres and contains an interesting variety of habitats, including woodland, two lakes and the remains of a pond designed by Capability Brown. The Visitors' Centre to this superb park can be found at the main entrance off Romford Road. Belhus Park Golf Course is a well-established 18-hole course set within this beautiful parkland.

Grangewaters Country Park, also in South Ockendon, has two lakes. Managed by Thurrock Environmental and Outdoor

Education Centre, it offers watersports such as windsurfing, sailing and canoeing, as well as off-road biking, climbing and other outdoor pursuits. Brannetts Wood is one of the oldest recorded ancient woodlands in South Essex. It can be reached from the Mardyke Way, or from South Road here in South Ockendon.

The village Church of St Nicholas has one of only six round church towers in Essex. This one was built in the 13th century and used to have a spire, which was sadly destroyed by lightning in the 17th century.

HORNDON-ON-THE-HILL
6 miles NE of Grays off the B1007/A13

🍀 Langdon Hills

Listed in the *Domesday Book* as *Horninduna*, a name which also appears on a Saxon coin of Edward the Confessor, it is said to have once been the site of a Royal Anglo-Saxon mint. The town's 16th century Woolmarket indicates the importance of the wool trade to the region, and is one of the area's historical treasures. The upper room served as Horndon's manor courtroom, while the lower, open area was used for trading in woollen cloth.

The main entrance and Visitors' Centre for **Langdon Hills Conservation Centre and Nature Reserve** are located off the Lower Dunton Road north of Horndon-on-the-Hill. A bridleway and footpaths lead visitors to meadows, a pond and outstanding ancient woods. Also within the reserve is the Plotlands Museum, housed in an original 1930s plotland bungalow known as the Haven.

LINFORD
3 miles NE of Grays off the A13/A1013

🏛 Walton Hall Museum

Walton Hall Museum on Walton Hall Road has a large collection of historic farm machinery in a 17th century barn. It affords visitors the opportunity to watch traditional craftsmen, such as a blacksmith, saddlemaker, printer and wheelwright, together with a printing shop, baker's, dairy and nursery.

STANFORD-LE-HOPE
4 miles NE of Grays off the A1014

🐦 Stanford Marshes

Stanford Marshes is an area to the south of Stanford-le-Hope, next to the Thames. The Marshes are home to a variety of wildlife and are an ideal location for birdwatching. Grove House Wood in Stanford-le-Hope is a nature reserve managed by Essex Wildlife Trust and the local Girl Guides. A footpath here leads to reed beds, a pond and a brook as well as an area of woodland.

The graveyard of St Margaret's Church has an unusual half-barrelled tomb, for one James Adams (d. 1765), that is decorated with gruesome stone-carved symbols of death.

CORRINGHAM
7 miles NE of Grays off the A13/A1014

🌳 Langdon Hills Country Park

Corringham has a picturesque cluster of timber-framed houses in the old village, leading up to its medieval church, which retains some Saxon and Norman features. **Langdon Hills Country Park** north of Corringham is 400 acres of ancient woodland and meadows. It has many rare trees and spectacular views of the Essex countryside.

CANVEY ISLAND
10 miles NE of Grays off the A130

🏛 Dutch Cottage Museum

🏛 Castle Point Transport Museum

Canvey Island is a peaceful and picturesque

stretch of land overlooking the Thames estuary with views to neighbouring Kent. The island boasts two unusual museums: **Dutch Cottage Museum** is an early 17th century eight-sided cottage built by Dutch workmen for Dutch workmen and boasting many traditional Flemish features. **Castle Point Transport Museum** is housed in a 1930s bus garage. It houses an interesting collection of historic and modern buses and coaches, mainly of East Anglian origin. The Canvey Miniature Railway at the Waterside Farm Centre has two steam miniature railways guaranteed to delight the child in all of us. The Island's most famous son is Dean Macey, the world-class decathlete.

WEST TILBURY
3 miles E of Grays off the A1089

West Tilbury was the site chosen for the Camp Royal in 1588, to prepare for the threatened Spanish invasion. Queen Elizabeth I visited the army here, and made her famous speech,

"I know I have the body but of a weak and feeble woman: but I have the heart and stomach of a king, and a king of England too."

Hidden away in rural tranquillity overlooking the Thames estuary, West Tilbury remains unspoilt in spite of its proximity to busy, industrial Tilbury. The former local church (now a private dwelling) in this quaint little village is a nautical landmark used for navigation. The list of Rectors of the church, dating from 1279-1978, when the church was disestablished, can be seen in The King's Head Pub.

EAST TILBURY
5 miles E of Grays off the A13

🏛 Thameside Aviation Museum 🏰 Coalhouse Fort

Coalhouse Fort is considered to be one of

the best surviving examples of a Victorian Casement fortress in the country. As such it is a protected Scheduled Ancient Monument. Built between 1861 and 1874 as a first line of defence to protect the Thames area against invasion, it stands on the site of other defensive works and fortifications dating back to around 1400. Even before the Middle Ages, this was an important site.

Part of the construction work on the Fort was overseen by Gordon of Khartoum. It was constructed to be a dedicated Artillery casement fortress, which meant that the guns were housed in large vaulted rooms with armour-plated frontages. Beneath these rooms lies an extensive magazine tunnel system to service the artillery.

Over the years many alterations were made to the Fort to accommodate new artillery. The Fort was manned during both World Wars, and is now owned by Thurrock Borough Council and administered by The Coalhouse Fort Project, a registered charity run entirely by volunteers. Open to the public, it contains reconstructions of period guns and other displays, and also houses the **Thameside Aviation Museum**, with a large collection of local finds and other aviation material. In the two parade grounds visitors will find various artillery pieces and military vehicles. One recent addition to the many pieces of historical military equipment is a Bofor Anti-Aircraft Gun of the Second World War. The site also offers visitors the chance to handle period equipment or try on a period uniform.

During the year the Fort hosts a range of shows, including an historic artillery rally when various big guns are fired by crews in the uniforms of the period, including a Second World War crew firing a 1940 25pdr field gun.

A guided tour (included in the price of admission) allows visitors to see the magazine tunnels beneath the gun casements and offer a feel for the work and conditions of a Victorian gunner. The tour also takes in the roof of the Fort, from which you will be able to judge for yourself the value of a fortification at this point along the Thames. The view from here is outstanding, taking in the two sister forts in Kent and, on a clear day, Southend.

The Fort is set in a lovely riverside park with walks and a children's play area, as well as other items of military history including a Quick Fire Battery and Minefield Control box. You can also follow the old railway tracks from the Fort to the side of the old jetty, where many of the armaments and supplies for the fort were shipped in.

It is possible that East Tilbury's St Catherine's church occupies the site of one of the first Christian monasteries in the 7th century. Its half-built tower was constructed by the First World War Garrison of Coalhouse Fort.

The Bata Estate is a conservation area of architectural and historical interest. Established in 1933, the British Bata Shoe Company was the creation of Czech-born Thomas Bata, who also developed a housing estate for his workforce. This range of uniform flat-roofed houses can still be seen on site.

TILBURY
3 miles SE of Grays off the A1089

🏛 Tilbury Fort

Tilbury Fort (see panel opposite) is a well-preserved and unusual 17th century structure with double moat. The largest and best example of military engineering in England at that time, the fort also affords tremendous

🏛 historic building   🏛 museum   🏛 historic site   🏛 scenic attraction   🏛 flora and fauna

Tilbury Fort

Tilbury, Essex RM18 7NR
Tel: 01375 858489

Ever wanted to fire a real anti-aircraft gun? Come to Tilbury Fort and you can. Discover the history of this most impressive of English artillery forts, from Henry VIII's time right up to World War II. Walk through Charles II's imposing Water Gate, noticing the mighty gun emplacements which protected London against attack by warships. Tour the ramparts and inspect the guns, while enjoying the panoramic views across the Thames, near the place where Queen Elizabeth I made her famous 'Armada Speech',

The audio tour leads you round the site step by step. In the museum and exhibition housed in the East Gunpowder magazine, you can follow the fortunes of Tilbury, from the creation of its first fortifications in the 16th century, to the two World Wars.

views of the Thames estuary. The most violent episode in the fort's history occurred in 1776, during a particularly vociferous cricket match which left three people dead. For a small fee visitors to the fort can fire a 1943 3.7mm anti-aircraft gun - a prospect most children and many adults find irresistible! Owned by English Heritage, the site was used for a military Block House during the reign of Henry VIII and was rebuilt in the 17th century. It remains one of Britain's finest examples of a star-shaped bastion fortress. Extensions were made in the 18th and 19th centuries, and the Fort was still being used in the Second World War.

Tilbury Festival is held every year in July in the field near the fort, and features arena events, craft and food stalls, and living history re-enactments. Tilbury Energy and Environment Centre at Tilbury Power Station provides a nature reserve and study centre for schools and community education. There is a flat two-mile nature trail leading to and from the Centre.

Southend-on-Sea

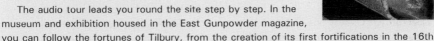

Central Museum · Southchurch Hall Museum

Prittlewell Pirory Museum · Saxon Cemetery

Pier & Museum · Beecroft Art Gallery

Kursaal

To be beside the seaside at Southend-on-Sea means that there is always plenty to do and see, and many events throughout the year to ensure its continuing appeal and popularity. The town is one of the best loved and friendliest resorts in Britain, featuring the very best ingredients for a day or a break at the seaside. With seven miles of beaches and a European Blue Flag Award, this treasure trove boasts Adventure Island theme park, Cliffs Bandstand, Cliffs Pavilion (the largest purpose-built performing arts venue in Essex), a distinguished art gallery and several interesting museums.

Southend Pier and Museum brings to life the fascinating past of the longest Pleasure

stories and anecdotes · famous people · art and craft · entertainment and sport · walks

Pier in the world. The Pier itself is 1.33 miles long; visitors can either take a leisurely walk along its length or take advantage of the regular train service that plies up and down the pier. One of the trains is named after Sir John Betjeman, a frequent visitor to the town; he once said, (perhaps underestimating the town's many other attractions?): "The Pier is Southend, Southend is the Pier". The pier has survived several major fires and is currently recovering from the latest conflagration in October 2005.

Beecroft Art Gallery boasts the work of four centuries of artistic endeavour, with some 2,000 works including those by Lear, Molenaer, Seago and Constable.

Sealife Adventure employs the most advanced technology to bring visitors incredibly close to the wonders of British marine life, offering fun ways of exploring life under the waves, with concave bubble windows helping to make it seem you're actually part of the sea-creatures'

environment. Another exhibit features a walk-through tunnel along a reconstructed seabed. The Shark Exhibition is not to be missed.

A floral trail guided tour around the parks and gardens will reveal why Southend has won the Britain in Bloom Awards every year since 1993, as well as medals at the Chelsea Flower Show.

The Kursaal on the Eastern Esplanade is an indoor entertainment complex, one of the largest in the country, with indoor bowling, synthetic ice and roller rink, a fun casino, children's play area, snooker and pool, arts and crafts, retail units and theme restaurants.

Boat trips in summer include occasional outings on a vintage paddle steamer. Ferry trips to Felixstowe are also available from Southend.

The **Southchurch Hall Museum** in Park Lane is a delightful 13th to 14th century timber-framed manor house with various displays and landscaped gardens. Period room settings are among this museum's many

Southend-on-Sea

delights. The museum also includes the Discovery Centre, which includes a section for 'hands-on' learning, and a Planetarium.

Prittlewell Priory Museum, slightly north of Southend town centre in Priory Park, is a well-preserved 12th century Cluniac Priory set in lovely grounds and housing collections of the Priory's history, natural history and the

🏛 historic building   🏛 museum   🏛 historic site   🞿 scenic attraction   🌱 flora and fauna

Caten collection of radios and communications equipment. Southend's award-winning coastline supports a number of important habitats, and the foreshore is an international SSSI (Site of Special Scientific Interest).

Leigh-on-Sea at Sunrise

Long before the name of Southend existed, Prittlewell was established as a Saxon settlement between 500 and 850, and the first signs of its Saxon past were unearthed in 1923. By far the most important discovery came in 2004, when a wood-lined chamber in a **Saxon Cemetery** came to light filled with gold and bronze ornaments, glass vessels, weapons and other treasures. The chief archaeologist at English Heritage described the find as "a discovery of international importance which stunningly illuminates the rich and complex world of the so-called Dark Ages". Many of the finds are on display in the British Museum, but there are plans to bring them to a special site in Southend.

Around Southend-on-Sea

OLD LEIGH
½ mile W of Southend off the A13

The unspoilt fishing village of Old Leigh has a long and distinguished history. It is picturesque, with sea front houses and narrow winding alleys. It has also earned its place in history: The pilgrim ship *The Mayflower* restocked here en route to the New World of America back in the mid-17th century, and the Dunkirk rescue embarked from here, as commemorated by plaques, flags and a memorial at St Clements Church.

LEIGH-ON-SEA
2 miles W of Southend off the A13

Leigh-on-Sea has quite a character quite different from Southend, being more intimate and serene, with wood-clad buildings and shrimp boats in the working harbour. The shellfish stall on the harbourside is justly famous. The Leigh Heritage Centre, housed in an ancient former smithy in the waterside High Street of the Old Town, is now home to historical artefacts and a photographic display of the history of Leigh-on-Sea.

stories and anecdotes · famous people · art and craft · entertainment and sport · walks

ROCHFORD
3 miles N of Southend off the B1013

The Old House, at 17 South Street, is an elegant, lovingly restored house originally built in 1270. The twisting corridors and handsome rooms of this fine structure offer a glimpse into the past; the building now houses some District Council offices, and is said to be haunted.

HADLEIGH
5 miles NW of Southend off the A13

🏛 Castle 🦌 Country Park

Hadleigh Castle, built originally for Edward III, is owned by English Heritage and once belonged to Anne of Cleves, Catherine of Aragon and Katherine Parr. The ruins were also immortalised in a painting by Constable. The remains of this once impressive castle can still be seen. The curtain walls towers, which survive almost to their full height, overlook the Essex marshes and the Thames estuary.

Hadleigh Castle Country Park offers a variety of woodland and coastal walks in grounds overlooking the Thames estuary. A Guided Events programme runs throughout the year.

HOCKLEY
6 miles NW of Southend off the A129

🐾 Hockley Woods

Hockley Woods is a 280-acre ancient woodland, managed for the benefit of wildlife and for the public. Traditional coppice management encourages a diverse array of flora and fauna, including the nationally rare Heath Fritillary butterfly.

Volpaia in Woodlands Road is a lily specialist's small but beautiful woodside garden, with rare collected species and own-bred hybrid lilies, shade-loving shrubs and plants for sale.

RAYLEIGH
6 miles NW of Southend off the A1016

Dutch Cottage at Crown Hill in Rayleigh is a tiny traditional Flemish eight-sided cottage based on a 17th century design created by Dutch settlers.

Rayleigh Mount is a prominent landmark in this part of the county. Once a motte-and-bailey castle built in the 11th century, it was abandoned some 200 years later. Rayleigh Windmill, in Bellingham Lane close to Rayleigh Mount, was built around 1809; the tower mill houses a fascinating collection of bygones mostly used in and around Rayleigh. Refreshments are available from the coffee shop adjacent to the Mill.

HULLBRIDGE
8 miles NW of Southend off the A132

Jakapeni Rare Breed Farm at Burlington Gardens in Hullbridge is a pleasant small-holding set in 30 acres of rolling countryside. Specialising in sheep and pigs, with other pets and wildlife, there's also a fishing lake, country walk and pets corner. Snacks and light refreshments are available from the café, and there's an attractive shop.

Chelmsford

🏛 Cathedral 🏛 Museum

Roman workmen cutting their great road linking London with Colchester built a fort at what is today called Chelmsford. Then called *Caesaromagus*, it stands at the confluence of the Rivers Chelmer and Can. The town has always been an important market centre and is now the bustling county town of Essex. It is also directly descended from a new town planned by the Bishop of London in 1199. At its centre are the principal inn, the Royal Saracen's Head, and the elegant Shire Hall of 1791. Three plaques situated high up on the eastern face of the Hall overlooking the High Street represent Wisdom, Justice and Mercy. The building now houses the town magistrates court.

Christianity came to Essex with the Romans and again, later, with St Cedd (AD 654); in 1914 the diocese of Chelmsford was created. **Chelmsford Cathedral** in New Street dates from the 15th century and is built on the site of a church constructed 800 years ago. The cathedral is noted for the harmony and unity of its perpendicular architecture. It was John Johnson, the distinguished local architect who designed both the Shire Hall and the 18th century Stone Bridge over the River Can and who also rebuilt the Parish Church of St Mary when most of its 15th century tower fell down. The church became a cathedral when the new diocese of Chelmsford was created. Since then it has been enlarged and re-organised inside. The cathedral boasts memorial windows dedicated to the USAAF airmen who were based in Essex between 1942 and 1945.

The Marconi Company, pioneers in the manufacture of wireless equipment, set up the first radio company in the world here in Chelmsford, in 1899. Exhibits of those pioneering days of wireless can be seen in the **Chelmsford Museum** in Oaklands Park, Moulsham Street, as can interesting displays of Roman remains and local history. Fine and decorative arts (ceramics, costume, glass), coins, natural history (live beehive, animals, geological exhibits) rub shoulders with displays exploring the history of the distinguished Essex Regiment. The museum is set in a lovely park complete with children's play area.

Also in the town, at Parkway, is Moulsham Mill Business & Craft Centre, set in an early 18th century water mill that has been renovated and now houses a variety of craft workshops and businesses. Crafts featured include jewellery, pottery, flowers, lace-making, dolls houses and bears, and decoupage work. There is a charming picnic area nearby, and a good café.

Three modern technologies - electrical engineering, radio, and ball and roller bearings

Chelmsford Cathedral

SPARHAM'S DÉCOR

126 Main Road, Broomfield, nr Chelmsford,
Essex CM1 7AG
Tel: 01245 444100
website: www.sparhamsdecor.co.uk

Opened by Barry and Tracey Sparham in July 2005 Sparham's Décor specialises in antique pine and painted furniture, clocks and other fine pieces for the home. The range on display is chosen to fit timelessly into any period home and the owners take pride in finding unique pieces of furniture from the Continent and the UK. The furniture ranges from tables and chairs to food cupboards, dressers, trunks, wardrobes and chest of drawers, all hand finished in traditional wax or the classic French distressed paint style.

To compliment their furniture Sparham's also stocks a small selection of reproduction French upholstered furniture including Louis XIV chairs and chaise longues. Smaller items in the impressive show includes lamps, mirrors, trugs, French fabric cushions, enamelware, pictures and picture frames. There is a wide selection of clocks from restored good quality antique slate, wood and porcelain mantel clocks to reproduction French wall clocks.

Barry and Tracey invite you to come and leisurely browse within the friendly atmosphere of their shop which is open from Tuesday to Saturday. Also on offer is free parking at the front of the shop and free local delivery. To view a range of current stock visit the website which details sizes and prices where possible.

- began in Chelmsford. At the Engine House Project at Sandford Mill Waterworks, museum collections from the town's unique industrial story provide a fun and fascinating insight into the science of everyday things.

Around Chelmsford

GREAT BADDOW
1 mile S of Chelmsford off the A12/A130

Baddow Antiques Centre at The Bringy, Church Street, is one of the leading antiques centres in Essex. Here, 20 dealers offer a wide selection of silver, porcelain, glass, furniture, paintings and collectibles. There is also a collection of 300 Victorian brass and iron bedsteads on display.

SANDON
2 miles SE of Chelmsford off the A414

The village green here in Sandon has produced a notable Spanish oak tree, the biggest in the country, planted in the centre of the village green. This oak tree is remarkable not so much for its height as for the tremendous horizontal spread of its branches. Around the green are a fine church and a number of attractive old houses, some dating back to the 16th century when Henry VIII's Lord Chancellor, Cardinal Wolsey, was Lord of the Manor of Sandon.

SOUTH HANNINGFIELD
6 miles S of Chelmsford off the A130

The placid waters of nearby Hanningfield Reservoir were created by damming Sandford

Brook, and transformed the scattered rural settlement of Hanningfield into a lakeside village. Now on the shores of the lake, the 12th century village church's belfry has been a local landmark in the flat Essex countryside for centuries. Some of the timbers in the belfry are said to have come from Spanish galleons, wrecked in the aftermath of Sir Francis Drake's defeat of the Armada.

The Visitor Centre at the Reservoir overlooks the 870-acre reservoir and the gateway to the 100-acre woodland beyond. The Centre also offers refreshments, a gift shop and toilet.

HIGHWOOD
3 miles SW of Chelmsford off the A414

Hylands House

Hylands House was built in 1728, a beautiful neo Classical Grade II listed villa set in over 500 acres of parkland landscaped by Repton. Rooms that are open to the public include the Blue Room, Entrance Hall, Library, Saloon, Boudoir and Drawing Room. Host to many outdoor events, including the annual 'V' concerts (V98 was a particularly great success) and the Chelmsford Spectacular, Hylands Park features lawns, rhododendron bushes, woodland paths, ornamental ponds and Pleasure Gardens adjacent to the house.

WRITTLE
2 miles W of Chelmsford off the A414

From a tucked-away corner of St John's Green in this village came Britain's first regular broadcasting service; an experimental 15-minute programme beamed out nightly by Marconi's engineers. Opposite the Green, the Cock

& Bell is reputed to be haunted by a young woman who committed suicide on the railway. Further along this street is the Wheatsheaf, one of the smallest pubs in the country.

Writtle's parish church of St John features a cross of charred timbers, a reminder of the fire which gutted the chancel in 1974. Ducks swim on the pond of the larger and quite idyllic main village green, which is surrounded by lovely Tudor and Georgian houses.

WITHAM
6 miles NE of Chelmsford off the A12/B1018

Dorothy L Sayers Centre

The River Brain flows through this delightful town; a continuous walk has been created along its length for a distance of about three miles. The settlement dates back to at least the 10th century; remains of a Roman temple

Witham

have been found at Ivy Chimneys, off Hatfield Road. Blackwater Lane leads to Whetmead, a nature reserve of 25 acres between the rivers Blackwater and Brain.

The **Dorothy L Sayers Centre** in Newland Street houses a collection of books by and about Sayers, the theologian, Dante scholar and novelist/creator of the Lord Peter Wimsey mysteries, who lived in Witham for many years.

LITTLE BRAXTED
6 miles NE of Chelmsford off the A12/B1018

Little Braxted has been voted the best-kept village on a regular basis since 1973. St Mary's chapel was built in 1888, and can accommodate only 12 people at a time. Services are held every Wednesday. The village church of St

Nicholas is mentioned in the *Domesday Book*, and is famous for its murals.

TIPTREE
11 miles NE of Chelmsford on the B1023

As all true jam-lovers will know, Tiptree is famed as the home of the Wilkin and Son Ltd jam factory, a Victorian establishment which now boasts a fascinating visitors' centre in the grounds of the original factory.

KELVEDON
11 miles NE of Chelmsford off the A12

 Museum

This village alongside the River Blackwater houses the **Feering and Kelvedon Museum**, which is dedicated to manorial history and houses artefacts from the Roman settlement

---

CARTOUCHE

10 The Centre, Church Street, Tiptree, Essex CO5 0HF
Tel: 01621 815302 Fax: 01621 819897
e-mail: Lawrence@ryan3939.fsnet.co.uk
website: www.ugem-cartouche.co.uk

For many years, Valerie and Lawrence Ryan traded in Hatton Garden as manufacturing jewellers before moving to Tiptree in 2000 to open **Cartouche**. Lawrence designs, makes, re-fashions and repairs all forms of jewellery – in gold, silver, platinum and other metals. The shop, in custom-built modern premises in the heart of town, also sells a fine range of precious and semi-precious stones and giftware, including glass, crystal, pewter, ceramics and leather.

There are pictures and prints, picture and photo frames in all sizes, handmade greetings cards, scented and plain wax candles, leather jewellery boxes, bronze figures and collectables and much more besides. All items purchased are beautifully gift wrapped free of charge.

Among the many suppliers are Royal Selangore, Dulwich Designs, LSA Glass, Gleneagles Crystal, Widdop Bingham, Citizen Watches and Junction 18. Cartouche also stocks a wide range of trophy ware and engrave onto glass and metal. Browsers are welcome, and for a special treat or a gift to remember, Cartouche is definitely the place to look.

THE PRINCE OF WALES

Kelvedon Road, Inworth, Essex CO5 9SP
Tel: 01376 570813
e-mail: enquiries@princeofwalesinworth.co.uk
website: www.princeofwalesinworth.co.uk

The Prince of Wales is a charming country inn and family restaurant set in the lovely Essex countryside in the village of Inworth near Kelvedon. It lies on the B1023, just off Junction 23 of the A12 equidistant from Chelmsford and Colchester. It has been recently acquired by new owners, Andy and Lindsay, and lovingly restored, revealing the traditional charming features whilst at the same time introducing a modern contemporary feel. The bar and restaurant are open six days a week (11am to 11pm, Tuesday to Saturday and midday to 10.30 Sunday), serving a range of fine food including all day, a la carte and Sunday roast. New menus are introduced every 8-10 weeks, providing a range of traditional and international cuisine. The menus are complemented by an extensive range of coffees, wines, ales and beers. Adjacent to the bar and restaurant is a 16th century barn which is a self contained function room suitable for both social and business events and catering for up to 40 a la carte or 70 for a buffet. The Prince of Wales is a lovely setting for drinks, meals, weddings, christenings, parties and any other gathering to celebrate a special occasion.

of Canonium, agricultural tools through the ages and other interesting exhibits.

LITTLE BADDOW
5 miles E of Chelmsford off the A414

Blakes Wood is a designated Site of Special Scientific Interest, an ancient woodland of hornbeam and sweet chestnut renowned for its bluebells. There is a good circular way-marked one-and-a-half mile walk.

Cruising along the Chelmer and Blackwater Canal provides the visitor with a unique view of this part of rural Essex. Chelmer Cruises & Canal Centre at Paper Mill Lock in Little Baddow offers the barge *Victoria* for group hire (seats 48). Individual day trips at weekends and bank holidays can also be arranged. There's also an island picnic area, lockside tea room, walks and fishing.

DANBURY
5 miles E of Chelmsford off the A414

🌿 Common, Country Park

This village is said to take its name from the Danes who invaded this part of the country in the Dark Ages. In the fine church, under a rare 13th century carved effigy, a crusader knight was found when the tomb was opened in 1779, perfectly preserved in the pickle which filled his coffin. Fine carving is also a feature of the bench ends; the oldest among them have inspired modern craftsmen to continue the same style of carving on all the pews. In 1402, *'the devil appeared in the likeness of Firor Minor, who entered the church, raged insolently to the great terror of the parishioners ... the top of the steeple was broken down and half the chancel scattered abroad.'* And, in 1941, another harbinger of disaster, a 500lb German bomb, reduced the east end to ruins.

Danbury

At **Danbury Common**, acres of gorse flower in a blaze of golden colour for much of the year. Along with Lingwood Common, Danbury Common is at the highest point of the gravel ridge between Maldon and Chelmsford. There is evidence here of Napoleonic defences and old reservoirs. Circular nature trails make exploring the area easily accessible. To the west, **Danbury Country Park** offers another pleasant stretch of open country, boasting woodland, a lake and ornamental gardens. Guide available by appointment.

WOODHAM WALTER

6 miles E of Chelmsford off the B1010

Woodham Walter is a small village which lies two-and-a-half miles west of the ancient market town and coastal port of Maldon. It is rumoured that Henry VIII hunted in Woodham Walter during his reign. During the troubled times after Henry's death, Mary Tudor was concealed in Woodham Walter Hall, from whence she was planning to escape from England in 1550. The church in Woodham, St Michael's, was constructed in April 1564 and is said to be one of the oldest still standing in the world.

MALDON

10 miles E of Chelmsford on the A414

Museum   Heritage Centre

Maldon's High Street has existed since medieval times, and the alleys and mews leading from it are full of intriguing shops,

welcoming old inns and good places to eat. One of the most distinctive features of the High Street is the Moot Hall. Built in the 14th century for the D'Arcy family, this building passed into the hands of the town corporation and was the seat of power in Maldon for over 400 years. The original brick spiral staircase (the best-preserved of its kind in England) and the 18th century courtroom are of particular interest. Guided tours are available on Saturdays in summer and by appointment with Maldon Town Council (01621 857373) at other times.

A colourful appliqued embroidery made to commemorate the 1,000th anniversary of the crucial Battle of Maldon (see Northey Island below) is on display at the **Maeldune Heritage Centre** (Maeldune being the Saxon name for Maldon). The Centre is housed in the Grade I listed St Peter's Building, erected in the 17th century by a local benefactor when the nave of the church that had once stood on this site collapsed. It can be found at the junction

MALDON DELICATESSEN

Wenlock Way, High Street, Maldon, Essex CM9 5AD
Tel/Fax: 01621 842637

Owner Liz Murphy had long experience in the hotel and catering trade, and it was her passion for top-quality food that led her to opening the brand new **Maldon Delicatessen** in December 2004. The interior of her shop is fresh, bright and modern, with gleaming display units and spotless food preparation areas. Ninety percent of the comestibles in the shop comes from top-quality private independent sources, and many items are organic and additive-free, home cooked and ready to take away.

There's a colourful array of Italian meats and cheeses, olives and antipasti, organic Welsh cheeses and sandwiches made to order, and for office lunches and home parties the staff will make up cheeseboards, starter platters and hampers. There are herbs, ceramics and a small, well-chosen selection of kitchen accessories. The shop has a comfortable coffee lounge/snacking area with a menu of soup, panini, baguettes, tortilla wraps and salads from a self-service bar; when the weather is kind, these tasty bites can be enjoyed at tables set outside on a traffic-free paved area. The staff do an excellent job, and Liz arranges monthly food tastings in the summer. The shop is easily accessible to buggies and wheelchairs.

of the High Street and the steep and architecturally interesting Market Hill. The benefactor, one Thomas Plume, erected the building to house his collection of 6,000 books and a school; The Plume Library in St Peter's Building is open to the public.

A few minutes' walk down one of the small roads leading from the High Street brings you to the waterfront, where the old wharves and quays are still active. Moored at Hythe Quay are several Thames sailing barges, all over 100 years old and still boasting their traditional rigging and distinctive tan sails. The barges and quay are overlooked by two pubs, the Queen's Head and the Jolly Sailor. Maldon, famous for its sea salt, is the only place in England still making salt from sea water. Salt production in Maldon dates from Roman times, and from its current premises on the waterfront has continued uninterrupted since 1882.

Promenade Park lies adjacent to Hythe Quay. This attractive park next to the River Blackwater opened in 1895. The Edwardian-style gardens include a marine lake where children can paddle and a sandy play-space by the waterside. Also in the park are an adventure playground, picnic site, amusement centre, tennis courts and mini-golf. A varied programme of events takes place in the park throughout the year, including the Mad Maldon Mud Race and the RNLI Rowing Race, both held annually over the Christmas and New Year holidays.

Housed in what was originally the park-keeper's lodge, by the park gates, **Maldon District Museum** looks back on the colourful history of the town through permanent and changing displays of exhibits and objects associated with the area and the people of Maldon.

📰 stories and anecdotes   🐦 famous people   🖌 art and craft   🍃 entertainment and sport   🥾 walks

Ruins are all that remain of the St Giles the Leper Hospital, founded by King Henry II in the 12th century. As with all monastic buildings, it fell into disuse after Henry VIII's Dissolution of the Monasteries, though it retained its roof and was used as a barn until the late 19th century. Many other buildings in the town, almost as old, fortunately remain - including two fine churches.

GOLDHANGER
4 miles NE of Maldon off the B1026

🏛 Agricultural & Domestic Museum

Maldon District Agricultural & Domestic Museum, at 47 Church Street in Goldhanger, features a large collection of vintage farm tools and machinery manufactured locally, as well as printing machinery and domestic artefacts.

TOLLESBURY
9 miles NE of Maldon on the B1023

Located at the mouth of the River Blackwater is the marshland village of Tollesbury. Tollesbury Marina has been designed as a family leisure centre for the crews and passengers of visiting yachts. The Marina, with its tennis courts, heated covered swimming pool, bar and restaurant is ideally located for exploring the Blackwater and the neighbouring estuaries of the Crouch, Colne, Stour and Orwell. Guests arriving by land are welcome to use some Cruising Club facilities.

LANGFORD
2 miles NW of Maldon off the B1019

🏛 Museum of Power

The **Museum of Power**, Hatfield Road, covers all aspects of power, from domestic

---

WICKS MANOR FARM

Witham Road, Tolleshunt Major, nr Maldon, Essex CM9 8JU
Tel:01621 860629
e-mail: rhowie@aspects.net
website: www.wicksmanor.co.uk

Three rooms in a 17th century moated farmhouse provide quiet, secluded and very comfortable accommodation at **Wicks Manor Farm**, a working mixed farm.

The beamed rooms are tastefully decorated and furnished in keeping with the age of the property, and amenities include excellent en suite power showers, hairdryers and beverage trays. The owner prepares a splendid breakfast using produce grown on the farm, served in the dining room overlooking the moat and garden.

The farm is an ideal place to relax, unwind and enjoy the rural peace, and to visit the many delightful places in the vicinity. The Blackwater Estuary, great for walking and birdwatching, is just two miles away, and the lovely gardens of Beth Chatto, Hyde Hall and Glen Chantry are all within an easy drive. The farm is located not far from the A12: take the small slip road exit at Rivenhall End between junctions 22 and 23; drive to the junction with the B1022 then follow signs for Tolleshunt Major and signs for the farm.

🏛 historic building   🏛 museum   🏛 historic site   🍃 scenic attraction   🌿 flora and fauna

Tollesbury

HEYBRIDGE BASIN
2 miles E of Maldon off the B1026

Here the Chelmer and Blackwater Canal meets the tidal estuary. The busy sea lock and the activities of crafts of all sizes provide an endlessly changing scene. A café and a shop selling local crafts occupy an old chandlery, and two pleasant inns overlook the water.

batteries to the massive machines that powered British industry. It includes the steam-powered pumping-station machinery of the redundant waterworks in which the museum is housed.

NORTHEY ISLAND
1 mile SE of Maldon off the B1018

🌿 Northey Island

Northey Island, comprising mainly salt marsh, is owned by the National Trust. Access to this nature reserve is on foot via a causeway passable at low tide. It is a Site of Special Scientific Interest, an important stopover for wintering birds.

The sea walls of the Island make for an interesting walk, and were used as the camp base for the Viking army in AD991, when Byrhtnoth led the Saxons against the invading army. A fierce three-day battle took place, with Byrhtnoth's head eventually being cut off and the Viking warriors retreating despite their victory, leaving the English King Ethelred the Unready to pay an annual tribute, 'danegold', to the Danes to prevent further incursions.

PURLEIGH
3 miles SW of Maldon on the B1010

The first recorded vineyard in Purleigh was planted in the early 12th century, only 400 yards from the site of New Hall Vineyards in Chelmsford Road. It covered three acres of land next to Purleigh Church, where first US president George Washington's great-great-grandfather was the rector - until the time he was removed from this office for sampling too much of the local brew! Purleigh Vineyard became Crown property in 1163; subsequently the wines produced were taken each year to London to be presented to the monarch.

RETTENDON
6 miles SW of Maldon off the A130

🌿 RHS Garden

The **Royal Horticultural Society Garden** (see panel on page 284) at Hyde Hall comprises eight acres of year-round hillside colour, with a woodland garden, large rose garden, ornamental ponds with lilies and fish, herbaceous borders, shrubs, trees, and national collections of malus and viburnum. Meals and

🎬 stories and anecdotes   🦆 famous people   🎨 art and craft   ✏ entertainment and sport   🚶 walks

RHS Garden Hyde Hall

Rettendon, Chelmsford, Essex CM3 8ET
Tel: 01245 400256
e-mail: hydehall@rhs.org.uk
website: www.rhs.org.uk

RHS Garden Hyde Hall is the proud and impressive result of 40 years of dedication and inspiration, created despite its hilltop setting, heavy clay soil, low rainfall and frequent strong, drying winds. Donated to the Royal Horticultural Society in 1993, a programme of development and improvement has made this delightful and imaginatively planted garden a centre of excellence. Home to the National Plant Collection of viburnum, the garden is also well known for its superb collection of roses. The colour-themed herbaceous border and new plantings around the lower pond are also striking examples of garden design. The Farmhouse Garden features a formal design full of bold colour combinations and fascinating plant associations. The Dry Garden displays plants from a variety of arid areas. The Hilltop Garden provides year-round interest with its naturalised spring bulbs and late-flowering tender perennials producing a blaze of autumn colour.

The visitor centre offers a wealth of information on many subjects. In the Hyde Hall Garden Library, visitors are welcome to browse through books, journals and CD ROMs exploring a range of topics such as problem places, garden plants, pests and diseases, pruning and more. The Barn Restaurant, Tea Yard and Shop complete this fascinating day out which will delight not just gardeners but anyone with an eye for beauty. Open every day from 10am.

snacks are available in the attractive thatched barn; there is also a plant centre. Fine views can be had from this attractively landscaped hilltop garden.

SOUTH WOODHAM FERRERS
5 miles SW of Maldon off the B1012

The empty marshland of the Crouch estuary, a yachtsman's paradise, was chosen by Essex County Council as the site for one of its most attractive new town schemes. At its centre, this successful 20th century new town boasts a traditional market square surrounded by pleasant arcades and terraces built in the old Essex style with brick, tile and weatherboard.

Marsh Farm Country Park in Marsh Farm Road, South Woodham Ferrers, is a working farm and country park adjoining the River Crouch. Sheep, pigs, cattle and hens roam; visitors can also partake of the adventure play area, farm trail, visitors' centre, gift shop and tea rooms. Guided tours are available by prior arrangement. Special events are held throughout the year.

BATTLESBRIDGE
7 miles SW of Maldon off the A132

Battlesbridge Antiques Centre at Hawk Hill in Battlesbridge is the largest in Essex. Housed in five period buildings, more than 70 dealers display and sell their wares. The heart of the Centre is Cromwell House, its ground floor dedicated to specialist dealers with individual units. They will advise, value and give an expert opinion free of charge. They offer a wide variety of old and interesting pieces and collectables.

The Centre's Haybarn Cottages were constructed as dwellings, while, alongside, The Bridgebarn began life as a barn with thatched roof and dates from the 19th century, at which time there were lime kilns nearby. It was converted to its present tiled roof in the 1930s. The building retains some fine oak beamwork, and houses a small 'penny arcade' with working model roundabout, fortune teller, and 'What the Butler Saw' as well as a large collection of antiques for sale.

The Old Granary is nestled on the riverbank and houses five floors of dealers selling collectables, reproductions, antiques and crafts, including specialists in old phones, clocks, furniture, cigarette cards, jewellery, fireplaces, interior design, dried flowers and much more. There are superb views from the top floor of the River Crouch and surrounding area, to be enjoyed as you take tea in the top-floor coffee shop.

This superb location is also the site of a Classic Motor Cycle Museum, with displays evoking the history of motorcycling through the ages and some interesting memorabilia. Open on Sundays or by appointment. Three classic vehicle events are held annually.

MUNDON
3 miles SE of Maldon off the B1018

Mundon and the surrounding area boast some excellent walking. St Peter's Way, a long-distance path from Ongar to St Peter's Chapel, Bradwell-on-Sea, leads through the village and past the disused Church of St Mary. This 14th century church is maintained by the Friends of Friendless Churches and is open to the public. Tolstoy is known to have visited the village.

ALTHORNE
6 miles SE of Maldon on the B1012

Church of St Andrew

The Church of **St Andrew's**, some 600 years old, has a fine flint-and-stone tower, built in the perpendicular style. Inside the church there's a 15th century font which retains its original carvings of saints and angels. A brass plaque dated 1508 records that William Hyklott 'Paide for the werkemanship of the wall'; an inscription over the west door remembers John Wylson and John Hyll, who probably paid for the tower.

To the south, where Station Road meets Burnham Road, stands the villagers' own War Memorial. This solid structure of beams and tiles lends dignity and honour to the tragic roll-call of names listed on it.

To the north of the village is the golden-thatched and white-walled Huntsman and Hounds, an alehouse since around 1700.

STEEPLE AND ST LAWRENCE
8 miles SE of Maldon off the B1021

Public footpaths lead down to the water from the village of Steeple; the houses of St Lawrence stand close to the water. Several sailing clubs and some waterside caravan and camping parks ensure that there is plenty of activity on the adjacent stretch of the River Blackwater. The St Lawrence Rural Discovery Church, on high ground further inland, overlooks the villages and the River Blackwater to the north; it also offers views over the River Crouch to the south. Exhibitions with local themes are held in the church during the summer months.

stories and anecdotes   famous people   art and craft   entertainment and sport   walks

BRADWELL-ON-SEA/BRADWELL WATERSIDE

12 miles E of Maldon off the B1021

🏛 St Peter's on the Wall   🌱 Dengie Peninsula

A visit to Bradwell-on-Sea (the name derives from the Saxon words *brad pall*, meaning 'broad wall') is well worth the long drive for its sense of being right out on the edge of things – the timeless emptiness is if anything exaggerated by the distant views of buildings across the water on Mersea Island and the bulk of the nearby (now decommissioned) nuclear power station. A walk eastwards along the old Roman road across the marshes takes you to the site of their fort, 'Othona', on which the visitors of today will find the chapel of **St Peter's on the Wall**, built by St Cedd and his followers in AD654 using rubble from the ruined fort. In the 14th century the chapel was abandoned as a place of worship, and over the following centuries used at various times as a barn and a shipping beacon. Restored and re-consecrated in 1920, it is well worth the half-mile walk from the car park to reach it. It is the site of a pilgrimage each July.

There is an unusual war memorial marking the site of the Bradwell Bay Secret Airfield, used during the Second World War for aircraft unable to return to their original base.

Bradwell Lodge, in the village centre, is a part-Tudor former rectory that has known some famous visitors. Gainsborough, the Suffolk artist, used rooms as a studio, while the Irish writer Erskine Childers, who was shot by the Irish Free State in 1920 because he fought for the IRA, wrote *The Riddle of the Sands* here.

At Bradwell Waterside, a large marina has berths for 300 boats. The now-decommissioned nuclear power station has a visitor centre with an exhibition and high-tech audio-visual displays about electricity production and the decommissioning process. A nature trail is waymarked within the grounds of the station.

To the south of the village lie the remote marshes of the **Dengie Peninsula**, parts of which are important nature reserves The salty tang of sea air, brought inland on easterly winds, gives an exhilarating flavour to the marshlands. Like the Cambridgeshire and Lincolnshire fens, this once-waterlogged corner of Essex was reclaimed from the sea by 17th century Dutch engineers. The views across the marshes take in great sweeps of countryside inhabited only by wildfowl and seabirds.

BURNHAM-ON-CROUCH

12 miles SE of Maldon on the B1012

🏛 St Mary's Church   🏛 Museum

🏛 Mangapps Farm Railway Museum

Burnham-on-Crouch is attractively old-fashioned, and probably best known as a yachting venue. It is lively in summer, especially at the end of August when the town hosts one of England's premier regattas, Burnham Week. This week of racing and shore events attracts many visiting craft and landlubbers alike. In winter many yachts are left to ride at anchor offshore, and the sound of the wind in their rigging is ever-present.

Behind the gaily-coloured cottages along the Quay lies the High Street and the rest of the town, its streets lined with a delightful assortment of old cottages and Victorian and Georgian houses and shops.

In past times, working boats thronged the estuary where yachts now ply to and fro. Seafarers still come ashore to buy provisions, following a tradition that goes back to medieval times when Burnham was the market centre for

🏛 historic building   🏛 museum   🏛 historic site   🌀 scenic attraction   🌱 flora and fauna

the isolated inhabitants of Wallasea and Foulness Islands in the estuary. A ferry still links Burnham with Wallasea at weekends during the summer, and a programme of boat trips to see the seals on Foulness Sands operates from Burnham Quay.

Near the Yacht Harbour, west of the town and accessible along the sea-wall

Burnham-on-Crouch

path is Burnham Country Park. Also alongside the river can be found the Millfield Recreation Ground and a sports centre.

Burnham-on-Crouch & District Museum on The Quay features agricultural, maritime and social history exhibits relating to the Dengie Hundred. There is also a small archaeological collection. Special exhibitions are mounted periodically.

Mangapps Farm Railway Museum on the edge of town offers an extensive collection of railway relics of all kinds, including steam and diesel locos, carriages and wagons, relocated railway buildings, one of the largest collections of signalling equipment open to the public, a complete country station and items of East Anglian railway history. Train rides are available when the museum is open, and Thomas the Tank Engine weekends are held several times a year.

St Mary's Church is constructed of Kentish ragstone that was transported to Burnham by sea. Construction was begun in the 12th century and was completed in the 14th, but since that time the nucleus of the town has moved closer to the waterfront. The arches and pillars are particularly fine examples of medieval craftsmanship, hence the church being known as 'The Cathedral of the Dengie'.

LOCATOR MAP

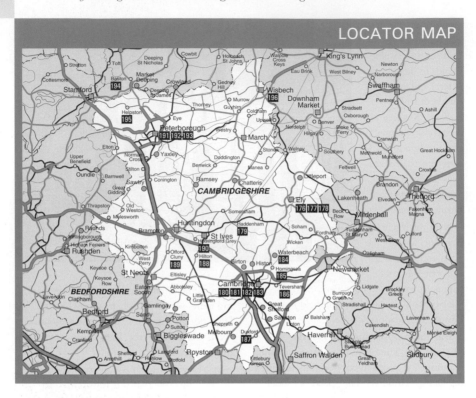

ADVERTISERS AND PLACES OF INTEREST

🏛 historic building   📷 museum   🏛 historic site   ♧ scenic attraction   🌱 flora and fauna

4 Cambridgeshire

Extending over much of the county from the Wash, the flat fields of the Fens are like a breath of fresh air, far removed from the hustle and bustle of modern life. These fields contain some of the richest soil in England, and villages such as Fordham and small towns like Ely rise out of the landscape on low hills.

Before the Fens were drained, this was a land of mist, marshes and bogs, of small islands inhabited by independent folk, their livelihood the fish and waterfowl of this eerie, watery place. The region is full of legends of web-footed people, ghosts and witchcraft. Today's landscape is the result of human ingenuity, with its constant desire to tame the wilderness and create farmland. This fascinating story spans the centuries from the earliest Roman and Anglo-Saxon times, when the first embankments and drains were constructed to lessen the frequency of flooding. Throughout the Middle Ages large areas were reclaimed, with much of the work being undertaken by the monasteries. The first straight cut bypassed the Great Ouse, allowing the water to run out to sea more quickly. After the Civil War, the New Bedford River was cut parallel to the first. These two still provide the basic drainage for much of Fenland. The significant influence of the Dutch lives on in some of the architecture and place names of the Fens. Over the years it became necessary to pump rainwater from the fields up into the rivers and, as in the Netherlands, windmills took on this task. They could not always cope with the height of the lift required, but fortunately the steam engine came along, to be replaced eventually by the electric pumps that can raise thousands of gallons of water a second to protect the land from the ever-present threat of rain and tide. The Fens offer unlimited opportunities for exploring on foot, by car, bicycle or by boat. Anglers are well catered for, and visitors with an interest in wildlife will be in their element.

Southeastern Cambridgeshire covers the

Mathematical Bridge, Cambridge

area around the city of Cambridge and is rich in history, with a host of archaeological sites and monuments to visit, as well as many important museums. The area is fairly flat, so it makes for great walking and cycling tours, and offers a surprising variety of landscapes. The Romans planted vines here and, to this day, the region is one of the main producers of British wines. At the heart of it all is Cambridge itself, one of the leading academic centres in the world and a city which deserves plenty of time to explore - on foot, by bicycle or by the gentler, more romantic option of a punt.

The old county of Huntingdonshire is the heartland of the rural heritage of Cambridgeshire. Here, the home of Oliver Cromwell beckons with a wealth of history and pleasing landscapes. Many motorists follow the Cromwell Trail, which guides tourists around the legacy of buildings and

places in the area associated with the man. The natural start of the Trail is Huntingdon itself, where he was born the son of a country gentleman. Other main stopping places are covered in this chapter.

The Ouse Valley Way (26 miles long) follows the course of the Great Ouse through pretty villages and a variety of natural attractions. A gentle cruise along this area can fill a lazy day to perfection, but for those who prefer something more energetic on the water there are excellent, versatile facilities at Grafham Water. The Nene-Ouse Navigation Link, part of the Fenland Waterway, provides the opportunity for a relaxed look at a lovely part of the region. It travels from Stanground Lock near Peterborough to a lock at the small village of Salters Lode in the east, and the 28-mile journey passes through several Fenland towns and a rich variety of wildlife habitats.

Ely

🏛 Cathedral 🏛 TIC 🏛 Ely Museum

🏛 Museum of Stained Glass

✎ Brass Rubbing Centre

Ely is the jewel in the crown of the Fens, in whose history the majestic **Cathedral** and the Fens themselves have played major roles. The Fens' influence is apparent even in the name: Ely was once known as Elge or Elig ('eel island') because of the large number of eels which lived in the surrounding fenland.

Ely owes its existence to St Etheldreda, Queen of Northumbria, who in AD673 founded a monastery on the 'Isle of Ely', where she remained as abbess until her death in AD679. It was not until 1081 that work started on the present Cathedral, and in 1189 this remarkable example of Romanesque architecture was completed. The most outstanding feature in terms of both scale and beauty is the Octagon, built to replace the original Norman tower, which collapsed in 1322.

Alan of Walsingham was the inspired architect of this massive work, which took 30 years to complete and whose framework weighs an estimated 400 tons. Many other notable components include the 14th century Lady Chapel, the largest in England, the Prior's Door, the painted nave ceiling and St Ovin's cross, the only piece of Saxon stonework in the building.

The Cathedral is set within the walls of the monastery, and many of the ancient buildings

FINE TABLE

4 High Street, Ely, Cambridgeshire CB7 4JU
Tel: 01353 650077 Fax: 01353 669137
e-mail: sales@finetable.co.uk
website: www.finetable.co.uk

Fine Table occupies High Street premises just 75 yards from Ely Cathedral and the Stained Glass Museum. Two floors of displays, well laid-out for the shopper, cover a unique selection of design-led dining accessories from across Europe. The stock is carefully sourced from companies large and small, and many individual pieces are the work of talented designers and artists. Among the many outstanding names featured are the stainless steel Nio range from Oliver Hemming, Laguiole cutlery with their famous bee logos, and a range of collectable functional art from Carrol Boyes, along with French porcelain, wine and bar accessories, traditional English forge work, candles and candle-holders, glassware, and kitchenware from Nigella Lawson and Emile Henry.

Fine Table is the ideal place to find the perfect wedding gift or a special gift for any occasion. The stock changes continuously, which means that every visit will reveal something out of the ordinary to enhance the home or to provide a gift which is both practical and beautiful.

🎞 stories and anecdotes 🐦 famous people ✎ art and craft ✒ entertainment and sport 🚶 walks

Ely Cathedral

still stand as a tribute to the incredible skill and craftsmanship of their designers and builders. Particularly worth visiting among these are the monastic buildings in the College, the Great Hall and Queens Hall.

Just beside the Cathedral is the Almonry, in whose 12th century vaulted undercroft visitors can take coffee, lunch or tea - outside in the garden if the weather permits. Two other attractions that should not be missed are the **Brass Rubbing Centre**, where visitors can make their own rubbings from replica brasses, and the **Museum of Stained Glass**. The latter, housed in

CHERRY HILL CHOCOLATES

28a High Street, Ely, Cambridgeshire CB7 4JU
Tel: 01353 666 617
e-mail: info@cherryhillchocolates.co.uk
website: www.cherryhillchocolates.co.uk

Centrally located on the High Street, Cherry Hill Chocolates is set amidst the ancient walls of Ely Cathedral. This historic shop with its magnificent vaulted ceiling houses the largest range of loose Belgium chocolates in the area. The superb selection includes, Valrhona from France, The Chocolate Society and coveted L'Artisan du chocolat of London.

Quality chocolates are not the only temptation. The shop also carries award winning luscious ice creams from Lovingtons of Somerset, loose teas and coffees from around the world to enjoy at home, and exquisite giftware, including limited edition teapots from The Teapottery in the Yorkshire Dales.

A recent addition to the services provided by the shop, is a bridal and special events department. Working with local suppliers, Cherry Hill Chocolates offers specially packaged chocolate gift boxes, bespoke cakes, floral arrangements and imported wines for weddings, special events and corporate functions. Gift hampers and chocolates can be purchased on-line, or by phone and mail order, and shipped to any location.

When visiting Ely, stop by this delightful shop to experience a part of the town's history, and treat yourself to the luxurious taste of Cherry Hill Chocolates – something wonderful for every occasion.

Shop hours are: Monday to Saturday: 9 to 6:00; Sunday 11:00 to 5:00

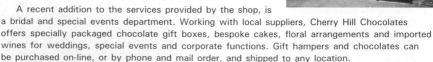

🏛 historic building 🏛 museum 🏛 historic site ⚘ scenic attraction � flora and fauna

the south Triforium of the Cathedral, is the only museum of stained glass in the country and contains over 100 original panels from every period, tracing the complete history of stained glass.

The Old Palace, the official residence of the Bishops of Ely until 1940, is now a hospice. It is fronted by two towers, and notable features inside include the Georgian sitting room and the Bishop's private chapel. In the garden is a giant plane tree that is claimed to be the oldest in Europe. The **Tourist Information Centre** is itself a tourist attraction, since it is housed in a pretty black-and-white timbered building that was once the home of Oliver Cromwell. It is the only remaining house, apart from Hampton Court, where Oliver Cromwell and his family are known to have lived; parts of it

trace back to the 13th century, and its varied history includes periods when it was used as a public house and, more recently, a vicarage. There are eight period rooms, including the room where he died, and a number of exhibitions and videos.

The Old Gaol, in Market Street, houses Ely Museum, with nine galleries telling the Ely story from the Ice Age to modern times. The tableaux of the condemned and debtors' cells are particularly fascinating and poignant.

Ely is not just the past, and its fine architecture and sense of history blend well with the bustle of the streets and shops and the riverside. That bustle is at its most fervent on Thursdays, when the largest general market in the area is held. Every Saturday there's a craft and collectables market, and on the

Wardy Hill

Distance: *5.5 miles (8.8 kilometres)*

Typical time: *120 mins*

Height gain: *0 metres*

Map: *Explorer 228*

Walk: *www.walkingworld.com ID:1170*

Contributor: *Joy & Charles Boldero*

ACCESS INFORMATION:

For information about bus routes ring 0870 6082608. There is parking on the very wide grass verge at By-way sign on the edge of Wardy Hill village, by Beumont Farm fence line. Wardy Hill is situated on a minor road off the A142 4 miles west of Ely.

ADDITIONAL INFORMATION:

Wardy Hill is set on an island above the fens, on what is known as the Isle of Ely. Wardy Hill means 'look out'. In centuries past this was to watch for cattle raiders coming across the fens. It is thought it was a Bronze Age settlement as shields and swords have been found here.

The New Bedford River, or Hundred-Foot Drain as it is also called, was built after the Old Bedford River, built by the Dutchman, Vermuydrn in the 1600s, was found to be inadequate. The land between the two rivers is a flood plain and part of the R.S.P.B. famous Welney Washes. To the left on the horizon Ely Cathedral can be seen.

The Three Pickerels pub at Mepal has an excellent menu. It is closed on Monday lunch times. It is open all day on Sundays.

DESCRIPTION:

This walk is beside the New Bedford River to Mepal, then returning by tracks, footpaths which can be muddy after heavy rain and country lanes.

FEATURES:

River, Pub, Toilets, Wildlife, Birds, Flowers, Great Views, Butterflies

WALK DIRECTIONS:

1 | Go westwards through the village, ignoring all footpaths off the country lane. Continue along Jerusalem Drove to lefthand bend.

2 | At bridleway sign go right along track passing Toll Cottage. Climb stile and cross to next one and climb it going up the bank.

3 | Turn left along river bank. Much further along go down bank to metal gate, climb stile. You can either continue along the track or climb the stile and go back onto bank. Climb stile.

4 | Turn right along road in Mepal, then almost immediately left to pub. Retrace steps to junction and turn right along pavement.

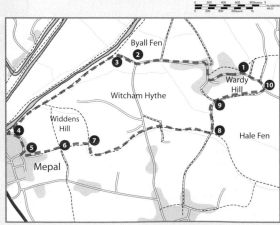

5 | Cross road by righthand bend and turn left along New Road. At end go around gate and cross field. Climb stile, cross second field, climb stile.

6 | Turn left along track then almost immediately right. Cross field and slippery bridge.

7 | Turn right along track. Cross road and continue along the track opposite. Cross track and continue along track. At fork either path can be used.

8 | Turn left at cross tracks.

9 | At T junction of tracks turn right.

10 | Turn left along country lane back to start of walk.

second and fourth Saturdays of the month Ely hosts a Farmers' Market.

At Babylon Gallery on Ely's Waterside, in a converted 18th century brewery warehouse, visitors will find an exciting collection of contemporary arts and crafts, in a programme of changing local and international exhibitions.

Around Ely

PRICKWILLOW
4 miles NE of Ely on the B1382

🏠 Museum

On the village's main street is the **Prickwillow Drainage Engine Museum**, which houses a unique collection of large engines associated with the drainage of the Fens. The site had been in continuous use as a pumping station since 1831, and apart from the engines there are displays charting the history of Fens drainage, the effects on land levels and the workings of the modern drainage system.

LITTLEPORT
6 miles N of Ely on the A10

🏠 St George's Church

St George's Church, with its very tall 15th century tower, is a notable landmark here in Littleport. Of particular interest are two stained-glass windows depicting St George slaying the dragon. Littleport was the scene of riots in 1861, when labourers from Ely and Littleport, faced with unemployment or low wages, and soaring food prices, attacked houses and people in this area, causing several deaths. Five of the rioters were hanged and buried in a common grave at St Mary's church. A plaque commemorating the event is attached to a wall at the back of the church.

LITTLE DOWNHAM
3 miles N of Ely off the A10

Little Downham's Church of St Leonard shows the change from Norman to Gothic in church building at the turn of the 13th century. The oldest parts are the Norman tower and the elaborately carved south door. Interior treasures include what is probably the largest royal coat of arms in the country. At the other end of the village are the remains (mainly the gatehouse and kitchen) of a 15th century palace built by a Bishop of Ely. The property is in private hands and part of it is an antiques centre.

COVENEY
3 miles W of Ely off the A10

🏠 Church of St Peter-ad-Vincula

A Fenland hamlet on the Bedford Level just above West Fen, Coveney's **Church of St Peter-ad-Vincula** has several interesting features, including a colourful German screen dating from around 1500 and a painted Danish pulpit. Unusual figures on the bench ends and a fine brass chandelier add to the opulent feel of this atmospheric little church.

SUTTON
6 miles W of Ely off the A142

A very splendid 'pepperpot' tower with octagons, pinnacles and spire tops marks out Sutton's grand church of St Andrew. Inside, take time to look at the 15th century font and a fine modern stained-glass window.

The reconstruction of the church was largely the work of two Bishops of Ely, whose arms appear on the roof bosses. One of the Bishops was Thomas Arundel, appointed at the age of 21.

A mile further west, there's a great family

attraction in the Mepal Outdoor Centre, an outdoor leisure centre with a children's playpark, an adventure play area and boat hire.

HADDENHAM
5 miles SW of Ely on the A1123

 Great Mill

More industrial splendour: **Haddenham Great Mill**, built in 1803 for a certain Daniel Cockle, is a glorious sight, and one definitely not to be missed. It has four sails and three sets of grinding stones, one of which is working. The mill last worked commercially in 1946 and was restored between 1992 and 1998. Open on the first Sunday of each month and by appointment.

The Church of St Andrew stands on a hillside in Haddenham. Look for the stained-glass window depicting two souls entering

---

HADDENHAM GALLERIES

20 High Street, Haddenham, nr Ely, Cambridgeshire CB6 3XA
Tel: 01353 749188 Fax: 01353 740688
e-mail: haddenhamgallery@dial.pipex.com
website: www.haddenhamgallery.co.uk

The **Creative Art Gallery** is set in the centre of Haddingham, with fine views across the Fens, and with a natural meadow set out as a sculpture garden. The gallery holds 10 selling exhibitions each year, exploring all aspects of creative art from a wide source of makers. Wherever possible it supports emerging artists, encourages new work and provides a valuable stepping stone in exhibiting affordable work to the public. In conjunction with the exhibitions it runs workshops for local children and adults, and is regularly involved in regional arts events and working open days. Eight studios are let to local artists/craftspeople working in a variety of disciplines.

The **Ethnic Gallery** adjoins the Creative Art Gallery through a 17th century carved doorway from Afghanistan. Alastair Hull, veteran traveller and writer, collects at source all the unusual and exciting items in this colourful gallery. He frequently travels through remote bazaars and villages within Central Asia and the East Indies archipelago and has built up a unique collection and deep knowledge of the people, their culture and traditions.

Heaven, and the memorial (perhaps the work of Grinling Gibbons) to Christopher Wren's sister, Anne Brunsell.

STRETHAM
5 miles S of Ely off A10/A1123

🏛 Sretham Old Engine

The **Stretham Old Engine**, a fine example of a land-drainage steam engine, is housed in a restored, tall-chimneyed brick engine house. Dating from 1831, it is one of 90 steam pumping engines installed throughout the Fens to replace some 800 windmills. It is the last to survive, having worked until 1925 and still under restoration. During the great floods of 1919 it really earned its keep by working non-stop for 47 days and nights.

This unique insight into Fenland history and industrial archaeology is open to the public on summer weekends, and on certain dates the engine and its wooden scoop-wheel are rotated (by electricity, alas!). The adjacent Stoker's Cottage contains four plainly

appointed rooms with period furniture and old photographs of fen drainage down the years.

Downfield Windmill, six miles southeast of Ely on the A142 bypass, was built in 1726 as a smock mill, destroyed by gales and rebuilt in 1890 as an octagonal tower mill. It still grinds corn and produces a range of flours and breads for sale (open Sundays and Bank Holidays).

WICKEN
9 miles S of Ely off the A1123

🏠 St Lawrence's Church 🌱 Wicken Fen

Owned by the National Trust, **Wicken Fen** is the oldest nature reserve in the country, celebrating its centenary in 1999. Its 600 acres of wetland habitats are famous for their rich plant, insect and bird life and a delight for both naturalists and ramblers. Features include boardwalk, adventurer's and nature trails, hides and watchtowers, wild ponies, a cottage with 1930s furnishings, a working wind pump (the oldest in the country), a visitor centre and a shop. Open daily, dawn to dusk.

St Lawrence's Church is well worth a visit, small and secluded among trees. In the churchyard are buried Oliver Cromwell and several members of his family. One of Cromwell's many nicknames was 'Lord of the Fens': he defended the rights of the Fenmen against those who wanted to drain the land without providing adequate compensation.

Wicken Windmill is a fine and impressive smock windmill restored back to working order. One of only four smock

Old Engine House, Stretham

windmills making flour by windmill in the UK, it is open the first weekend of every month and every Bank Holiday (except Christmas and Good Friday) from 11am until 5pm, and also over the National Mills Weekend the second week in May.

ISLEHAM
10 miles SE of Ely off the B1104

The remains of a Benedictine priory, with a lovely Norman chapel under the care of English Heritage, are a great draw here in Isleham. Also well worth a visit is the Church of St Andrew, a 14th century cruciform building entered by a very fine lychgate. The 17th century eagle lectern is the original of a similar lectern in Ely Cathedral.

SNAILWELL
12 miles SE of Ely off the A142

Snailwell's pretty, mainly 14th century Church of St Peter on the banks of the River Snail

boasts a 13th century chancel, a hammerbeam and tie beam nave roof, a 600-year-old font, pews with poppy heads and two medieval oak screens. The Norman round tower is unusual for Cambridgeshire.

Cambridge

- 🏠 The Colleges 🏠 University Library
- 🏠 Bridge of Sighs 🏠 Mathematical Bridge
- 🏛 Fitzwilliam Museum 🏛 Museum of Zoology
- 🏛 Museums of Archaelology & Anthropolgy
- 🏛 Museum of Technology 🏛 Whipple Museum
- 🏛 Museum of Earth Sciences
- 🏛 Scott Polar Research Institute
- 🏛 Cambridge & County Folk Museum
- 🌿 University Botanic Gardens 🎨 Kettle's Yard

There are nearly 30 Cambridges spread around the globe, but this, the original, is the one that the whole world knows as one of the leading university cities. Cambridge was an important town many centuries before the scholars arrived, standing at the point where forest met fen, at the lowest fording point of the river. The Romans took over a site previously settled by an Iron Age Belgic tribe, to be followed in turn by the Saxons and the Normans.

Soon after the Norman Conquest, William I built a wooden motte-and-bailey castle; Edward I built a stone replacement: a mound still marks the spot. The town flourished as a market and river trading centre, and in 1209 a group of students fleeing the Oxford riots arrived.

Drainage Windmill, Wicken Fen

🏠 historic building 🏛 museum 🏛 historic site 🌿 scenic attraction 🌿 flora and fauna

The first College was **Peterhouse**, founded by the Bishop of Ely in 1284, and in the next century **Clare, Pembroke, Gonville & Caius, Trinity Hall** and **Corpus Christi** followed. The total is now more than 30; the most distinctive of the modern colleges is **Robinson College**, built in striking post-modern style in 1977; it has the look of a fortress, its concrete structure covered with a 'skin' of a million and a quarter hand-made red Dorset bricks. It was the gift of the self-made millionaire engineer and racehorse owner David Robinson. All the colleges are all well worth a visit, but places that simply must not be missed include **King's College Chapel** with its breathtaking fan vaulting, glorious stained glass and Peter Paul Rubens'

Adoration of the Magi; **Pepys Library**, including his diaries, in **Magdalene College**; and Trinity's wonderful **Great Court**. A trip by punt along the 'Backs' of the Cam brings a unique view of many of the colleges and passes under six bridges, including the **Bridge of Sighs (St John's)** and the extraordinary wooden **Mathematical Bridge at Queens**.

Cambridge has nurtured more Nobel Prize winners than most countries - 32 from Trinity alone - and the list of celebrated alumni covers every sphere of human endeavour and achievement: Byron, Tennyson, Milton and Wordsworth; Marlowe and Bacon; Samuel Pepys; Sir Isaac Newton and Charles Darwin; Charles Babbage, Bertrand Russell and Ludwig Wittgenstein; actors Sir Ian McKellen,

Sir Derek Jacobi and Stephen Fry; Lord Burghley; Harold Abrahams, who ran for England in the Olympics; and Burgess, Maclean, Philby and Blunt, who spied for Russia. The 'Cambridge Mafia' was the title given to a group of senior Conservatives at Cambridge together in the early 1960. Their number included Ken Clarke, John Gummer, Norman Lamont, Peter Lilley and Michael Howard, all in John Major's 1992 cabinet, Norman Fowler and Leon Brittan.

The Colleges apart, Cambridge is packed with interest for the visitor, with a wealth of grand buildings both religious and secular, and some of the country's leading museums, many of them run by the University. The **Fitzwilliam Museum** is renowned for its art collection, which includes works by Titian, Rembrandt, Gainsborough, Hogarth, Turner, Renoir, Picasso and Cezanne, and for its antiquities from Egypt, Greece and Rome. **Kettle's Yard** has a permanent display of 20th century art in a house maintained just as it was when the Ede family donated it, with the collection, to the University in 1967. The **Museum of Classical Archaeology** has 500 plaster casts of Greek and Roman statues, and the **University Museum of Archaeology and Anthropology** covers worldwide prehistoric archaeology with special displays relating to Oceania and to the Cambridge area. The **Museum of Technology**, housed in a Victorian sewage pumping station, features an impressive collection of steam, gas and electric pumping engines and examples great and small of local industrial technology. Anyone with an

---

ORANGERIE INTERIORS

69/71 Lensfield Road, Cambridge, Cambridgeshire
Tel: 01223 314377   Fax: 01223 462980
e-mail: info@orangerie.co.uk

Birgit Berry trained as an accountant, ran her own software company, married and raised a family before becoming the owner of **Orangerie Interiors**. The shop was established in 1988 as the Pine Merchant selling 19th century and reproduction pine furniture.

The previous owner retired in 2003 and Birgit updated and extended the range, and changed the name. What started as more or less a hobby has become a full-time career in the shop, which sells antique pine furniture (English and Continental), made-to-measure furniture in hard and soft woods, freestanding kitchens and painted furniture. Smaller items include soft furnishings, home accessories, rugs, lamps, tableware and paints.

There is a workshop on the premises for waxing, painting and repairing, and the shop offers wedding lists and advice and help on many aspects of interior design. Orangerie Interiors is located on the south side of the city centre, with the Cam a short walk in one direction and Fenners cricket ground and Parker's Piece in the other.

🏛 historic building   🏛 museum   🏚 historic site   ♨ scenic attraction   🌱 flora and fauna

interest in fossils should make tracks for the **Sedgwick Museum of Earth Sciences**, while in the same street (Downing) the **Museum of Zoology** offers a comprehensive and spectacular survey of the animal kingdom. The **Whipple Museum of the History of Science** tells about science through instruments; the **Scott Polar Research** Institute has fascinating, often poignant exhibits relating to Arctic and Antarctic exploration; and the **University Botanic Garden** boasts a plant collection (more than 8,000 species) that rivals those of Kew Gardens and Edinburgh. The 40-acre site includes the National Collections of species tulips, fritillaries and hardy geraniums.

Trinity College, Cambridge

The work and life of the people of Cambridge and the surrounding area are the subjects of the **Cambridge and County Folk Museum**(see panel below), housed in a 16th century building that for 300 years was the White Horse Inn. It traces the everyday lives of the local people from 1700 onwards, with sections devoted to crafts and trades, town & gown, witchbottles, skating, and eels. One of the city's greatest treasures is the **University Library**, one of the world's great research libraries with six million books, a million maps and 350,000 manuscripts.

Cambridge also has many fine churches, some of them used by the colleges before they built their own chapels. Among the most notable are St Andrew the Great (note the memorial to Captain Cook); St Andrew the Less; St Benet's (its 11th century tower is the oldest in the county); St Mary the Great, a

Cambridge & County Folk Museum

2-3 Castle Street, Cambridge, Cambridgeshire CB3 0AQ
Tel: 01223 355159
website: www.folkmuseum.org.uk

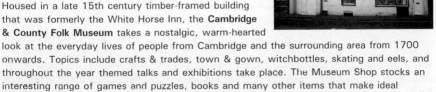

Housed in a late 15th century timber-framed building that was formerly the White Horse Inn, the **Cambridge & County Folk Museum** takes a nostalgic, warm-hearted look at the everyday lives of people from Cambridge and the surrounding area from 1700 onwards. Topics include crafts & trades, town & gown, witchbottles, skating and eels, and throughout the year themed talks and exhibitions take place. The Museum Shop stocks an interesting range of games and puzzles, books and many other items that make ideal Christmas stocking fillers, all with a nostalgic feel.

📖 stories and anecdotes 🦜 famous people 🎨 art and craft 🎭 entertainment and sport 🚶 walks

marvellous example of Late Perpendicular Gothic; and St Peter Castle Hill. This last is one of the smallest churches in the country, with a nave measuring just 25 feet by 16 feet. Originally much larger, the church was largely demolished in 1781 and rebuilt in its present diminished state using the old materials, including flint rubble and Roman bricks. The Church of the Holy Sepulchre, always known as the Round Church, is one of only four surviving circular churches in England.

Around Cambridge

GIRTON
3 miles NW of Cambridge off the A14

The first Cambridge college for women was founded in 1869 in Hitchin, by Emily Davies. It moved here to Girton in 1873, to be *'near enough for male lecturers to visit but far enough away to discourage male students from doing the same'*. The problem went away when Girton became a mixed College in 1983.

RAMPTON
6 miles N of Cambridge off the B1049

🏛 Giant's Hill

A charming village in its own right, with a tree-fringed village green, Rampton is also the site of one of the many archaeological sites in the area. This is **Giant's Hill**, a motte castle with part of an earlier medieval settlement.

MILTON
3 miles N of Cambridge off the A10

⚲ Milton Country Park

Milton Country Park offers fine walking and exploring among acres of parkland, lakes and woods. There's a visitor centre, a picnic area and a place serving light refreshments.

WATERBEACH
6 miles NE of Cambridge on the B1102

🏠 Denny Abbey 🏛 Farmland Museum

Denny Abbey (see panel below), easily accessible on the A10, is an English Heritage Grade I listed Abbey with ancient earthworks.

Farmland Museum & Denny Abbey

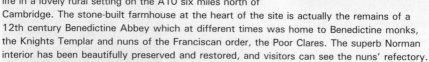

Ely Road, Waterbeach, Cambridgeshire CB5 9PQ
Tel/Fax: 01223 860988
website: www.dennyfarmlandmuseum.org.uk

Two thousand years of history are brought fascinatingly to life in a lovely rural setting on the A10 six miles north of Cambridge. The stone-built farmhouse at the heart of the site is actually the remains of a 12th century Benedictine Abbey which at different times was home to Benedictine monks, the Knights Templar and nuns of the Franciscan order, the Poor Clares. The superb Norman interior has been beautifully preserved and restored, and visitors can see the nuns' refectory.

On the same site, and run by English Heritage as a joint attraction, is the Farmland Museum. Old farm buildings have been splendidly renovated and converted to tell visitors about the rural history of Cambridgeshire from early days to modern times. The museum is ideal for family visits, with specially designed activities for children, and among the top displays are a village shop, agricultural machinery and a magnificent 17th century stone barn. The Museum is open from noon to 5pm April to October.

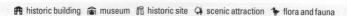

🏠 historic building 🏛 museum 🏛 historic site 🝙 scenic attraction 🌱 flora and fauna

CAMBRIDGE GARDEN PLANTS

The Lodge, Clayhithe Road, Horningsea, nr Cambridge, Cambridgeshire CB5 9JD
Tel: 01223 861370

As featured in *The Garden Magazine*, **Cambridge Garden Plants** specialises in hardy perennials, spring and summer flowering bulbs, herbaceous plants and some more unusual plants. Among these is an excellent selection of old-fashioned roses, including Lady Hillingdon, one of the original tea roses, and the shrub rose Rosa Gallica Mundi, which dates back to Plantagenet times.

The nursery has been a thriving concern since 1989, and owner Kit Buchdahl and his friendly, well informed staff offer a high standard of quality and service and advice on many aspects of plants.

The soil here is sandy, so they know all about dry soil plants, and the 3½-acre site includes a large pond, so a variety of pondside plants is available.

The nursery, a popular place with local garden clubs and societies as well as individual visitors, is open from 11am to 5.30pm Thursday to Sunday, March to October; other times by appointment.

On the same site, and run as a joint attraction, is the **Farmland Museum**. The history of Denny Abbey runs from the 12th century, when it was a Benedictine monastery. It was later home to the Knights Templar, Franciscan nuns of the Poor Clares order and the Countess of Pembroke, and from the 16th century was a farmhouse. The old farm buildings have been splendidly renovated and converted to tell the story of village life and Cambridgeshire farming up to modern times. The museum is ideal for family outings, with plenty of hands-on activities for children and a play area, gift shop and weekend tearoom.

LODE
6 miles NE of Cambridge on the B1102

🏠 Anglesey Abbey

Anglesey Abbey dates from 1600 and was built on the site of an Augustinian priory, but the house and the 100-acre garden came together as a unit thanks to the vision of the 1st Lord Fairhaven. His mother was American, his father English, and when he left the Abbey to the National Trust in the 1960s he wanted the house and garden to be kept to 'represent an age and way of life that is quickly passing'. The garden, created in its present form from 1926, is a wonderful place for a stroll, with 98 acres of landscaped gardens including wide grassy walks, open lawns, a riverside walk and one of the finest collections of garden statuary in the country. Lode Mill is a working watermill that runs on the first and third Saturdays of each month. There's also a plant centre, shop and restaurant. In the house itself is Lord Fairhaven's magnificent collection of

paintings (a seascape by
Gainsborough, landscapes by
Claude Lorraine), sumptuous
furnishings, tapestries, Ming
porcelain and clocks.

BOTTISHAM
*5 miles E of Cambridge on the
A1303*

🏛 Holy Trinity Church

John Betjeman ventured that
Bottisham's **Holy Trinity
Church** was 'perhaps the best
in the county', so time should
certainly be made for a visit.
Among the many interesting
features are the 13th century
porch, an 18th century

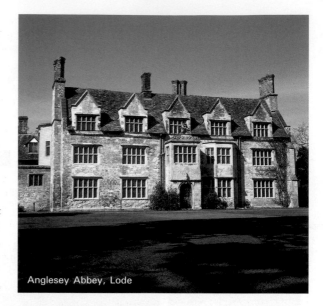

Anglesey Abbey, Lode

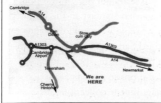

DARWIN NURSERIES AND FARM SHOP
*5 Quy Waters, Newmarket Road, Teversham,
Cambridgeshire CB1 5AT
Tel/Fax: 01223 293911
e-mail: Christine.millar@cambsmh.nhs.uk*

Darwin Nurseries and Farm Shop is a horticultural centre where the
workers are mainly young adults who have learning disabilities
and/or mental health issues. Manager Christine Millar and her staff
provide skills training and an opportunity for the workers to be
involved in all aspects of growing plants and selling them to the
public. The summer and winter bedding seasons are always busy
times, and on average 500 hanging baskets are made and sold
each year. Vocational courses are organised in partnership with
Huntingdon Regional College, designed for young people and
adults who wish to develop their personal and vocational skills.
Training is also given in animal husbandry, and the animal farm on
the site is a great attraction for visitors, particularly for children;
the turf maze also adds to the fun of a visit.

The Farm Shop is stocked with fresh fruit and vegetables,
much of it home or locally grown, jams, preserves and other
foodstuffs, along with plants and seeds, fertilisers, garden
accessories and pet foods. The centre enjoys a picturesque
setting close to the Newmarket Road (A1303) between the
Cambridge Airport roundabout and the roundabout at Junction
35 of the A14. Opening hours are 9am to 5pm Monday to
Saturday, 10am to 4pm Sunday.

🏛 historic building 📷 museum 🏛 historic site 🗿 scenic attraction 🦋 flora and fauna

monument to Sir Roger Jenyns and some exceptionally fine modern woodwork in Georgian style.

SWAFFHAM PRIOR
8 miles NE of Cambridge on the B1102

Swaffham Prior gives double value to the visitor, with two churches in the same churchyard and two fine old windmills. The churches of St Mary and St Cyriac stand side by side, a remarkable and dramatic sight in the steeply rising churchyard. One of the mills, a restored 1850s tower mill, still produces flour and can be visited by appointment.

At Swaffham Bulbeck, a little way to the south, stands another church of St Mary, with a 13th century tower and 14th century arcades and chancel. Look for the fascinating carvings on the wooden benches and a 15th century cedarwood chest decorated with biblical scenes.

BURWELL
10 miles NE of Cambridge on the B1102

Church of St Mary Museum Devil's Dyke

Burwell is a village of many attractions with a history going back to Saxon times. **Burwell Museum** reflects many aspects of a village on the edge of the Fens up to the middle of the 20th century. A general store, model farm, local industries and children's toys are among the displays.

Next to the museum is the famous Stephens Windmill, built in 1820 and extensively restored.

The man who designed parts of King's College Chapel, Reginald Ely, is thought to have been responsible for the beautiful **St Mary's Church**, which is built of locally quarried clunch stone and is one of the finest examples of the Perpendicular style. Notable

internal features include a 15th century font, a medieval wall painting of St Christopher and roof carvings of elephants, while in the churchyard a gravestone marks the terrible night in 1727 when 78 Burwell folk died in a barn fire while watching a travelling Punch & Judy show.

Behind the church are the remains of Burwell Castle, started in the 12th century but never properly completed.

The **Devil's Dyke** runs through Burwell on its path from Reach to Woodditton. This amazing dyke, 30 yards wide, was built, it is thought, to halt Danish invaders.

REACH
8 miles NE of Cambridge off the A4280

The charming village of Reach is home to the oldest fair in England, which celebrated its 800th anniversary on 1st May, 2000.

LINTON
10 miles SE of Cambridge on the B1052

Bartlow Hills Zoo

The village is best known for its zoo, but visitors will also find many handsome old buildings and the church of St Mary the Virgin, built mainly in Early English style.

A world of wildlife set in 16 acres of spectacular gardens, **Linton Zoo** is a major wildlife breeding centre and part of the inter-zoo breeding programme for endangered species. Collections include wild cats, birds, snakes and insects. For children there is a play area and, in summer, pony rides and a bouncy castle.

Chilford Hall Vineyard, on the B1052 between Linton and Balsham, comprises 18 acres of vines, with tours and wine-tastings available. Some two miles further off the A1307, **Bartlow Hills** are the site of the largest Roman burial site to be unearthed in Europe.

DUXFORD
8 miles S of Cambridge off A505 by J10 of the M11

🏛 Duxford Aviation Museum

Part of the Imperial War Museum, **Duxford Aviation Museum** (see panel below) is Europe's premier aviation heritage complex, with an outstanding collection of 200 historic aircraft, more than 60 of which are in airworthy condition. First World War bi-planes join with the Lancaster, Concorde, Gulf War jets and the SR-71 Blackbird spyplane in this extraordinary collection, which is located on a former key Battle of Britain airfield.

The American Air Museum, where many of the aircraft are suspended as if in flight, is part of this terrific place, and the centrepiece of this part of the complex is a B-29A Suprefortress, the only example of its kind outside the United States. Major air shows take place several times a year, and

Imperial War Museum Duxford

Duxford, Cambridgeshire CB2 4QR
Tel: 01223 835000
Fax: 01223 837267

A branch of the **Imperial War Museum**, Duxford is Europe's premier aviation museum. It was built on a former RAF and USAF fighter base that saw that service throughout the Second World War, and the preserved hangars, a control tower and operations room retain a period atmosphere and from the historic heart of the 85-acre complex.

Over 400,000 visitors come to Duxford each year to see the bi-planes and the Spitfires, the Concorde and the Gulf War jets that are among the 180 historic aircraft on show. A major exhibition on the Battle of Britain charts events of 1940, giving an insight into life at the time, and features an RAF Hurricane and a Luftwaffe Messerschmitt 109 that saw action in the battle. An award-winning modern building designed by Lord Foster houses the American Air Museum with aircraft both on the ground and suspended from the roof as though in flight. Exhibits here range from a U2 Spyplane to a T-10 Tankbuster and the mighty B-52 Stratofortress. Tanks and artillery are on show in the exciting Land Warfare Hall, which houses 50 military vehicles and artillery pieces in a series of realistic and authentic battlefield scenes.

Major attractions are being added each year, and among the latest is an exhibition focusing on Monty and the D-Day landings. Important air shows take place several times each year, featuring resident aircraft, current military aircraft, civilian display teams and solo aerobatic performers. This wonderful museum, which lies south of Cambridge at Junction 10 of the M11, is open throughout the year apart from three days at Christmas.

🏛 historic building   🏛 museum   🏛 historic site   🐊 scenic attraction   🌿 flora and fauna

among the permanent features are a reconstructed wartime operations room, a hands-on exhibition for children and a dramatic land warfare hall with tanks, military vehicles and artillery. Everyone should take time to see this marvellous show - and it should be much more than a flying visit! But it can actually be just that, as Classic Wings offers visitors the chance to fly over Duxford in an elegant 1930s de Havilland Rapide.

At nearby Hinxton, a few miles further south, is another mill: a 17th century water mill that is grinding once more.

SHEPRETH
8 miles S of Cambridge off the A10

🐾 Nature Reserve   🐾 Wildlife Park

🐾 Docwra's Manor

A paradise for lovers of nature and gardens and a great starting point for country walks, **Shepreth L Moor Nature Reserve** is an L-shaped area of wet meadowland - now a rarity - that is home to birds and many rare plants. The nearby **Shepreth Wildlife Park** is a haven in natural surroundings to a wide variety of animals, which visitors can touch and feed. The 18th century **Docwra's Manor** is a series of enclosed gardens with multifarious plants that is worth a visit at any time of year. Fowlmere, on the other side of the A10, is another important nature reserve, with hides and trails for the serious bird-watcher.

GRANTCHESTER
2 miles SW of Cambridge off the A603

🐾 Paradise Nature Reserve   🐦 The Orchard

A pleasant walk by the Cam, or a punt on it, brings visitors from the bustle of Cambridge to the famous village of Grantchester, where

Rupert Brooke lived and Byron swam. The walk passes through **Paradise Nature Reserve**.

Rupert Brooke, who spent two happy years at Grantchester, immortalised afternoon tea at **The Orchard** and wrote of his love of the place in a poem while staying in Berlin.

> *God! I will pack, and take a train,*
> *And get me to England once again!*
> *For England's the one land I know,*
> *Where men with splendid hearts may go;*
> *And Cambridgeshire, of all England,*
> *The shire for men who understand;*
> *And of that district I prefer*
> *The lovely hamlet of Grantchester.*

And of the afternoon tea experience:

> *Stands the church clock at ten to three*
> *And is there honey still for tea?*

The Orchard, first planted ain 1868, became a tea garden by chance in 1897 when a group of Cambridge students asked the owner, a Mrs Stevenson, if she could serve them tea under the trees in the orchard rather than on the front lawn. So started a great tradition that continues to this day. Brooke died at sea in 1915 on his way to the Dardanelles and is buried on the island of Scyros.

Time should also be allowed in Grantchester for a look at the church of St Andrew and St Mary, in which the remains of a Norman church have been incorporated into the 1870s main structure.

BARTON
3 miles SW of Cambridge off the A603

Looking south from this pleasant village you can see the impressive array of radio telescopes that are part of Cambridge

University's Mullard Radio Astronomy
Observatory.

ARRINGTON

11 miles SW of Cambridge off the A603

🏠 Wimpole Hall   🐦 Wimpole Home Farm

🚶 Wimpole Park

Arrington's 18th century **Wimpole Hall**,
bequeathed to the National Trust by Elsie
Bambridge, a daughter of Rudyard Kipling, is
probably the most spectacular country
mansion in the whole county, and certainly the
largest 18th century country house in
Cambridgeshire. The lovely interiors are the
work of several celebrated architects, and
there's a fine collection of furniture and
pictures. The magnificent formally laid-out
grounds include a Victorian parterre, a rose
garden and a walled garden.

Landscaped **Wimpole Park**, with hills,
woodland, lakes and a Chinese bridge,
provides miles of wonderful walking and is
perfect for anything from a gentle stroll to a
strenuous hike.

A brilliant attraction for all the family is
Wimpole Home Farm, a working farm that
is the largest rare breeds centre in East Anglia.
The animals include Bagot goats, Tamworth
pigs, Soay sheep and Longhorn cattle, and
there's also a pets corner, mini pedal tractors
and horse-drawn wagon ride. Children can
spend hours with the animals or in the
adventure playground.

CAXTON

*6 miles W of Cambridge off the
A12198/A428*

Caxton is home to Britain's oldest surviving
post mill, and at Little Gransden, a couple of
miles further southwest on the B1046, another
venerable mill has been restored. A scheduled
ancient monument, it dates from the early
17th century and was worked well into the
early years of the 20th century.

MADINGLEY

4 miles W of Cambridge on the A428

🏛 American Cemetery

The **American Cemetery** is one of the
loveliest, most peaceful and most moving
places in the region, a place of pilgrimage for
the families of the American servicemen who
operated from the many
wartime bases in the
county. The cemetery
commemorates 3,811
dead and 5,125 missing
in action in the Second
World War.

Madingley Hall is a
Tudor mansion set in a
Capability Brown
garden. It was leased in
1861 by Queen Victoria
and Prince Albert for
the use of their son the
Prince of Wales during

Wimpole Hall, Arrington

his brief spell as an undergraduate. The Hall was acquired by Cambridge University in 1948.

Huntingdon

📷 Cromwell Museum 🏃 Spring Common

🐾 Hinchingbrooke Country Park

⛪ All Saints Church ⛪ St Mary's Church

The former county town of Huntingdonshire is an ancient place first settled by the Romans. It boasts many grand Georgian buildings, including the handsome three-storeyed Town Hall.

Oliver Cromwell was born in Huntingdon in 1599 and attended Huntingdon Grammar School. The schoolhouse was originally part of the Hospital of St John the Baptist, founded during the reign of Henry II by David, Earl of Huntingdon. Samuel Pepys was also a pupil here.

Cromwell was MP for Huntingdon in the Parliament of 1629, was made a JP in 1630 and moved to St Ives in the following year. Rising to power as an extremely able military commander in the Civil War, he raised troops from the region and made his headquarters in the Falcon Inn.

Appointed Lord Protector in 1653, Cromwell was ruler of the country until his death in 1658. The school he attended is now the **Cromwell Museum**, located on Huntingdon High Street, housing the only public collection relating specifically to him, with exhibits that reflect many aspects of his political, social and religious life. The museum's exhibits include an extensive collection of Cromwell family portraits and personal objects, among them a hat and seal, contemporary coins and medals, an impressive Florentine cabinet - the gift of the Grand Duke of Tuscany - and a surgeon's chest made by Kolb of Augsburg. This fine collection helps visitors interpret the life and legacy of Cromwell and the Republican movement.

All Saints Church, opposite the Cromwell Museum, displays many architectural styles, from medieval to Victorian. One of the two surviving parish churches of Huntingdon, All Saints was considered to be the church of the Hinchingbrooke part of the Cromwell family, though no memorials survive to attest to this. The Cromwell family burial vault is contained within the church, however, and it is here that Oliver's father Robert and his grandfather Sir Henry are buried. The church has a fine chancel roof, a very lovely organ chamber, a

🎭 stories and anecdotes 🐦 famous people 🎨 art and craft 🎶 entertainment and sport 🏃 walks

truly impressive stained-glass window and the font in which Cromwell was baptised, as it's the old font from the destroyed St John's church, discovered in a local garden in 1927.

Huntingdon's other church, **St Mary's**, dates from Norman times but was almost completely rebuilt in the 1400s. It boasts a fine Perpendicular west tower, which partially collapsed in 1607.

Hartford Marina, Huntingdon

The damage was extensive, and the tower was not completely repaired until 1621. Oliver Cromwell's father Robert contributed to the cost of the repairs, as recorded on the stone plaque fixed to the east wall on the nave, north of the chancel arch.

Cowper House (No 29 High Street) has an impressive early 18th century frontage. A plaque commemorates the fact that the poet William Cowper (pronounced 'Cooper') lived here between 1765 and 1767.

Among Huntingdon's many fine former coaching inns is The George Hotel. Although badly damaged by fire in 1865, the north and west wings of the 17th century courtyard remain intact, as does its very rare wooden gallery. The inn was one of the most famous of all the posting houses on the old Great North Run. It is reputed that Dick Turpin used one of the rooms here. The medieval courtyard, gallery and open staircase are the scene of annual productions of Shakespeare.

Along the south side of the Market Square, the Falcon Inn dates back in parts to the

1500s. Oliver Cromwell is said to have used this as his headquarters during the Civil War.

About half a mile southwest of town stands Hinchingbrooke House, which today is a school but which has its origins in the Middle Ages, when it was a nunnery (ghostly nuns are said to haunt the building to this day). The remains of the Benedictine nunnery can still be seen. It was given to the Cromwell family by Henry VIII in 1538. Converted by the Cromwell family in the 16th century and later extended by the Earls of Sandwich, today's visitors can see examples of every period of English architecture from the 12th to early 20th centuries. King James I was a regular visitor, and Oliver Cromwell spent part of his childhood here. The 1st Earl of Sandwich was a central figure in the Civil War and subsequent Restoration, while the 4th Earl (inventor of the lunchtime favourite that bears his name) was one of the most flamboyant politicians of the 18th century. The house is open for guided tours, including lovely cream teas served in the Tudor kitchens.

Hinchingbrooke Country Park covers

180 acres of grassy meadows, mature woodland, ponds and lakes. There is a wide variety of wildlife including woodpeckers, herons, kestrels, butterflies and foxes. The network of paths makes exploring the park easy, and battery-powered wheelchairs are provided for less able visitors. The Visitors' Centre serves refreshments at peak times.

Half a mile north, **Spring Common** offers another chance to enjoy some marvellous Cambridgeshire countryside. Covering 13 acres, its name comes from the natural spring that runs constantly and has long been a gathering place. The town developed around, rather than within, this area of rural tranquillity, which boasts a range of diverse habitats including marsh, grassland, scrub and streams. Plant life abounds, providing food and shelter for a variety of animals, amphibians, birds and invertebrates.

Around Huntingdon

HARTFORD
½ mile N of Huntington off the B1514

At just half a mile from Hartford Marina, this lovely village offers plenty of excellent riverside walks.

BARHAM
6 miles W of Huntingdon off the A1/A14

This delightful hamlet boasts 12 houses, 30 people and an ancient church with box pews, surrounded by undulating farmland. Nearby attractions include angling and sailing on Grafham Water, go-karting at

Kimbolton and National Hunt racing at Huntingdon.

WARBOYS
7 miles NE of Huntingdon off the B1040

An interesting walk from Warboys to Ramsey takes in a wealth of history and pretty scenery. St Mary Magdalene's church has a tall, very splendid tower.

RAMSEY
9 miles NE of Huntingdon on the B1040

🏛 Abbey 🏛 Rural Museum

🏛 Church of St Thomas à Becket of Canterbury

A pleasant market town with a broad main street down which a river once ran, Ramsey is home to the medieval **Ramsey Abbey**, founded in AD969 by Earl Ailwyn as a Benedictine monastery. The Abbey became one of the most important in England in the 12th and 13th centuries, and as it prospered, so did Ramsey, so that by the 13th century it had become a town with a weekly market and an annual three-day festival at the time of the feast of St Benedict. After the Dissolution of

Ramsey Abbey

🎭 stories and anecdotes 🐦 famous people 🎨 art and craft 🏃 entertainment and sport 🚶 walks

the Monasteries in 1539, the Abbey and its lands were sold to Sir Richard Williams, great-grandfather of Oliver Cromwell. Most of the buildings were then demolished, the stones being used to build Caius, King's and Trinity Colleges at Cambridge, the towers of Ramsey, Godmanchester and Holywell churches, the gate at Hinchingbrooke House and several local properties. In 1938 the house was converted for use as a school, which it remains to this day.

To the northwest are the ruins of the once magnificent stone gatehouse of the late 15th century - only the porter's lodge remains, but inside can be seen an unusual large carved effigy made of Purbeck marble and dating back to the 14th century. It is said to represent Earl Ailwyn, founder of the Abbey. The gatehouse, now in the care of the National Trust, can be visited daily from April to October.

The church of **St Thomas à Becket of Canterbury** forms an impressive vista at the end of the High Street. Dating back to about 1180, it is thought to have been built as a hospital or guesthouse for the Abbey. It was converted to a church to accommodate the many pilgrims who flocked to Ramsey in the 13th century. The church has what is reputed to be the finest nave in Huntingdonshire, dating back to the 12th century and consisting of seven bays. The church's other treasure is a 15th century carved oak lectern, thought to have come from the Abbey.

Most of **Ramsey Rural Museum** is housed in an 18th century farm building and several barns set in open countryside. Among the many fascinating things to see are a Victorian home and school, a village store, and restored farm equipment, machinery, carts and wagons. The wealth of traditional implements used by local craftsmen such as

the farrier, wheelwright, thatcher, dairyman, animal husbandman and cobbler offer an insight into bygone days.

The unusual Ramsey War Memorial is a listed Grade II memorial consisting of a fine bronze statue of St George slaying the dragon atop a tall, octagonal pillar crafted of Portland stone.

UPWOOD
8 miles NE of Huntingdon off the B1040

Upwood is a pleasant, scattered village in a very tranquil and picturesque setting. Woodwalton Fen nature reserve is a couple of minutes' drive to the west.

SAWTRY
8 miles NW of Huntingdon on the A1

The main point of interest here has no point! All Saints Church, built in 1880, lacks both tower and steeple, and is topped instead by a bellcote. Inside the church are marvellous brasses and pieces from ancient Sawtry Abbey.

Just south of Sawtry, Aversley Wood is a conservation area with abundant birdlife and plants.

HAMERTON
9 miles NW of Huntingdon off the A1

🐾 Zoological Park

Hamerton Zoological Park has hundreds of animals from tortoises to tigers. Specially designed enclosures make for unrivalled views of the animals, and the park features meerkats, marmosets and mongooses, lemurs, gibbons, possums and sloths, snakes and even creepy-crawlies such as cockroaches.

STILTON
12 miles NW of Huntingdon off the A1

Stilton has an interesting high street with many fine buildings, and is a good choice for the hungry or thirsty visitor, as it has been since the heyday of horse-drawn travel. Journeys were a little more dangerous then, and Dick Turpin is said to have hidden at the Bell Inn.

ELLINGTON
4 miles W of Huntingdon off the A14

Ellington is a quiet village just south of the A14 and about a mile north of Grafham Water. Both Cromwell and Pepys visited, having relatives living in the village, and it was in Ellington that Pepys' sister Paulina found a husband, much to the relief of the diarist, who had written: '*We must find her one, for she grows old and ugly.*' All Saints church is magnificent, like so many in the area, and among its many fine features are the 15th century oak roof and the rich carvings in the nave and the aisles. The church and its tower were built independently.

WOOLLEY
5 miles W of Huntingdon off the A1/A14

This quiet and secluded hamlet attracts a broad spectrum of visitors including anglers, golfers, walkers and riders, drawn by its lush and picturesque beauty and rural tranquillity.

SPALDWICK
6 miles W of Huntingdon off the A14

A sizable village that was once the site of the Bishop of Lincoln's manor house, Spaldwick boasts the grand church of St James, which dates from the 12th century and has seen restoration in most centuries, including the 20th, when the spire had to be partly rebuilt after being struck by lightning. Two miles further west, Catworth is another charming village, regularly voted Best Kept Village in Cambridgeshire and well worth exploring.

KEYSTON
12 miles W of Huntingdon off the A14

🏠 Church of St John the Baptist

A delightful village with a pedigree that can be traced back to the days of the Vikings, Keyston has major attractions both sacred and secular: the **Church of St John the Baptist** is impressive in its almost cathedral-like proportions, with one of the most magnificent spires in the whole county, while the Pheasant is a well-known and very distinguished pub-restaurant.

BRAMPTON
2 miles SW of Huntingdon off the A1

Brampton is where Huntingdon Racecourse is situated. An average of 18 meetings (all jumping) are scheduled every year, including Bank Holiday fixtures (extra-special deals for families) In November, the Grade II Peterborough Chase is the feature race.

Brampton's less speculative attractions include the 13th century church of St Mary, and Pepys House, the home of Samuel's uncle, who was a cousin of Lord Sandwich and who got Samuel his job at the Admiralty.

GRAFHAM
5 miles SW of Huntingdon on the B661

🐦 and 🏃 Grafham Water

Created in the mid-1960s as a reservoir, **Grafham Water** offers a wide range of outdoor activities for visitors of all ages, with 1,500 acres of beautiful countryside, including the lake itself. The 10-mile perimeter track is great for jogging or cycling, and there's excellent sailing, windsurfing and fly-fishing.

The area is a Site of Special Scientific Interest, and an ample nature reserve at the western edge is run jointly by Anglian Water

and the Wildlife Trust. There are nature
trails, information boards, a wildlife garden
and a dragonfly pond. Many species of
waterfowl stay here at various times of the
year, and bird-watchers have the use of six
hides, three of them accessible to
wheelchairs. An exhibition centre has
displays and video presentations of the
reservoir's history, a gift shop and a café.

KIMBOLTON
8 miles SW of Huntingdon on the B645

🏛 Castle

Kimbolton Castle

History aplenty here, and a lengthy pause is
in order to look at all the interesting
buildings. St Andrew's Church would head
the list were it not for **Kimbolton Castle**
which, along with its gatehouse, dominates
the village. Parts of the original Tudor
building are still to be seen, but the
appearance of the castle today owes much
to the major remodelling carried out by
Vanbrugh and Nicholas Hawksmoor in the
first decade of the 18th century. The
gatehouse was added by Robert Adam in
1764. Henry VIII's first wife Catherine of
Aragon spent the last 18 months of her life
imprisoned here, where she died in 1536. The
castle is now a school, but can be visited on
certain days in the summer (don't miss the
Pellegrini murals).

BUCKDEN
4 miles SW of Huntingdon on the A1

🏛 Buckden Towers

This historic village was an important
coaching stop on the old Great North Road. It

THE CRAFT SHOP

*199 High Street, Offord Cluny, nr St Neots,
Cambridgeshire PE19 5RT
Tel: 01480 812422
e-mail: thecraftshop@hotmail.co.uk*

The **Craft Shop** is a new and exciting venture for owner
Denise Heath, based in a distinctive little redbrick building
with decorative half-timbering and a steeply raked tiled
roof. Inside, all is cosy and welcoming, a great place for
browsing through the range of gifts and craftware, along with materials and ideas for craft
making, card making and scrap booking. Services include workshops, make & take sessions,
bespoke wedding stationery and children's parties.

🏛 historic building   🏛 museum   🏛 historic site   ⚘ scenic attraction   🌿 flora and fauna

is known particularly as the site of **Buckden Towers**, the great palace built for the Bishops of Lincoln. In the splendid grounds are the 15th century gatehouse and the tower where Henry VIII imprisoned his first wife, Catherine of Aragon, in 1533 (open only on certain days of the year).

ST NEOTS
10 miles SW of Huntingdon off the A1

🏛 Church of St Mary the Virgin 🏛 Museum

St Neots dates back to the founding of a Saxon Priory, built on the outskirts of Eynesbury in AD974. Partially destroyed by the Danes in 1010, it was re-established as a Benedictine Priory in about 1081 by St Anselm, Abbot of Bec and later Archbishop of Canterbury. For the next two centuries the Priory flourished. Charters were granted by Henry I to hold fairs and markets. The first bridge over the Great Ouse, comprising 73 timber arches, was built in 1180. The name of the town comes from the Cornish saint whose remains were interred in the Priory some time before the Norman Conquest. With the Dissolution of the Monasteries, the Priory was demolished. In the early 17th century the old bridge was replaced by a stone one. This was then the site of a battle between the Royalists and Roundheads in 1648 - an event sometimes re-enacted by Sealed Knot societies.

St Neots repays a visit on foot, since there are many interesting sites and old buildings tucked away. The famous Market Square is one of the largest and most ancient in the country. A market has been held here every Thursday since the 12th century. The magnificent parish **Church of St Mary the Virgin** is a very fine edifice, known locally as the Cathedral of Huntingdonshire. It is an outstanding example of Late Medieval architecture. The gracious interior complements the 130-foot Somerset-style tower, with a finely carved oak altar, excellent Victorian stained-glass and a Holdich organ, built in 1855.

St Neots Museum - opened in 1995 - tells the story of the town and the surrounding area. Housed in the former magistrates' court and police station, it still has the original cells. Eye-catching displays trace local history from prehistoric times to the present day. Open Tuesday to Saturday.

LITTLE PAXTON
2½ miles N of St Neots off the A1/A428

🐐 Paxton Pits Nature Reserve

Fewer than three miles north of St Neots at Little Paxton is **Paxton Pits Nature Reserve**. Created alongside gravel workings, the Reserve attracts thousands of water birds for visitors to observe from hides. The wealth of wildlife means that the area is an SSSI (Site of Special Scientific Interest) and ensures a plethora of colour and activity all year round. The site also features nature trails and a visitors' centre. It has thousands of visiting waterfowl, including one of the largest colonies of cormorants, and is particularly noted for its wintering wildfowl, nightingales in late spring and kingfishers. There are about four miles of walks, some suitable for wheelchairs. Spring and summer also bring a feast of wild flowers, butterflies and dragonflies.

Just north again is the Great Paxton church, originally a Saxon Minster.

EYNESBURY
1 mile S of St Neots on the A428

Eynesbury is actually part of St Neots, with only a little stream separating the two. Note the 12th century Church of St Mary with its Norman tower. Rebuilt in the Early English period, it retains some well-preserved locally sculpted 14th century oak benches.

History has touched this quiet and lovely village from time to time: it was the home of the famous giant James Toller, who died in 1818 and is buried in the middle aisle of the church. Only 21 when he died, he measured some 8 feet tall - it is said he was buried here to escape the attention of body-snatchers, whose activities were widespread at the time. Eynesbury was also the birthplace of the Miles' Quads, the first-ever surviving quadruplets in Britain.

BUSHMEAD
4 miles W of St Neots off the B660

The remains of Bushmead Abbey, once a thriving Augustinian community, are well worth a detour. The garden setting is delightful, and the surviving artefacts include some interesting stained-glass. Open weekends in July and August.

GODMANCHESTER
2 miles SW of Huntingdon off the A1

🏠 Island Hall   🐾 Wood Green Animal Shellter

🐾 Port Holme Meadow

Godmanchester is linked to Huntingdon by a 14th century bridge across the River Ouse. It was a Roman settlement and one that continued in importance down the years, as the number of handsome buildings testifies. One such is **Island Hall**, a mid-18th century mansion built for John Jackson, the Receiver General for Huntingdon; it contains many interesting pieces. This family home has lovely Georgian rooms, with fine period detail and fascinating possessions relating to the owners' ancestors since their first occupation of the house in 1800. The tranquil riverside setting and formal gardens add to the peace and splendour - the house takes its name from the ornamental island that forms part of the grounds. Octavia Hill was sometimes a guest, and wrote effusively to her sister that Island Hall was 'the loveliest, dearest old house, I never was in such a one before.' Open only to pre-booked groups.

Wood Green Animal Shelter at Kings Bush Farm, Godmanchester is a purpose-built, 50-acre centre open to the public all year round. Cats, dogs, horses, donkeys, farm animals, guinea pigs, rabbits, llamas, wildfowl and pot-bellied pigs are among the many creatures for visitors to see, and there is a specially adapted nature trail and restaurant.

Godmanchester

St Mary's Church is Perpendicular in style, though not totally in age, as the tower is a 17th century replacement of the 13th century original. A footpath leads from the famous Chinese Bridge (1827) to **Port Holme Meadow**, at 225 acres one of the largest in England and the site of Roman remains. It is a Site of Special Scientific Interest, with a huge diversity of botanical and bird species. Huntingdon racecourse was once situated here, and it was a training airfield during the First World War. Another site of considerable natural activity is Godmanchester Pits, accessed along the Ouse Valley Way and home to a great diversity of flora and fauna.

PAPWORTH EVERARD
6 miles S of Huntingdon on the A1198

One of the most recent of the region's churches, St Peter's dates mainly from the mid-19th century. Neighbouring Papworth St Agnes has an older church in St John's, though parts of that, too, are Victorian. Just up the road at Hilton is the famous Hilton Turf Maze, cut in 1660 to a popular medieval design.

BOXWORTH
7 miles SE of Huntingdon off the A14

🐦 Overhall Grove

A village almost equidistant from Huntingdon and Cambridge, and a pleasant base for touring the area, Boxworth's Church of St Peter is unusual in being constructed of pebble rubble.

A mile south of Boxworth is **Overhall Grove**, one of the largest elm woods in the country and home to a variety of wildlife.

The Great Ouse Valley

HEMINGFORD ABBOTS
3 miles SE of Huntingdon off the A14

🏠 Hemingford Grey Manor

Once part of the Ramsey Abbey Estate, Hemingford Abbots is set around the 13th century church of St Margaret, along the banks of the Great Ouse. Opportunities for angling and boating facilities, including rowing boats for hire, as well as swimming, country walks, golf and a recreation centre are all within a couple of miles. The village hosts a flower festival every two years.

Just to the east is Hemingford Grey, with its church on the banks of the Ouse. **The Manor** (see panel on page 318) at Hemingford Grey is reputedly the oldest continuously inhabited house in England, built around 1130. Visits (by appointment only) will reveal all the treasures in the house and garden.

River Ouse, Hemingford Grey

📖 stories and anecdotes　🐦 famous people　🎨 art and craft　🎭 entertainment and sport　🚶 walks

THE MANOR

Hemingford Grey, Cambridgeshire PE28 9BN
Tel: 01480 463134 Fax: 01480 465026
e-mail: diana_boston@hotmail.com
website: www.greenknowe.co.uk

Built about 1130 **The Manor** is one of the oldest continuously inhabited houses in the country. It was the home of Lucy Boston from 1939 and the setting for her *Green Knowe* children's books: going round the house and garden readers feel that they are walking into the books. In the winter Lucy Boston sewed exquisite patchworks. They form the only collection of this calibre worldwide which can be seen in the house where they were made.

The three-and-a-half acre garden is bordered by a moat on three sides and the river Great Ouse on the other. It is approached by walking along the towpath beside the river, where visitors get a glimpse of the long herbaceous borders filled with mainly scented plants of year round interest. The garden contains coronation and chess topiary, as well as Lucy Boston's beautiful collection of old roses and irises.

Opening times:

House: All year to individuals or groups strictly by appointment only.

Garden: All year daily 11am-5pm (dusk in winter).

FENSTANTON

7 miles SE of Huntingdon off the A14 bypass

🌱 Capability Brown

Lancelot Capability Brown (1716-1783) was Lord of the Manor at Fenstanton from 1768, and served for a time as High Sheriff of Huntingdonshire. Born in Northumberland, Brown started his working life as a gardener's boy before moving on to Stowe, where he worked under William Kent. When Kent died, Brown set up as a garden designer and soon became the leading landscape artist in England, known for the natural, unplanned appearance of his designs. His nickname arose from his habit of remarking, when surveying new projects, that the place had 'capabilities'. Brown, his wife and his son are buried in the medieval church. His grave is inscribed with a eulogy by the poet and landscape gardener William Mason. Any visit here should also take in the 17th century manor house and the red-brick Clock Tower.

HOUGHTON

5 miles E of Huntingdon on the A1123

🏚 Houghton Mill

Houghton is a popular tourist destination thanks to its proximity to Houghton Mill and opportunities for riverside walks, as well as its charming thatched buildings and shops. Milling takes place on Sundays and Bank Holiday Mondays. Houghton Meadows is a Site of Special Scientific Interest with an abundance of hay meadow species. One of the most popular walks in the whole area links Houghton with St Ives.

ST IVES

6 miles E of Huntingdon off the A1123

📷 Norris Museum   🐾 Wilthorn Meadow

🐾 Holt Island Nature Reserve

This is an ancient town on the banks of the Great Ouse which once held a huge annual fair and is named after St Ivo, said to be a Persian bishop who came here in the Dark Ages to spread a little light.

In the Middle Ages, kings bought cloth for their households at the village's great wool fairs and markets, and a market is still held every Monday. The Bank Holiday Monday markets are particularly lively affairs, and the Michaelmas fair fills the town centre for three days.

Seagoing barges once navigated up to the famous six-arched bridge that was built in the 15th century and has a most unusual two-storey chapel in its middle. Oliver Cromwell lived in St Ives in the 1630s; the statue of him on Market Hill, with its splendid hat, is one of the village's most familiar landmarks. It was made in bronze, with a Portland stone base, and was erected in 1901. It was originally designed for Huntingdon, but they wouldn't accept it!

The beautiful parish church in its churchyard beside the river is well worth a visit. The quayside provides a tranquil mooring for holidaymakers and there are wonderful walks by the riverside.

Clive Sinclair developed his tiny TVs and pocket calculators in the town, and another famous son of St Ives was the great Victorian rower John Goldie, whose name is remembered each year by the second Cambridge boat in the Boat Race.

The **Norris Museum**, in a delightful setting by the river, tells the story of Huntingdonshire for the past 175 million years or so, with everything from fossils, mammoth tusks and models of the great historic reptiles through flint tools, Roman artefacts and Civil War armour to lace-making and ice-skating displays, and contemporary works of art. A truly fascinating place that is open throughout the year, admission is free. Exhibitions include a life-size replica of a 160-million-year-old ichthyosaur. There are remains of woolly mammoths from the Ice Ages, tools and pottery from the Stone Age to Roman times and relics from the medieval castles and abbeys. Also on show are toys and models made by prisoners of the Napoleonic Wars.

St Ives

🎬 stories and anecdotes   🦜 famous people   🎨 art and craft   🎵 entertainment and sport   🚶 walks

As I was going to St Ives
I met a man with seven wives.
Each wife had seven sacks,
each sack had seven cats, each cat had seven kits.
Kits, cats, sacks and wives,
how many were going to St Ives?

- Only the man who put the question, of course, but today's visitors are certain to have a good time while they are here.

Just outside St Ives are **Wilthorn Meadow**, a Site of Natural History Interest where Canada geese are often to be seen, and **Holt Island Nature Reserve**, where high-quality willow is being grown to reintroduce the traditional craft of basket-making. Take some time for spotting the butterflies, dragonflies and kingfishers.

BLUNTISHAM
3 miles NE of St Ives on the A1123

There's an impressive church here in Bluntisham, with a unique 14th century chancel that ends in three sides. The rector in times past was the father of Dorothy L Sayers – creator of nobelman sleuth Lord Peter Wimsey - and Dorothy once lived in the large Georgian rectory on the main road.

EARITH
4 miles E of St Ives on the A1123

The Ouse Washes, a special protection area, runs northeast from the village to Earith Pits, a well-known habitat for birds and crawling creatures; some of the pits are used for fishing. The Washes are a wetland of major international importance supporting such birds as ruffs, Bewick and Whooper swans, and hen harriers. The average bird population is around 20,000. Some of the meadows flood in winter, and ice-skating is popular when the temperature really drops. There's a great tradition of ice-skating in the Fens, and Fenmen were the national champions until the 1930s.

SOMERSHAM
4 miles NE of St Ives on the B1040/B1060

🦅 Raptor Foundation

The **Raptor Foundation** is located here, a major attraction where owls and other birds of prey find refuge. There are regular flying displays and falconry shows. Somersham once had a palace for the Bishops of Ely, and its splendid church of St John would have done them proud.

Peterborough

🏛 Cathedral 🏛 Museum 🏛 Railworld

🔲 Thorpe Meadows Sculpture Park

The second city of Cambridgeshire has a long and interesting history that can be traced back to the Bronze Age, as can be seen in the archaeological site at Flag Fen. Although a cathedral city, it is also a New Town (designated in 1967), so modern development and expansion have vastly increased its facilities while retaining the quality of its historic heart.

Peterborough's crowning glory is, of course, the Norman **Cathedral**, built in the 12th and 13th centuries on a site that had seen Christian worship since AD655. Henry VIII made the church a cathedral, and his first queen, Catherine of Aragon, is buried here, as for a while was Mary Queen of Scots after her execution at Fotheringay. Features to note are the huge (85-foot) arches of the West Front, the unique painted wooden nave ceiling, some exquisite late 15th century fan vaulting, and the tomb of Catherine.

Though the best-known of the city's landmarks, the Cathedral is by no means the only one. The **Peterborough Museum and Art Gallery** (see panel on page 322) covers all aspects of the history of Peterborough from the Jurassic period to Victorian times.

The Gildenburgh Gallery at 44 Broadway boasts a good collection of fine art from the 20th and 21st centuries and a design-led craft shop. The views of Peterborough to be had from the gallery are panoramic and impressive.

There are twin attractions for railway enthusiasts in the shape of **Railworld**, a hands on exhibition open daily dealing with modern rail travel, and the wonderful Nene Valley Railway, which operates 15-mile steam-hauled trips between Peterborough and its HQ and museum at Wansford. A feature on the main railway line at Peterborough is the historic Iron Bridge,

Peterborough Cathedral

part of the old Great Northern Railway and still virtually as built by Lewis Cubitt in 1852.

Just outside the city, by the river Nene, is **Thorpe Meadows Sculpture Park**, one of several open spaces in and around the city

---

INJABULO

Tel/Fax: 01832 274881
e-mail: info@injabulo.com website: www.injabulo.com

Injabulo – it's the Zulu word for happiness – offers secure online shopping of craft products made in South Africa using fair trade policies. The main specialities include fabulous handmade ceramic buttons for use in knitting and sewing or to embellish scrap booking, card making, cross-stitch, patchwork and stationery. Handmade paper and paper products originate from two main projects – one in Kwa Zulu Natal helping HIV/Aids victims, the other a women's project in Cape Town. Other delightful ranges include baskets woven from natural materials, silk flower and organza corsages and enchanting Christmas decorations.

🎦 stories and anecdotes   🐦 famous people   🎨 art and craft   ✆ entertainment and sport   🚶 walks

Peterborough Museum & Art Gallery

Priestgate, Peterborough PE1 1LF
Tel: 01733 343329
e-mail: museum@peterborough.gov.uk   website: peterboroughheritage.org.uk

At the Museum & Art Gallery, visitors will see an exciting picture of the region's development - from ancient marine reptiles to its modern commercial growth and cultural diversity. There is a lively changing programme of exhibitions and events, many based upon the interests, art and cultures of the wide-ranging local communities.

This beautiful building is one of the finest examples of Georgian architecture in the city. It dates from 1816, when it was built as the private residence of Squire Cooke, magistrate of Peterborough, and his family. After his death, the mansion was acquired by the 3rd Earl Fitzwilliam, and became the City Infirmary. During The Great War, a mortally wounded Anzac soldier was brought to the infirmary, where he later died. His tragic story has inspired a local legend - it is said his ghost still haunts the stairwells. The building became the city's museum in 1931. In 1939, the Art Gallery extension was added, but due to the war, did not house its first exhibition until 1952. Many original features are still evident inside, including magnificent pillars, panelled doors and intricate cornices.

Browse in the museum shop and take a look at the Art Gallery, containing works from the permanent collection along with contemporary exhibitions - now including multi-media art. Follow the stairs up, or take the lift from the Art Gallery or the second exhibition Gallery.

The Geology & Wildlife Gallery houses one of the most impressive collections of marine reptile fossils in the world. In the Archaeology Gallery, discover the impressive Water Newton Silver, and other interesting local relics from Roman, Medieval and Anglo-Saxon times. Tiny tots are welcome in the award-winning Mini Museum, while adults can get nostalgic in the Period Shop.

Bone and straw marquetry items made by Napoleonic prisoners-of-war are on display in the Norman Cross Gallery. The depot opened on the site in 1797, so the collection, one of the largest in existence, dates back over two hundred years. The Social History Gallery traces the region's industrial and economic development, as well as aspects of education and entertainment and contains objects some visitors may find familiar.

with absorbing collections of modern sculpture.

Around Peterborough

PEAKIRK
7 miles N of Peterborough off the A15

A charming little village, somewhat off the beaten track, Peakirk boasts a village church of Norman origin that is the only one in the country dedicated to St Pega, the remains of whose hermit cell can still be seen.

CROWLAND
10 miles NE of Peterborough off the A1073

🏫 Trinity Bridge 🏛 Abbey

It is hard to imagine that this whole area was once entirely wetland and marshland, dotted with inhospitable islands. Crowland was one such island, then known as Croyland, and on it was established a small church and hermitage back in the 7th century, which was later to become one of the nation's most important monasteries. The town's impressive parish church was just part of the great edifice which once stood on the site. A wonderful exhibition can be found in the **Abbey** at Crowland, open all year round. The remains cover a third of the Abbey's original extent.

Crowland's second gem is the unique **Trinity Bridge** - set in the centre of town on dry land. Built in the 14th century, it has three arches built over one over-arching structure. Before the draining of the Fens, this bridge crossed the point where the River Welland divided into two streams.

THORNEY
8 miles E of Peterborough on the A47

🏫 Abbey 🏛 Heritage Museum

Thorney Abbey, the Church of St Mary and St Botolph, is the dominating presence even though what now stands is but a small part of what was once one of the greatest of the Benedictine abbeys. Gravestones in the churchyard are evidence of a Huguenot colony that settled here after fleeing France in the wake of the St Bartholomew's Day massacre of 1572 and to settle the drained fenland at the request of Oliver Cromwell.

The **Thorney Heritage Museum** is a small, independently-run museum of great fascination, describing the development of the village from a Saxon monastery, via Benedictine Abbey to a model village built in the 19th century by the Dukes of Bedford. The main innovation was a 10,000-gallon water tank that supplied the whole village; other villages had to use unfiltered river water. Open Easter to the end of September.

WHITTLESEY
5 miles E of Peterborough off the A605

🏛 Museum 🎭 Straw Bear Procession

The market town of Whittlesey lies close to the western edge of the Fens and is part of one of the last tracts to be drained. Brick-making was a local speciality, and 180-foot brick chimneys stand as a reminder of that once-flourishing industry. The church of St Andrew is mainly 14th century, with a 16th century tower; the chancel, chancel chapels and naves still have their original roofs.

A walk around this charming town reveals an interesting variety of buildings: brick, of course, and also some stone, thatch on timber frames, and rare thatched mud boundary walls.

The **Whittlesey Museum**, housed in the grand 19th century Town Hall in Market Street, features an archive of displays on local archaeology, agriculture, geology, brick-making and more. Reconstructions include a

🎭 stories and anecdotes 🦢 famous people 🎨 art and craft ✏ entertainment and sport 🚶 walks

1950s corner shop and post office, blacksmith's forge and wheelwright's bench.

A highlight of Whittlesey's year is the **Straw Bear Procession** that is part of a four-day January festival. A man clad in a suit of straw dances and prances through the streets, calling at houses and pubs to entertain the townspeople. The origins are obscure: perhaps it stems from pagan times when corn gods were invoked to produce a good harvest; perhaps it is linked with the wicker idols used by the Druids; perhaps it derives from the performing bears which toured the villages until the 17th century. What is certain is that at the end of the jollities the straw suit is ceremoniously burned.

Whittlesey was the birthplace of the writer L P Hartley (*The Go-Between*) and of General Sir Harry Smith, hero of many 19th century campaigns in India. He died in 1860, and the south chapel off St Mary's church (note the beautiful spire) was restored and named after him.

FLAG FEN

2 miles E of Peterborough signposted from the A47 and A1139

🏛 Bronze Age Centre

Flag Fen Bronze Age Centre (see panel below) comprises massive 3,000-year-old timbers that were part of a major settlement and have been preserved in peaty mud. The site includes a Roman road with its original surface, the oldest wheel in England, re-creations of a Bronze Age settlement, a museum of artefacts, rare breed animals, and a

Flag Fen Bronze Age Centre

The Droveway, Northey Road, Peterborough PE6 7QJ
Tel: 91733 313414   Fax: 01733 349957
e-mail: office@flagfen.co.uk
website: www.flagfen.com

Flag Fen is one of Europe's most important Bronze Age sites; this archaeological jewel is situated on the outskirts of the Cathedral

City of Peterborough. This Bronze Age religious site pre-dates the Cathedral by nearly 2,000 years. The Museum of the Bronze Age contains artefacts found on the site over the last 20 years of excavating.

The park is entered through a uniquely designed 21st century roundhouse; this visitor centre is your portal to the past, with information boards, and pictures. Once out on the park you will be stepping back into the past, and have the chance to see how your ancestors used to live, as you explore the Bronze Age and Iron Age roundhouses in their landscape setting.

The Preservation Hall contains undercover archaeology, along with a 60 metre mural painting depicting life in the Bronze Age in the Fens. During the summer months, archaeologist's can often be seen at work, uncovering Peterborough's past.

Workshops and lectures are among our full programme of events, which include sword and bronze casting, flint knapping and theatre in the park.

🏛 historic building   🏛 museum   🏛 historic site   🐸 scenic attraction   🌱 flora and fauna

March Town Centre

Betjeman declared the church to be 'worth cycling 40 miles into a headwind to see'.

The **Nene-Ouse Navigation Link** runs through the town, affording many attractive riverside walks and, just outside the town off the B1099, Dunhams Wood comprises four acres of woodland set among the Fens. The site contains an enormous variety of trees, along with sculptures and a miniature railway.

visitor centre with a shop and restaurant. Ongoing excavations, open to the public, make this one of the most important and exciting sites of its kind.

MARCH
14 miles E of Peterborough off the A141

🏠 St Wendreda's Church 📷 Museum

🚶 Nene-Ouse Navigation Link

March once occupied the second-largest 'island' in the great level of Fens. As the land was drained the town grew as a trading and religious centre, and in more recent times as a market town and major railway hub. **March and District Museum**, in the High Street, tells the story of the people and the history of March and the surrounding area, and includes a working forge and a reconstruction of a turn-of-the-century home.

The uniquely dedicated **Church of St Wendreda**, at Town End, is notable for its magnificent timber roof, a double hammerbeam with 120 carved angels, a fine font and some impressive gargoyles. John

STONEA
3 miles SE of March off the B1098

📷 Stonea Camp

Stonea Camp is the lowest hill fort in Britain. Built in the Iron Age, it proved unsuccessful against the Romans. A listed ancient monument whose banks and ditches were restored after excavations in 1991, the site is also an increasingly important habitat for wildlife.

CHATTERIS
8 miles S of March off the A141

📷 Museum

A friendly little market town, where the **Chatteris Museum and Council Chamber** features a series of interesting displays on Fenland life and the development of the town. Themes include education, agriculture, transport and local trades, along with temporary exhibitions and local photographs, all housed in five galleries.

The church of St Peter and St Paul has some 14th century features but is mostly more modern in appearance, having been substantially restored in 1909.

LONGTHORPE
2 miles W of Peterborough off the A47

🏛 Longthorpe Tower

Longthorpe Tower, part of a fortified manor house, is graced by some of the very finest 14th century domestic wall paintings in Europe, featuring scenes both sacred and secular: the Nativity, the Wheel of Life, King David, the Labours of the Months. The paintings were discovered during renovations after the Second World War.

ELTON
6 miles SW of Peterborough on the B671

🏛 Elton Hall

Elton is a lovely village on the river Nene, with stone-built houses and thatched roofs.

Elton Hall is a mixture of styles, with a 15th century tower and chapel, and a major Gothic influence. The grandeur is slightly deceptive, as some of the battlements and turrets were built of wood to save money. The hall's sumptuous rooms are filled with art treasures (Gainsborough, Reynolds, Constable) and the library has a wonderful collection of antique tomes.

THORNHAUGH
8 miles NW of Peterborough off the A1/A47

🌿 Sacrewell Farm

Hidden away in a quiet valley is **Sacrewell Farm and Country Centre**, whose centrepiece is a working watermill. All kinds of farming equipment are on display, and there's a collection of farm animals, along with gardens, nature trails and general interest trails, play areas, a gift shop and a restaurant

THE BASKERVILLES HOTEL
Main Street, Baston, Peterborough PE6 9PB
Tel: 01778 560010   Fax: 01778 561147
e-mail: info@baskervilles.vispa.com
website: www.thebaskervilles.co.uk

The **Baskervilles Hotel** is an early 19th century redbrick building, partly creeper-clad, on the main street of Baston, less than half a mile off the A15 between Market Deeping and Bourne. The hotel sign depicts the dreaded Hound of the Baskervilles, immortalised by Sir Arthur Conan Doyle in the best known of his Sherlock Holmes adventures. The hotel has nine en suite rooms for bed & breakfast guests, including two family rooms.

The bar is well stocked with cask ales, beers, lagers and wines, and the food options range from bar snacks and light meals to traditional favourites such as steaks and chicken, and a popular Sunday carvery. The Baskervilles has a large car park and a garden with seating and an area where children can play. The hotel has facilities for business meetings and receptions, and the main-road links in all directions (A15 and A16) make it a very convenient base for both business people and tourists.

🏛 historic building　🏛 museum　🏛 historic site　🌄 scenic attraction　🌿 flora and fauna

WILLOW BROOK FARM SHOP

Scotsman's Lodge, Stamford Road, Helpston Heath,
Peterborough PE6 7EL
Tel: 01780 740261 Fax: 01780 740493
website: www.willowbrookfarm.co.uk

Top-quality home-reared and locally-reared meats are the mainstay of
Willow Brook Farm Shop, a third generation family business close to the A15 and just off the
B1443 midway between Peterborough and Stamford. Beef and lamb are raised on the farm using
traditional methods, and locally reared pork includes the rare-breed Gloucester Old Spot. Game is
available in season, and among other offerings are home-cured hams, ox tongues, haslet, hand-
raised pork pies and meat pies made in the farm's kitchens. Open every day except Monday.

serving light refreshments.

BURGHLEY

14 miles NW of Peterborough off the A1

🏠 Burghley House

The largest and grandest house of the Elizabethan Age, **Burghley House** presents a dazzling spectacle with its domed towers, walls of cream coloured stone, and acres of windows. Clear glass was still ruinously expensive in the 1560s so Elizabethan grandees like Cecil flaunted their wealth by having windows that stretched almost from floor to ceiling.

Burghley House also displays the Elizabethan obsession with symmetry - every tower, dome, pilaster and pinnacle has a corresponding partner.

Contemporaries called Burghley a "prodigy house", a title shared at that time with only one other stately home in England - Longleat in Wiltshire. Both houses were indeed prodigious in size and in cost. At Burghley, Cecil commissioned the most celebrated interior decorator of the age, Antonio Verrio, to create rooms of unparalleled splendour. In his Heaven Room, Verrio excelled even himself, populating the lofty walls and ceiling with a dynamic gallery of mythological figures.

The 18 State Rooms at Burghley house a vast treasury of great works of art. The walls are crowded with 17th century Italian paintings, Japanese ceramics and rare examples of European porcelain grace every

Burghley House

🎬 stories and anecdotes 🦜 famous people 🎨 art and craft 🎭 entertainment and sport 🚶 walks

table, alcove and mantelpiece, and the wood carvings of Grinling Gibbons and his followers add dignity to almost every room. Also on display are four magnificent state beds along with important tapestries and textiles.

In the 18th century, Cecil's descendants commissioned the ubiquitous Capability Brown to landscape the 160 acres of parkland surrounding the house. These enchanting grounds are open to visitors and are also home to a large herd of fallow deer which was first established in Cecil's time. Brown also designed the elegant Orangery which is now a licensed restaurant overlooking rose beds and gardens.

A more recent addition to Burghley's attractions is the Sculpture Garden. Twelve acres of scrub woodland have been reclaimed and planted with specimen trees and shrubs and now provide a sylvan setting for a number of dramatic artworks by contemporary sculptors.

Throughout the summer season, Burghley hosts a series of events of which the best known, the Burghley Horse Trials, takes place at the end of August.

Wisbech

🏦 Peckover House   🏛 Octavia Hill Museum

🏛 Wisbech & Fenland Museum   🎭 Angles Theatre

One of the largest of the Fenland towns, a port in medieval times and still enjoying shipping trade with Europe, Wisbech is at the centre of a thriving agricultural region. The 18th century in particular saw the building of rows of handsome houses, notably in North Brink and South Brink, which face each other across the river. The finest of all the properties is undoubtedly **Peckover House** (see panel below), built in 1722 and bought at the end of the 18th century by Jonathan Peckover, a member of the Quaker banking family. The family gave the building to the National Trust in 1948. Behind its elegant façade are splendid panelled rooms, Georgian fireplaces with richly carved overmantels, and ornate plaster decorations. At the back of the house is a beautiful walled garden with summerhouses and an orangery.

No 1 South Brink Place is the birthplace of Octavia Hill (1838-1912), co-founder of the National Trust and a tireless worker for the

Peckover House & Garden

North Brink, Wisbech, Cambridgeshire PE13 1JR
Tel: 01945 583463
website: www.peckoverhouse.co.uk

This lovely Georgian brick townhouse, built c. 1722, is renowned for its very fine plaster and wood Rococo decoration and includes displays on the Quaker banking family who owned it and the Peckover Bank. The outstanding two acre Victorian garden includes an orangery, summer houses, roses, herbaceous borders, fernery, croquet lawn and 17th century thatched barn, which is available for weddings and functions.

🏦 historic building   🏛 museum   🏛 historic site   🍃 scenic attraction   🌿 flora and fauna

cause of the poor, particularly in the sphere of housing. The house is now the **Octavia Hill Museum** with displays and exhibits commemorating her work.

More Georgian splendour is evident in the area where the Norman castle once stood. The castle was replaced by a bishop's palace in 1478, and in the 17th century by a mansion built for Cromwell's Secretary of State, John Thurloe. Local builder Joseph Medworth

River Nene, Wisbech

built the present Regency villa in 1816; of the Thurloe mansion, only the gate piers remain.

The **Wisbech and Fenland Museum** is one of the oldest purpose-built museums in the country, and in charming Victorian surroundings visitors can view displays of porcelain, coins, rare geological specimens, Egyptian tomb treasures and several items of national importance, including the manuscript of Charles Dickens' *Great Expectations*, Napoleon's Sèvres breakfast set captured at Waterloo, and an ivory chess set that belonged to Louis XIV.

Wisbech is the stage for East Anglia's premier church Flower Festival, with flowers in four churches, strawberry teas, crafts, bric-a-brac, plants and a parade of floats. The event takes place at the beginning of July. The most important of the churches is the church of St Peter and St Paul, with two naves under one roof and an independent tower with a peal of 10 bells. Note the royal arms of James I and, in the north chancel, a mosaic by Salviati of Leonardo's *Last Supper*.

Other sights to see in Wisbech include

Elgoods Brewery on North Brink and the impressive 68-foot limestone memorial to Thomas Clarkson, one of the earliest leaders of the abolitionist movement. The monument was designed by Sir George Gilbert Scott in Gothic style.

Still a lively commercial port, Wisbech boasts a restored Marina and new facilities for small craft that include floating pontoons with berths for 75 yachts. River trips are available from the yacht harbour.

The **Angles Theatre** – one of the oldest working theatres in Britain – is a vibrant centre for the arts located in a Georgian building with a history stretching back over 200 years. Some of the best talent in the nation, from poets and musicians to dance, comedy and theatrical troupes come to perform in the intimate 112-seat auditorium.

Wisbech's Lilian Ream Photographic Gallery is named after a daughter of Wisbech born in the late 19th century who at the time of her death in 1961 had amassed a collection of over 1,000 photographs of Wisbech people, places and events, making for a unique

Wisbech

Distance: *3.1 miles (4.83 kilometres)*

Typical time: *120 mins*

Height gain: *5 metres*

Map: *Explorer 235*

Walk: *www.walkingworld.com ID:739*

Contributor: *Joy & Charles Boldero*

Bus service: ring the Tourist Information Centre in Wisbech on 01945-583263. There are several free car parks in the town. The walk starts from the large Love Lane car park off Alexandria Road, near the church.

Wisbech is an ancient port and has many historic buildings. There is a fine brass on the floor of St Peter and St Paul's Church of Thomas de Braustone, Constable of Wisbech Castle in the 1400s .

The Norman Castle was replaced by a Bishop's Palace in 1478 and in the 17th century this was replaced by a mansion house built for John Thurloe, who was Oliver Cromwell's Secretary of State. Later this was replaced by the Georgian Crescent in 1816. Along New Inn Yard on the left is one of the oldest timber-framed buildings in the town.

Along South Brink on the left is the house where Octavia Hill was born, now a museum. She was one of the founder members of the National Trust. Along North Brink there are many old historic houses including the 18th Century Peckover House, owned by the NT. Elgood's Brewery has a museum; the brewery has functioned for the last 200 years. The Wisbech and Fenland Museum has many interesting items including the manuscript of *Great Expectations* by Charles Dickens.

River, Pub, Toilets, Museum, Church, Castle, Stately Home, National Trust/NTS, Good for Wheelchairs

1 | Turn right into Love Lane, going towards the church. At the church turn right , then left along the street that leads to the Market Place. Turn left into Market Street.

2 | At the T-junction turn left around The Crescent. Turn right along High Street, then left along the alley, New Inn Yard. Turn left along River Nene Quay to the statue. Cross the road and continue along Post Office Lane, crossing the road to the car park. Cross the car park, keeping to the right-hand side. Turn right from the car park, then left along Somers Road and continue along Coal Wharf Road.

3 | Turn right at T-junction along South Brink with the river on the left. Cross road at traffic-lights, turn left along North Brink. Cross two

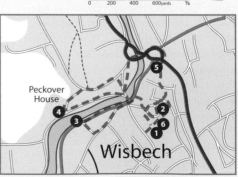

roads. At Elgood's Brewery retrace your steps, crossing one road.

4 | Turn left along Chapel Road. Turn right up Exchange Square, then left at road, left again along Old Market. Cross the road and continue along North Street. Go over the river bridge and keep right beside it for a short distance.

5 | Cross the road and turn left signed 'Pedestrian Zone'. Cross School Lane and turn right along Scrimshire's Passage. Turn left along Hall Street. Turn right by Boots the Chemist, cross the market square and go along Market Street opposite.

6 | Turn left, then left again going down steps. Turn right into Love Lane which leads to the car park.

and fascinating insight into the history and culture of the town. The gallery is housed in the Tourist Information Centre in Bridge Street, and offers changing exhibitions from this treasure trove of pictorial memorabilia.

The Fens Around Wisbech

WEST WALTON AND WALTON HIGHWAY
3 miles NE of Wisbech off the A47/B198

🏛 Fenland & West Norfolk Aviation Museum

Several attractions can be found here, notably the Church of St Mary the Virgin in West Walton with its magnificent 13th century detached tower that dominates the landscape. Walton Highway is home to the **Fenland and West Norfolk Aviation Museum**, whose exhibits include Rolls-Royce Merlin engines, a

Lightning jet, a Vampire, crashed aircraft, a Jumbo jet cockpit simulator, uniforms and memorabilia. The museum is open weekends in summer.

LEVERINGTON
1 mile NW of Wisbech off the A1101

The tower and spire of the church of St Leonard date from the 13th and 14th centuries. The most exceptional feature of an exceptionally interesting church is the 15th century stained-glass Jesse window in the north aisle. There are many fine memorials in the churchyard. Oliver Goldsmith wrote *She Stoops to Conquer* while staying in Leverington.

PARSON DROVE
6 miles W of Wisbech on the B1187

Parson Drove is a Fenland village which Samuel Pepys visited in 1663. He stayed at the village's Swan Inn, and mentions it in his diaries, though he was not complimentary. It was a centre of the woad industry until 1914, when the last remaining woad mill was demolished. Parson Drove is most certainly not the 'heathen place' once described by Pepys!

The Parson Drove Visitors' Centre is set in the old Victorian lock-up on the village green, a building with an unusual 170-year history. Photographs and documents trace the story of this lovely Fens village.

WELNEY
12 miles S of Wisbech off the A1101

🦢 Wildfowl & Wetlands Trust

The Wildfowl & Wetlands Trust in Welney is a nature reserve that attracts large numbers of swans and ducks in winter. Special floodlit 'swan evenings' are held, and there is also a wide range of wild plants and butterflies to be enjoyed.

TOURIST INFORMATION CENTRES

Cambridgeshire

CAMBRIDGE
Wheeler Street, Cambridge, Cambridgeshire CB2 3QB
Tel: 0871 2268006 Fax: 01223 457549
e-mail: tourism@cambridge.gov.uk

ELY
Oliver Cromwell's House, 29 St Mary's Street, Ely
Cambridgeshire CB7 4HF
Tel: 01353 662062 Fax: 01353 668518
e-mail: tic@eastcambs.gov.uk

HUNTINGDON
The Library, Princes Street, Huntingdon,
Cambridgeshire PE29 3PH
Tel: 01480 388588 Fax: 01480 388591
e-mail: Hunts.TIC@huntsdc.gov.uk

PETERBOROUGH
3-5 Minster Precincts, Peterborough,
Cambridgeshire PE1 1XS
Tel: 01733 452336 Fax: 01733 452353
e-mail: tic@peterborough.gov.uk

ST NEOTS
The Old Court, 8 New Street, St Neots,
Cambridgeshire PE19 1AE
Tel: 01480 388788 Fax: 01480 388791
e-mail: stneots.tic@huntsdc.gov.uk

WISBECH
2-3 Bridge Street, Wisbech, Cambridgeshire PE13 1EW
Tel: 01945 583263 Fax: 01945 427199
e-mail: tourism@fenland.gov.uk

Essex

BRAINTREE
Town Hall Centre, Market Place, Braintree,
Essex CM7 3YG
Tel: 01376 550066 Fax: 01376 344345
e-mail: tic@braintree.gov.uk

BRENTWOOD
Pepperell House, 44 High Street, Brentwood,
Essex CM14 4AJ
Tel: 01277 200300 Fax: 01277 202375
e-mail: tic@brentwood.gov.uk

CLACTON-ON-SEA
Town Hall, Station Road, Clacton-on-Sea,
Essex CO15 1SE
Tel: 01255 423400 Fax: 01255 253842
e-mail: emorgan@tendringdc.gov.uk

COLCHESTER
Tymperleys Clock Museum, Trinity Street, Colchester,
Essex CO1 1JN
Tel: 01206 282920 Fax: 01206 282924
e-mail: vic@colchester.gov.uk

HARWICH
Iconfield Park, Parkeston, Harwich, Essex CO12 4EN
Tel: 01255 506139 Fax: 01255 240570
e-mail: harwichtic@btconnect.com

MALDON
Coach Lane, Maldon, Essex CM9 4UH
Tel: 01621 856503 Fax: 01621 875873
e-mail: tic@maldon.gov.uk

SAFFRON WALDEN
1 Market Place, Market Square, Saffron Walden,
Essex CB10 1HR
Tel: 01799 510444 Fax: 01799 510445
e-mail: tourism@uttlesford.gov.uk

SOUTHEND-ON-SEA
Pier Entrance, Western Esplanade, Southend-on-Sea,
Essex SS1 1EE
Tel: 01702 215620 Fax: 01702 611889
e-mail: vic@southend.gov.uk

WALTHAM ABBEY
Unit B, 2-4 Highbridge Street, Waltham Abbey,
Essex EN9 1DG
Tel: 01992 652295 Fax: 01992 652295
e-mail: tic@walthamabbey.org.uk

Norfolk

AYLSHAM
Bure Valley Railway Station, Tourist Information Centre, Norwich Road, Aylsham, Norfolk NR11 6BW
Tel: 01263 733903 Fax: 01263 733922
e-mail: aylsham.tic@broadland.gov.uk

BURNHAM DEEPDALE
Deepdale Farm, Burnham Deepdale, Norfolk PE31 8DD
Tel: 01485 210256 Fax: 01485 210158
e-mail: info@deepdalefarm.co.uk

CROMER
Prince of Wales Road, Cromer, Norfolk NR27 9HS
Tel: 0871 200 3071 Fax: 01263 513613
e-mail: cromertic@north-norfolk.gov.uk

DISS
Meres Mouth, Mere Street, Diss, Norfolk IP22 3AG
Tel: 01379 650523 Fax: 01379 650838
e-mail: dtic@s-norfolk.gov.uk

DOWNHAM MARKET
The Priory Centre, 78 Priory Road, Downham Market, Norfolk PE38 9JS
Tel: 01366 383287 Fax: 01366 385 042
e-mail: downham-market.tic@west-norfolk.gov.uk

GREAT YARMOUTH
Maritime House, 25 Marine Parade, Great Yarmouth, Norfolk NR30 2EN
Tel: 01493 846345 Fax: 01493 858588
e-mail: tourism@great-yarmouth.gov.uk

HOLT
3 Pound House, Market Place, Holt, Norfolk NR25 6BW
Tel: 0871 200 3071 Fax: 01263 713100
e-mail: holttic@north-norfolk.gov.uk

HOVETON
Station Road, Hoveton, Norfolk NR12 8UR
Tel: 01603 782281 Fax: 01603 782281
e-mail: hovetoninfo@broads-authority.gov.uk

HUNSTANTON
Town Hall, The Green, Hunstanton, Norfolk PE36 6BQ
Tel: 01485 532610 Fax: 01485 533972
e-mail: hunstanton.tic@west-norfolk.gov.uk

KING'S LYNN
The Custom House, Purfleet Quay, King's Lynn, Norfolk PE30 1HP
Tel: 01553 763044 Fax: 01553 819441
e-mail: kings-lynn.tic@west-norfolk.gov.uk

NORWICH
The Forum, Millennium Plain, Norwich, Norfolk NR2 1TF
Tel: 01603 727927 Fax: 01603 765389
e-mail: tourism@norwich.gov.uk

SHERINGHAM
Station Approach, Sheringham, Norfolk NR26 8RA
Tel: 0871 200 3071
e-mail: sheringhamtic@north-norfolk.gov.uk

SWAFFHAM
The Shambles, Market Place, Swaffham, Norfolk PE37 7AB
Tel: 01760 722255 Fax: 01760 723410
e-mail: swaffham@eetb.info

THETFORD
4 White Hart Street, Thetford, Norfolk IP24 2HA
Tel: 01842 820689 Fax: 01842 820986
e-mail: info@thetfordtourism.co.uk

WELLS-NEXT-THE-SEA
Staithe Street, Wells-next-the-Sea, Norfolk NR23 1AN
Tel: 0871 200 3071 Fax: 01328 711405
e-mail: wellstic@north-norfolk.gov.uk

WYMONDHAM
Market Cross, Market Place, Wymondham, Norfolk NR18 0AX
Tel: 01953 604721 Fax: 01953 604721
e-mail: wymondhamtic@btconnect.com

TOURIST INFORMATION CENTRES

Suffolk

ALDEBURGH
152 High Street, Aldeburgh, Suffolk IP15 5AQ
Tel: 01728 453637 Fax: 01728 453637
e-mail: atic@suffolkcoastal.gov.uk

BECCLES
The Quay, Fen Lane, Beccles, Suffolk NR34 9BH
Tel: 01502 713196 Fax: 01502 713196
e-mail: becclesinfo@broads-authority.gov.uk

BURY ST EDMUNDS
6 Angel Hill, Bury St Edmunds, Suffolk IP33 1UZ
Tel: 01284 764667 Fax: 01284 757084
e-mail: tic@stedsbc.gov.uk

FELIXSTOWE
91 Undercliff Road West, Felixstowe, Suffolk IP11 2AF
Tel: 01394 276770 Fax: 01394 276984
e-mail: ftic@suffolkcoastal.gov.uk

FLATFORD
Flatford Lane, Flatford, East Bergholt, Suffolk CO7 6UL
Tel: 01206 299460 Fax: 01206 299973
e-mail: flatfordvic@babergh.gov.uk

IPSWICH
St Stephens Church, St Stephens Lane, Ipswich,
Suffolk IP1 1DP
Tel: 01473 258070 Fax: 01473 432017
e-mail: tourist@ipswich.gov.uk

LAVENHAM
Lady Street, Lavenham, Suffolk CO10 9RA
Tel: 01787 248207 Fax: 01787 249459
e-mail: lavenhamtic@babergh.gov.uk

LOWESTOFT
East Point Pavilion, Royal Plain, Lowestoft,
Suffolk NR33 OAP
Tel: 01502 533600 Fax: 01502 539023
e-mail: touristinfo@waveney.gov.uk

NEWMARKET
Palace House, Palace Street, Newmarket,
Suffolk CB8 8EP
Tel: 01638 667200 Fax: 01638 667415
e-mail: tic.newmarket@forest-heath.gov.uk

SOUTHWOLD
69 High Street, Southwold, Suffolk IP18 6DS
Tel: 01502 724729 Fax: 01502 722978
e-mail: southwold.tic@waveney.gov.uk

STOWMARKET
at the Museum of East Anglian Life, Stowmarket,
Suffolk IP14 1DL
Tel: 01449 676800 Fax: 01449 614691
e-mail: tic@midsuffolk.gov.uk

SUDBURY
Town Hall, Market Hill, Sudbury, Suffolk CO10 1TL
Tel: 01787 881320 Fax: 01787 242129
e-mail: sudburytic@babergh.gov.uk

WOODBRIDGE
Station Buildings, Woodbridge, Suffolk IP12 4AJ
Tel: 01394 382240 Fax: 01394 386337
e-mail: wtic@suffolkcoastal.gov.uk

INDEX OF ADVERTISERS

INDEX OF ADVERTISERS

JEWELLERY

PLACES OF INTEREST

SPECIALIST FOOD AND DRINK

INDEX OF ADVERTISERS

INDEX OF WALKS

Looking for more walks?

The walks in this book have been gleaned from Britain's largest online walking guide, to be found at *www.walkingworld.com*.

The site contains over 2000 walks from all over England, Scotland and Wales so there are plenty more to choose from in this book's region as well as further afield - ideal if you are taking a short break as you can plan your walks in advance. There are walks of every length and type to suit all tastes.

Want more detail for the walks in this book? Next to every walk in this book you will see a Walk ID. You can enter this ID number on Walkingworld's 'Find a Walk' page and you will be taken straight to the details of that walk.

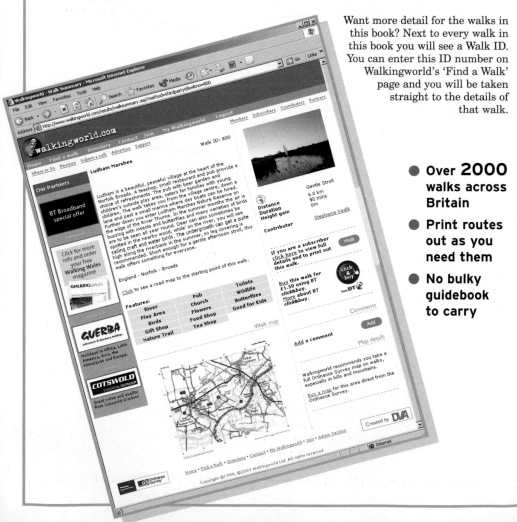

- Over **2000** walks across Britain
- **Print routes out as you need them**
- **No bulky guidebook to carry**

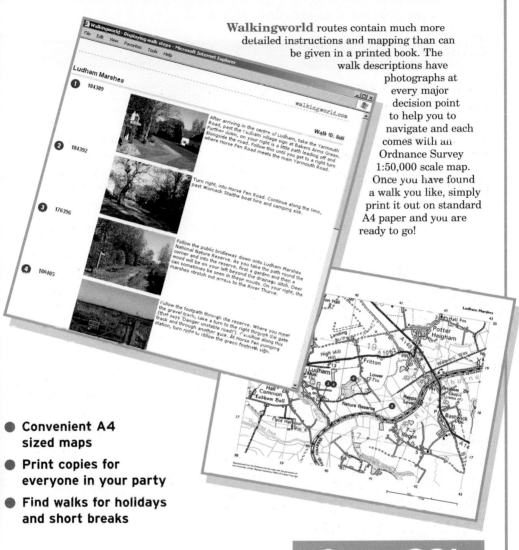

Walkingworld routes contain much more detailed instructions and mapping than can be given in a printed book. The walk descriptions have photographs at every major decision point to help you to navigate and each comes with an Ordnance Survey 1:50,000 scale map. Once you have found a walk you like, simply print it out on standard A4 paper and you are ready to go!

- **Convenient A4 sized maps**
- **Print copies for everyone in your party**
- **Find walks for holidays and short breaks**

A modest annual subscription gives you access to over 2000 walks, all in Walkingworld's easy to follow format. The database of walks is growing all the time and as a subscriber you gain access to new routes as soon as they are published.

Visit the Walkingworld website at *www.walkingworld.com*

ORDER FORM

To order any of our publications just fill in the payment details below and complete the order form. For orders of less than 4 copies please add £1 per book for postage and packing. Orders over 4 copies are P & P free.

Please Complete Either:

I enclose a cheque for £ [_____] made payable to Travel Publishing Ltd

Or:

CARD NO: [_____]   EXPIRY DATE: [_____]

SIGNATURE: [_____]

NAME: [_____]

ADDRESS: [_____]

TEL NO: [_____]

Please either send, telephone, fax or e-mail your order to:

Travel Publishing Ltd, 7a Apollo House, Calleva Park, Aldermaston, Berkshire RG7 8TN
Tel: 0118 981 7777 Fax: 0118 940 8428 e-mail: info@travelpublishing.co.uk

	Price	Quantity		Price	Quantity
HIDDEN PLACES REGIONAL TITLES			**COUNTRY PUBS AND INNS TITLES**		
Cornwall	£8.99	....	Cornwall	£5.99	....
Devon	£8.99	....	Devon	£7.99	....
Dorset, Hants & Isle of Wight	£8.99	....	Sussex	£5.99	....
East Anglia	£8.99	....	Wales	£8.99	....
Lake District & Cumbria	£8.99	....	Yorkshire	£7.99	....
Northumberland & Durham	£8.99	....	**COUNTRY LIVING RURAL GUIDES**		
Peak District and Derbyshire	£8.99	....	East Anglia	£10.99	....
Yorkshire	£8.99	....	Heart of England	£10.99	....
HIDDEN PLACES NATIONAL TITLES			Ireland	£11.99	....
England	£11.99	....	North East of England	£10.99	....
Ireland	£11.99	....	North West of England	£10.99	....
Scotland	£11.99	....	Scotland	£11.99	....
Wales	£11.99	....	South of England	£10.99	....
HIDDEN INNS TITLES			South East of England	£10.99	....
East Anglia	£7.99	....	Wales	£11.99	....
Heart of England	£7.99	....	West Country	£10.99	....
South	£7.99	....	**OTHER TITLES**		
South East	£7.99	....	Off The Motorway	£11.99	....
West Country	£7.99	....			

TOTAL QUANTITY [_____]

TOTAL VALUE [_____]

READER REACTION FORM

The **Travel Publishing** *research team would like to receive readers' comments on any visitor attractions or places reviewed in the book and also recommendations for suitable entries to be included in the next edition. This will help ensure that the* **Country Living series of Rural Guides** *continues to provide its readers with useful information on the more interesting, unusual or unique features of each attraction or place ensuring that their visit to the local area is an enjoyable and stimulating experience. To provide your comments or recommendations would you please complete the forms below and overleaf as indicated and send to:*

The Research Department, Travel Publishing Ltd, 7a Apollo House, Calleva Park, Aldermaston, Reading, RG7 8TN

YOUR NAME:

YOUR ADDRESS:

YOUR TEL NO:

Please tick as appropriate: COMMENTS ☐   RECOMMENDATION ☐

ESTABLISHMENT:

ADDRESS:

TEL NO:

CONTACT NAME:

PLEASE COMPLETE FORM OVERLEAF

READER REACTION FORM

COMMENT OR REASON FOR RECOMMENDATION:

....

....

....

....

....

....

....

....

....

....

....

READER REACTION FORM

The **Travel Publishing** *research team would like to receive readers' comments on any visitor attractions or places reviewed in the book and also recommendations for suitable entries to be included in the next edition. This will help ensure that the* **Country Living series of Rural Guides** *continues to provide its readers with useful information on the more interesting, unusual or unique features of each attraction or place ensuring that their visit to the local area is an enjoyable and stimulating experience. To provide your comments or recommendations would you please complete the forms below and overleaf as indicated and send to:*

The Research Department, Travel Publishing Ltd, 7a Apollo House, Calleva Park, Aldermaston, Reading, RG7 8TN

YOUR NAME:

YOUR ADDRESS:

YOUR TEL NO:

Please tick as appropriate: COMMENTS ☐   RECOMMENDATION ☐

ESTABLISHMENT:

ADDRESS:

TEL NO:

CONTACT NAME:

PLEASE COMPLETE FORM OVERLEAF

READER REACTION FORM

COMMENT OR REASON FOR RECOMMENDATION:

....

....

....

....

....

....

....

....

....

....

....

READER REACTION FORM

The **Travel Publishing** *research team would like to receive readers' comments on any visitor attractions or places reviewed in the book and also recommendations for suitable entries to be included in the next edition. This will help ensure that the* **Country Living series of Rural Guides** *continues to provide its readers with useful information on the more interesting, unusual or unique features of each attraction or place ensuring that their visit to the local area is an enjoyable and stimulating experience. To provide your comments or recommendations would you please complete the forms below and overleaf as indicated and send to:*

The Research Department, Travel Publishing Ltd, 7a Apollo House, Calleva Park, Aldermaston, Reading, RG7 8TN

YOUR NAME:

YOUR ADDRESS:

YOUR TEL NO:

Please tick as appropriate: COMMENTS ☐ RECOMMENDATION ☐

ESTABLISHMENT:

ADDRESS:

TEL NO:

CONTACT NAME:

PLEASE COMPLETE FORM OVERLEAF

READER REACTION FORM

COMMENT OR REASON FOR RECOMMENDATION:

....

....

....

....

....

....

....

....

....

....

....

READER REACTION FORM

The **Travel Publishing** *research team would like to receive readers' comments on any visitor attractions or places reviewed in the book and also recommendations for suitable entries to be included in the next edition. This will help ensure that the* **Country Living series of Rural Guides** *continues to provide its readers with useful information on the more interesting, unusual or unique features of each attraction or place ensuring that their visit to the local area is an enjoyable and stimulating experience. To provide your comments or recommendations would you please complete the forms below and overleaf as indicated and send to:*

The Research Department, Travel Publishing Ltd, 7a Apollo House, Calleva Park, Aldermaston, Reading, RG7 8TN

YOUR NAME:

YOUR ADDRESS:

YOUR TEL NO:

Please tick as appropriate: COMMENTS ☐   RECOMMENDATION ☐

ESTABLISHMENT:

ADDRESS:

TEL NO:

CONTACT NAME:

PLEASE COMPLETE FORM OVERLEAF

READER REACTION FORM

COMMENT OR REASON FOR RECOMMENDATION:

READER REACTION FORM

The **Travel Publishing** *research team would like to receive readers' comments on any visitor attractions or places reviewed in the book and also recommendations for suitable entries to be included in the next edition. This will help ensure that the* **Country Living series of Rural Guides** *continues to provide its readers with useful information on the more interesting, unusual or unique features of each attraction or place ensuring that their visit to the local area is an enjoyable and stimulating experience. To provide your comments or recommendations would you please complete the forms below and overleaf as indicated and send to:*

The Research Department, Travel Publishing Ltd, 7a Apollo House, Calleva Park, Aldermaston, Reading, RG7 8TN

YOUR NAME:

YOUR ADDRESS:

YOUR TEL NO:

Please tick as appropriate: COMMENTS ☐   RECOMMENDATION ☐

ESTABLISHMENT:

ADDRESS:

TEL NO:

CONTACT NAME:

PLEASE COMPLETE FORM OVERLEAF

READER REACTION FORM

COMMENT OR REASON FOR RECOMMENDATION:

....

....

....

....

....

....

....

....

....

....

....

READER REACTION FORM

The **Travel Publishing** *research team would like to receive readers' comments on any visitor attractions or places reviewed in the book and also recommendations for suitable entries to be included in the next edition. This will help ensure that the* **Country Living series of Rural Guides** *continues to provide its readers with useful information on the more interesting, unusual or unique features of each attraction or place ensuring that their visit to the local area is an enjoyable and stimulating experience. To provide your comments or recommendations would you please complete the forms below and overleaf as indicated and send to:*

The Research Department, Travel Publishing Ltd, 7a Apollo House, Calleva Park, Aldermaston, Reading, RG7 8TN

YOUR NAME:

YOUR ADDRESS:

YOUR TEL NO:

Please tick as appropriate: COMMENTS ☐ RECOMMENDATION ☐

ESTABLISHMENT:

ADDRESS:

TEL NO:

CONTACT NAME:

PLEASE COMPLETE FORM OVERLEAF

READER REACTION FORM

COMMENT OR REASON FOR RECOMMENDATION:

....

....

....

....

....

....

....

....

....

....

....

TOWNS, VILLAGES AND PLACES OF INTEREST

TOWNS, VILLAGES AND PLACES OF INTEREST

TOWNS, VILLAGES AND PLACES OF INTEREST

TOWNS, VILLAGES AND PLACES OF INTEREST

TOWNS, VILLAGES AND PLACES OF INTEREST

TOWNS, VILLAGES AND PLACES OF INTEREST

TOWNS, VILLAGES AND PLACES OF INTEREST